Sound Pleasure

Sound Pleasure

Sound Pleasure

A Prelude to Active Listening
Second Edition

Donald Ivey
University of Kentucky

SCHIRMER BOOKS
A Division of Macmillan, Inc.
NEW YORK
Collier Macmillan Publishers
LONDON

Schirmer Books
A Division of Macmillan, Inc.
866 Third Avenue, New York, N.Y. 10022

Collier Macmillan Canada, Inc.

Library of Congress Catalog Card Number: 84–10483

Printed in the United States of America

printing number
          4 5 6 7 8 9 10

Library of Congress Cataloging in Publication Data

Ivey, Donald.
  Sound pleasure.

   1. Music—Analysis, appreciation.   I. Title.
MT6.I95S7 1985   780'.1'5   84–10483
ISBN 0–02–872270–1

To Jonse, Elizabeth, Jonathan, Laura, and Christopher,
who have furnished much of the consonance and
dissonance in my life

Contents

Listening Selections

Part One

Primary: Anton Webern, Concerto, Opus 24
Supplemental: Arnold Schoenberg, *Variations for Orchestra;* Quintet for Wind Instruments; Alban Berg, Violin Concerto

31 *Multithematic Forms: Movements of the Symphony*
Primary: Mozart, Symphony No. 40; Beethoven, Symphony No. 5
Supplementary: Symphonies by Mozart, Haydn, and Beethoven

32 *Sonata-Allergo in the Overture*
Primary: Tchaikowsky, *Romeo and Juliet Overture*
Supplemental: Felix Mendelssohn, *Hebrides Overture; A Midsummer Night's Dream*

33 *Sonata-Allegro in Chamber Music*
Primary: Fanny Mendelssohn Hensel, *Trio,* Opus 11, first movement
Supplemental: *Women's Work; Jazz Women*

34 *The Concerto*
Primary: Antonin Dvořák, Concerto for Cello, Opus 104, first movement
Supplemental: Sergei Rachmaninoff, Piano Concerto No. 2, C minor; Mendelssohn, Violin Concerto in E minor; Alban Berg, Concerto for Violin; George Gershwin, Piano Concerto in F major
Primary: George Frederic Handel, Concerto in B$^\flat$ major, Opus 3, No. 2
Supplemental: Handel, Concerti Grossi, Opus 6; Bach, Brandenburg Concerti; Arcangelo Corelli, Concerti, Opus 6

35 *Rondo*
Primary: Mozart, Concerto for Horn and Orchestra in E$^\flat$ major, K. 417, third movement
Supplemental; Mozart, Rondo in D Major, K. 382; Rondo in A major, K. 386; Beethoven, Rondo in C major

36 *Sectional Forms: March, Rag, Dixieland, Mozart*
Primary: John Philip Sousa, "El Capitan"; Scott Joplin,

"Maple Leaf Rag," solo piano version and Dixieland band version

Supplemental: "Sensation Rag"; "Froggie Moore"; "The Pearls"; "High Society"

Primary: Igor Stravinsky, *Ragtime*

Supplemental: Stravinsky, *L'Histoire du soldat; Ebony Concerto;* Darius Milhaud, *La Création du monde;* George Gershwin, *Rhapsody in Blue*

Primary: Mozart, *Eine kleine Nachtmusik,* third movement

Acknowledgments

I deeply appreciate the kindness of the following publishing houses for granting permission to quote passages from music for which they control the copyrights: Bärenreiter, Edwin F. Kalmus, Strong Arm Music, Harvard University Press, Breitkopf & Haertel, Friedrich Gennrich, Universal Editions, Royal Musical Association, Chappell & Co., Inc., MCA Music, C. F. Peters Corp., International Music Co., G. Schirmer, Inc., Carl Fischer, Inc., Stainer and Bell, Ltd., European American Music Distributors Corp., Ernst Eulenberg, Ltd., Boosey and Hawkes, Inc., Mercury Music, Inc., PWM Editions and Deshon Music, Inc., Colfranc Music Publishing Corp., E. C. Kerby, Ltd., Warner Bros., Inc., Harms, Inc., Belwin-Mills Publishing Corp., Golden West Melodies, Inc., MJQ Music, Inc., Essex Music of Australia, Pty, Ltd., Theo. Presser, Inc., Galaxy Music Corp., and Kensington Music Ltd.

For permission to reproduce prints of paintings and other art works, I am indebted to the following: Cincinnati Art Museum, J. B. Speed Art Museum, Hirmer Verlag, Harper and Row, Instituto Geografico de Agostini, A. F. Kersting, Rizzoli International Publications, Inc., National Gallery of Art, University of Kentucky Art Museum, Dover Publications, Inc., and Chas. E. Tuttle Co.

I am especially indebted to the editorial and production staff at Schirmer Books and at Columbia Special Products for their advice and superb assistance at every stage of the preparation of the book and its accompanying record set.

Many of my colleagues at the University of Kentucky have offered encouragement and professional expertise. Of these, I thank especially Cathy Hunt and Pam Fields of the Music Library staff. I would like, too, to recognize Dr. Carol Quin whose research into the life and works of Fanny Mendelssohn Hensel formed the basis for much of the discussion of that composer.

Since much of the second edition is based on material from the first edition, I wish to continue my expression of indebtedness to Donna Boyd for her suggestions, corrections, criticism, and support. Mistakes of fact and interpretation are probably unavoidable in the writing of a book; I would like to reiterate that there would be many more in this one had it not been for Donna's knowledge and insight.

Finally I wish to thank the students who have allowed me to experiment on them through the years of teaching introductory music courses. Of additional and invaluable assistance have been the comments of teaching assistants who have been assigned to our music appreciation course at the University of Kentucky and have used the first edition of *Sound Pleasure* for a number of years. In particular, I have benefited from the experiences and counsel of Margaret Doutt.

Introduction

Everyone who listens to any kind of music at all has some reaction to it, which can range from intense enjoyment to absolute rejection or even boredom, but to explain our response can be difficult. On the other hand, explanation can be unnecessary, as long as we limit our statements to expressions of personal preference. Aside from music, there is no need to explain why we like roast beef rare, or why blue is our favorite color, or why tennis is our preferred sport. Similarly, we need no defense at all when our reaction to a piece of music is "I really get into that," or "I can't stand that," or "That doesn't do a thing for me."

But there are other kinds of verbalization, just as common, that are not as defensible. Some of them seem only silly or trite or thoughtless, but they reveal a kind of thinking that can have dangerous implications. Such a statement might be "I hate Mozart and all that long-hair junk!" Because we are going to be discussing Mozart along with numerous other composers and various types of music, it might be profitable to examine that statement and some of its implications.

The kind of thinking behind the remark is a result of the way we organize our world. One thing this involves is what we call categorization or classification, which can serve many good purposes. In order to keep things and ideas arranged in some sort of order, we put them into classes or categories, within each of which there is presumably a common denominator. Thus a chair may take many forms, but the thing that all chairs have in common is that they provide a place to sit, other than the floor. A table is something to put things on. A table has this in common with all other tables, or it couldn't be called a table to begin with. And this is all very helpful. If we were not aware of the difference between tables and chairs, we might easily do some rather hilarious things at a dinner party.

However, the security that classification offers as an organizing device involves some built-in restrictions. Once we have defined the characteristics of a category, we are apt to guard it carefully. Innovative designs in chairs are often met with remarks like *"That's a chair?"* This simply means we have relied so heavily on our classification that we cannot gracefully include anything that fails to meet our particular definitions and preconceptions. To this extent our categorization can be restrictive, even prohibitive; it can place very real limits on our imagination and our vision of the world and the people, things, and ideas in it.

Now in the statement we are examining, "Mozart and all that long-hair" is a category. For the person who made it, the category probably includes all the music more traditionally classified as "serious," "classical," or "art." But indeed all these terms, including the phrase "Mozart and all that long-hair," are so vague that they are practically meaningless. What meaning they may have is an imagined one or, worse, one that we assign and accept simply because we don't know what *else* to call the music we are trying to classify. This is faulty thinking, because although it gives us a label, it tells us nothing we really want to know about the music. Specifically, it ignores the vast differences within the category. Presumably "Mozart and all that long-hair" takes in the music of Beethoven, Palestrina, Tchaikowsky, Britten, Penderecki, Bach, and thousands of other composers. But the fact is that their music doesn't sound at all alike. There are as many differences between Beethoven and Palestrina as there are between midnight and noon (even though both of those occur at 12 o'clock), and the differences are significant. These can even be *seen*, whether or not you can read music. If you can't, the music of both composers may look like chicken scratches, but at least the scratches are *different* (Examples 1 and 2). And to relate the differences to the similarities that also exist is so confusing that it is better not to try to work both Beethoven and Palestrina into the same category in the first place.

We fall into the same trap with people. We classify one another as students, parents, teachers, Protestants, Jews, Englishmen, barbers— all sorts of things. So a student is somebody who goes to school. What do we do with people who study on their own? A parent can also be a teacher, or even an English Protestant barber. How is an English Jew different from a Russian Jew? What is a Russian Jew the day after he or she emigrates to Israel, or America? All our helpful little classification systems begin to break down, of course, and we are in a rat's nest of symbolism. In addition, our systems of easy identification almost never tell us anything we really want to know about people *as people*. When we identify someone as a student, what does that tell us that really matters? Is he sensitive to beauty, to pain, to love? What is her capacity for understanding, compassion, ecstasy? Does she beat her dog? Is he the sort of person you could go to when your dreams are in shreds? Would he care?

EXAMPLE 1
Palestrina, *Missa in Duplicibus.*
Aus der Musik in Geschichte
und Gegenwart, Bd. 10, Spalte
698, Bärenreiter-Verlag, Kassel
und Basel.

It is possible for us to be enticed into a false sense of clear identification brought on by the ease of "tagging" things and people. That, fortunately, is not particularly dangerous because all it leads to is some degree of misinformation or incomplete information. The danger comes when we begin to make evaluations using our tags as criteria. That's exactly what happened to the person who made the "Mozart" statement. Not only does he take literally millions of

EXAMPLE 2
Beethoven, *Missa Solemnis.*
Kalmus score, p. 5. Used by permission.

musical compositions and lump them into "Mozart and all that long-hair"; but he also makes a one-word evaluation of them: "junk." Why junk? According to the statement, because he hates them. Or does he hate them because they're junk? In the end, the result is the same: an evaluation arrived at in an easy but capricious manner.

There's the danger. The thinking behind the kind of identification and evaluation we are discussing is the sort of thinking that leads to calling all students "effete snobs," all Jews "kikes," all politicians "crooks," all Negroes "niggers." These terms are all evaluative—and derogatory. Given the proper environment and the requisite authority, the next steps are frighteningly easy: physical and spiritual segregation; Auschwitz; hell.

All of which is preamble to explaining the first objective of this book and the course of study. We will be listening to and discussing many musical compositions. The temptation will be to classify them into easily managed types in order to help with identification or style or period or whatever. Because of our experience, our training, our preconceptions, our habits of thinking and organizing, it will be impossible, maybe even undesirable, to avoid a certain amount of categorization. At the same time we will be discovering that particular pieces of music are quite distinctive *in themselves*, even though they may share features in common with other compositions. What makes all music interesting and worth discussing is both the differences and the similarities. We need to work very hard at avoiding the trap of evaluating solely on the basis of categories. To that end, let's agree right at the beginning not to concern ourselves with whether Mozart is better or worse than Blood, Sweat and Tears, for instance, and just agree that they are different. But not *totally* different; otherwise they wouldn't both be music. Our principal goal is to understand what there is about particular music that identifies it as music, how it is similar to other music, and, at the same time, what makes it sound distinctive.

In order to reach the goal, we need to develop a vocabulary appropriate to the description of music. Such a vocabulary includes many terms—melody, harmony, rhythm, texture, thematic contrast, and many others. Acquiring the vocabulary will be no problem if we follow a simple procedure: first, listen to a composition carefully enough to *hear* what happens in it, and second, learn the words or phrases that *describe* what happens in it. Only in this way will the words have any relationship to the music. And more important, only in this way can we be reasonably certain that we are all hearing and discussing the same thing.

The most rewarding thing about developing a vocabulary of description for music is that once it is acquired, it serves for *all* music. If we can learn to distinguish the melody, for instance, from everything else that is happening, and if we can learn the words that properly describe it, then we have verbal tools for discussing melody in music of all sorts—sonatas from the nineteenth century, folk songs from Bali, jazz from Kansas City, religious chant from the medieval period. This is true simply because some of the differences among musics can be described in terms of the melodies they employ, as well as what happens to the melodies in the course of the composition or performance. At the back of the book is a glossary of terms. It is there to remind you what to call musical sounds you have heard. It is *not* there to help you memorize definitions. We need the words in order to describe and discuss; but without the sound itself, we have no music and the words become merely jargon.

In addition, numerous examples of music scores will be printed in the book, like those from Palestrina and Beethoven that we have already compared. In the development of musical procedure in Western civilization, notation came after actual music making. The problem was to find a way to put down on paper the symbols that would adequately represent the music that people were already performing. When innovations were made in musical practice, new notational signs had to be conceived to symbolize those practices. As a result, the development of notation has been a laborious process, involving a great deal of trial and error, many false starts, and much just plain fumbling; not surprisingly, this has been the history of written language as well. However, once a usable system was established, notational devices could be put to use in a number of ways. The two most obvious and frequent uses are to preserve a record of the music—bookkeeping—and to provide directions for performers. Neither one of these may be particularly important to us if our main concern is to train ears instead of eyes. However, music scores can be useful in another way. They can add a visual dimension to the music being listened to, and in that way they can be interesting even though most of the concentration is aural.

Appendix 1, "Theory and Notation," interprets some of the most important notational symbols. It is there to use if that fits in with the objectives you have. But keep in mind that unless we are performers, theorists, or musicologists, we will very likely never see the musical scores for most of the music we hear during our lives. The main responsibility is to our ears, though if our eyes can help, well and good.

So listen first, then learn to describe or identify, and you will be equipped to approach the almost limitless world of music on your own and able to arrive at your own conclusions about relative values. Most important of all, you will gain some assurance that you not only can discuss and articulate your conclusions but can *understand* them as well.

Now that last statement takes some explanation:

We contact and use music in many ways, and all of them must

be attractive because they are all so popular. Sometimes music serves as an indispensable accompaniment to other activity—as in dancing. Sometimes it is merely a background to other activity—as at a cocktail party or in a bull session or even as atmosphere for study. Sometimes it enhances another activity, gives it an additional dimension—as in watching a film or listening to a radio drama. Sometimes it actually motivates another activity—as when we use music to stimulate daydreaming or even a seduction. In all such cases, music is being employed for extramusical purposes rather than solely for its own sake.

But we also listen to music purely for the enjoyment or stimulation of it, without any motivation except in terms of how it makes us feel, how it affects us. At such times we are contacting music most subjectively, and it is operating at what is very likely the ideal level—as expression of feeling. The response we feel on such occasions is what we call the affective response. All art strives to operate forcefully at this level, and many people believe that art is not art at all unless it meets with such a response. When it does, we become impatient with anything that intrudes between us and music. We resent discussion and description, we reject analysis, we couldn't care less about vocabulary or musical device. We know very well that all the discussion and description, all the analysis, all the words do not make us like the music one bit more. And we are on solid ground: total emotional involvement has a valid place in human experience and often needs no verbalization to justify it or even to explain it.

But we are also, we like to think, rational. Unfortunately, we often stop short of rationality in the area of our preferences, and that can get us into some pretty sorry predicaments. For instance, "Well, I don't know anything about it but I do know what I like, and I don't like that!" Which is not very rational. Nor does it help us understand ourselves.

This is where music can serve another extramusical purpose. Discussion and description can provide tools for self-examination and evaluation of responses. They can goad you, if you have them at your command, into wondering why some music is appealing to you and other music repels you or leaves you unmoved. They can help you recognize and sort out those purely musical characteristics that attract and stimulate you. In the process you may learn to understand yourself better, perhaps even run into questions that have never occurred to you. You may well discover that you have fenced yourself in too closely, restricted your musical awareness too rigidly to certain types of music, blocked out too much of the musical world as well as the kind of understanding of people that music can lead to. You may even discover sensitivities that were never exposed before.

But even if this does not happen—even if you find yourself unable to relate to *anything* you listen to in following the suggestions in this book—that in itself will inform you of something you need to know: the limits of your capacity to respond to music. We all have those limits, as we have limits in other areas of human activity, understanding, and feeling. Tragically, we as individuals are seldom pushed into questioning the fences behind which we spend our lives or wondering what might lie beyond them. If we go about it intelligently and with integrity, abandoning as many preconceptions as possible, we can use music to help us locate some of our fences. That would be more valuable than learning to like "Mozart and all that long-hair junk."

Because of the diversity of our backgrounds and our exposure to music, it might appear difficult to find some common ground that we can occupy with comfort. In order to minimize that difficulty, we will begin with *music that is accompanied by words*. We will assume that all of us can reach agreement about what the words mean and what the expressive intent of them seems to be. That should provide us with a handle for trying to understand the music. In most cases, when a composer adds music to a set of words that already exists, or even composes the words and music at the same time, he or she must believe that the music can add something to the text. Otherwise why fool around with music at all? So by examining the relationship between words and music, we ought to be able to at least guess what expressive importance is being assumed by the music.

Next we will examine a number of compositions without words but with some sort of story line or specified mood or dramatic concept we can deduce from the title. Such musical compositions are called *program music* because the composer uses an extra-musical idea on which to structure musical ideas. To some degree, then, the program explains the music and the music intensifies the program. This will give us quite a bit to think about, because the extramusical ideas in program music are often not as specific as the words of a song or chorus.

Finally we will examine some examples of music that have neither words nor program—what we call *absolute music*. In doing this, we will need to discuss music as an internally coherent art and try to find out what holds it together, without reference to outside influences. This is a real challenge. However, if we have laid the groundwork carefully and have prepared the necessary vocabulary and developed the necessary listening skills, the investigation of absolute music should present few hazards.

Although these three large groupings—music with words, program music, and absolute music—provide general guidelines for organization, there are occasions when the discussion will not remain rigidly within them. The chaconne, for instance, is a musical form coherent enough to be self-sufficient without words or programmatic ideas to explain its meaning, and we will consider it first as absolute music. However, the principle of harmonic repetition which forms the basic of its structure is sometimes used in vocal music, most strikingly in the classic blues formula. There is no contradiction, then, in considering both the chaconne and the blues as sharing a purely musical concept, even though one may be wordless and the other not. Throughout the book there is an attempt to avoid the kind of stringent compartmentalization that might inhibit free investigation and so the groupings indicated above should not be seen as mutually exclusive ones. Music, like nearly everything else, defies exact categorization.

The pieces of music that are most extensively discussed in the book are also the primary selections for your record listening. These selections are identified under the heading "Primary Listening" at appropriate points in the discussion (see, for example, pages 14–15). Many of them are included in the accompanying record set, and when this is so, the words "record set" appear in the "Primary Listening" note. The rest of these selections are available on records, in many cases in numerous versions. But also the book presents "Supplemental Listening" selections that in some cases you may want to listen to, which are also available on records (see page 10).

A final word about the exploration ahead. One could spend a lifetime listening and never contact more than a small portion of the music that is available. Because of this, we need not set a goal of covering a vast amount of musical composition. Neither is it necessary to hear a sample of the music of all composers. It is to be hoped that each of us has a long life ahead and will spend some of it listening to and trying to understand music. What we need is to acquire some tools *now* that will help us *then*. That means that we should be most interested in discovering musical ideas, devices, procedures, and relationships. These are the keys that open the doors to the music of the world. In the course of looking for them we will contact a number of significant composers and a good many varied compositions. Many composers will not be discussed, and many compositions will not be investigated, but that is a relatively minor matter. There are millions of records and thousands of books that you can call upon to stimulate your own explorations and musical experiences in the years ahead. What we want to gain from the work here is an awareness of the kinds of experiences that are waiting once we have become equipped with the necessary tools. So we will spend this time opening our ears and stretching our minds—and perhaps even sharpening our emotional sensitivities.

Part One
Music with Words

Chapter 1
Monophonic Texture: One Melody Alone

Kyrie eleison	Lord, have mercy upon us
Kyrie eleison	Lord, have mercy upon us
Kyrie eleison	Lord, have mercy upon us
Christe eleison	Christ, have mercy upon us
Christe eleison	Christ, have mercy upon us
Christe eleison	Christ, have mercy upon us
Kyrie eleison	Lord, have mercy upon us
Kyrie eleison	Lord, have mercy upon us
Kyrie eleison	Lord, have mercy upon us

This is the text of the first listening selection, the "Kyrie eleison" from the medieval Mass for the Dead. How to approach it? It would be easy to overlook one of the most important points about it—the fact that it cannot function ideally in the modern classroom and in the midst of people with varying religious backgrounds and persuasions. It was never intended for use in that context. Only if we can ignore our own immediate environment and our own religious preconceptions can we hope to relate in any important way to the "Kyrie" text.

PRIMARY LISTENING:
"Kyrie eleison" from Mass for the Dead, Gregorian chant (record set)

How much imagination are you carrying with you? Can you transport yourself back in time to the early medieval period, around the eighth century? Summon up all the awareness you can of the concept of God as a distant and almost unapproachable monarch-creator exerting eternal control over His creatures, one of whom is you yourself. How to capture the attention of such a being? If you are a medieval man or woman, your approach is mostly indirect, through the priesthood, a group of intermediaries who will assume most of the responsibility for uttering the necessary prayers. You are allowed only occasional and limited rights of access. Because of the particular theological stance into which you have been educated, you will trust the priesthood almost completely to intercede with God for you, through ritual. And the "Kyrie" is part of one of its rituals of intercession. It is one part of a multi-sectioned ritual called the Mass and although most of that service is in Latin, the "Kyrie eleison" itself is Greek. Neither language, however, is familiar to you. Very likely you are unable to read or write in any language at all; certainly you cannot even speak or understand the language of the worship services you attend. But no matter. The carrying out of the ritual is not really your affair—it is between the priests and God. The *effectiveness* of the ritual, however, is very much your affair! In this sense, nothing else in life matters quite as much as the ritual, poses so many threats, offers so many rewards. Within this framework, what is the "Kyrie"?

It is first of all a prayer. It is one of thousands of prayers and religious statements that were adopted by the Catholic Church for use in its worship services. It took many centuries for such a body of approved ritual utterances to develop, and in the course of that development music was added to the words in some cases. By the time of Pope Gregory I, who occupied the papacy from 590 to 604, the number of melodies, or tunes, used to sing the ritual was enormous. They varied from place to place, and some of them had slipped in without official approval of the ecclesiastical authorities. So Pope Gregory set about standardizing the chant, the collected body of these melodies, and editing it. Some of this he did himself; some of it he merely supervised. But because of his influence over the final catalogue, the chant itself bears his name: *Gregorian chant*. It has other titles as well: *plain chant* and *plainsong*. To complicate matters, there were, and are, other bodies of chant used in the various branches of the church; Ambrosian and Mozarabic are the most important. Trying to understand and interpret all of these has been a lifetime's work for many monks, religious scholars, and musicologists.

Among the various types of chant, however, the similarities are greater than the variations, so that by using the Gregorian "Kyrie" as an example, we can discover some of the characteristics of all of them. But it should be kept in mind that we will be considering just one chant taken from many Gregorian settings of the "Kyrie" text. It is extracted from a series of prayers used in the Mass for the Dead, or Requiem Mass, a service conducted on All Souls' Day (November 2), at funeral services, and at anniversaries of the death of individuals.

If we were setting out to learn to read this Gregorian chant as a set of instructions for a performance, such as the performance of it on our record, there are many things we would need to discuss and clarify (Example 3). If we were studying the history or notation, there are many points of interest here. If we were studying the score in order to discuss pitch identification and relationships in a theoretical sense, there would be much to investigate. But assuming only the most general objectives, perhaps only the satisfying of curiosity, the score can be used simply for assurance that there is some sort of correlation between the way the music sounds and the way it looks on the page.

As for the sound of the "Kyrie," several things are absent that we have become accustomed to in music. One is *meter*, an important aspect of rhythm. The basis of musical rhythm is a sense of forward motion, most often measured in regular beats or pulses. Over these beats, sounds of varying duration occur, some the length of the pulse, some longer, some shorter. These variations produce rhythmic interest, and they are heard and notated in quantitative terms—how long or short a time the individual notes last (see appendix 1). When the underlying pulses are arranged in groups containing accented and unaccented units, we identify the result as having meter or as being metered. From the standpoint of meter, music and poetry

Example 3
"Kyrie eleison" from the
Requiem Mass.

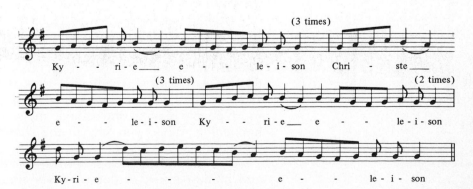

work much alike. In poetry, for instance, the following lines illustrate syllables divided into groups of two, the first of which is accented:

> Má–ry hád a lít–tle lámb;
> Its fleéce was white as snów. . . .

Try singing the familiar nursery song with this text and notice how the verbal accents coincide with the musical ones. In this case, we would say that the musical meter matches the poetic meter. It's also possible to have a meter that is made up of groups of three.

> Mér–ri–ly, mér–ri–ly,
> Mér–ri–ly, mér–ri–ly . . .

Meter can become quite complex, but the thing to keep in mind is very simple: it involves dividing up beats into groups of accented and unaccented units. When the meter remains the same, we feel a resulting regularity and consistency of accent that provides much of the momentum in music.

What about the meter in the Gregorian "Kyrie"? Can you feel any regular organization of metric patterns, as in the nursery rhymes? Unlikely. And for this reason you are probably not inclined to start clapping your hands or stomping your feet—the rhythmic feeling is just not that sort. So if we were to describe this piece of chant in terms of one of its rhythmic characteristics, we'd simply say it is unmetered.

Another element of rhythm involves the varying time values of the different notes. In singing the nursery songs, we sing some notes faster than others and sustain some for an especially long time. These variations in rhythmic values help create musical interest, and some compositions are immensely complex in this regard. But how about the chant? It would be possible to say of this that the rhythms are generally unvaried, most of the notes lasting for about the same length of time.

How about the harmony? To have harmony at all in music, you need at least two different pitches occurring at the same time. In the chant everybody is singing the same melody (the same series of pitches) together. So we say simply that this music is unharmonized. Or we say, more articulately, that the *texture* of the music is *monophonic* (*mono* means "one"). Music is monophonic when one or more people play or sing a single melodic line without anything else happening. When you sing in the shower, you are making mono-phonic music.

How about the melodic *range*—the distance between the lowest and highest notes? It doesn't cover much space, either visually or

Illustration 1. HOLY WOMEN AT THE SEPULCHRE.
Master of San Baudelio, mid-twelfth century. This *fresco secco* (literally *dry fresco*, a watercolor painting on dry plaster) was originally on the wall of a medieval structure. Painters of the period had not yet mastered the art of perspective—the illusion of depth—and the figures are therefore "flat." The relationship to unharmonized Gregorian chant is strong.
Cincinnati Art Museum. Gift of Elija B. Martindale.

aurally, in comparison with a lot of music we are more familiar with. For instance, people complain about our national anthem partly because of the range: it goes too high for some of us and too low for others. This Gregorian "Kyrie," in contrast, covers a very limited range.

Notice, too, how smooth the melody sounds, how easily it moves from pitch to pitch without big jumps. Again, compare it with "The Star Spangled Banner." The smooth melody of the chant is properly described as *conjunct*, while the beginning of the national anthem has a *disjunct* melody.

To describe this Gregorian chant fairly completely and use the proper vocabulary, you might say, "This piece is monophonic, monotonous rhythmically, and unmetered, covers a relatively small range, and is melodically conjunct." And in fact this is a description that fits most Gregorian chant. In some ways this presents us with a parallel to the two-dimensional art of the medieval era, most of which lacked perspective—the illusion of depth that we might associate with harmonic richness (Illustration 1).

In broader terms, the piece can be described as function—part of the ritual—and as music. Is there a way to relate these two, a way to theorize about what effect they have on one another? We might agree that the words of the prayer themselves are expressive, and if we are inspired to plead for mercy, we want to convey some sort of urgency. In speaking, formally or otherwise, we usually raise and lower our voices pitchwise in direct relation to our emotional or expressive intent. (Volume is affected too, but here let's concentrate on pitch.) Have you noticed how shrill people often sound during arguments, how we tend to raise the pitch of a question, how we lower our pitch when we are trying to be seductive? These pitch changes are involved with the expressive use of the voice and the degree of our emotional involvement. So with this chant. The melodic style is simply that of heightened speech, somewhat controlled, as befits religious ritual. There are no accents other than those that might fall naturally on important syllables. A syllable is emphasized by singing it through several consecutive notes, that is, lengthening the syllable rather than landing on it heavily. That's appropriate, too, because regular accents might encourage us to tap our feet, which would be out of place in terms of this kind of ritual. There is no harmony because it just doesn't seem necessary: the prayer itself is felt to be effective with God. Harmony might make it more *musically* interesting for us, and harmony did develop later, using chant as its basis. But the *function* is served excellently without it because this whole exercise between the priests and God is not intended to stimulate us at all, artistically.

The practice of chanting or speaking prayers is closely involved with the theology of the time. The rationale was that the mere utterance was effective and necessary in and of itself. So necessary, in fact, that the days and nights were divided into periods marked by certain hours at which a series of prayers *had* to be said or chanted. Monks spent much of their time carrying out this function; many still do. All of this had a great deal to do with the development of music in Western civilization, as we shall see later.

But we have still not exhausted the descriptive possibilities in this one short Gregorian chant. We have not thought about the form of the words and the form of the music and how they relate to one another.

The words are arranged in groups of threes—three times "Kyrie," three times "Christe," and three times "Kyrie" again. Altogether they make up a larger group of three. This is related to the concept of the Trinity (Illustration 2). So we can say that the text is *ternary* or *tripartite*—made up of three parts. Even within the parts, the text occurs three times, adding yet another Trinitarian

Illustration 2. MADONNA AND CHILD ENTHRONED. About 1360. This altarpiece is a reflection of the medieval interest in carrying Trinitarian and ternary design into the visual arts. The entire work is tripartite, and two of its parts are in that form also, with figures of equal stature on either side of a central elevated figure. The only contradiction is in the binary grouping on the left panel. Collection of the J. B. Speed Art Museum, Louisville, Kentucky.

reference. The music, however, uses the same tune throughout except for the very last statement of "Kyrie eleison," where it becomes more dramatic, even disjunct. In the other two parts, there is no change except the deletion of one note during the chanting of "Christe eleison." Why is that note left out? Why the drama in the music at the very end?

Another interesting aspect of this performance is the use of a leader and chorus, which adds some variation in dynamic level. Interplay between a soloist and a group is sometimes referred to as "call–response" and is a feature of many types of musical performance. Such interplay is properly called *antiphony* and music that uses it is *antiphonal* music. It also happens when group answers group, as well as in the leader-chorus framework. The antiphonal process occurs on a worldwide scale, as we shall see. What do you think makes the procedure so universally appealing?

This is a lot of verbiage to expend on a composition that lasts only two minutes, but it will not be wasted if two things are established by it. First, control over the descriptive terminology involved. The terms will occur again and again in different contexts, but they will be usable only if they are understood and applied accurately. Second, awareness of the complexity of even such a brief work of art as this one.

Almost any Gregorian "Kyrie" will illustrate the same principles at work, and if you listen to a number of them, you will discover a fundamental fact: they all share many characteristics, but they are each different in some way from all the others.

SUPPLEMENTAL LISTENING   Recorded anthologies that include examples of Gregorian chant of varying types, including settings of the "Kyrie" text, are:

> *History of European Music,* vol. 1. Musical Heritage Society: OR 349.
> *Masterpieces of Music before 1750.* Haydn Society: HSE 9038.
> *History of Music in Sound,* vol 2. RCA Victor: LM 6015.
> *History of Music in Performance: Early Medieval Music,* parts 1 and 2. Pleiades Records: P 247 and 248.

A GLANCE AT HISTORY   The early part of the medieval period is given different dates by different historians. Many identify it as running from A.D. 400 to A.D. 1100; others begin it about the year 450, still others with 500. Certainly the main event to suggest the beginning of a new period was the fall of the Roman empire in A.D. 476. It was from that date forward that social, political, and cultural life in Europe changed dramatically.

The breakdown of the empire was brought on by the advances made by various barbarian tribes: Angles, Saxons, Vandals, Huns, Franks, Vikings. However, the chaos they created was gradually offset by the growing strength of the Roman Catholic Church. Although the Romans could no longer offer protection to the populace, the church was able to do so to some extent. It moved even into the political arena to convert a number of barbarian leaders and their heirs: Charlemagne, Clovis, Alfred the Great, among others. Thus there was a combination of the powers of the rulers with the powers of the church, even though there was not the same consistency that existed under the government of the Roman empire.

The era we are looking at is called the Romanesque period (c. 450–1100), largely because many aspects of Roman life persisted, at least in principle. For instance, the legal system of Rome vanished with the empire itself, but the church was able to substitute its own system of laws, rewards, and punishments. Here, as in all of society, it was the principal element in whatever unification was achieved. Also, because the church at Rome was the most important one, the architecture that typified the period is Roman in style (Illustration 3). Notice the rounded arches, the squat appearance, the heaviness. It is almost as though the church is bearing the weight of heaven, pressed down by all the threats and restrictions typical of the theology of the period.

Because there were no states, the political structure was feudal. Each political territory was governed by an hierarchy consisting of kings, lords, vassals, sub-vassals, and peasants, all relating to one another in a system of loyalties that attempted to insure the protection of everyone. Because illiteracy was the norm rather than the exception outside the clergy, there was little attempt to preserve secular art of any kind, including music. Certainly there must have been a thriving body of secular music used for dancing, celebrations of all sorts, and just plain socializing. Much of it would have been influenced, as was religious music, by the broadening cultural awareness brought on by the Crusades. Returning crusaders carried with them new concepts of art, new musical sounds, new instruments, and new life styles. Some of this we know through contemporary reports, but very little is preserved on paper.

On the other hand, the church built up a network of monasteries, not only to provide sanctuary for the monks but also to provide an environment conducive to scholarship, worship, and the preservation of sacred documents. Since the monks were among the very few people who could read and write, such preservation fell naturally to them.

By the year 1000, the dominance of the church in all the arts, in architecture, and in philosophy (theology), as well as in social and political life, was almost complete. We have already seen an example of the importance of Roman Catholic theology to the arts. The mystery of the Trinity was one of the strongest dogmas of the time, and we have encountered its reflection in the "Kyrie eleison" and the visual arts. The doctrine was established at the Council of Nicaea in 325, following extensive and bitter arguments about the nature of God and Christ. After the doctrine was adopted, any concept of God that separated him from Christ and the Holy Spirit was looked upon as heresy. Such an emphasis in the arts was one way of educating the church members to the "proper" beliefs. Among many other doctrines that were all-pervasive were the glories of heaven and the terrors of hell, both of which were given graphic illustration in the rituals, the music, and the other arts.

Along with strengthening its influence in the areas of politics, the arts, and social life, the church gradually gained control over the forms of worship that were acceptable to the hierarchy. The principal form, and one that persists to the present day, is the Mass. By the year 1000, its structure was well established.

The two main types of Mass are the regular one, which is used in the day-to-day worship services, and the Requiem Mass. Some portions are common to both types, and the "Kyrie eleison" is one such portion. We have already discussed its nature and its function in the service. Let's broaden our perspectives enough to briefly look at the ritual of which it is a part.

As the word "Mass" is used, it means several things. First, it is the name of a church service; in this sense, one "goes to Mass" at 9 A.M., for instance. In another sense, the Mass is that part of the service that involves the serving of the sacrificial elements, the bread and wine; in this context one "takes Mass" or "serves Mass" or "celebrates Mass." Another meaning, the one usually used in the musical sense, involves the various prayers and liturgical statements that make up the entire worship service. These are divided into two large groups: the Ordinary and the Proper.

The Proper is that portion of the liturgy that changes from day to day and from hour to hour. It is a set of approved readings and prayers that are "proper" to a particular service. The Ordinary is a series of prayers and statements that remain the same from service to service, and that occur no matter what day or hour the Mass is celebrated. When a Mass is set to music other than chant, it is the various segments of the Ordinary that are mostly used.

In the regular day-to-day services of the church, the Ordinary of the Mass consists of five parts:

Kyrie eleison: we are already familiar with that.

Gloria: beginning "Glory to God in the Highest," this section continues in a mood of exultant praise and thanksgiving.

Credo: beginning "I believe in one God," the statement continues with an extended series of beliefs which underlie the faith of the church members and the clergy.

Sanctus: beginning "Holy, Holy, Holy," this section continues in a mood of praise. It is very closely associated with the consecration of the elements of sacrifice, the bread and wine. It is succeeded immediately by the Benedictus, which begins "Blessed is he who comes in the name of the Lord," and which again relates to the partaking of the elements of the Mass. The Sanctus and Benedictus are normally set as a two-part unit.

Agnus Dei: beginning "Lamb of God, who takest away the sins of the world," this final part of the Ordinary continues as a prayer for mercy and pease and directly precedes the distribution of the Eucharist.

You can easily figure out why composers want to spend their efforts on the Ordinary rather than the Proper. Thus, there is such a composition as the Bach Mass in B minor or the Beethoven *Missa Solemnis* (Solemn Mass). In the course of our investigations, we will encounter musical settings of other portions of both the regular Mass and the Requiem.

PEOPLE AND EVENTS TO INVESTIGATE:

MUSICIANS:

Boethius: c. 475–525
Guido d'Arezzo: c. 995–1049

CHURCHMEN IMPORTANT FOR MUSIC:

Ambrose of Milan: Bishop 340–397
Gregory I: Pope 590–604

EVENTS: Barbarians overrun Europe: 3rd–6th centuries
                First Crusade: 11th century
                Monasteries inaugurated: 4th century
                Norman conquest of England: 1066
                Rome sacked: 476

Illustration 3. COLOGNE: ST. MARIA IN CAPITOLIO, MID-ELEVENTH CENTURY. This is a clear example of the rounded arches and the earth-bound, heavy type of architecture associated with the Romanesque period. Used by permission of Hirmer Verlag, München.

Each of the sections entitled "A Glance at History," found at appropriate places throughout part 1, is followed by a list of people and events like the one above. These are given in alphabetical order under each subheading. However, in order to place them in chronological order, appendix 2 lists the same people and events by date. You might want to consult that appendix as you run into the historical information you will encounter in the text.

PRIMARY LISTENING
"Mercedes Benz," Janis
Joplin (record set)

For a big change of pace as well as period, listen to Janis Joplin singing "Mercedes Benz." Although separated widely in time and style, the pieces are comparable in many ways. Both are monophonic. How about vocal range, rhythm, meter? How about vocal style? (Example 4.)

Rock vocalist Janis Joplin (1943–1970) was one of the most flamboyant and emotive of the rock stars of the 1960s, and her erratic life style symbolized the mood of that turbulent era. She was a favorite at rock festivals and on recordings. Those unfamiliar with Joplin and the temper of the rock scene of the sixties would be well rewarded by reading Myra Friedman's *Buried Alive: The Biography of Janis Joplin* (New York: Morrow, 1974) or Michael Lyndon's *Janis Joplin: Her Life and Times* (New York: Paperback Library, 1971). "Mercedes Benz" was recorded shortly before Joplin's death; the album of which it is a part was not really finished when she died although recording on it had begun in 1969.

Consider, for a moment, the nature of ritual. Webster defines it as "the form of conducting worship; religious ceremonial. . . . A code of ceremonies observed." Is there a sense in which rock festivals or concerts can be related to ritual or are in themselves ritualistic? To some degree, we tend to deify our popular idols in many areas—sports, movies, vocal and instrumental performance. Did Joplin

Example 4
Janis Joplin, "Mercedes Benz."

Oh, Lord, won't you buy me a Mer-ce-des Benz? My

friends all drive Por-sches, I must make a-mends. Worked hard all my life-time, no

help from my friends so Oh, Lord, won't you buy me a Mer-ce-des Benz?

become a goddess—or perhaps a sort of priestess in the eyes of much of the public? Her prayer, ironic and caricatured as it is, speaks to many twentieth-century attitudes even years after her death. Do we all want essentially what Joplin is after? Is she praying for us too?

Even in the most primitive societies we study, music often plays an important part in intensifying or elaborating on spiritual rites. If Gregorian chant can be seen as an idealization of the medieval approach to God, it is not too farfetched to wonder whether "Mercedes Benz" tells us something about our current religious concepts—to each his own and all of us free to express ourselves without fear of official reprisals. But what medieval person would *dare* sing this song in public, in the face of the church's authority and power over even the temporal rulers themselves?

PRIMARY LISTENING: "The Farmer's Curst Wife," Child ballad 278 sung by Horton Barker (record set)

Listen next to a ballad, "The Farmer's Curst Wife," sung by a traditional folk singer, Horton Barker. Just as the Gregorian "Kyrie" serves as a prototype for plain chant, so this ballad illustrates many of the characteristics of that genre.

You will notice immediately that the texture is monophonic. The traditional style of ballad performance is without accompaniment, although in some localities singers sometimes play an instrument as they sing. This is true in Kentucky, for instance, where it is not at all unusual for a folk singer to strum a dulcimer for accompaniment.

A ballad is a type of folk song that tells some sort of story, very often dealing with love and most often ending unhappily, even tragically with the death of one or more characters in the drama. There are not too many humorous ballads, but "The Farmer's Curst Wife" is certainly one.

Because most ballads have come down to us through many years, even centuries of tradition, they use some musical idioms that are associated more with the distant past than with the present. "The Farmer's Curst Wife," for instance, uses a type of scale that we call *gapped*, because it contains fewer than the seven pitches we normally include in a scale (see appendix 1). In other words, there are some notes skipped, leaving gaps. In this case, there are only five notes; such a scale we identify as *pentatonic* (*penta* means "five," *tonic* means "tone"). There are various kinds of pentatonic scales, depending upon which notes of the full seven-tone scale are omitted. Here the missed notes are the fourth and seventh steps or degrees. Pentatonic scales are very prevalent in folk cultures around the world for some reason that musicologists have not explained satisfactorily. Some think they are just more primitive than our seven-tone scale—incomplete or unfinished, as it were.

Whatever the reason, they are in wide use in the British and American folk tradition. The type used here can be played using only the black keys on the piano—there are five black keys to each octave. That means that there are no half-step intervals; in a full seven-tone scale there are two. Barker's tune, then, can be played entirely on black keys (Example 5).[1]

Strangely enough, Janis Joplin uses a pentatonic scale for "Mercedes Benz," too, but we can be pretty sure she wasn't trying to imitate ballad style! More important to us as listeners, though, is the fact that we probably don't even miss those omitted pitches unless we are being very analytical and are more interested in theory than in enjoying the story of the ballad. One thing we know for certain: the folk who sing and listen to songs like this as a regular part of their life style couldn't care less about theory. They are one hundred percent involved with the tale.

And that leads to another feature of traditional ballad style. The story seems to carry its own weight as far as performers and listeners are concerned. Even though some ballads are highly dramatic, there is usually no attempt on the part of the singer to make the performance theatrical or filled with emotion. The same is true of humorous ballads like "The Farmer's Curst Wife." Even though there might be a chance for a good bit of horseplay and cutting up, Barker avoids indulging in it. Apparently the people who enjoy ballads as an ongoing part of everyday living feel no need for dramatization beyond what the words and music themselves express.

Related to the emotional detachment in ballad style is the lack of dynamic variation from stanza to stanza. The delivery is traditionally

[1] The example is written in the key used by Barker. To use only black keys, start the tune on D♭.

Example 5
"The Farmer's Curst Wife."

There was an old man at the foot of the hill, if he ain't moved a - way, he's liv - ing there still, Sing Hi, did - dle - eye, did - dle - eye, fie, did - dle - eye, did - dle - eye, day.

straight-forward without vocal manipulations from loud to soft in order to illustrate the text. Just sing the words and the tune—leave the fireworks off.

Another term that helps describe this ballad is *strophic*. This simply means that the piece includes a number of different stanzas of the poem but each stanza uses the same music. Just about all folk songs work this way and for a very good reason. They have been handed down by ear from generation to generation and from person to person, and it would be much too difficult to remember the music if it got too complicated. Types of song other than folk song are strophic, too. Check on "Mercedes Benz."

Even within the strophic framework, notice that Barker does use slight variations from stanza to stanza. Most of this is probably not deliberate—some stanzas apparently call for slight modifications in rhythm and notes, and these things are not out of place when a person is singing from memory rather than from notation. Actually, folk song collectors have discovered that the same person singing a song one day is very apt to vary it somewhat when singing it another day. The variations are never very severe, however, and no one would have difficulty recognizing the piece. In fact, most of us would probably be unaware of the changes unless we had recorded the song both times and compared the versions very carefully.

Try investigating other aspects of the music and words. Is the rhythm strong metrically? Are the verbal accents matched by the musical accents? How would you describe the melody—conjunct, disjunct, or a combination of these?

Many of the ballads still being sung in America are quite old, having been brought from England and Scotland and other countries by colonists and immigrants. Because folk songs are passed from person to person and learned by ear, there are numerous different versions of any given piece in both text and tune. People forget, or they add new stanzas, or they vary the tune to suit themselves, or the words have no immediate association for them so they change them to make more sense—lots of reasons for the changes that take place in the course of time. But the many variations have been of great interest to scholars of folklore.

Toward the end of the last century, interest in folk song led collectors to travel about in search of singers who still sang the old pieces. Perhaps the most important of the English-speaking collectors of ballads was Francis James Child (1825–1896), a Harvard scholar, who published a ten-volume set of ballads, *English and Scottish Popular Ballads*, between 1882 and 1898. He identified each one by a number and gave all the various versions of the text that he could find. He was the first scholar to give such enormous attention to the old ballads and his work was so thorough that the pieces are still referred to by the number assigned them by Child. Thus, "The Farmer's Curst Wife" is Child 278, and Horton Barker's is only one of many variants.

Because he was a literary scholar, the *tunes* of the ballads did not interest Child, and so his publications gave only the words. It was not until 1959 that Bertrand Bronson supplied music for the texts. His four-volume work, *The Traditional Tunes of the Child Ballads*, includes all the different melodies that he could find to match the various texts in the Child collection. The number of variations can be pretty overwhelming. The different tunes and texts to "Barbara Allen," probably the best-known of all ballads, add up to a total of about 230, and more have been springing up since the book's publication.

One of the earliest collectors to concentrate his activities within a limited area of the United States was Cecil Sharp (1859–1924), an English folklorist. He spent three years in several remote parts of the southern Appalachian mountains and in 1917 published *English Folk Songs from the Southern Appalachians*, a large collection giving both words and melodies. Many of the songs were Child ballads still being sung by the rural folk in their own homes as part of social gatherings, or just to pass the time pleasantly during the evening hours. It was within such an environment that Horton Barker learned the many ballads he knew.

Barker (1889–1973), born in the eastern Tennessee mountains, was blind from childhood. He lived during the latter part of his life in St. Clair's Creek, Virginia, and sang for a number of collectors including Alan Lomax of the Library of Congress. The recording on the record set was made in 1961 at a session lasting several days during which he sang many of the ballads and other folk songs in his repertoire.

SUPPLEMENTAL LISTENING

Monophonic singing with varying degrees of rhythmic freedom, contrasts of vocal range and style, function in ritual, and quite accessible formal characteristics can be found among recordings of rural blues and black church music. The following make interesting counterparts to the music discussed above:

Leadbelly (Huddie Ledbetter). Among his best-known unaccompanied blues are "Looky, Looky Yonder" and "Black Betty," available on *Leadbelly*. Everest: FS 202. A blues singer and guitarist, Leadbelly (1888–1949) was associated most strongly with the Texas rural blues style. He was a prodigious drinker and a resident of many jails. He was brought to attention and some commercial success as a result of recordings he made for the Library of Congress in the late 1930s at the invitation of John Lomax, a leader in the collection and preservation of American folk and ethnic music of all sorts. A movie based on Leadbelly's life, released in 1976, brought him to the attention of millions who were unaware of his contribution to folk art.

Roots of the Blues. Atlantic: S–1348. Good examples of field hollers which make an interesting contrast to other types of monophony.

The Real Bahamas. Nonesuch: H–72013

Negro Church Music. Atlantic: S–1351. Many points of comparison: call–response (leader–group) format, monophonic texture, ritual function, vocal range. Also many easy-to-hear contrasts.

PRIMARY LISTENING:
Juba dance from Haiti
(record set)

In Haiti, Harold Courlander recorded a Juba dance in 1949 and included it in a collection of music illustrative of African influences in the Americas. He tells us that the Juba dance is semireligious—often used in festivals celebrating the spirit's departure from the body of a recently deceased person. To this extent there is a contact point with the Gregorian chant, although the differences in mood and musical device are enormous. The Juba dance is very far removed from the cultural environment of most of us, musically as well as spiritually. It takes a great deal of concentration for us to even absorb the sort of musical framework within which the performance works. More than that, this music provides an exercise in abandoning preconceptions about what music is and what is "proper" to it.

The exact translation of the words is less important than the fact that even though we cannot understand the language we can catch the repetitive nature of the text. Remember that the text of the Gregorian "Kyrie" was equally repetitive. It would be appropriate to ask whether repetition itself plays some significant role in ritual and the music that accompanies it. We have been considering music in terms of rhythm, harmony, and melody; this more exotic piece can be discussed in the same terms (Example 6).

Rhythmically, it is organized around a steadily recurring beat, one that is easy to locate and that encourages foot tapping. But how about the meter? Try keeping up with the accents. Do they occur regularly? Can you anticipate all of them? There are a number of different drums at work. Careful listening will reveal that there are

Example 6
Juba Dance, Haiti.

* Indicates microtonally inflected pitch.

sections of the performance where each drum is accenting within its own pattern rather than in exact concert with the other drums. Such a procedure creates a mixture of meters, and this mixture is one of the reasons for the rhythmic complexity of this recording.

The practice of using several different meters at the same time has a technical name, *polymetric* (*poly* means "many"). Some people believe that this kind of metric maneuvering led to the great amount of syncopation in black American music, particularly jazz. Syncopation is the shifting of accents to normally unaccented beats, and it happens in much music from around the world. In the Juba dance, the accents sometimes contradict one another in the relationships among the drums. So to add to the description of the rhythmic characteristics of this piece, we could say that it includes a lot of syncopation. This is a characteristic of African rhythms, perhaps the most important characteristic, and was a direct influence on early jazz and associated musical styles that developed in America.

It is important in trying to understand the particular style of performance in the Juba dance to realize that the complexity is arrived at through the participation of a group. In fact, it would probably be impossible to achieve without such community of effort. This sense of community and group involvement is also a characteristic of much African and African-derived musical practice and one that was significant for black American music.

Like the Gregorian chant, "Mercedes Benz," and the ballad, the Juba dance uses no harmony. Also like the chant, it is performed by a leader and chorus.

Melodically there is a lot going on in the Juba dance that calls for close listening. Concentrate first on the soloist. It is obvious not only that the melody is repetitive, like the words, but that it covers a limited range. That relates it to the "Kyrie." In addition, it divides into some sort of *phrases*, or, putting this another way, arrives at pausing points periodically, as did the other songs. Phrasing is another feature of music from all parts of the world, and the type of phrasing is important in the description of music and how it differs from other music. In singing, this is a very functional matter—singers need to breathe. But even in instrumental music phrasing is important: its regularity or irregularity, strength or weakness, helps describe style and form and often the effect on the listener. You might want to listen carefully enough to determine the pitches on which the phrases in the Juba dance end. Are they always the same?

Now add another bit of vocabulary and call the end of the phrase a *cadence*. There are a number of ways to use that word: a cadence marks the end of a phrase; a phrase lasts from one cadence to another; cadences help determine phrase lengths. There are many types of cadences, as there are many types of phrases.

Perhaps the most interesting thing about the cadences in the Juba dance is that the soloist sustains the final note of the phrase for varying periods of time. Assuming all our preconceptions about pitch and the proper way to perform vocally or instrumentally, we would probably conclude that the poor woman is having trouble singing the pitch accurately. Her voice wavers up and down, and she seems unable to maintain the right level. We are led to suspect that she is simply untrained—and even that this fact couldn't matter much in this sort of primitive music, anyway. So we might dismiss her performance as being out of tune or off pitch. So much for that.

In this case, carrying our cultural criteria into another cultural environment would send us down entirely the wrong road and rob us of a full appreciation of the performance. In music the term *pitch* is used to identify a tone in terms of the frequency of vibrations set up when it is sounded (see Glossary.) Listen again—*very* carefully— and you may notice that although the soloist's sustained notes do vary quite minutely in pitch, just at the point of release she "kicks" the pitch back to what we think she should have been singing all along. This is not accidental. The manipulation of pitch by varying degrees, some so small that it is difficult or impossible for us to identify them exactly, is an important expressive device in this musical style. We are trained almost completely to hear half-steps as the smallest acceptable interval, or distance between pitches. This is simply a result of musical practice in the West. Except for some avant-gardists, musicians through whom we trace our cultural backgrounds didn't use smaller intervals. This custom has been reinforced strongly by our keyboard instruments, none of which are normally tuned to intervals smaller than half-steps. (Thus the distance between two neighboring notes on a piano is a half-step.) As a result, we naively interpret very minute variations of pitch as being performing errors.

Many other cultures are not oriented in those terms. For them, the manipulation of pitch is an important musical device and one without which the music would seem flat and expressionless—actually unacceptable. Some of this is related to language: many languages of the world rely on pitch to establish meaning. In such cultures, a syllable or word spoken on one pitch level means something different from the same syllable or word spoken on another pitch level. The proper term for such languages is "inflected," and those who use them develop a great sensitivity to pitch variations. We never cultivate this, because we can say or sing, for instance, "cat on a hot tin roof" on any pitch or pitches we want and everyone knows that it means the same thing all the time.

For many cultures with inflected languages the discrimination developed through speech carries over into musical practice. In the Juba dance, this is what has happened. And one of the fascinating things about cultural developments of this sort is that their abandonment in one area does not necessarily eliminate them in another. The ethnic background of the performers in the Juba dance is African. However, the subtleties of their inflected African language have mostly disappeared in the process of acculturation in Haiti, and it thus is no longer an inflected one. On the other hand, musical practices have been handed down from generation to generation in the true folk fashion—by ear and by imitation. As a result, minute pitch manipulation has retained its fascination and remains as a musical characteristic in spite of the fact that pitch variation no longer has a functional value in the spoken language.

If you have listened closely, you will have realized that the soloist is not the only one who manipulates the pitch. The same expressive device is carried over into the chorus sections, which helps to identify it as a significant part of the entire musical culture rather than just an artistic device peculiar to solo performers. Many scholars who have tried to locate the roots of the blues have suggested that the pitch manipulations associated with that idiom are carry-overs from African sensitivities and practices.

In this context it might pay to reconsider our concept of "primitivism." On casual listening, we would probably classify this performance of the Juba dance as primitive. But it involves rhythms that are more complex than most of those we are accustomed to using. In fact, we have no rhythmic notation that can symbolize them without a great deal of cumbersome manipulation. Also, in spite of our elaborate system of pitch notation, we have no symbols to represent this sort of pitch variation. As a result, we could not transfer this sound to paper at all accurately. Is it fair to dismiss it as primitive, then, or does it instead contain some elements that are too sophisticated for us to accommodate?

Actually, the music is not notated in Haiti or Africa, either—it is kept alive in the folk manner. Is it possible that notational systems, where they exist, exert a negative control over musical practice, weeding out those procedures that cannot be accommodated by notation?

It would be easy to oversimplify this. I referred to avant-garde musicians who have experimented with intervals smaller than a half-step. That kind of interval is called a *microtone;* where such intervals are used as a way of organizing the pitches, the result is properly identified as microtonality. In the late nineteenth century a large amount of manipulation of this type began to be done by Western composers. As is the case with much experimentation, however, microtonality never "caught on" except among a relatively few devotees. As a result it hasn't become an important element of our musical culture.

The Juba dance (named for an African spirit) itself was carried over into the United States by slaves, and the word "Juba" occurs in the folklore of the South. Eventually the association of the Juba dance with postfuneral rites was lost and it became simply a dance with a rhythm that was created mostly by patting the thighs and clapping hands. The practice was actually called "patting Juba." One of the most successful black minstrel show dancers of the nineteenth century was William Henry Lane, and he was known professionally as Juba. According to all the references to him, he was extremely skillful at translating the rhythmic complexities of Juba into his exciting dance routines.

SUPPLEMENTAL LISTENING   There are excellent examples of some of the above musical characteristics on the following albums:

> *Negro Folk Music of Africa and America.* Folkways: FE–4500
> *African and Afro-American Drums.* Folkways: FE–4502. This collection contains some Juba dances without singing.
>
> The last movement of Nathaniel Dett's *In the Bottoms: Suite for Piano* is a Juba dance. The Canadian-born Dett (1882–1943) was an important black American composer who successfully combined Negro musical idioms and themes with music based essentially on European models.

Chapter 2
Polyphonic Texture: Horizontal Harmony

Let's return to Western music and investigate some of the changes that took place in the use of Gregorian chant. These played a very important role in the development of Western music, and for practical reasons. As we know, most of what we have preserved of our earliest musical heritage is religious in character, and it was necessary to write it down, not only as a guide for performance but also as a means of ensuring its proper liturgical usage. Folk and popular music has always existed, but in most cases the people who used it were not able to transfer it to paper, and until recently few others took enough interest in it to preserve it. What we know, then, of early musical developments in the West we know through manuscripts of a religious nature. From these we learn that one of the most significant innovations in the chant was the addition of a second melodic line. That created one kind of harmony, and the importance that harmony assumed in our music is unique in the history of world musics.

To experience this change, listen to two different settings of a liturgical text, "Benedicamus Domino":

Benedicamus Domino	Let us praise the Lord
Deo gratias	Thanks be to God

Example 7
"Benedicamus Domino."

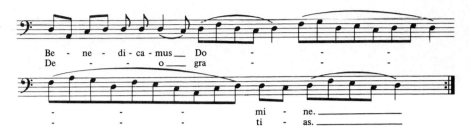

Be - ne - di - ca - mus — Do - - -
De - - o — gra - - -

- - - mi - ne. —
- - - ti - as. —

PRIMARY LISTENING:
"Benedicamus Domino,"
Gregorian chant
(record set)

The first setting is Gregorian chant, or plainsong, and has characteristics that we are already familiar with (Example 7). But notice that one syllable (the first one of "Domino") assumes great importance because of the many notes sung on it. This not only provides a quantitative accent—an accent of length, duration, number of notes—but also serves to emphasize "Domino," the word for "Lord." Because the music remains the same for both lines of the text, the initial syllable of "gratias" receives the same accentuation, which is appropriate to it. The musical figure (group of notes) is called a *melisma,* and the proper way to identify this type of singing is to call it *melismatic.* There were shorter melismas in the Gregorian "Kyrie," you may recall. But this is not something that happens only in Gregorian chant; it occurs in many types of vocal music. In any case, this piece is still the unmetered monophony we expect from Gregorian.

PRIMARY LISTENING:
"Benedicamus Domino,"
two-voice organum, School
of Notre Dame (record set)

The second setting is strikingly different in many respects, and even though this is only a portion of the entire piece, we can get a good idea of what is going on (Example 8).

To begin with, the performer singing the text of "Benedicamus Domino" is not using the Gregorian tune at all. *That* melody is in the organ but is moving at a snail's pace. This is related closely to religion and ritual. The medieval prescriptions for worship were very exact, and the utterance of the text, once it was established and approved, became something of an end in itself. So did the music to which the text was sung: in the thinking of the time, certain tunes were appropriate for each particular text, including, of course, "Benedicamus Domino." Several tunes were available for each text, but they were the *only* ones. The choice of which one to use was determined by the day and hour the text was to be chanted. In the setting of "Benedicamus Domino" we're now considering, the organ is using the proper tune but the singer is supplying the words. Thus

c. Two-voice organum

School of Notre Dame (*c.* 1175)

Example 8
"Benedicamus Domino," two-voice organum, School of Notre Dame.
Archibald T. Davison and Willi Apel, *Historical Anthology of Music.* Harvard University Press, 1962. Copyright 1946, 1949 by the President and Fellows of Harvard College. Used by permission.

the letter of the liturgical law is being observed: the words and the tune are both there. But they are not in the same place at the same time.

It is important to realize here that *both* the organ and the singer are using a melody and that whatever harmony occurs is a result of this fact. The simultaneous use of two melodies creates harmony, though the harmony is not *conceived* as harmony, in spite of the fact that we hear it that way. This might seem an unnecessarily sticky point to worry about, but it is an important one. For many centuries Western music developed along just such lines. Melodies were not harmonized by adding chords as we do when we strum along on a guitar to increase the musical interest of a song. Melodies were combined. And that is a big difference in musical thinking and practice.

This performance style has a name, *organum*, of which our example is just one of a number of types. Organum is the first kind of harmony we know about in Western music. As far as we can tell from contemporary sources, it began around the ninth century, but the example we are considering dates from about 1175. Even though our example has a relatively free sound—sometimes this type is called *free organum*—the music follows certain rigidly prescribed rules about what notes and intervals are permitted at what points in the composition. Unless you want to get deeply into theory, the rules themselves are of little interest. It is helpful to know, though, that the prescriptions existed and that music developed along the lines it did largely because there *were* approved procedures.

What about the rhythmic style of the singer and his music? Notice that his melody moves along in a metered style, and in very fast groups of three pulses. Is this a reference to the Trinity as it may have been in the "Kyrie eleison" discussed in chapter 1? It may be, because this triple kind of rhythmic quality was called *tempus perfectum* (perfect time), while groups of two pulses were called *tempus imperfectum* (imperfect time). At any rate the rhythmic style adds a new dimension to the music.

The School of Notre Dame in Paris, of which this organum is an example, was an important one. Among other contributions made there was the introduction of rhythmic notation, without which combinations of musical lines would not be possible in any kind of controlled way.

Here the relationship between rules of procedure and innovations becomes relevant. We are not sure how or why musical practices developed as they did, but their development has some interesting human implications. Although conducting public worship was one of the responsibilities of the priesthood—and the choirs of churches (often the same personnel)—it was not their only task. They were also expected to participate in the rituals observing the various Hours of the day, and these were often conducted without a congregation in attendance. There were eight different Hours, each with its own name—Matins and Vespers were two—during which services were prescribed, and these were in addition to the Mass. The "Benedicamus Domino" is an important text because it occurs in all the Hours.

Is it possible that during these periods the human urge to "make music," to create, was combined with the desire to make the offering more acceptable to God? We cannot know, of course, but we do know that the end result was to add through music an urgency to the words. It was inevitable, however, that the rules governing the musical procedures would become just as strict as those controlling the liturgy—and so Western musical theory was advanced through the combination of innovation and organizational control. The interplay between them has always been one of the most complex elements in the conduct of human affairs, and is one that still occupies us all, as we find, for instance, when we try to get a rule changed!

Now the particular musical practice we are considering, organum, creates a musical *texture* that is called *polyphony*. Polyphony is the texture that results from combining melodies. When there is significant melodic interest in the various voices or instrumental lines of a composition, we identify it as being *polyphonic*. Polyphony and the musical devices that derive from it have played an extremely important part in the development of music in the West and in some other parts of the world as well. We will encounter it frequently in the course of this book and in some surprising contexts. For now, we can describe the organum we have just been listening to as polyphonic. We could say further that various kinds of organum represent not only the earliest examples of harmony in Western music but also the earliest examples of polyphony. Polyphonic texture is not peculiar to vocal music, but as far as we know it had its beginning there.

As a reminder, we have encountered two types of texture so far: monophonic and polyphonic. These are extremely useful descriptive words because they permit very precise and brief identification without paragraphs of accompanying explanation and they also happen to be common terms throughout the world wherever informed people discuss musical practices.

Take notice of one important thing at this point: we have here, and as early as the twelfth century, the basic materials from which the music of the West was to derive its characteristics, and in terms of which we can discuss all music. These materials are melody, harmony, and rhythm, and they are all clearly recognizable in this work. And although the relationship among these three things is an ever-changing and fascinating one, by discussing one or all of them we can make verbal sense out of any music we hear. In other words, we can explain in these terms why a piece sounds the way it does and how the various sounds that occur relate to one another.

We are tempted to see the medieval period as an extremely untutored one; we used to refer to it as the Dark Ages. However, it was a time of enormous and vigorous creative activity, and during it the groundwork was laid for much of our musical practice and thinking. The typical medieval man may have been severely limited and controlled by the prevailing aura of mysticism and ecclesiastical authority, but his imagination was as great as ours. The innovative use of music in the service of religious ritual is merely one evidence of that fact.

SUPPLEMENTAL LISTENING Written examples of various types of organum abound in anthologies that illustrate the development of Western musical history and practice. The principles discussed above apply to innumerable compositions, although each composition has its own special points of interest. Among the most accessible recorded anthologies, the following are suggested:

History of European Music, vol. 2. Musical Heritage Society: OR–350.
A Treasury of Early Music, vol. 1. Haydn Society: HSE–9100.

History of Music in Sound, vol. 2. RCA Victor: LM–6015.
Ars Antiqua. Telefunken: SAWT–9530/31–B.

Almost 200 years later than the "Benedicamus Domino" we listened to, another French composer, Guillaume de Machaut, composed a mass of considerable historical significance. In order to appreciate the advances that had been made in polyphony and the growing complexity involved in the music, listen to one of the movements from Machaut's *Notre Dame Mass,* the "Agnus Dei," composed about 1364.

PRIMARY LISTENING:
Guillaume de Machaut, "Agnus Dei" from *Notre Dame Mass,* about 1364

The text is in three sections as follows:

Agnus Dei, qui tollis peccata mundi; miserere nobis.

Lamb of God, who takest away the sins of the world, have mercy upon us.

Agnus Dei, qui tollis peccata mundi; miserere nobis.

Lamb of God, who takest away the sins of the world, have mercy upon us.

Agnus Dei, qui tollis peccata mundi; dona nobis pacem.

Lamb of God, who takest away the sins of the world, grant us peace.

[1]In musical terminology, melodic lines are often referred to as "voices," so that the organ part in "Benedicamus Domino" is a voice, although certainly not a human one.

A lot of action has been added during the two centuries that separate this composition and the "Benedicamus Domino." For one thing, there are four voices rather than only two.[1] That means there has to be a great deal more organization involved. It also means that with so many different melody lines going on, it is more difficult for the listener to take in all the activity. The words are no help, either, because about the only time all the singers are singing the text together is at the beginning of each phrase and at the cadences. But the sound is a lot fuller than when there are only two lines, richer and more varied in every way. That's one of the principal reasons for adding voices, of course. We are led to suspect that interest in music, almost for its own sake alone, is beginning to take precedence over the mere utterance of the liturgy.

Another difference is in the addition of instruments. If you listen closely, you will hear that the instruments are playing the same melodies that the voices are singing, rather than having independent parts. This is quite typical of medieval music. The score provides only part of the story (Example 9). Depending upon what recording of this piece you happen to be using, you may be surprised to hear things that are very different from what you see on the page. That's because present-day performances usually follow the medieval practice, if they are reliable performances, and one of the things

peculiar to medieval music is the fact that the notes are given but
what instruments might be involved are not indicated, nor does the
composer let you know what he wants sung and what he wants
played. As a result, performances then and now are apt to be quite
different from one another. Sometimes all four parts will be sung,
sometimes only two, sometimes only one. The slack is taken up by
instruments, and it is even possible to have all parts sung *and* played.

Example 9
Machaut, "Agnus Dei" from
Notre Dame Mass.
Copyrighted by Breitkopf & Haertel,
Wiesbaden.

5 Agnus Dei

Vg f. 294ʳ- 295, A f. 449ʳ- 450, G f. 132ʳ-138, E f. 170.

The "arrangement" is open wide to interpretive differences, partly because we have only slender bits of information about how music of the period was conceived and performed. Musicologists work at this constantly; for some it is almost their sole concern, and they are gradually pushing back the fog of incomplete information. A glance at the original manuscript will show why the problems are not easily solved (Example 10).

Example 10
Machaut, "Agnus Dei"
from *Notre Dame Mass*.
From *Summa Musicae Medii Aevi*,
vol. 1. Facsimile edition published
by Friedrich Gennrich,
Darmstadt, Germany.

This all takes a lot of deciphering, and there is still a lot of wrangling among scholars about just what to make of it. Little wonder, then, that performances vary. But it was the same in the medieval period and for a functional reason: performing forces varied from place to place and from time to time. Therefore the treatment of the notes depended on who was available to sing and play, and also what instruments might be on hand.

The *Notre Dame Mass* is a significant one for our history of music. It is the first polyphonic setting of the entire Mass by a single composer who can be identified. There is an earlier Mass, but the composer remains anonymous. As a result, Machaut, while probably not an innovator, assumes considerable importance as a musical figure.

Machaut (about 1300–1377) was a member of the Roman Catholic clergy, and was attached to several royal personages including princes and kings. Also a poet, he set many of his own verses and composed ballads and much sacred music.

A GLANCE AT HISTORY

The year 1000 was anticipated with fear by some and with hope by others. Many true believers assumed that it would mark the return of Christ, an assumption based upon scriptural references to a millennium. The year came and went, and as the century wore on, people relaxed their vigils and began to take a closer look at man and his environment. The church was still an enormously powerful force in the affairs of earth, but there was less tendency to feel the power as an oppressive force and even somewhat less struggle to carry the weight of a threatening heaven. Thus a new God–man relationship developed and the almost joyous outreach toward heaven was reflected in all the arts. It is particularly visible in the change of architectural style, wherein during the period from 1100 to about 1400, the Gothic era, the high, pointed arches of the cathedrals seemed to be trying to touch the heavens themselves (Illustration 4).

Along with the thrust toward the sky in architecture, all the arts became more decorative, more expressive of beauty as man beheld beauty, more involved with humanity and the concerns of people. Although the movements were halting and not fully developed, they were a beginning of the awakening of humanism that was to come to full flower in the next period, the Renaissance.

Among the many new emphases in human relationships were the strengthening of political forces and a growing independence of secular rulers from the dominance of the church. Under the sponsorship of the nobility, explorations were undertaken in an attempt to broaden knowledge of the world. The second Crusade got under way and even more interaction with non-European cultures resulted. Although still guided strongly by the influence of the church, universities with strong secular interests were

**Illustration 4. THE
CATHEDRAL AT COLOGNE,
1248–1322.**
The pointed spires, stretching
toward heaven, identify this
cathedral as among the most
striking examples of Gothic
architecture.
Used by permission of Hirmer Verlag,
München.

founded, and subjects other than theology occupied the attention of scholars.

With the growing control over musical notation came a greater concern for preserving secular music. Among the legacies we have from the Gothic period are the poems and songs of the Troubadours and Trouvères in France and the Minnesingers in Germany. Many of the Troubadours were actually well-educated dropouts from the priesthood, disenchanted with the restrictions of the monastic life. Because they were well trained musically, their works are of more than passing interest, and if you want to investigate, there are many fine recordings.

All of the activity that centered on the pleasures of man rather than the total fear of God led quite naturally to the increased complexity of music that we have seen in the Machaut Mass. Although it would be unfair to summarize the musical character of an entire historical period through the impressions of one small excerpt, it is fair to say that in some ways Machaut is the culmination of the medieval period musically. Throughout the Gothic era, artists of all sorts came out from under the cloud of anonymity that was typical of the early Middle Ages. We have a relatively large body of works from Machaut, more than from any of his contemporaries, and he stands, then, as the prototype of the artist as a distinctive personality.

PEOPLE AND EVENTS TO INVESTIGATE:

MUSICIANS:

Franco of Cologne: 13th century
Adam de la Halle: c. 1240–1287
Léonin: 12th century
Guillaume de Machaut: c. 1300–1377
Pérotin: 13th century

ARTISTS AND LITERARY FIGURES:

St. Thomas Aquinas: c. 1225–1274
Roger Bacon: c. 1214–1294
Giovanni Boccaccio: 1313–1375
Geoffrey Chaucer: c. 1340–1400
Dante Alighieri: 1265–1321
Giotto: c. 1266–1337
Francesco Petrarch: 1304–1374
John Wycliffe: c. 1320–1384

EVENTS:

Avignon Captivity: 1309–1377
Hundred Years' War: 1337–1453
Magna Carta: 1215
Plague of the Black Death: 1347–1350
Marco Polo: c. 1254–1324 (Journeys 1271–1295)
Second Crusade: 12th century
Universities established, including Oxford: 12th century

Once introduced and adopted as a musical texture and procedure, polyphony underwent a number of changes that added to its complexity and sophistication, as we have seen. During the course of the Renaissance period, roughly spanning the fifteenth and sixteenth centuries, a new concept of melodic combinations developed. This involved the use of a single melody but beginning in different voices at different times. This process is called *imitative polyphony* because all the voices are imitating the one that begins the whole procedure. Most of us have sung rounds and we will deal more fully with them later in the book. But now it is enough to point out that when we sing a round we are singing in imitative polyphony.

By the last half of the sixteenth century, polyphonic imitation was very much the order of the day. The Renaissance is often referred to as the Golden Age of Polyphony, in fact. A common practice was to use one melodic idea for each section of the text, changing that melody as the text changed but allowing all voices to use it in turn. The "Agnus Dei" from the *Missa Brevis* by Giovanni Pierluigi da Palestrina will illustrate this.

The text is the same tripartite one that we know from Machaut's setting, but Palestrina breaks each of the three sections into three smaller segments, treating each one individually.

PRIMARY LISTENING:
Giovanni Pierluigi da
Palestrina, "Agnus Dei"
from *Missa Brevis*, 1570

Agnus Dei	Lamb of God
Qui tollis peccata mundi	Who takest away the sins of the world,
Miserere nobis	Have mercy on us.

Each section of the text has its own particular melody, and the voices all get their turn with it in an imitative fashion. The opening section establishes the process (Example 11).

The order of entry is alto, tenor, soprano, bass. When the words change to "Qui tollis peccata mundi," a different melody is used, entering in the order bass, alto, tenor, soprano. Then at "Miserere nobis" the musical idea is changed again, and the various vocal lines carry on the process of imitation. Notice the continuous nature of the sound. Is this related in any way to the matter of cadences? How, then, do cadences help define structure in a composition like this?

Although the concept of combining melodies is the same here as in the "Benedicamus Domino" and Machaut's Mass from the medieval period, notice how much richer the effect is. Some of that is due to the changing ideas about harmony and the relationship among the various voices. More and more rules and theories developed during the Renaissance period, some relating to worship rituals—remember that the Protestant Reformation began in 1517. Without getting too deeply into theory, you might simply be aware

Example 11
Palestrina, "Agnus Dei" from
Missa Brevis.
Kalmus score, pp. 21–22. Used by
permission.

that the sonorities here involve many more intervals of thirds and sixths than in the Machaut piece, where there was an abundance of fourths and fifths (see appendix 1). If you play a series of thirds and sixths on the piano, followed by a series of fourths and fifths, you will understand why Palestrina sounds richer than Machaut. At the same time, you might miss some of the rugged vigorous and forthright quality in Machaut. And thus the changes in musical practice help to define the differences between medieval and Renaissance style.

What is the metric character of Palestrina's piece? How can this *tempus* be used in a religious context? Which voice is most important in this performance: soprano, alto, tenor, or bass?

The Italian organist and composer Giovanni Pierluigi da Palestrina (1525–1594), normally called simply Palestrina, began his career as organist and teacher at the cathedral in Palestrina, his native town. He moved to Rome to direct the choir at St. Peter's Cathedral, left to accept several other posts, and returned to St. Peter's in 1570. He was assigned the task of "purifying" and reediting the body of church chant, partially in response to the Reformation and the Roman Catholic reaction to it. The complexity of the task, however, made it impossible to complete until some time after Palestrina's death. Meanwhile, he achieved wide fame as a composer and in 1588 began publishing his accumulated works. This task, too, was incomplete at his death. He composed many Masses, motets, madrigals, miscellaneous service music, and a few secular works.

SUPPLEMENTAL LISTENING

Any Renaissance Mass or motet will illustrate the devices found in Palestrina's *Missa Brevis*. Among the most accessible on records is the same composer's *Missa Papae Marcelli*. Other important composers of the Renaissance period who wrote Masses as well as other sacred and secular music of a polyphonic nature include Josquin des Prez, Johannes Ockeghem, Jacob Obrecht, and Tomás Luis de Victoria.

Examples of compositions by all these composers may be found on recordings of the *Historical Anthology of Music* on Pleiades: 250 through 257.

A GLANCE AT HISTORY

Renaissance means revival or reawakening. The period from about 1400 to 1600 was characterized by the coming to full fruition of the increased interest in humanity that was begun on a smaller scale during the Gothic period. Philosophers, scholars, artists all turned their attention to the patterns of creativity and inquiry that had developed so strikingly during the classic era in Greece. Following those guidelines, humanism came into its own as a force behind man's ideas and activities. Uppermost among the motivations was the belief that rational thought and the intellect were the sources of knowledge. This replaced the earlier reliance on divine revelation, most of which was not open to question without fear of reprisals. With this belief and the scientific and philosophical gains that gave it credibility came an associated sense of the worth of human values and even of material things, including the world itself.

Among the many results was artistic control over perspective in painting and an intense interest in the human body as an art object (Illustrations 5 and 6). Complementing the fascination with man and his immediate environment was the search for new worlds, new trade routes, new

Illustration 5. THE ADORATION OF THE MAGI.

Follower of Dirck Bouts (1400–1475). Renaissance painters such as Bouts were fascinated with their newly developed control over perspective. Not yet free enough to indulge in pure landscapes, they were tied to subject matter that was usually sacred in nature and was commissioned for religious use. But it is evident that the real interest here is not the Holy Family, but rather the figures receding into the distance, many caught in the act of natural movements. Nor is the city Bethlehem, of course. Compare this to El Greco's *Crucifixion* (page 150), for evidence that the overlap of sacred and secular interests was not short-lived. Cincinnati Art Museum. Bequest of Mrs. Mary M. Emery.

Illustration 6. GROUP OF FIGURES SEATED, DISPUTING. Baccio Bandinelli (1493?–1559/60). The growing interest in real-life subjects during the Renaissance led naturally into an enchantment with the human body and techniques for representing it realistically. Its musculature in action was a favorite subject, as Bandinelli's work illustrates. Cincinnati Art Museum. Gift of Emily Poole.

geographical vistas that led to many voyages of exploration. Reaching even beyond the confines of earth, astronomers sought to fathom the heavens, and in spite of opposition from the church, did develop theories that persist to this day.

On the political side, feudalism vanished almost completely in the West, replaced by a system of city-states and ever-strengthening monarchies. The freedom to explore as well as to exploit led to the gradual development of a merchant class as well as an embryonic middle class of artisans and other folk attached to the various enterprises created by the new commercialism.

There was an enormous amount of artistic activity, most of it still under the patronage of the church and the aristocracy. In music as in sculpture and painting and architecture, the period can be truly called the seedbed for the modern era. The invention of printing aided greatly in the dissemination of music throughout Europe, so that a common practice developed giving a new stability to musical style. A whole new body of composition grew in support of the worship patterns of the Reformation. At the same time, the reforms in the Roman Catholic church led to innovations also.

Although most of the music, sacred and secular, was still conceived with vocal ideals in mind, there was a growing interest in instrumental music and an accompanying development in instruments themselves. Ranges were increased, playing techniques became more virtuosic, and there was a corresponding production of music to accommodate the advancements.

Because of the growing independence of the individual and the general broadening interest in the affairs of man and his world, the list of significant people lengthens with each new historical period. Even a cursory examination of the achievements of the musicians, artists, and scientists below will give you an idea of the stimulating physical and mental activity of the Renaissance.

MUSICIANS:

William Byrd: c. 1540–1623	Claudio Monteverdi: 1567–1643
Guillaume Dufay: c. 1400–1474	Thomas Morley: 1557–1603
Carlo Gesualdo: c. 1560–1613	Jacob Obrecht: 1430–1505
Josquin des Prez: c. 1445–1521	Giovanni Palestrina: c. 1526–1594

Tomás Luis de Victoria: c. 1535–1611

ARTISTS, LITERARY FIGURES AND OTHERS:

Sandro Botticelli: c. 1444–1510
Benvenuto Cellini: 1500–1571
Nicolaus Copernicus: 1473–1543
Donatello: c. 1386–1466
Albrecht Dürer: 1471–1528
Galilei Galileo: 1564–1642
Matthias Grünewald: c. 1470–1528
Johannes Gutenberg: c. 1400–1468
Leonardo da Vinci: 1452–1519
Michelangelo Buonarotti: 1475–1564
Francois Rabelais: c. 1490–1553
Raphael: 1483–1520
William Shakespeare: 1564–1616
Titian: c. 1477–1576

EVENTS:

Christopher Columbus (c. 1446–1506), voyages: 1492–1504
Vasco de Balboa discovers Pacific Ocean: 1513
Hernando Cortes (1485–1547) invades Mexico: 1519
Fernando Magellan voyages: 1520–1521
Council of Trent: 1545–1563
Sir Francis Drake (1540–1596) sails around the world: 1577–1580

Chapter 3
Homophonic Texture: Vertical Harmony

Let's dip back in time to the beginning of the sixteenth century. Most of us will remember King Henry VIII of England (1491–1547) for his political and religious activities and, even more likely, will remember that he had difficulty finding a wife he could endure for very long. But it may come as a surprise to know that he was intensely interested in music and tried his hand at composing as well as performing. Henry was originally destined for service in the church and as a part of his preparation he was trained in music. Although he was sidetracked from ecclesiastical pursuits into the monarchy, he remained a patron and participant in musical performance and composition.

He was only 18 when he ascended the throne in 1509 to rule until he died, and many of the more dramatic and sordid events with which he is associated were in the future. The temper of the early years of his reign was often one of youthful gaiety, characterized by dancing, drinking, and the lusty sort of lovemaking that was typical of Renaissance Europe. All of this is in keeping with the spirit of the period as discussed in chapter 2.

One of Henry VIII's compositions, "Pastime with Good Company" (Example 12), reflects some of this spirit, in its words as well as in the music. It is from a manuscript collection that is dated by scholars as between 1510 and 1520.

Example 12
Henry VIII, "Pastime with
Good Company."

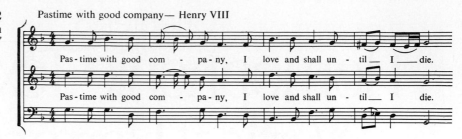

Pastime with good company— Henry VIII

Pas - time with good com - pa - ny, I love and shall un - til _ I _ die.

Pas - time with good com - pa - ny, I love and shall un - til _ I die.

PRIMARY LISTENING:
HENRY VIII, "Pastime with
Good Company"
(record set)

Pastime with good company,
I love and shall until I die.
Gruch who lust, but none deny;
So God be pleased, thus live will I;

For my pastance,
Hunt, sing, and dance;
My heart is set
All goodly sport
For my comfort:
Who shall me let?

Youth must have some dalliance,
Of good or ill some pastance;
Company me thinks then best
All thoughts and fancies to digest.

For idleness
Is chief mistress
Of vices all;
Then who can say
But mirth and play
Is best of all?

Company with honesty
Is virtue, vices to flee;
Company is good and ill,
But every man hath his free will.

The best ensue,
The worst eschew,
My mind shall be;
Virtue to use,
Vice to refuse,
Thus shall I use me.

Some of the words are no longer in English usage. "Gruch" means "to complain about or condemn." Our word "grouch" comes from this. The sense of the third line, then, is "Condemn those who lust, but no one can deny having some lust." "Pastance" means "recreation," and "let" means "to hinder or obstruct." Clearly Henry is putting his best foot forward and wants good companionship in his pleasures, although declaring himself for virtue rather than vice.

Notice how spritely the music is, how filled with good spirits, how much less repetitious the rhythmic figures are than in some of the music we listened to. Is that because this is a secular piece? The percussion keeps the beat steady, while above it the voices and instruments follow the accents of the words. What is the meter? As we listen and perhaps tap our feet, it seems to swing along in groups of two pulses. In spite of the meter signature, which suggests groups of four, we *feel* two. Does the tempo have something to do with this?

Perhaps the symbols for meter do not always indicate what the metric sensations will be.

Whatever the apparent contradictions, we can certainly say that the musical accents do match the verbal ones, and this is often the case in vocal music. The poetry also affects the musical phrasing, long poetic lines resulting in long musical phrases, short lines in short phrases. It is possible that much of our feeling for musical phrasing developed through this sort of literal extension of poetic phrasing. Although there is a tendency toward irregularity of phrase length in Renaissance music, a greater consistency emerges during the later Classic period, and we will discuss this fully later.

Listen carefully to the instruments. There is a soprano recorder and a tenor recorder—termed soprano and tenor because they match the range of those human voices. The recorder is one of the forerunners of the modern flute and is used in public schools as well as in some rock bands, of all things. The lowest instrument is not well known except in university chamber ensembles that specialize in music of the early periods. It's a krummhorn and is an ancestor of the double-reed instruments of today, the bassoon and oboe. *Krumm* means "bent," and the instrument was just that, curving upward in a U toward the end (Illustration 7).

As in the Machaut Mass, this music was not composed for a specific set of instruments in the way more modern music is. If the performers wanted to omit a part, that was fine. In this performance of "Pastime with Good Company," notice that the ranges are not large in any one melody; this makes it possible for most people to sing along without a great deal of vocal training. The instruments were also restricted in range at this midpoint in the Renaissance; anyone who really wanted to could master them, although some performers were naturally better than others, even as now. Finally, the notes were there in the score, but not the performance directions—it was just a matter of sing it, play it, or mix and match at will.

But this was good-fellowship music—music just to gather round and have fun with. We later lost much of this in our musical experience because the music gradually became more complex and the performers developed a corresponding skill. And people responded by listening and enjoying music more as consumers than as makers. This has not been true in all cultures, and perhaps we have added one dimension at the sacrifice of another. The very fact that one takes a course of this kind using a book like this speaks to that point.

There is an additional musical factor here that deserves some attention. Our ears tend to be most attracted to the highest voice; if we were going to join in singing this piece, we would most likely

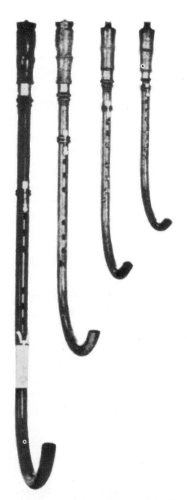

Illustration 7.
KRUMMHORNS.
Like recorders, krummhorns were divided into families that approximated the ranges of the human voice. From left to right, those pictured are bass, tenor, alto, and soprano.

follow along with that part. Also, all the voices and words move along together rather than going their more or less separate ways as in the polyphonic music we heard. To some degree, then, the two lower melodic lines are subservient to the top voice. They tend to harmonize it by supplying supporting parts rather than to harmonize it because they have an important melody of their own. The kind of musical texture created is called *homophonic*, and it raises a real question of identification because it overlaps so much with polyphony and yet it sounds so different.

If you happen to sing along with the bass here, you will probably think that the tune you sing is pretty good and interesting—and you'll be right. The same thing goes on when we sing hymns. In a harmonization that is musically stimulating, all the parts—soprano, alto, tenor, bass—have an interesting melody. But again there is a question of degree. If you are singing bass, tenor, or alto in a hymn, you are most often fulfilling a harmonic function in support of the soprano, like it or not. And that makes the musical texture essentially homophonic. It's easy to check this out. Ask 10 people the question "How does "America" go?" Chances are they will all sing the melody—the soprano part—instead of the alto or tenor or bass. Ergo "America" is homophonic. As in all matters of music, it pays not to get too involved with terminology. The best approach is simply to realize that textural characteristics "feel" different from one another, that much music uses mixtures of texture for purposes of musical variety and interest, and that the vocabulary has more to do with discussion and description than with our responses to music. It helps us to intellectualize and is most valuable in that context.

One more observation about texture: Palestrina was a Renaissance composer and his "Agnus Dei" was polyphonic. What is Henry VIII doing writing homophonic music in the Renaissance, a period that we have already identified as the Golden Age of Polyphony? Well, another category shot down! Although it was not to come to its fullest development until the Baroque period which succeeded the Renaissance, homophony was slipping gradually into the texture of music even before Henry wrote his piece. As in so many other things, we'd best be very cautious in our generalizations.

Notice what the instruments are doing in the different stanzas. Particularly in the third one some *ornamentation*—embellishment of the original tune—is taking place. During the Renaissance the practice was a common one, and performers were expected to improvise in this way. Indeed, different recordings or live performances of a piece like this are apt to sound quite different because of improvisation. We will encounter it in many situations because it has a long history in our own music as well as in the music of other lands.

We have now at our command all the vocabulary of texture we will need—monophonic, polyphonic, and homophonic. We have also some descriptive terminology for melody, harmony, and rhythm, the three most important materials of music. These things reinforce one another and have a cross-relationship that is useful in discussion.

But perhaps more important from the human perspective, we have met a new composer, and he has turned out to be none other than the much-married King Henry VIII of England.

SUPPLEMENTAL LISTENING   Again, historical anthologies of music from the Renaissance will illustrate the points discussed above. The mixture of homophony and polyphony is a common one during the period, particularly the later years, and the investigation of that mixture can be quite rewarding.

Henry VIII's complete works have been recorded by the Musical Heritage Society on *Henry VIII: Complete Works*. MHS–1530.

Additional recorded anthologies of Renaissance music include:

History of Music in Sound, vol 3. RCA Victor: LM–6016.
History of Music in Sound, vol. 4. RCA Victor: LM–6029.
Historical Anthology of Music. Southern Illinois University
Press. Pleiades: P–252/3/4/5/6. These recordings cover the
period from the late fifteenth century to the late sixteenth
century.

A GLANCE AT HISTORY   By the time of Henry VIII's rule in England, the monarchy had become immensely strong and stable. As a result, it was possible for the courts to turn their attention to aspects of life other than an almost total involvement with protecting property, life, and limb from invaders and marauders as had been the preoccupations of much of the medieval period. With considerably more time on hand, it was natural that the members of the courts should turn their energies to various phases of the arts, including the performance and creation of music. Practically all establishments were able to retain some sort of musical force, including composers as well as performers. They provided entertainment and ceremonial music for state occasions and similar celebrations. But they also served in a tutorial capacity for those members of the monarchic entourage who were interested enough to cultivate their musical abilities.

The period of the professional artist was not yet at hand. What patronage was not available from the church (and there was a lot that was) could be enhanced by commissions from the aristocracy and even to some extent from the rising merchant classes.

Unlike the general illiteracy of the rulers of the medieval period, especially those with a heritage drawn from the barbarian tribes, the Renaissance kings, queens, lords, and ladies were relatively well educated in literature, history, and general culture. It was by this route, of course, that Henry had the background to indulge his interests in both composition and performance.

Although much of the motivation for the break with the Roman Catholic church that was a high point in Henry's reign was economic and connubial, there was a solid undergirding of educated maneuvering that allowed for the success of the enterprise. He was not able, however, to bring the sort of stability to the church–state relationship that was to come with the reign of Elizabeth. But his movement toward independence of the church in England was certainly the beginning of a new era in the arts as well as in the politics of that nation.

In spite of the fact that homophonic texture began early in the Renaissance, it appeared most often as contrast to what was principally a polyphonic practice. It was not really until the outset of the Baroque period that homophony gained its first truly secure foothold. And here, as in so many innovations in music and the other arts, the reason was functional.

Polyphony has its advantages, especially for the performer; for one, everybody gets to sing or play a satisfying melody. However, it can be disconcerning to the listener in some ways. One of these has to do with understanding the text, as we have seen. The words do get a bit garbled when each voice is about its own business rather than singing the text together. We noticed in Henry VIII's piece the clarity that homophony can bring.

Something happened to intensify the search for clear verbal delivery: the birth of opera. Because opera is essentially drama, the singers and the audience insisted on a clear understanding of the words. What resulted was an entirely new concept of the relationship between melody and harmony.

PRIMARY LISTENING: Claudio Monteverdi, "Tu se' morta" from *L'Orfeo* (record set)

The next listening selection, "Tu se' morta," is from *L'Orfeo*, one of the first operas—although it wasn't called an opera when it was first performed for a small Italian audience in 1607 and later for a larger group in 1609. Then it was called a *favola*, meaning "tale" or "fable."

It was composed by Claudio Monteverdi (1567–1643), who served as court musician to the Duke of Mantua from 1602 to 1613, when he was appointed chapelmaster at St. Mark's Cathedral in

Venice. He is considered one of music's great innovators because of his influence over the transition from Renaissance polyphony to the new Baroque styles and forms. Especially important was his expressive use of homophonic style and his use of instruments in more dramatic ways than doubling or otherwise simply supporting the vocal parts. He composed many operas and ballets, as well as sacred and secular choral pieces including numerous madrigals.

Without getting into elaborate detail about the plot of the opera, it would be helpful to know that the singer, Orpheus, is grieving because his wife, Eurydice, has been bitten by a snake and has died. Orpheus is determined either to rescue her from the underworld, the realm of the dead, or to join her there rather than live on earth without her. He sings these words:

Tu se' morta, mia vita, ed io respiro?	You are dead, my life, and I breathe?
Tu se' da me partita	You have left me
Per mai più non tornare, ed io rimango?	Never to return, and I must remain?
Nò, che se i versi alcuna cosa ponno,	No, if there is any power at all in my verses,
N'andrò sicuro a' più profondi abissi,	I will go down to the deepest depths,
E, intenerito il cor del rè de l'ombre,	And, having melted the heart of the King of Shadows,
Meco trarrotti a riveder le stelle;	Bring you back with me to see the stars again;
O, se ciò negherammi empio destino,	Or, if this is denied to me by unkind fate,
Rimarrò teco in compagnia di morte,	Remain with you in the company of death.
Addio, terra, addio cielo e sole, addio.	Farewell earth, farewell sky and sun, farewell.

The tale is based on Greek sources, and that has something to do with the objectives and style of early opera in the first place. As we have discussed above, the Renaissance was called that because in philosophy, architecture, and many of the arts it was characterized by an intense interest in the ideals and practices of the Greeks (Illustration 8). As is often the case, music was a little while really catching up with the changing movements in the other arts. Not until the Renaissance had reached a climax and turned somewhat from its course did music adopt what the musicians and playwrights took to be the Greek ideals. They were aware that the Greeks had used poetry, music, and drama as a unified type of artistic expression, all these elements operating with equal importance. In an attempt to

Illustration 8. THE KING AND MARS.
Philippe Behagle (died 1704). The Renaissance interest in classic Greek models carried over into the Baroque in the visual arts where it complemented the later-born musical interest in the same subjects. This tapestry depicts Louis XIV (1638–1715) about to set out on one of his military exploits accompanied by Mars, the god of war. The musical instruments and cupids are symbols of the love and peace he leaves behind but to which he will presumably return. The instruments are a cross section of those of the period. Among them are a viol d'amore, bagpipe, soprano viol, lute, recorder, cornetto, flute, and tambourine.
Collection of the J. B. Speed Art Museum, Louisville, Kentucky.

recapture that, the opera was born, and even most of the characters were drawn from Greek mythology and drama. And thus we find Orpheus and his troubles in Monteverdi's *favola*.

So much for the literary and dramatic elements. The musical style is in strong contrast to anything we've heard so far. If you follow the score of "Tu se' morta" as you listen (Example 13), you will probably hear some repetition of words, always in the interest of dramatic emphasis. You will be aware, too, that what is being played by the lute and organ is not exactly what is on the page. The reasons have to do with the mechanics of writing the music for this particular type of composition. What the composer put on paper during much of this period, particularly for solo pieces, consisted of only two lines of music: the melody and the accompanist's bass notes. Above or below the bass notes, he put some numbers—figures—that helped the accompanist identify the chords that were to be played as an accompaniment for the melody. The part was called, logically, the *figured bass* or *continuo*.

This created several problems. A good accompanist was able to translate the figures into the proper chords and arrive at the right harmony. But he was free, even encouraged, to add some notes of his own as long as they didn't change the harmony. As a result, each performer probably played something a bit different from what was played by other performers. The whole process of choosing just what to play was called *realizing the figured bass*, and if one is to perform this music today, he either has to do the realization himself or rely on what somebody else has provided on paper by editing. So the score that is reproduced here is merely one person's idea of what to add to the bass and its figures. Other editors would undoubtedly work it out differently.

The editor of the recorded performance you are listening to was not the same person as the one who provided the score you are looking at, and therefore there are some differences here too. As you can imagine, a lot is left to the performer or editor. A different recording would probably sound at odds with the notation in other ways, just as different performances did during the medieval, Renaissance, and Baroque periods. It is all such a tricky business that some scholars are involved with almost nothing except trying to work out the problems presented by what we would call incomplete notation.

If you listen and watch carefully, you will realize that most of the discrepancies here are in the harmony. The chords being played are not those on the page. The reason for this is in Monteverdi's figures, with which he was very sparing. He relied on the performer

Example 13
Monteverdi, "Tu se' morta"
from *L'Orfeo*.
The Complete Works of Monteverdi,
vol. 11, ed. Malipiero. Used by
permission of European American
Music Distributors Corporation, sole
U.S. agent for Universal Edition.

Example 13, *cont.*

stel _ le,   O se ciò ne _ ghe _ rammi em _ pio de _ sti _ no,

ri _ marrò te _ co   in compagnia   di mor _ te   a dio ter _ ra

a   dio cie _ lo   e So _ le,   a Di _ o.

to compensate out of his knowledge of current style, using the "right" chords even when they were not given in complete figures. But notice that the bass line is exactly what is on the page. Monteverdi put *that* down in musical notation, so it's not open to interpretation.

Listening to this music, we immediately become aware that the accompaniment (i.e., the chords) has only one main function; it supplies a harmonic background that supports the vocal melody but does not get in the way too much. This leaves the singer free to project the meaning of the text in order to get the message across; our ears are not distracted with a lot of musical complexity. The advantage of this homophonic style over polyphony, especially in a dramatic presentation such as an opera, is clear. All this was actually the thinking behind this method of composing and performing. Whatever polyphonic writing there was in early opera was reserved for choruses that merely commented on the dramatic action rather than contributing strongly to the plot development. The solo singing style was called *recitative*, and was more a way of reciting on pitch, as the term indicates, than of trying to build an exciting melody. The rhythms are pretty close to speech rhythms, although elongated, and the rise and fall in pitch is pretty much like heightened speech. One is reminded of chant, of course, and can see the relationship between that and recitative.

Thus the effect of the recitative style on musical thinking was to focus attention on the melody and the words. But there was a side effect that was important to our music: melody and harmony became separated in everyone's mind and ears. Recall the very beginning of Western harmony, where that separation was merely a result of combining melodies, and it will be evident that our fascination with harmony as a specific musical tool probably gained much impetus from the innovations of the early Italian opera composers.

Do you see the relationship to strumming chords on a guitar as a way of accompanying songs? In fact, have you been aware that the discussion of "Tu se' morta" is the first discussion to include a reference to chords at all? That's because previous musical periods did not develop that concept—they heard mainly the combinations of melodic lines even within a homophonic texture. But once there developed the awareness of sonorities completely independent of the melody even while supporting it, then musicians were into another avenue of harmonic exploration altogether.

SUPPLEMENTAL LISTENING   Any aria from *L'Orfeo* will illustrate the same style of delivery and the same melodic–harmonic relationships. Complete recordings of the opera are:

> *L'Orfeo.* Telefunken: SKH 21/1–3.
> *L'Orfeo.* Archive: ARC 3035–36.
> Also of interest is the opera *L'Euridice* by the Italian composer Jacopo Peri. This is the earliest opera for which we have the complete music preserved. It was first performed in 1600 and published in 1601. Like *L'Orfeo* it is characterized by recitative vocal delivery over a principally chordal accompaniment. It is available on Orpheus: OR 344–345 S. Peri (1561–1633) was most active in Florence, where he contributed to the establishment of opera as a member of the group of artists and intelligentsia known as the Camerata. His opera *Dafne* on a libretto by Ottavio Rinuccini, is thought to be the first in that genre. The music for it is lost. *L'Euridice* is his second opera.

The attention given to chords as harmonic entities rather than merely kissing cousins of melodic lines naturally led to theories about their function in music. You might want to refer to appendix 1 at this point in order to track down what some of those theories are and also check on how chords are built and how they relate to one another. But whether or not you want to pursue the matter in detail, you should know that by various main roads and byways, Western music settled for three centuries on the concept that three chords in any given key constitute the backbone of that key. Those three chords are the *tonic* (I), the *subdominant* (IV), and the *dominant* (V). The manner in which they interact helps to clarify the harmonic sense of the key more than any other factors. They are so important, in fact, that many kinds of music use *only* those three chords.

Tonic, subdominant, and dominant are used to properly identify the most important steps of a scale. The tonic is the first step, the subdominant is the fourth step, and the dominant is the fifth step. If you build a chord on the tonic note, you have a tonic chord—also called the I chord for obvious reasons. A chord built on the fourth step is a subdominant chord—the IV chord. The dominant is the V chord.

Among the kinds of music that use only those three chords is the blues. The blues is many things. It is a mood, a state of being—as when we say, "I've really got the blues" or "I feel sort of blue today." It is also a traditional way of communicating within the black community, and in this sense it has a meaning and a richness of association that whites can never fully relate to. There is even a language of symbolism that runs through its history, and the failure to understand that symbolism will obscure the meaning of many of the lyrics.

But not all blues have words—some are purely instrumental. In either case, the blues is a form, one of the most important elements of which is the harmonic background.

PRIMARY LISTENING:
Traditional, "How Long Blues," Jimmy Yancey, piano (record set)

Listen now to "How Long Blues," an instrumental rendition of a traditional blues that originally had words (Example 14). The melodic outline that is given here is that of the traditional "How Long Blues." You will notice that Yancey adds some harmonizing notes and that he also uses some octave exchanges. None of this upsets the harmonic progression, of course. Assuming that your ears are able to separate the left-hand from the right-hand piano parts, you will notice that the left is playing what musicians call chord outlines. That is, the notes of several different chords are being played, but successively, like a melody, instead of all sounding together. We hear such chord outlines played by guitar and banjo pickers, by the bass in rock bands, by folk singers who might be accompanying them-

Example 14
"How Long Blues."

selves on the guitar, by all sorts of performers. Now if you follow the left-hand music carefully you can tell that Yancey is playing only three different chords, and they are the ones discussed above. They form the harmonic vocabulary of the blues when they remain in the strictly classic style of that form. In an eight-bar blues, like the one Yancey is playing, the pattern works like this for each eight measures:

> Two measures of tonic (I chord)
> Two measures of subdominant (IV chord)
> One measure of tonic (I chord)
> One measure of dominant (V chord)
> Two measures of tonic (I chord)

If you play the guitar, the three chords we are talking about are usually the first ones that need to be mastered in any key. "How Long Blues" is in F major, so the chords here are F major, B♭ major, and C major. If you can play those three chords, you can "jam" along with Yancey. The only problem might be the fancy sort of thing that he does in the seventh and eighth bars of each chorus.[1] That's called a *break*, and it is a standard device in many blues performances as well as a favorite way to end each chorus with a little added musical interest.

Another term to get familiar with is *changes*. The changes are simply chord changes. Going from the tonic to the subdominant in the third measure is a change. Jazz and rock musicians often tune up or warm up by playing the changes, usually involving I, IV, and V chords, in several different keys. Some jazz soloists had to work pretty hard to learn to keep up with the changes in the pieces they played so that they wouldn't contradict the harmony with their

[1]In jazz and blues terminology, each eight bars of an eight-bar blues is called a chorus, so that this performance consists of a long series of choruses, each eight bars long and each following the same harmonic procedure.

melodic improvisations. And many of them were doing it entirely by ear, without knowing the exact musical vocabulary that described them. But then, their ears were great.

These three basic chords are the most important ones in defining any key, because among them they contain every step of the scale. So any melody that stays within the notes of the scale (does not use chromatics, in other words) can be harmonized by these three chords. For this reason, they are the most common ones in folk song, rock, gospel songs, bluegrass, and country western. During some periods, these three chords exerted an enormous amount of control over the harmonic movement of even the most "serious" music. So they are important ones to hear in many different styles if you are interested in following the harmonic progressions. And if you are ever going to *play* a blues, you'd better be able to hear the changes!

Notice that the left hand doesn't always play *exactly* the same notes. Sometimes there are rhythmic variations in the pattern and sometimes it is put into a higher register without losing its basic shape. None of this affects the harmony. The chords are still the tonic, subdominant, and dominant.

Of course, it is possible to use many other different chords within a given key, and much music that we will be encountering does just that. It is even possible to leave a key altogether and move into a different one—and even back again. We'll look into that, too. But as a background for experiencing all the adventures that harmony can bring, it is well to remember that the more different chords are used, the more different keys are visited, the further away we get from just the tonic, subdominant, and dominant, the richer the harmony becomes, and that is one factor to consider seriously when discussing a piece of music.

To return to "How Long Blues," the most important of Yancey's variations take place in the right hand. The melody is the most uncomplicated sort of descending pattern that might be imagined. Out of this material Yancey builds a wealth of varying ideas and never loses the easy, relaxed mood. There is no attempt to make a virtuoso piece out of it, no getting in the way of the expression. This is typical of most authentic blues. They came out of a unique shared experience, and the public for which they were intended neither expected nor demanded any great display of emotionalism. Honesty, yes. Fireworks, not usually. There was (and is) no need for fireworks because the blacks who shared the blues already knew the mood and feeling and the experience that inspired them.

When the changes cling to only the three chords discussed above, we can say that the performer is adhering to the classic form of the blues. The progression is sometimes departed from, but such cases are exceptions—which makes them worth noticing when they occur. For instance, Jelly Roll Morton and Duke Ellington are two performers who got quite carried away sometimes when they performed the blues. We will meet others later in the book. But the kind of enrichment they indulged in helps to describe their approach rather than helping to describe the basic harmonic character of the blues.

The restricted harmonic vocabulary is partially involved with the fact that the blues are a folk type, learned and played most often by ear rather than from notes. Also, many people believe that the harmony was strongly influenced by gospel songs and spirituals, both of which use mostly I, IV, and V chords. All three types of expression—blues, gospel songs, spirituals—circulated among a people who were more interested in honest communication than they were in highly involved artistic expression. It was entirely appropriate, then, that the musical fabric should be simple and direct and comfortable.

Nobody really knows how these formal characteristics developed and became solidified enough to identify the blues in terms of standard musical procedures—form, that is. Behind them were histories of field hollers, work songs, and solitary singers and players working out their frustrations alone or in small groups. Even further back were the residues of language inflections that persisted in the transfer from Africa to the Americas. Street-corner minstrels, often blind, performers in black carnival and tent shows, church musicians—all had some role in the evolving styles that eventually came to focus in a form that we can describe as being typical of the blues. Once established, that form and that style of expression became so intertwined with jazz that it is impossible to discuss or understand jazz without reference to the blues. All of this will be fully discussed and investigated later.

What we need to remember here, aside from the high points of blues form, is that the sort of harmonic organization that depends on chords and chord progressions could not have developed without the dominance of one melodic line with supporting sonorities. And this is the very backbone of homophony, a texture that has been a strong feature of our music since the Baroque.

SUPPLEMENTAL LISTENING

Joe Turner: Boss of the Blues. Atlantic: 1234. This album contains a vocal version of "How Long Blues." It makes a nice contrast to Yancey's version because Turner is accompanied by a group of instrumentalists and they add a great deal of richness to the harmony while at the same time keeping the

main features of the original piece. Another classic eight-bar blues is "Baby, Please Don't Go," which is on the following two albums:
Muddy Waters. Chess: LPS–127.
Big Bill Broonzy. Scepter: SRX–529.

Chapter 4
Textural Mixtures

Since we have now contacted all the important textures in music—polyphonic, monophonic, and homophonic—it would be well at this point to acknowledge the fact that mixtures of these textures are far more common than the dogmatic adherence to any one of them. The trend toward mixtures started in the high Renaissance, reached a crescendo in the Baroque, and has persisted to the present. It is this tendency toward textural mixtures that we will investigate in this chapter.

By the end of the sixteenth century, there were a host of composers and performers (often the same person) whose principal importance was musical—they were, in other words, professionals rather than amateurs like King Henry VIII. One such person was John Dowland (1563–1626). An English (or possibly Irish) lutenist and composer, widely travelled and urbane, Dowland is best known for his lute pieces and his solo and/or ensemble songs with lute accompaniment (Illustration 9). His lute accompaniments are generally more interesting than those of his contemporaries, probably because of his own virtuosity on the instrument.

Although there is some disagreement about his true nationality and ancestry, his most significant musical work was published in England. He was attached to a wide variety of royal and aristocratic personages throughout Europe, including Italy, Germany, Spain, Denmark, and Norway. In the process of fulfilling his duties to them, he gained an enviable reputation as a lutenist and composer. During the last part of his life he was engaged as one of the king's musicians in England.

In 1603, while Dowland was part of the musical establishment for King Christian IV of Denmark and Norway, he published in

Illlustration 9. A MUSIC PARTY.
Gerard Ter Borch (1617–1681). The obviously aristocratic lady here may well be about to launch into a lute song, perhaps John Dowland's "What if I Never Speed." The painter and his subjects are Dutch, the song is English, but this does not contradict the possibility. Publications of lute songs were widely circulated throughout Europe and accessible in all its countries. Compare the mood of this party to that of Dirck Hals's *The Merry Company* (page 318), which is from the same period.
Cincinnati Art Museum. Bequest of Mrs. Mary M. Emery.

London a collection of songs, his third such volume. They were so arranged that they could be sung in four vocal parts or as solos with lute accompaniment. Perhaps it was because of this flexibility in performance that Dowland's songs were so popular and so widely circulated during his lifetime.

PRIMARY LISTENING:
John Dowland, "What if I Never Speed?" (record set)

Listen to one of the pieces, "What if I Never Speed," in its four-part vocal version (Example 15). The sentiment is clear. Either try to win love or make up your mind to walk away from it without too much bitterness. The musical texture here includes two types with which

What if I never speed

we are familiar: the opening section is homophonic and the final section tends to be more polyphonic.

The meter is strong and has a regularity that we feel comfortable with. And notice how subtle and varied the rhythms are, especially in the latter half of the song where the parts stand in polyphonic contrast to one another. Systems of notation have become quite sophisticated in keeping with the growing complexity of musical practice. These two factors go hand in hand, although, as we have seen and will observe often, there are some musical practices that we are not even yet able to capture completely on paper.

Concentrate on the last half of the song. Can you listen carefully enough to follow one individual line and be aware of its relationship to the other three? Of all the four voice parts, which one seems to have the most independence? Even though all the voices appear to have a rhythmic and melodic life of their own, can some be considered as relatively supportive rather than taking the "leading role"? This mixture of leading and supportive functions among the various melodic lines is quite characteristic of late Renaissance and early Baroque music.

What this all means is that the transition from the Renaissance to the Baroque, like most periods in music history, was characterized by no one general style. Even the types of polyphony were not totally standardized. For instance, imitation plays only a small part in Dowland's song as compared to Palestrina's "Agnus Dei." Still, both of them are polyphonic and both are from the late Renaissance period. This lack of real consistency is simply part of the reaching out for new musical materials and it belongs to no particular era. But it does belong to something without which art could never survive: creativity.

Although Dowland called his compositions of this type "Songs and Ayres," they are in the character of madrigals, part-songs designed for social singing by four, five, or more solo voices. But the fact that he also provided for solo performance with an accompanying lute indicates that there is more than one way to enjoy his compositions.

PRIMARY LISTENING: John Dowland, "What if I Never Speed?" with lute accompaniment (record set)

Listen now to such a solo version with lute accompaniment and notice the striking difference in effect. And also in the notation (Example 16).

One needs more than the usual amount of musical training to decipher the lute notation. The proper name for that notation is

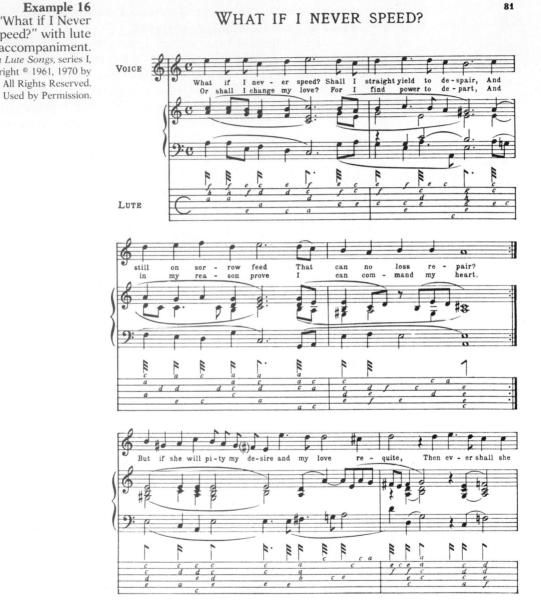

WHAT IF I NEVER SPEED?

81

tablature, and it employs a set of symbols peculiar to that instrument. There are other types of tablature, as we will discover later. Perhaps the most familiar is the kind used for guitar, in which the strings are pictured and dots placed on them where the player's fingers belong. In general, this is the way many tablatures work: they are diagrams showing the fingering, and for one who knows how to tune the instrument, the rest comes naturally if the symbolism is familiar.

The tablature in Example 16 is given as it appeared in the original edition of Dowland's song, where the voice part was the only other thing printed, but notes have been editorially added to show how the pitches for the lute would look if transcribed for a piano keyboard.

There is more to notice than the difference in sound between this performance and the four-part vocal one. The solo line is not doubled in the instrument—more evidence of the growing independence and dominance of the most important melodic segment of the musical fabric. Can you listen closely enough to both performances to discover whether or not the editor has transferred the exact notes of the lute tablature to the four-part vocal arrangement? In other words, is the difference *only* in the substitution of an instrument for voices or are there other *musical* differences too?

If the notes in both versions are the same, then the difference is one of *timbre*—the tonal color—since the acoustical properties of the lute are quite different from those of the human voice. Substituting one for the other changes timbre, and the effect is therefore not the same. This is not, however, a purely musical matter. Acoustics affect the expressive characteristics, but they do not alter the elements— the melodies, rhythms, and harmonies—by which we describe or analyze the structures of the music itself—unless, that is, you want to take timbre in as an important part of the musical characteristics, which some commentators do. That might get you into trying to decide exactly what music *is*—a difficult but stimulating sort of intellectual problem to solve.

SUPPLEMENTAL LISTENING Many part-songs, lute songs, and madrigals illustrate the type of polyphonic complexity mixed with homophonic directness that are found in "What if I Never Speed." Recorded examples include:

> *John Dowland: Songs and Ayres.* Nonesuch: H 71167.
> *An Evening of Elizabethan Music.* RCA Victor: LD 2656.
> *Renaissance Vocal Music.* Nonesuch: H 71097. This collection,
> including English, Italian, French, and German pieces, offers
> a fine opportunity to contact and contrast the varying national
> styles.
> *Kissing, Drinking, and Insect Songs.* Turnabout: TV–S 34485.
> This set includes compositions from several countries as well as
> spanning the transition period from the Renaissance to the
> early Baroque.

Having established the musical advantages of contrasting textures within the same composition, composers from the late Renaissance onward exploited the varieties of sound that such contrasts provided. Our next listening example is only one of thousands that might be chosen to illustrate how combinations of texture can serve expressive purposes.

Richard Wagner (1813–1883) was particularly interested in heightening the expression in his music. He was primarily an opera composer, and his objectives all focused on integrating the various elements that constitute that musical-dramatic genre. He sought a balance between the vocal and instrumental forces, a balance in which neither would dominate the fabric of sound. In seeking to unite the music and the drama, he needed to give all elements in the music a significance beyond themselves—a dramatic meaning, in other words. Moreover, he wanted the musical drama to unfold in a continuous line, uninterrupted by pauses in the action that would allow a singer to simply stand and exhibit his or her virtuosity. What he was after ultimately was a unified expression that was essentially indivisible, a complete experience rather than a series of events.

To achieve his objectives, he devised a system of musical motives, called *leitmotifs*, each of which had some particular meaning within the drama and its characters. These were not confined to the vocal parts alone but were shared equally between orchestra and vocalists. They represented all sorts of things: dramatic elements, objects, ideas, persons. By means of the *leitmotifs*, melodic material was given dramatic significance, and by assigning this material to both orchestra and singers, the orchestra was promoted to full partnership rather than serving merely as an accompanying group.

In order to assure a continuous unfolding of the music and drama, Wagner put harmony to use in what was then a new way. Almost every cadence is evaded or elided in some manner. Not only does the sense of key keep shifting from phrase to phrase, but the chords that end most of the phrases are the "wrong" ones, not those we are led to expect. Usually this is coupled with melodic function. A melody in one voice or instrument will overlap with those in other voices or instruments. The effect is a continuous unfolding of harmony and melody, so that all the seams in the music are smoothed over and the musical movement never seems to stop—even during actual silences. This melodic process has a name: *unending melody*. Its basis is the constant overlapping of polyphonic lines. Thus, the music is just as continuous as the drama. But it is important to realize, too, that harmony is playing a part as well as melody.

The style Wagner developed was particularly effective in his 1859 opera, *Tristan und Isolde,* from which the Prelude and *Liebestod* are used as our listening example. The story concerns love pursued with great passion but fulfilled completely only after death. This sort of glorification of tragic love has been a favorite theme from the Greeks through Shakespeare and right up to the present.

Briefly, the plot concerns the bethrothal of Isolde, an Irish princess, to King Mark of Cornwall. Tristan is sent to bring her to Mark, against her will, for the wedding festivities. Isolde asks her lady-in-waiting to prepare a death potion for Tristan and herself, but the servant prepares a love potion instead. The stage is set for tragedy in the Romantic vein. Under the spell of the potion, Tristan and Isolde arrive at Mark's castle deeply impassioned with love for one another. They have an intensely emotional scene in the garden but are interrupted by Mark and his court followers. In the aftermath Tristan is mortally wounded. He is taken back to his own castle, where he feverishly relives in memory his love scene with Isolde. She pursues him there but arrives only in time to see him die. The final scene consists of her singing the *Liebestod* (Love Death), in which she mourns her loss but is transported into an imagined reunion with Tristan beyond the grave. After finishing her aria in ecstatic anticipation, she falls dead across the prostrate body of her beloved Tristan.

Here are the words of the *Liebestod:*

Mild und leise wie er lächelt,	How softly and gently he smiles,
Wie das Auge hold er öffnet—	How fondly he opens his eyes—
Seht ihr's, Freunde? Seht ihr's nicht?	Do you see, friends? Do you not see?
Immer lichter wie er leuchtet,	Always brighter, how he shines,
Stern-umstrahlet hoch sich hebt?	Glowing in starlight, soaring on high?
Seht ihr's nicht?	Do you not see?
Wie das Herz ihm mutig schwilt,	And how his heart bravely swells,
Voll und hehr im Busen ihm quilt?	Full and calm it throbs in his breast?
Wie den Lippen, wonnig mild,	How from his lips blissfully mild,
Süsser Atem sanft entweht—	Sweet breath softly flutters—
Freunde! Seht! Fühlt und seht ihr's nicht?	Friends! See! Do you not feel and see?
Hör' ich nur diese Weise	Do I alone hear this melody
Die so wundervoll und leise,	So wonderful and gentle,
Wonne klagend, alles sagend,	Moaning bliss, saying all things,
Mild versöhnend aus ihm tönend,	Sweetly reconciling, welling from him,
In mich dringet, auf sich schwinget,	Penetrating me, rising upward,
Hold erhallend um mich klinget?	Echoing fondly, ringing around me?
Heller schallend, mich unwallend,	Sounding more clearly, drifting around me,

Sind es Wellen sanfter Lüfte?	Are they waves of gentle breezes?
Sind es Wogen wonniger Düfte?	Are they clouds of delightful perfumes?
Wie sie schwellen, mich umrauschen,	As they swell and roar around me,
Soll ich atmen, soll ich lauschen?	Shall I breathe, shall I listen?
Soll ich schlürfen, untertauchen?	Shall I sip, plunge beneath?
Süss in Düften mich verhauchten?	Breathe my last in sweet fragrance?
In dem wogenden Schwall, in dem tönenden Schall,	In the surging waves, the resounding tumult,
In des Welt-Atems wehendem All—	In the vastness of the infinite world-spirit,
Ertrinken, Versinken—	To drown, sink down—
Unbewusst—	Unconscious—
Höchste Lust!	Supreme bliss!

PRIMARY LISTENING:
Richard Wagner, Prelude and *Liebestod* from *Tristan und Isolde*

Although the Prelude and the *Liebestod* are the first and last parts of Wagner's three-act music drama, they are usually played and sung as one uninterrupted piece in concert. Their moods are similar because the Prelude is a forecast of the drama as well as of musical motives that pervade the work, and the *Liebestod* is the dramatic and musical culmination of the tragedy.

The *leitmotifs* that are most prominent in the Prelude have been given different meanings by different commentators, but the meanings are similar enough to convey the emotional intent. The sense of longing and desire that is involved throughout the work is established at the very outset by two of the motives (Example 17). "Longing" is associated with Tristan; "Desire" is associated with Isolde. Some analysts call the first motive "Grief" and associate it with both lovers. Some have even taken the two motives as a single entity and identified it as the "Love-Potion" which the lovers drink. Thus the perils of analysis. In any case, you can see and hear the melodic overlap already at work in these few measures.

In true Wagnerian style, the motives grow slowly, almost imperceptibly into a new musical idea—that of the "Glance of love" (Example 18), which, once again, is sometimes referred to as "Love's longing."

Example 17
Wagner, Prelude to *Tristan und Isolde.*

Example 18
Wagner, Prelude to *Tristan und Isolde.*

Glance of love

Following a long, increasingly passionate working out of these ideas and their extensions, another melody emerges, prophetic in its importance to the drama. It expresses what is known as the "Deliverance by death" motive (Example 19).

All of the polyphonically organized activity eventually subsides with a few restatements of the "Longing" and "Desire" motives, and the *Liebestod* begins, transplanted here from its rightful place at the end of the music drama. The opening vocal motive had occurred earlier in the drama during the love scene in the garden. There the melody was shared by Tristan and Isolde to words that expressed their wish to die together rather than face the possibility of separation in life. It is entirely appropriate to build on it here, of course. But notice its similarity to the "Longing" motive from the Prelude. This sort of musical continuity and coherence is a Wagnerian trademark and a tribute to that composer's ability to carry out his own objectives (Example 20).

The other important motive in the *Liebestod* represents the transfiguration of love by death, a highly Romantic notion, certainly with something of ecstasy in it if you happen to share the mood (Example 21). Introduced quietly in the orchestra at first, it soon becomes quite exalted and Isolde takes it up in a dialogue with the instruments. After a soaring climax, the music sinks with the dying Isolde.

The alternation of textures throughout this portion of *Tristan und Isolde* are invaluable in reflecting the expressive changes in the drama, including even the purely orchestral Prelude which introduces many of the dramatic elements to come. Polyphony,

Example 19
Wagner, Prelude to *Tristan und Isolde.*

Deliverance by death

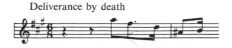

Example 20
Wagner, *Liebestod* from *Tristan und Isolde.*

Liebestod

Mild und lei - se wie er lä - chelt

Example 21
Wagner, *Liebestod* from *Tristan und Isolde.*

Love's transfiguration

homophony, monophony, and antiphony keep our attention engaged equally with all elements of the music.

Wagner was an author as well as a composer, and he put his artistic ideas into a number of weighty volumes. He was also a pure egotist, convinced that the world owed him a living because of his genius. He was convincing enough to talk his supporters into financing a theater built to his specifications in Bayreuth, Germany. The theater is still used, and one of its most popular functions is an annual festival devoted entirely to the operas and music dramas of Wagner. His most ambitious work was a cycle of four music dramas, *Der Ring des Nibelungen* (The Ring of the Nibelung), based on Norse mythology. The four separate works are unified through the use of an enormous catalogue of motives that appear in many transformations. The complexity of Wagner's artistic ideals and the manner in which he attempted to realize them has encouraged a great deal of scholarship and analysis. If you care to plunge into his other music dramas, there are many studies that describe the stories and the *leitmotifs*, presenting their meaning and the use to which the composer puts them.

Wagner's demands on the human voice are as great as those of any composer and far greater than those of most. The fact that his orchestra is huge and that often the voice is all but buried in the torrent of sound and competing melodies has put a great challenge before his singers. Only the heartiest souls can muster up the requisite volume. As a result, Wagnerian singers tend to be large—the waggish stereotype is of someone six feet, six inches tall and weighing at least three hundred pounds.

Wagner's style too is "heavy" for many listeners, and the slow pace of his dramas has come in for some criticism. It has been claimed that it's entirely possible to leave the opera house, go to a neighboring bar, enjoy three leisurely martinis, and return to find the same singer in the same spot as when you left. Nevertheless, as the ultimate expression of Romanticism, Wagner's particular kind of musical longing, frustration, and passion is successful.

SUPPLEMENTAL LISTENING   The most logical place to begin a further acquaintance with Wagner is the *Ring*. Many of the same characters with their same musical identities run throughout all four dramas. This is true of the *leitmotifs* also, and the interested investigator can expect a real challenge tracing them through the four works. The dramas, best heard in the following sequence, are *Das Rheingold (The Rhine Gold)*, *Die Walküre (The Valkyrie)*, *Siegfried*, and *Die Götterdämmerung (The Twilight of the Gods)*.

Chapter 5

Monody: Text Illustration and the Aria in Baroque Opera

Let's return once more to the Baroque period for some new investigation of melody and harmony and their interaction. The increased attention given to the melody line, when it was freed from competition with other melodies, brought new concepts of the relationship between tune and words. Another listening selection—Marco da Gagliano's "Valli profonde," composed in 1625—illustrates this.

Gagliano lived from about 1575 to 1642. Educated as a priest, he was attached to various chapels as well as to the Accademia degl' Elevati in Florence, which he was instrumental in founding. The Academia degl' Elevati (Academy of the Elevated Ones) was one of many similar organizations dedicated to the advancement of music and other fine arts. A leader in the musical life of Florence, Gagliano is best known for his opera *Dafne* and for his numerous part-songs and other vocal works for from one to five voices.

PRIMARY LISTENING:
Marco da Gagliano, "Valli profonde" (record set)

The words of "Valli profonde," a song for one voice, are colorful, as poetry from this period is apt to be, and the melody does some interesting things about that (Example 22).

Example 22
Marco da Gagliano, "Valli
profonde."

Valli profonde, al sol nemiche,	Deep valleys, enemies of the sun,
Rupi, ch'el ciel superbe minacciate,	Boulders that proudly threaten the sky,
Grotte, onde non parte mai silentio e notte,	Caves where silence and night are supreme,
Aer, che d'altra nube il ciel occupi,	Winds that cover the sky with black clouds,
Precipitanti sassi, alte dirupi,	Crashing stones, lofty rocks,
Ossa insepolte, herbose muta e rotte,	Bones unburied, walls covered with rotten weeds,
D'huomini albergo gia hor par condotte	Former dwelling of men, so forsaken
Che temon gir tra voi serpenti e lupi.	That even serpents and wolves are afraid to enter.

This is only the first half of Gagliano's song, but the rest of the piece continues in much the same vein. This sounds like a bad place to spend the night.

As in any group of words, some here are more important than others, and notice that Gagliano tries to write a tune for the more important ones that illustrates them in some way. The melody of the very first words, for instance, is in the shape of a "deep valley," and sometimes the word "ciel" (sky) is put to very high pitches. "Precipitanti sassi" (crashing stones) tumble down melodically, and "serpenti" (serpents) wind around just like snakes. This kind of maneuvering is called *text illustration,* and it was one of the favorite ways for Baroque composers to match the music with the words. It happens to some extent in all periods of music history, but it was almost a cliché in the seventeenth and eighteenth centuries. It is quite different from recitative, because it is more musical than speech-like—the emphasis is more on tune than on appropriate verbal inflection. Notice the many melismas. This kind of florid melodic style is typical of much Baroque music, as we have indicated, and it is found very highly developed in Bach, Handel, and many others late in the period.

Because of its tuneful character, this kind of song was known as an *aria*—the Italian word meaning "air." Though not confined to opera, it was very important in that genre. It was used there for contrast to the recitatives, which carried the storytelling parts of the libretto and the dialogues among the actors. The arias were inserted to increase the musical beauty as well as to give the singers a chance to display their talents.

Vocally, these florid passages call for a lot of technical skill, and it wasn't long before the singers who could manage them became real stars throughout Europe. Composers produced music that could be exploited by the performers, and the audiences expected the singers to add even more runs, trills, and other ornaments to what the composer had written. This led not only to a very sophisticated use of the voice, but even to a new form, the da capo aria.

PRIMARY LISTENING:
George Frederic Handel, "Lascia ch'io pianga," from *Rinaldo* (record set)

With J. S. Bach, George Frederic Handel (1685–1759) is considered a figurehead of the Baroque. His style is often more homophonic than Bach's because of Handel's concern for opera and its demands for spotlighting the solo voice. German-born, Handel began his opera composition while an instrumentalist in the Hamburg opera; later he spent considerable time composing and performing in Italy. Handel visited London several times, finally staying on as court musician for George I and director of the Royal Academy of Music. He became an English citizen. Later travels took him to Ireland and back to the continent.

Listen to "Lascia ch'io pianga," from *Rinaldo*, Handel's first opera in Italian during his years in London. The first performance was in 1711, but it was performed frequently for some years after that. The accompaniment is scored for violins, viola, and continuo. As in most concerted pieces from the period, the continuo given by Handel is merely a bass line, but it is usually performed by a cello and a harpsichord, the latter filling in the chords (Example 23). The text is:

Lascia ch'io pianga mia cruda sorte,	Let me cry for my cruel fate,
E che sospiri la libertà!	And sigh for liberty!
Il duolo infranga queste ritorte	May grief break these chains
De' miei martiri, sol per pietà.	Of my torment in pity.

You will notice immediately that the texture here is completely homophonic. That's because the focus of attention is almost totally on the voice. The first violin does double the vocal part, but that in

Example 23
Handel, "Lascio ch'io pianga."

no way detracts from the importance of the singer. Also, at least in this performance, the harmony is clearly given in the instruments so the person at the harpsichord doesn't have to interpret numbers as the accompanist did for "Tu se' morta."

After some attention to the first two lines of the poem, including a bit of text repetition, the music changes in several ways for the last two poetic lines (Example 24). How about instrumentation? If it changes, that would be one clue that the four-line poem is being treated as though it were in two separate sections. And what about the melody? If it changes, then that means still more evidence that there is sectionalization going on.

Now something surprising happens. The opening section returns, but with some striking differences. Are the accompanying instruments less perceptible here? Is the singer adding anything to the original melody of the first two lines? If you are listening closely you will know that she certainly is. Runs that extend the range, trills, turns—all sorts of devices to elaborate on Handel's original tune. It becomes apparent, then, that the repetition of the first section serves two purposes, one formal and the other virtuosic.

From the formal standpoint, if we call the first section A and the middle section B, we can diagram the entire aria as:

A   B   A

That is exactly how musicians go about identifying forms of a certain type, and the proper name for this particular arrangement is *ternary*, or *three-part*, although here it has no relationship to the Trinity as there was in the structure of the "Kyrie eleison." In this case, the arrangement serves what appears to be one of man's most persistent artistic needs: a balance between unity and variety. The return of the A section seems to "tie up" the formal package satisfactorily. We will encounter this A B A structure time and again in all kinds of musical styles. When it occurs within large vocal forms like the opera or oratorio, this is often in what is called a *da capo aria*. In Italian, a language often used for musical terminology for reasons of convention, *da capo* means "from the head" or, in other words, "from the beginning." The statement usually appears just after the B

Example 24
Handel, "Lascio ch'io pianga."

Il duo - lo in - fran - ga que - ste ri - tor - te de' miei — mar - ti - ri sol per — pie - ta, _____

section in the score, and anyone who understands the directions will go back and repeat the A section. The repeated A section is often referred to as the *da capo* section. That is where Baroque opera singers had their shining moments.

Because of the stress put upon virtuosity, the singers were expected to perform all sorts of vocal gymnastics in the *da capo* section. Sometimes they added some ornamentation to the B section too, especially if the musical mood changed drastically. But because ornamentation was improvised by the performers, different performances of the same aria involved different trills and runs and so on, depending on the particular performers.

The ornamenting of the *da capo* section of an aria thus demanded both great technical competence and considerable skill at improvisation. The improvisation, however, took place within the framework of well-defined conventions. Those conventions were dictated by the musical practice of the Baroque period, and present-day singers of Baroque opera must learn and abide by them if they are to meet with the approval of critics and other knowledgeable listeners. Some Baroque composers furnished written instructions for adding ornamentation to their music. When these guidelines are available, performers can use them to great advantage. Most composers of the period, however, left no such directions. As a result, performers usually rely heavily on the advice of scholars, editors, and coaches, many of whom are skilled in applying the appropriate conventions. In post-Baroque opera, the use of improvisation and ornamentation gradually diminished as time went on. Other demands, dictated by the composers and conductors, had to be met by the performers, as we saw in Wagner's *Tristan und Isolde*. But virtuosity remained, and still remains, a decisive factor.

The demand for virtuosity raises some questions about artistic and human integrity. During the Baroque period, some of the most famous opera stars were *castrati*—men who had been castrated as boys because they showed above-average vocal and musical ability. Castration had exactly the same physical effect on the boys as it does on cattle or sheep today. It induced greater growth—and a correspondingly greater lung power. At the same time, it eliminated the change of vocal quality that normally accompanies adolescence, since the men retained the pure voice of a child. As a result they were able to perform the elaborate vocal feats that the public was interested in hearing. The operation was not confined to opera singers alone. In fact, the practice was borrowed from the church, where the purity of a boy's voice was thought to be more suitable for the high parts of liturgical music than the warmer, more sensual sound of a mature woman. For quite different reasons, of course, the practice was common in cultures that used eunuchs to guard harems. With a destruction of the sexual drive, the eunuchs presented no threat to the supremacy of the sultan in the bedroom.

The human question, as distinguished from the artistic one, is very pointed in the case of the operatic castrati. The rewards for the successful singers were enormous financially as well as in terms of public adulation. They were among the most idolized individuals in all Europe, rivaling even the aristocracy in the luxury of their life style. Italian opera was far and away the most popular form of theatrical entertainment on the continent and in England. Without virtuoso singers it could not have thrived, and without castrati much of the virtuosity would have been diminished. Because of the lure of possible success, thousands of boys were castrated as the initial step in pursuit of vocal fame. Unfortunately, most of them failed to develop all the vocal and musical skills needed for success in opera, and these spent their lives not only deprived of their dreams of artistic triumphs but also without their virility. It is a sobering example of the many complexities created by the frequent conflict between art and life.

Although we are "civilized" enough now to abhor the process of emasculation for such purposes, it is worth wondering whether there may not be a sort of psychological castration involved in our treatment of idols in the present-day world of entertainment. In other than physical ways it is possible to rob individuals of their identity as individuals, of their psychic virility, so to speak. In the quest for public acclamation, how much does a performer have to relinquish in order to meet the demands of his or her worshipers? In some symbolic sense, do we castrate our performing gods and goddesses? What price do we exact of them for our approval?

SUPPLEMENTAL LISTENING   Other examples of varying degrees of florid singing may be found on:

> *The Art of Ornamentation and Embellishment in the Renaissance and Baroque.* Bach Guild: BGS 70697/8.
> *George Frederic Handel.* Musical Heritage Society: MHS 722.
> *Italian Songs.* Vanguard: BG 565.
> *Italian Chamber Music.* Vanguard: BG 566.
> *Chamber Music for Soprano and Continuo.* Pleiades: P 103.

The *da capo* aria became so conventional during the high Baroque era that numerous examples are to be found in recordings of music from that period, including those indicated above. Handel's *Messiah* is already familiar to many listeners because of its popularity at the Christmas and Easter seasons of the church year. It includes *da capo* arias as well as other types; a recent recording of superior quality is *Handel: Messiah.* RCA Victor: LSC 6175.

A secular work by Handel, the opera *Julius Caesar*, also includes many *da capo* arias. Among the most spectacular is Cleopatra's plaintive "Piangerò," magnificently ornamented in the *da capo* section by Beverly Sills on *Handel: Julius Caesar*. RCA Victor: LSC 6182.

A GLANCE AT HISTORY

The Baroque period (c. 1600–1750) brings us full-tilt into the modern era. Glance at the people and events that are listed below. They will be a clue to the amazing amount of intellectual, political, and artistic activity that was characteristic of the era. Although much patronage of the arts was still lodged in the church and the aristocracy, there was an increasingly large audience drawn from the general populace. Some of this was due to the strengthening middle class, some simply to the ever-growing and efficient avenues of communication and travel.

The word "Baroque" derives from a Portuguese word meaning rough or irregularly shaped pearl. Its initial use was in a derogatory sense, meant to ridicule the elaborate ornamentation and ornately decorative style of the painters, sculptors, architects, and musicians of the time.

Illustration 10. MUNICH: INTERIOR OF THE CHURCH OF ST. JOHN NEPOMUK, 1733 (DETAIL). The elaborate detail here is typical of what many thought to be the excesses of the Baroque period. From A. Blunt, *Baroque and Rococo Architecture and Decoration* (New York: Harper & Row, 1978).

In music, there was a sort of paradox at the outset of the period. On the one hand was a simplicity of texture with the increased use of homophony, and one might see this as an attempt to erase the polyphonic complexity of the preceding period. However, the attention given to the melody soon gave rise to excesses of virtuosity which almost totally eradicated the artistic objectives with which the movement began. At the same time, it invited the sort of ornamentation of the melody that corresponded closely to the decorative nature of the other arts. But polyphony was far from dead, and as the period advanced into the early years of the eighteenth century, the complexities of that texture grew more and more pronounced, as we will see later in the book when we are concentrating on instrumental music.

In architecture, the classic lines of the Renaissance gave way to an abundance of curves and even grotesque sculpture and carvings in churches and public buildings (Illustration 10). Painters produced art works that featured brilliant colors, flamboyant subjects, and a spectacular and highly decorative style. One of the best examples of the extravagance of the Baroque is the palace built by Louis XIV, King of France from 1643 to 1715, at Versailles (Illustration 11). The main structure is enormous enough, but

Illustration 11. THE PALACE AT VERSAILLES, FRANCE, 1680s.
The enormous scope of this complex of buildings is an example of the extravagance found in many Baroque works of art and architecture.
Reproduced by kind permission of Istituto Geografico de Agostini, Milan, Italy. From Michael Raeburn, ed., *Architecture of the Western World*, Rizzoli International Publications, Inc., New York, 1980.

there is a separate, very palatial building where Louis' mistress was housed and which he used as a place to escape from the throngs of his court.

Our experience with Baroque music has been limited at this point to vocal types. One of the great developments of the period, however, was a sudden outburst of purely instrumental music. Much of this was due to the increased potential of the instruments themselves, not only in types but also in the more brilliant tone quality and extended ranges. A corresponding emphasis on virtuosity accompanied these advances, so that instrumentalists fully rivaled vocalists in their performance powers. We will investigate all of this later.

MUSICIANS:

Johann Sebastian Bach: 1685–1750
Giulio Caccini: 1548–1618
François Couperin: 1668–1733
Giovanni Gabrieli: 1557–1612
George Frederic Handel: 1685–1759
Jean-Baptiste Lully: 1632–1687

Jacopo Peri: 1561–1633

Henry Purcell: c. 1659–1695
Jean-Phillipe Rameau: 1683–1764
Domenico Scarlatti: 1685–1757
Heinrich Schütz: 1585–1672

Antonio Vivaldi: c. 1676–1741

ARTISTS, LITERARY FIGURES, AND OTHERS:

John Bunyon: 1628–1688
Miguel de Cervantes: 1547–1616
René Descartes: 1596–1650
Franz Hals: c. 1581–1666
John Milton: 1608–1674
Jean Molière: 1622–1673

Isaac Newton: 1642–1727
Blaise Pascal: 1623–1662
Rembrandt van Rijin: 1606–1669
Peter Paul Rubens: 1577–1640
Baruch Spinoza: 1632–1677
Jonathan Swift: 1667–1745

Jean Watteau: 1684–1721

EVENTS:

Founding of Academies and Universities:
  Académie Française: 1635
  Harvard University: 1636
  Yale University: 1701
Bay Psalm Book printed: 1640
Commonwealth/Restoration in England: 1649–1660
Hudson River explored and charted: 1609
King James Bible printed: 1611
Manhattan Island purchased: 1626
Pilgrims landed on Cape Cod: 1620
Thirty Years' War: 1618–1648
Witchcraft trials in Salem, Mass.: 1692

Chapter 6
Ornamentation and Improvisation in Non-Western Music

A *thumri* song is a style of performance rather than a particular form like a *da capo* aria. Thumri is what we would probably classify in our Western tradition as light classical music, more sophisticated than folk song but not as highly stylized as the Handel aria "Lascia ch'io pianga." The most important accompanying instrument on our recording (which presents only a short portion of a thumri song) is a sarangi, which has several main strings, usually three or four, and a larger number of additional strings that vibrate sympathetically (Illustration 12). It is played with a bow, but the sympathetic strings are controlled by the fingers. The reverberations that are so evident in the sound are partially due to the "echoing" effect of the sympathetic vibrations. Another stringed instrument is involved in this performance: a tambura, sometimes spelled tamboura. This is strung with four wires, and is a relatively large instrument held in performance with the large belly at the bottom and the long neck in a vertical position. Because of the continuous strumming of the strings, it produces a drone sound that emphasizes the most important note or notes of the scale being used in the song.

The drum is a tabla—really two drums, one for the right hand and one for the left. The right-hand one is made of wood and tuned

Illustration 12. SARANGI.
William P. Malm, *Music Cultures of the Pacific, the Near East, and Asia* © 1967.

to the tonic note. The left-hand drum, which is metal, serves as a sort of bass drum and has a warmer color.

So much for the bare mechanics. The structural basis for this music, as for much Indian music, is the *raga*, which is a group of from five to seven different notes arranged in a definite relationship to one another and to a tonic. This is roughly comparable to a scale in Western music (see appendix 1 for a full discussion of scales).

But the sequence of scale pitches used in India as contrasted to Western music has very profound ramifications expressively. In Western music, for over three centuries we have used the scale of C major, for instance, for innumerable compositions and in many differing moods. Within some of our conventions, mood has been associated with key or scale, but these associations have not been guarded carefully from period to period. As a result, keys and scales tend to define mood and style in certain periods within our tradition rather than through the entire tradition. This is not true in India. Each raga, through association and tradition, carries with it a definite built-in expressive character. That character is appropriate for specific times of day or occasions, and "mixing up" the ragas—using them at the wrong time or in the wrong place or as a basis for the wrong composition—is severely frowned upon.

To illustrate, we can sing "The Star Spangled Banner," built on the scale of B♭ major, without concern for time of performance. We are just as comfortable singing "Silent Night" in B♭ major, again at no particular time. But the moods of these pieces, regardless of when performed, are sharply different from each other. The Indian is not as free and easy with such interchanges. Because the raga *does* equate with mood and expressive content, a morning raga is not used in the evening, and the words are not allowed to contradict the sentiment appropriate to a particular raga. If we were to use this same principle, our national anthem and "Silent Night" would call for different scales and keys because their moods are different. In addition, we would need to restrict their use to particular times of the day or night.

There are other differences. In performance, the singer and players begin with a rhythmically free statement of the notes of the raga and later launch into improvisations. But in the use of the raga for improvisations very rigid conventions are exercised. Certain notes should be ornamented, others must not be. Certain melodic progressions may be exploited, others must be carefully avoided. Some notes are more important than others, and these must be dealt with in a particular fashion.

There are literally hundreds of ragas, each with a mood and expression inherent within it. Many performances are enormously extended, often continuing for an hour or more. The singer or player explores all the raga's melodic implications, seeks to develop the expression fully through ornamentation and other manipulations of the tonal material. When the performance is a vocal one, the quality of singing is also brought to bear on the expression. Here, as in all other facets of the music, there are ingrained conventions that govern the delivery.

Another difference between this performance and a Western performance is in the rhythmic system. Most of our music is arranged metrically in such a way that the accents are quite regular and also relatively strong. Indian rhythms are organized around a *tala*, which is a series of beats arranged in groups but carrying a much more subtle accent than our measures carry. The divisions here are additive, so that one tala may be made up, for instance, of five plus five plus two plus two beats. This corresponds roughly to our phrase, but the tala is repeated literally throughout each section of a performance that involves the accompaniment of the percussion instrument. There is therefore a sense of great repetition around a steady pulse. In western music the phrasing tends to contrast regularity with irregularity, including even music from periods when regular phrasing was a characteristic of the style. But under the control of the tala, Indian music is highly repetitive in its organization of rhythmic groupings.

Still another contrast is in the use of melody versus harmony. The latter is foreign to Indian music. It occurs only incidentally (even accidentally, as it were) as a result of the use of a drone instrument—in our recording a tambura. The real interest is in melodic manipulation of the raga and the rhythmic improvisation of melodist and percussionist within the restrictions of the tala. In contrast to Western practice, then, where so much of the expressive content is enhanced by harmonic color, the performance of a raga must be contacted in terms of its melody and rhythm alone.

In listening to an Indian performance, we are probably most impressed by the sense of repetition, and all of the above musical factors contribute to this. The drone reinforces what sounds like the tonic note, and that note pervades the entire texture of the music. The melody returns at regular intervals to it. The sense of phrase is constant, almost unremitting. The tonal material of the raga is adhered to closely, so that after a while we are almost mesmerized by the reiteration of sounds, even though they are extensively varied in rhythm. Many of the melodic variations are so subtle that our ears have difficulty really distinguishing one from another. The pitch manipulations are more minute than our ears are accustomed to: the Indian systems use as many as 22 pitches within an octave; we normally use only 12.

And so the differences between this musical tradition and ours are vast, even though we can delineate them in terms of rhythm, harmony, and melody, and can even refer them to the concepts of improvisation and ornamentation. This is theory, and with it we can describe, but such description, even in terms of the theory involved, is the most rash oversimplification. The nuances at work within the application of theory to performance in *any* musical tradition are enormous. But that in itself is valuable to know. It is also good to recognize that the musical system of another culture is in some ways so infinitely more complex than ours that we cannot even describe it adequately with the concepts we have at our command. In the same sense, it is almost impossible to articulate our own complexities to others. The differences and the communication traps create the problems of understanding and response. This is not confined to music alone, of course. The implications are ever-present in international politics, religion, and dozens of other areas.

The subject of the song is love—a thumri is, in fact, a love song. As in so many love songs from all corners of the world, including our own, the singer is lamenting the absence of the loved one. Although sung here by a man, the words are those of a woman. This does not create a contradiction in terms of Indian vocal practice. The lover has left the singer and moved to another town, leaving behind only memories of happier days and a passionate relationship. Although we may understand and sympathize with the sentiment being expressed, it is unlikely that we can fully understand the mode of imparting that sentiment.

From the humanistic standpoint, the important question is how to respond to this music. We are fond of referring to music as the universal language, and we like to think that we can understand something of other cultures by exposing ourselves to some of their art. It is valid to wonder whether this is true, except in some superficial way. Does verbal description really lead to anything more than a purely intellectual rapport—if that? Even in our own music, using idioms that have become familiar to us because of our own heritage, mere description often fails to get to the bottom of what music is all about. For instance, when we have said that Beethoven's Fifth Symphony is in the key of C minor, have put the C minor scale on paper, have notated the themes, and have shown some of the rhythmic motives from which the melodies are derived, what have we said about the Fifth Symphony that really matters? We have described some of the theoretical principles and some of the musical material, but we have not even come close to explaining why that composition affects us the way it does, no matter what its effect may be, negative or positive.

I have not indicated the scale structure that identifies this particular raga, or described the metric organization of this tala.

That kind of detailed analytical description will come later in the book when varying principles of musical organization are under more careful scrutiny. The point now is to examine our psychological responses to what is surely strange music to our ears but which, at the same time, carries great expressive reality to people of another cultural environment and background. We are familiar with many types of singing and many varying uses of the voice, but the quality of Indian singing is an unusual one for us, and the performance may strike some of us as funny or even foolish.

These would be perfectly human reactions, based on problems of what we find acceptable—a kind of problem we all carry around with us. There is no reason to beat our breasts about such reactions or to do penance for our limited perceptions. But there *is* something to learn from the experience beyond the fact that Indian thumri style strikes a discordant note in terms of our musical sensibilities—if, indeed, it does.

In her book *The Music of India* Peggy Holroyde writes:

> Without some knowledge of the mainstream of Indian thought, and the atmosphere which Hindu philosophy engenders into everything Indian, even Muslim society, nothing can ever really fit together and make sense to strangers in India.
>
> The whole temper of thinking and the very atmosphere one breathes in moving around daily among Indians, are wholly different from those of the West.
>
> The psychological impulses that influence an Indian's outlook on life, and therefore his culture, are obviously present in the music also. Our cultures are created from the nature of our respective environments. . . .[1]

[1]Peggy Holroyde, *The Music of India,* Praeger, New York, 1972, p. 19.

And later:

> We can only become aware of the inward exploration of Indian music if we comprehend the metaphysical urges that are so part and parcel of the thinking of each individual Asian. These urges gave rise to the principles of the music many thousands of years ago, and have remained consistent, coherent and contemporary for a longer stretch of time here than anywhere else in the world, except China.[2]

[2]Ibid. p. 33.

Does this mean that it is hopeless to seek understanding and psychological contact? Not really. What it means is that superficial explanations and contact can lead only to superficial results. *The Music of India* is one of the finest books on the subject because it recognizes the danger of dealing in superficialities. It explains the relationship between musical practice and many of the cultural aspects of Indian life, including its philosophies. Speaking of the effect of music on the listener and the role of improvisation, the author writes:

> This creates a compulsive hypnotic effect. The listener sinks deeper and deeper into himself, almost in meditation. The result is profoundly emotional. This is part of the fabric of India where everything is permeated by this timelessness and this intensity of serious thought.[3]

[3]Ibid, pp. 44–45.

The connection is to yoga, perhaps the most fashionable and even faddish element of Indian philosophy to be adopted by the West. The danger is precisely in the appeal it exercises as a fad. In his quest for a clearer vision of reality, for synthesis of intellectual and emotional forces, the Indian seeks within himself. This is entirely foreign to most of us; our realities are more apt to be expressed in terms of externals, the things we can feel and see and smell. Another way of putting the matter might be to admit that though we are just as intent as the Indian on "getting our head together" or "putting the world in order," very few of us try to do so by a lifetime of yoga and the inner (and outer) disciplines it enforces; we are much more apt to buy another car or a color TV, or a new deodorant, or find a job in another locality, or make some new friends.

At the same time, we might well wonder if the Indian accent on inwardness is at all related to the socioeconomic nature of that country. The tolerance of one of the world's most severe levels of poverty may well be merely a reflection of psychological isolationism. The intense subjectivism described in *The Music of India* may help account, too, for the perpetuation of the caste system and all it implies about the human condition.

The point here is that when we listen to improvisation and ornamentation in our own tradition, if that is involved in a given performance, we are apt to relate to it in a rather objective way; each nuance fills us with admiration for the skill and imagination of the performer. That doesn't mean that we get no emotional kick out of it, but it does mean that we are not totally immersed spiritually, not in touch with a meditative synthesis as is the Indian described by Holroyde.

By exposing ourselves to other cultural forces, even if we cannot relate to them on the richest possible expressive level, we can at least realize that there *are* realities other than those we are aware of and insist upon. That is only a beginning, of course—a starting point for tracking down some of those realities if we wish to.

In considering all this, it may add confusion—or perhaps comfort—to learn that in fact many Indians are just as at sea in regard to their own classical music as many of us are in regard to ours. There are even "music appreciation" books written by Indians *for* Indians. That must mean that in India, as in our own country, the preservation and transmission of a cultural heritage and background cannot come about in a haphazard way. Apparently we all need some sort of structured educational process in order to help us understand and appreciate our past and present.

SUPPLEMENTAL LISTENING

A growing number of recordings of non-Western music are being issued by commercial as well as educational companies. The points above are general enough to apply to almost any vocal piece based on an Indian raga. The following are suggested as especially worthwhile:

> *South Indian Vocal Music.* Nonesuch: H–72018.
> *South Indian Instrumental Music.* Nonesuch: H–72019. This disc contains vocal as well as instrumental selections.

PRIMARY LISTENING:
"Another Hard Day's Night," The Beatles (*HELP!*—Capitol: MAS–2386)

In a capricious mood and in order to bolster some of the carrying-on in their move *HELP!*, the Beatles resorted to Indian musical idioms. "Another Hard Day's Night" uses part of a song from an earlier movie. Even though this is all done with tongue in cheek, the reference points are there—the drone, the variations on the original musical material, the instrumental characteristics. It all has a rock flavor, but the fact that we immediately recognize the Eastern influence is evidence that there is some cultural exchange going on, even though it may be in a superficial way. Some rock groups have gotten into a more serious attempt to exploit Indian musical practice. Among the better known ones are the Who, the Rolling Stones, and Pink Floyd, all of whom have included the sitar, the Indian string instrument, on occasion. One of the organizations that has leaned strongly toward Indian idioms is the Mahavishnu Orchestra. Perhaps the richest work has been done by jazz musicians like John Mayer and Joe Harriott in England. One of their most stimulating albums is *Indo-Jazz Suite* (Atlantic: 1465). Jazzmen are often out front on serious explorations of new musical ideas, and the idea of adapting new thematic material for use in improvisational variations is particularly appropriate to jazz.

SUPPLEMENTAL LISTENING

George Harrison, a member of the now-defunct Beatles group, has gotten involved in some serious exploration of Indian idioms as well as those from the Far East. Among other examples of his work, the album *Wonderwall Music* (Apple Records: ST 3350) contains some interesting pieces that attempt a combination of Indian and other Easternisms with some of the vocabulary of rock. On that album, the following cuts are suggested: "Tabla and Pakavaj," "In the Park," "Greasy Legs," "Ski-ing and Gat Kirwani," "Dream Scene."

PRIMARY LISTENING:
Lullaby from Bali
(record set)

While we are exploring other cultures and their music, listen to a lullaby from Bali, sung by a child. We say that this is monophonic, that it is fluid rhythmically but lacks a strong metric sense, that there are melismas and much of it sounds improvised, that there is a sense of phrase and an attraction to a tonic note. Are the pitch manipulations really manipulations or simply insecurities? Is this enough to say or to wonder about? Having shared this song with the singer, what is your own feeling about Balinese folk song? How do you suppose this singer would relate to Dolly Parton or the Rolling Stones?

SUPPLEMENTAL LISTENING

The suggested Balinese lullaby is from a record set called *Music From the Morning of the World*. Nonesuch: H–72015. There is much to stimulate ears and minds on that record set as well as on the numerous others issued by Nonesuch in its Explorer series.

Another album worth investigating for its variety of non-Western music is *Music from the Distant Corners of the World*. Nonesuch Explorer: H 7–11.

Chapter 7
Jazz Improvisation and 32-Bar Pop Song Form

PRIMARY LISTENING:
Duke and Gershwin, "I Can't Get Started with You," Dizzy Gillespie Sextet, Gillespie solo trumpet (record set)

For an example of improvisation in twentieth-century America, try listening to Dizzy Gillespie's version of "I Can't Get Started with You." which he recorded on January 9, 1945 in New York City. He is accompanied by a group of excellent and well-known jazz musicians, but the recording is one that features Gillespie as soloist, the other men serving as back-up.

You will recognize that the piece opens with a totally homophonic section in which Gillespie solos and the group merely provides a series of chords under him. As in much jazz improvisation, his melody is based on the harmonic background and if you listen carefully, you can hear this clearly. The opening section is really an introduction, and if you look at the line score, you will be able to recognize when Gillespie launches into the song proper. Another clue is the call–response between him and the group at this point, breaking somewhat the homophony of the opening section. At the same time, you will see in what ways he alters the original melody—his improvisation is given immediately under the "real" tune (Example 25).

The structure of the song is a very common one in pop songs from the thirties and forties and even beyond. Since you are familiar with diagramming form with the use of letters, you will understand what's happening here if you know that the form is A A B A, and that each section is 8 bars (measures) long. That adds up to a total of 32

Example 25
Vernon Duke & Ira Gershwin,
"I Can't Get Started."
Copyright © 1935 by Chappell & Co.,
Inc. Copyright Renewed. International
Copyright Secured. All rights reserved.
Reprinted by permission.

bars, of course, and this form, so often used in popular music, is called a *32-bar pop song*. Other organizations are possible, but this is far and away the most common. If you try to count beats and bars, you will need a very slow four beats to a measure because the tempo is so slow.

The musical example shows the A section which remains the same on each of its occurrences in the original song. Since all the A sections are the same, you will recognize that Gillespie becomes much more daring in the second A than in the first, and even more so in the final one. This is typical of a skilled improviser. By staying relatively close to the tune on the first half of A, Gillespie is giving you a chance to learn the original just in case you don't know it already. But once having treated those 4 bars conservatively, he is free to take off on some very imaginative alterations without losing you—that is, if you can manage to hear the original tune inside your head as a reference point. That's not so easy to do, but with some practice, most people can handle it.

What happens at the B section is quite different. Gillespie never really does quote the original but goes flying off in all directions (Example 26). The B segment of a 32-bar pop song is called the *bridge,* and it's really difficult for some folks to remember because we get to hear the A section three times but the B only once in the course of the song.

All improvisers have to have some sort of guidelines for their improvisations. In the case of this particular style of jazz, and in many others as well, the guide is the harmonic background. If he is to be successful and not confuse his listeners, Gillespie must build his melody so that it is compatible with the harmony. In this performance, although there is some call–response going on, much of the time the group is simply playing a series of chords against which you can measure Gillespie's improvised melody. The form is of some support, too, because everyone can rely on that series of 8-bar phrases and the fact that the bridge comes at a predictable time.

You may have a little difficulty telling exactly where the 32 bars end because Gillespie runs right past the last cadence and into a sort of finishing-off section, usually referred to as a tag. Throughout the performance, the back-up group is probably playing from a score—very little of what they do seems improvised. If they are not actually reading their parts, it is certain that they have practiced the chords very carefully, deciding which instrument is responsible for which notes. Such a procedure is not at all unusual in the style represented by our recording, and it is also kind to the listener who has a harmonic background that helps interpret the improvisations of the soloist.

You will remember the term *chorus* from our discussion of "How Long Blues." In the same way that once through the 8 bars of an 8-bar blues constitutes a chorus, once through the 32 bars of a 32-bar pop song constitutes a chorus. You will see, then, that there are many more choruses in Yancey's version of "How Long Blues" than there are in Gillespie's version of "I Can't Get Started with You."

Example 26
Vernon Duke & Ira Gershwin,
"I Can't Get Started."
Copyright © 1935 by Chappell & Co.,
Inc. Copyright Renewed. International
Copyright Secured. All rights reserved.
Reprinted by permission.

Original (B section)

In fact, the latter performance consists of only one chorus preceded by an introduction and followed by a brief tag. Most jazz performances do consist of more than one chorus—sometimes as many as seven or eight or even more depending on the tempo. And the tempo is a factor here, because during the period when this was recorded, records were limited to about three minutes to a side. Long-playing or 33 1/3 rpm recordings did not appear until 1948, and this is a 1945 cut. So there actually wasn't enough time for more than one chorus at this tempo.

There are quite severe differences between the thumri song and this performance of "I Can't Get Started with You." One of the sharpest is the role of harmony, so important in jazz but of no consequence in a raga. You can think of other differences. But be aware that both pieces involve improvisation even though they may be worlds apart in other ways. Most of the differences are traceable to preconceptions about what is "right and proper" in music. East and West may never meet, as Rudyard Kipling has suggested. Still, we can admire and wonder at what seems to be a universal attraction to spontaneous creativity during performance. It happens from one period to the next and from one locality to the next. Sometimes the rules are strict, sometimes not so strict. The guiding elements within the music are often different. But most of us humans appreciate our performing artists when they are able to add their own individuality to the music they work with.

SUPPLEMENTAL LISTENING

There are literally thousands of jazz recordings that use 32-bar pop songs as a basis for improvisations. Many of them feature vocalists, of course, although the example above is purely instrumental. Among the most imaginative singers are Ella Fitzgerald and Billie Holiday, both of whom depart pretty far from the original tunes. For the uninitiated, the best contact with the many styles of jazz is through collections or historical sets. One of the most recent and complete is *The Smithsonian Collection of Classic Jazz.* Columbia: P–6 11891. The set includes extensive notes by the renowned jazz critic and author Martin Williams.

PRIMARY LISTENING:
"Lucretia MacEvil," Blood, Sweat and Tears (record set)

Although styles in rock change through the years, some of the principles that are characteristic of their organization have been rather consistent. Blood, Sweat and Tears have had a long and successful career, and part of their success can be laid to the skill with which their pieces are structured. If you listen to rock analytically, you will discover that most of it is put together in small chunks that make some formal sense—unless you are into the really psychedelic things and some of the punk rock. The same kind of sectionalizing that we found in "I Can't Get Started with You" is at work here, and the same sort of approach to diagramming will serve the purpose of describing the form. But because the sections are not the same length as in "I Can't Get Started," we need to look at them from a different perspective.

For the moment, forget about the instrumental postlude in "Lucretia MacEvil" and concentrate on the part that has words with brief instrumental interludes. If we were trying to label each little piece of musical variety, we might arrive at a diagram like this, with the words that begin the sections:

a. Lucretia MacEvil . . .
b. Tail-shakin', home-breakin' . . .
a. Lucretia MacEvil . . .
b. I hear your mother was the talk . . .
c. Devil got you, Lucy . . .
a. Lucretia MacEvil . . .
b. Daddy Joe's payin' your monthly rent . . .

That's a perfectly legitimate way to outline the composition. However, analysts often combine little pieces into larger pieces and arrive at a more comprehensive view of the structure. In "Lucretia MacEvil," we could consider the a and b sections as two sub-parts of a single unit. In that case, we'd have a diagram like this:

A   A   B   A
a b   a b   c   a b

The large pattern, then, would be A A B A, exactly like "I Can't Get Started" but with different proportions to each section.

As we move on in our study and begin to deal with longer compositions, this kind of amalgamation of small parts into larger ones will become more important, and so we need to know just what we're doing here with A and a and B and b. Actually, we're using the convention of formal description in which capital letters are used to indicate large sections and lower-case letters indicate the form of those large sections. Thus, in "Lucretia MacEvil" each of the three large A sections is in *binary* (two-part) form, indicated by a b. The entire song is A A B A.

There is a trick to this, though. Usually we use lower-case letters *only* when subdividing larger sections. When the sections do not subdivide, we use capitals regardless of length, as in "I Can't Get Started" and "Lascia ch'io pianga."

How long are the sections in "Lucretia MacEvil?" Does this piece have a 32-bar pop song form in the standard sense, or does it just use the principle of organization found in that form?

Perhaps you noticed that the B section beginning with "Devil got you, Lucy" is quite a bit different musically from the rest of the piece. Suddenly all the metric regularity drops out and the voice uses that speechlike delivery that we found in early opera—recitative. Then, when the A section returns with its driving rhythm and colorful brass interludes, the effect is striking in its contrast.

What sort of musical things are happening that help create all the excitement? Think about rhythm. But also think about the use of instruments as they might be related to the text. Is the brass there to match Lucretia's personality? She sounds like a brassy person. Or is it merely there to add the particular kind of excitement that brass creates? Blood, Sweat and Tears formed as a group in 1968 and they were one of the first internationally known bands to combine rock and jazz elements. The use of brass, for instance, is a nod in the direction of jazz, so perhaps it's Blood, Sweat and Tears that is brassy and not Lucretia at all. These are matters of expression and open to all sorts of interpretation. And if the music has a raunchy sound to it, if it hits us where we feel our earthier instincts at work, that's what the text is all about.

The final instrumental section doesn't seem to fit in anywhere as far as the form is concerned. It does have a function, though, and we will run into similar sections frequently when we dig into large instrumental works. The technical name is *coda*, meaning "tail." The coda often works as it does here: to merely polish off the piece, let it coast down, so to speak—though we shall find the coda being put to different uses by different composers.

A rock number as easily accessible as this one brings to mind the question of the relationship of form to expression. The fact that there is such an immediate appeal to rock probably accounts for its domination of the popular music scene. Almost anyone can respond to it. And if you put your mind to it, you can follow the form, assuming you understand the symbols and how they work. Does describing the form make you like the piece any more or less than you might have before knowing about it? Probably not. But it should give you some respect for the logical way Blood, Sweat and Tears can put a number together to satisfy one of our artistic urges for unity and variety. And that brings up another matter. Did Blood, Sweat and Tears really decide to write a composition in A A B A form? Did they really decide to use recitative in the B section in order to create a change of pace so that the return of A would be more exciting? Did they really choose brass for an expressive purpose? In other words, what might be the correlation between creativity and analysis?

In this case, *they* are the only ones who have the answers. But for us as listeners, this makes no difference as long as we understand the function of analysis and description. Description is merely verbalization of what happens in the music; it is totally objective. When we use it to venture into interpretation, as we have done here and elsewhere, that is a prerogative we are all free to use. Creativity is often an altogether different thing. Sometimes it is very deliberate, and artists can tell us in very precise terms what they had in mind and why they did what they did. In other cases, they are completely unable to rationalize, knowing only that what happened is what seemed inevitable at the time and was justified by some sense of the rightness of it all. None of that need interfere with the objective description. If the musical processes can be identified and described, so much the better for discussion. That is how we are operating now.

But we always need to be cautious about forcing something on the creators of music that they might be reluctant to accept: our interpretation of what they do. They deserve their creative privacy, and we, likewise, have the right to our objective observations, our individual interpretations, and our subjective responses. All this is one reason for the general antagonism among critics, performers, and composers, all of whom are jealous of encroachment on their territory and often impatient with perspectives other than their own.

SUPPLEMENTAL LISTENING   Almost any rock piece of a standard type will support the concept of organization described above. Not all are in A A B A form, of course. But most will be structured in sections, some of which repeat or are interspersed with different material. Rock-and-roll, on the other hand, very often follows the pattern of the 12-bar blues, a form that we will discuss in considerable detail later.

Chapter 8
The Classic Ideal in Song

Admiration for the performer's ability to create from scratch or to add something to the composer's creation has not remained as consistent a feature of Western "art" music as it was during the Baroque and earlier periods. In the course of the Classic period (about 1750 to 1827), composers exerted an increasing control over performances of their music, adding all sorts of directions to the score. This was largely a reaction to the flamboyance of the Baroque and an attempt to eliminate the excesses of that style. The Classicists, like the Greeks of antiquity after whom the movement was named, developed a style that emphasized clarity of formal ideals, and a disciplined balance among the elements of art. In the case of music, this meant a logical and clear relationship among melody, harmony, and rhythm.

The song "Plaisir d'amour," composed by Martini Il Tedesco in 1785, illustrates many characteristics of the classic style. A German organist and composer, Martini spent most of his life (1741–1816) in France. He wrote a number of operas, Masses, and miscellaneous sacred pieces, but is best remembered for "Plaisir d'amour." Here are its words:

Plaisir d'amour ne dure qu'un moment,
Chagrin d'amour dure toute la vie.

The pleasure of love lasts only a moment,
The sorrow of love lasts all life long.

J'ai tout quitté pour l'ingrate Sylvie;
Elle me quitte et prend un autre amant.
Plaisir d'amour, etc.
Tant que cette eau coulera doucement
Vers ce ruisseau qui borde la prairie,
Je t'aimerai, me répétait Sylvie;

L'eau coule encor, elle a changé pourtant.
Plaisir d'amour, etc.

I gave up everything for ungrateful Sylvia;
She left me and took another lover.
The pleasure of love, etc.
"As long as this water flows quietly
Toward the brook bordering the meadow,
I will love you," repeated Sylvia to me.
The water still flows, but she has changed.
The pleasure of love, etc.

PRIMARY LISTENING:
Martini Il Tedesco, "Plaisir d'amour" (record set)

In previous listening selections we have considered phrasing and cadences and how they relate to one another. This song illustrates one of the tendencies of the Classic period: the construction of four-measure phrases, often in pairs that balance one another. The first two lines of the poem are treated that way, for instance, and they are used in the song as a refrain (Example 27). The same phrase construction is repeated throughout the song—a line of poetry equals a phrase of music, and all the phrases are four measures long. At one point, right after "Toward the brook bordering the meadow," a measure of instrumental interlude is added in order to complete the four measures because the words use only three measures.

Thinking in terms of a large rhythmic feeling, the composers of this period must have felt a sense of satisfaction about arriving at cadences at four-measure intervals. It fits into the musical scheme of things so closely, in fact, that ever since that era, we speak of a "regular phrase" as being four measures in length. This is true even in most popular and folk song. For instance, in "I Can't Get Started with You," the A and B sections are each constructed of two four-measure phrases. Other types are referred to generally as "irregular."

Example 27
Martini, "Plaisir d'amour."

Plai - sir d'a - mour ___ ne du - re Qu'un mo - ment, ___ Cha -
grin d'a - mour du - re tou - te la vi   e.

How about the instrumental introduction in "Plaisir d'amour"? Is its phrasing regular or irregular? What is the purpose of this?

Notice the form. If the refrain is **A**, then the scheme would be:

A   B   A   C   A

That works for the words and the music both. But there are some things about the C section that make it rather important. For one thing, it is twice as long as A or B. Also, the accompaniment pattern gets more active and the bass line (played in this performance by the cello) runs in scales—in other words, becomes more impulsive. Perhaps the most striking thing is the harmonic change, because the C section is in minor, whereas A and B are in major (Example 28). Aurally, we are simply conscious that the color has changed from the beginning major. Most people are aware of the color change even though they may be completely unaware of what pitch modification creates it, and for the listener, hearing it is more important than analyzing it. Alternations between major and minor are an extremely popular musical factor in Western music, where there is a good deal of interest in harmony to begin with. Very often they work in an expressive way: many people associate major with joy or nobility or tranquility, while interpreting minor as sorrowful or threatening or some other darker emotion. This may very well be a matter of training, because many other cultures do not make these associations, and even in the West we have not always done so. The proper designation here is *mode*. Major is a kind of mode, and minor is a kind of mode. A change from one to the other, then, is a change of mode. For the theoretical basis for this, see appendix 1.

From about the mid-Baroque era until very near the end of the nineteenth century, these two modes—major and minor—formed the basis of harmonic practice in the West. Prior to that period of time there were many more than two modes in use, and there were long periods during which the mode was an important factor in defining the expression of any given piece of music. One reason why medieval and Renaissance music appears slightly archaic to many

Example 28
Martini, "Plaisir d'amour."

Tant   que cette eau   cou - le - ra   dou - ce - ment   Vers

ce   ruis-seau   qui   bor - de   la __ prai - ri - e,

listeners is the "strangeness" of the harmonic procedures, which are based on so-called modal harmonies. Because of the harmonic conventions established during the Baroque period, our ears are geared mostly to those chord progressions that are a part of the major–minor system. Paradoxically, many people are attracted to the harmonies of folk music, much of which does use modal colors. So, depending upon our exposure to different music, we may be cursed (or blessed) with split personalities, harmonically.

A lot of things happen in the C section of "Plaisir d'amour." It would be a fine exercise in interpreting to try to figure out why this is so, what it has to do with the words, if anything, and what it accomplishes in the way of purely musical expressiveness.

You can also add the formal term for A B A C A to your list of descriptions: *five-part song*. Five-part form, of course, carries even further than ternary form—A B A—the idea of variety within unity in art. Many larger works, vocal and instrumental, use the A B A C A principle of alternating sections between identical or similar music and different music. Sometimes the principle goes by another name, *rondo*, and compositions that use that principal are often called rondos, as we shall see later. All such organization seems to be built on the premise that we like to get away from something for a while but we also like to return to it. Who knows which came first, the urge or the artistic arrangement? Do we construct our forms to satisfy an inherent psychological need, or do we invent the form and then achieve a sense of satisfaction because of our response to it? That problem is handled in philosophy by the field of aesthetics, and, as you might imagine, there are many different points of view.

A GLANCE AT HISTORY   The period from about 1750 to 1827 (some suggest to 1800 or 1810) was marked by a reawakened interest in the classicism of ancient Greece. This is reminiscent of the Renaissance, of course, although some of the manifestations were not the same. The two periods do share the concept of rational thought as opposed to either divine or other more psychological/emotional sorts of revelation. Because of the fascination with Grecian precedents, the architecture returned to straight lines, balanced columns, and a general avoidance of the more spectacular displays of the Baroque (Illustration 13). The period was, in fact, a reaction against what many felt to be the extremes of the preceding era; often the vacillations from one historical and artistic period to another can be seen as chains of reactions.

While there was a great deal of artistic activity that would bear out the above generalizations, we must be careful about trying to date changes of periods too decisively. To do so encourages a distortion of the realities. There is a tremendous overlap of temper between the Classic (sometimes called the Neoclassic) period and the Romantic period which follows

Illustration 13. KENWOOD HOUSE, LONDON: LIBRARY, 1767.
The balance and clarity of design, including the borrowing of columns and the clean linear approach, are representative of the Greek-inspired classicism of the late eighteenth century.
Michael Raeburn, ed., *Architecture of the Western World*, Rizzoli International Publications, Inc., New York, 1980. Photograph by A.F. Kersting, London.

immediately after. As an example of how arbitrary these categorizations can be, consider how we arrive at the usual date for the end of the Baroque and the beginning of the Classic. It is based simply on the death of J. S. Bach in 1750, mainly because he is seen as the culmination of the musical principles of the Baroque. We will meet Bach later and will realize that there is some justification for this thinking. At the same time, there were many Classic characteristics brewing before his death. In the same vein, we most often date the end of the Classic period to coincide with the death of Beethoven in 1827. But again, Romanticism was well under way before that, and in many ways Beethoven can be seen as encompassing *both* the Classic and Romantic tempers in his work. We will pay more detailed attention to all of this in a later chapter, but it is well at this point to be cautious about placing artistic tempers too casually into boxes of time.

But the late eighteenth century was one of great political and social unrest and change. It was the period of not only the French and American Revolutions, but also the beginning of the Industrial Revolution which was to radically change the social climate during the succeeding century, bringing to fruition the definitions of class that had begun during the Baroque period and even earlier. The growth of the working class, the rise of wealthy industrialists, the growing sense of national identity, the disenchantment with the divine rights of monarchies and their figureheads—all may seem at odds with the serene ideals of classicism. But they also reflect the tendency of the period to categorize, to put things in their proper place, to create a more orderly and rational system of identification. What was not classic was the lack of restraint with which much of the shuffling was accomplished.

To put the people and events in some sort of perspective, you might want to look into some of the items on the following lists:

MUSICIANS:

Carl Phillip Emanuel Bach: 1714–1788
Ludwig van Beethoven: 1770–1827
William Billings: 1746–1800
Luigi Cherubini: 1760–1842

Christoph Gluck: 1714–1787
Franz Joseph Haydn: 1732–1809
Wolfgang Amadeus Mozart: 1756–1791
Johann Stamitz: 1717–1757

ARTISTS, LITERARY FIGURES AND OTHERS:

William Blake: 1757–1827
Robert Burns: 1759–1796
Jacques David: 1748–1825
Thomas Gainsborough: 1717–1788
Johann Wolfgang Goethe: 1749–1832

Immanuel Kant: 1724–1804
Thomas Paine: 1737–1809
Jean Jacques Rousseau: 1712–1778
Francois Voltaire: 1694–1778
William Wordsworth: 1770–1850

EVENTS:

American Revolution:
    Articles of Confederation: 1781
    Bill of Rights: 1791
    Constitution: 1787
    Continental Congress: 1774–1789
    Declaration of Independence: 1776
Discoveries:
    Hydrogen: 1776
    Oxygen: 1774
French Revolution: 1787–1815

Inventions:
  Cotton gin: 1793
  Electric battery: 1796
  Spinning jenny: 1770
  Steamboat: 1787
  Steam engine: 1769

PRIMARY LISTENING:
"Plaisir d'amour," as sung by Joan Baez (record set)

Joan Baez used "Plaisir d'amour" on one of her recordings, but being most strongly associated with folk song, she makes her own particular adaptation of Martini's music and words. Contrasting her version with the original gives us a good illustration of one of the prerogatives of all musical folk artists: to bring their own individual creativity to each performance. That is appropriate, because folk music is by its very nature an oral–aural art, one that is passed along without being written down, except by historians and collectors long after the songs have been in circulation. Even though Baez is using a "classical" composition, she treats it in a "folky" manner. If you listen carefully, though, you will realize that she keeps the original harmony, rhythm, and melody. All that changes is the form: she omits the B and C sections. Can you remember what the form of her version is properly called?

PRIMARY LISTENING:
"Everything's Alright" from *Jesus Christ, Superstar,* (Decca: DXSA–7206)

The principle of alternation of musical ideas is still very current, although the schemes that describe the total form are not always as consistent as in "Plaisir d'amour." Listen to "Everything's Alright" from the production *Jesus Christ, Superstar.* It's easy to hear the recurrence of the A section, and you should be able to tell that there is a change to the minor mode for B. Have you any idea why? Does the B section come around twice, or is the section different enough the second time to be called C? That's a hard decision, and probably only the most serious theorists will want to wrestle long with it. But it illustrates some of the analytical gray areas we can get into if we insist too dogmatically on putting all music into one or another formal category. Form gives us a handle on some elements of identification, and so it is often useful. How much can a composer push and pull inside a particular form, though, before he or she has broken free of it altogether? "Everything's Alright" is a good example of the kind of composition that leads to such questions.

Aside from form and the vacillation between major and minor, there is something interesting about the rhythm in Example 29. We talked earlier about regular and irregular phrases. There are such

Example 29
"Everything's Alright."
From the rock opera *Jesus Christ Superstar*. Lyrics by Tim Rice. Music by Andrew Lloyd Webber. © Copyright 1970 by MCA Music Ltd., London, England. Sole Selling Agent Leeds Music Corporation (MCA), New York, N.Y. for North, South, and Central America. Used by permission. All rights reserved.

things as regular and irregular meters, too, and what we have through much of this song is irregular. Regular meters are those in which the number of beats in a measure can be divided by 2 or 3. Thus $\frac{4}{4}$, $\frac{3}{4}$, and $\frac{6}{8}$, among many others, are all considered to be regular (see appendix 1). But when the number of beats is *not* divisible by 2 or 3, then we are into an irregular meter. Thus $\frac{7}{8}$, $\frac{5}{8}$, and $\frac{5}{4}$ are all considered to be irregular and, of course, there are many others. The meter in "Everything's Alright" happens to be $\frac{5}{4}$ and it feels a bit like groups of 2 and 3 beats alternating. But check carefully. Does the meter change at any time? To what? And is there an expressive purpose if it does?

Back to form: try paying attention to the formal arrangements of the particular kind of popular music to which you are most attracted. You may gain a new respect for the various composers and performing groups in terms of the way they organize their musical material. You may even discover that some of the artistic principles of the Classic period are still satisfying today.

SUPPLEMENTAL LISTENING

The five-part song has not been as widely used as its close relative the three-part, or ternary, song. One that has remained consistently popular in the concert repertoire, however, is "An Chloe" by Mozart. It has been recorded on *Mozart Songs*, Angel: 35270.

Irregular meters have been a characteristic of much music since the early years of the twentieth century. Among the popular recording stars who have used them is Dan Fogelberg. In jazz, Dave Brubeck plays tricks with meter on his album *Time Out* (Col. PC-8192). From that album, the piece "Take Five" is in $\frac{5}{4}$ meter. The big band leader, Don Ellis, has also done some rather esoteric experimenting with strange meters. The piece "Open Beauty" from his album *Electric Bath* (Col. CS–9585) is in $\frac{3\frac{1}{2}}{4}$—not an easy one to keep up with!

Chapter 9

The Romantic Ideal in Song

The Austrian composer Franz Schubert (1797–1828) was one of the most productive song composers of all time and led in the development of the Romantic lied, the German word for song. His style relied on expressive melody undergirded with an illustrative use of harmony that anticipated many of the expansions of the nineteenth century. He composed over 600 songs, some of them in cycles (*Die schöne Müllerin*, and *Winterreise*), chamber and piano music, and orchestral works which include his famous *Unfinished Symphony*.

PRIMARY LISTENING:
Franz Schubert,
"The Erl King"

One of Schubert's most famous songs, "Der Erlkönig" (The Erl King) (Example 30), makes extensive use of homophonic texture and vacillation of mode for expressive purposes. He was only 18 years old when he composed this piece in 1815, and he had already written many other songs. The poem is by the renowned German poet Wilhelm von Goethe, and is a ballad, or narrative lyric about a father and son riding frantically through a forest trying to escape from the Erl King who is threatening the child. The Erl King, a character drawn from German folklore, is the king of the elves and he was thought to prey on children and even to cause their death by his touch. Many ballads are highly dramatic, and this one is no exception:

Example 30
Schubert, "The Erl King."
From *Schubert Songs*, vol. 1. C. F.
Peters Corporation.

Ausgewählte Lieder.

1.
Erlkönig.

Goethe.

Op. 1.

(Orig. **G moll.**)

Schnell. (♩ = 152.)

59.

Wer rei - tet so spät   durch Nacht und

Wind?   Es   ist   der   Va - ter mit sei - nem

Example 30, *cont.*

Kind; er hat den Kna- ben wohl in dem

Arm, er faßt ihn si-cher, er hält ihn warm.

Wer reitet so spät durch Nacht und Wind?	Who rides so late through night and wind?
Es ist der Vater mit seinem Kind;	It is the father with his child;
Er hat den Knaben wohl in dem Arm,	He has the boy close in his arms,
Er fasst ihn sicher, er hält ihn warm.	He holds him safely, he holds him warmly.
Mein Sohn, was birgst du so bang dein Gesicht?	My son, why do you hide your face so fearfully?
Siehst, Vater, du den Erlkönig nicht?	Father, do you not see the Erl King?
Den Erlenkönig mit Kron' und Schweif?	The Erl King with crown and train?
Mein Sohn, es ist ein Nebelstreif.	My son, it is a streak of mist.
Du liebes Kind, komm, geh mit mir!	You lovely child, come, go with me!
Gar schöne Spiele spiel' ich mit dir,	All the most wonderful games I'll play with you,
Manch bunte Blumen sind an dem Strand,	Many colorful flowers are on the shore,
Meine Mutter hat manch gülden Gewand.	My mother has many golden robes.
Mein Vater, mein Vater, und hörest do nicht,	My father, my father, and do you not hear
Was Erlenkönig mir leise verspricht?	What the Erl King is gently promising me?

Sei ruhig, bleibe ruhig, mein Kind:	Be still, stay still, my child:
In dürren Blättern säuselt der Wind.	In the dead leaves, the wind is whispering.
Willst, feiner Knabe, du mit mir gehn?	Will you come with me, fine boy?
Meine Töchter sollen dich warten schön;	My daughters will wait upon you.
Meine Töchter führen den nächtlichen Reihn	My daughters lead the nightly dance,
Und wiegen und tanzen und singen dich ein.	And rock and dance and sing you to sleep.
Mein Vater, mein Vater, und siehst du nicht dort	My father, my father, and do you not see there
Erlkönigs Töchter am düstern Ort?	The Erl King's daughters in the shadowy place?
Mein Sohn, mein Sohn, ich seh' es genau:	My son, my son, I see it clearly;
Es scheinen die alten Weiden so grau.	The old willows appear so grey.
Ich liebe dich, mich reizt deine schöne Gestalt;	I love you, I am pleased by your lovely figure;
Und bist du nicht willig, so brauch' ich Gewalt.	And if you are not willing, I will use force.
Mein Vater, mein Vater, jetzt fasst er mich an!	My father, my father, he is taking me now!
Erlkönig hat mir ein Leids getan!	The Erl King has done me harm!
Dem Vater grauset's, er reitet geschwind,	The father shudders, he rides swiftly,
Er hält in Armen das ächzende Kind.	He holds in his arms the moaning child.
Erreicht den Hof mit Mühe und Not;	He reaches his house, troubled and distressed;
In seinen Armen das Kind war tot.	In his arms, the child was dead.

There's a lot going on musically in this song: that may be why it has remained so popular for over a century and a half. The long introduction establishes the mood in a hurry; because of the rhythm the music sounds as harassed as the father and son. Moreover, there is some text illustration involved if you are willing to accept the rhythm as representing the sound of the horse's hooves, which most people are. There is also some attempt at realism in the use of the voice. The father usually sings in a low register, the boy higher and more frantically, and the Erl King in a seductive sort of way.

In order to get the most out of the dramatic possibilities, Schubert uses a host of expressive devices. One of the most important is the vacillation between major and minor. The principal mode is minor, but because he is trying to lure the boy away with promises of various kinds, the Erl King always sings in major. This use of mode had much meaning to composers and audiences in the Romantic period, and Schubert comes right at the beginning of that era. The only time the Erl King gets into minor is when he resorts to a threat: "And if you are not willing, I will use force." At that cadence, the piano lands hard on a minor chord.

Without making any attempt to identify the exact keys involved, you may be able to hear that the key changes from stanza to stanza, and that the piano interludes help accomplish this. This song is through-composed, as contrasted with strophic, and the key changes are used to contribute to the variety among the strophes of the poem. If you can hear this kind of harmonic activity, it adds a dimension to your reactions to the song's expressiveness. Moving around from one key to another increases the feeling of restlessness in music—it helps create tension. Some keys are higher than others, and many people even believe that some keys sound brighter or darker than others. This may be imagination, or it may be a kind of superior sensitivity to the quality of sound, or it may even be a result of indoctrination. In any case, it is worth thinking about and listening for if you are trying to develop your ear.

Perhaps the most obvious instance of this in Schubert's song is that each time the boy cries, "My father, my father!" he does so on a higher pitch, because he is in a higher key. To add to the intensity of these places, the voice employs a sharp dissonance with the piano. Even if you are unable to read music, you can see that what the voice sings is not the same pitch as what the piano is playing in its highest part (Example 31). The interval between the voice and the piano is actually the smallest one we use in Western music, a half-step. When two pitches a half-step apart are sounding at the same time, we experience a very real sense of aural discomfort, and that is one of the purposes of dissonance when used expressively. There are many different kinds of dissonance, but the half-step is considered one of the sharpest.

Example 31
Schubert, "The Erl King."
From *Schubert Songs,* vol. 1. C. F.
Peters Corporation.

The concept of dissonance is a very controversial and complex one, but worth a little thought because it occurs so often and in so many kinds of music and for so many different reasons. Dissonance is widely contrasted with consonance: in a general sense, the first is considered harsh or unpleasant and the second is considered smooth and easy to take. The ideas about what is dissonant and consonant have changed often in the course of our music history, from country to country and from period to period. Whenever there is some sort of agreement about what constitutes dissonance and consonance, though, composers often use the former to express tension and the latter to express relaxation. Certainly that is what Schubert has in mind here; he is adding musical tension and discomfort to match the fear of the boy. Also, we can infer that he is adding greater excitement, even hysteria, by making the pitch on each successive outburst higher. So we can say that these cries of fright are dramatized by sharp dissonances, by changes of key, and by use of higher pitches. Exactly the same devices are used in purely instrumental music and for exactly the same expressive reasons. The only difference is that in the latter case, we do not have words to explain the specific cause of the tension. Then it is tension for its own sake. We will encounter that often when we get into absolute music.

All that has been said here about "The Erl King" indicates that Schubert had a large bag of tricks to use in adding music to Goethe's ballad. That is entirely in keeping with one of the artistic aims of the Romantic period, which was to intensify expression in all the arts following the relative restraint of the preceding Classic period. The Romantics did not throw away the musical ideas that had been accumulated and invent all new ones. For instance, in spite of the excitement most of the phrases are regular. Also, there is the familiar homophonic texture. But the piano is given a far more important part in the expression than we found in the accompaniment of "Plaisir d'amour." Because of that, it would be hard to imagine that a guitar could substitute as well as it did in Baez's recording of that song.

Another thing that fascinated artists of all sorts during the Romantic period was the mystery of death—and even the mystery of mystery itself. Many novels, for instance, were full of macabre situations, and the devil was very much in evidence. Perhaps Goethe's most famous work is the long poem *Faust,* in which Satan plays an indispensable role. The Erl King is obviously derived from fearful imaginings about otherworldly powers exercising some frightful control over the fate of humans. We seem to be having a resurgence of this theme with our interest in exorcism and with the hysteria that accompanies it. It may be that human nature really doesn't change so much with the changing centuries, in spite of our advancing knowledge. Think of the Salem witch hunts, Halloween imagery, and even, in a lighter vein, the television show *Bewitched*, still being seen on reruns. Not to mention the Hollywood film *The Exorcist* and the barrage of movies patterned on it. We still probe around for explanations of things that can't be readily explained. Goethe and his Erl King have lots of company still.

SUPPLEMENTAL LISTENING

Another Schubert song that makes similar use of slightly different material for dramatic purposes is "Gretchen am Spinnrade," based on a text from Goethe's *Faust*. It may be found, among other places, on *Schubert Lieder Recital.* Angel: 35022.

The German organist and composer Carl Loewe (1796–1869) is associated almost completely with ballad composition, although his works include symphonies and piano pieces. His setting of "The Erl King" is even more dramatic than Schubert's. It has been recorded on *Loewe: Ballads.* Deutsche Grammophon: DG 2530052.

There are many ballads in the folk repertoire, as we discussed in chapter 1. "Barbra Allen," just as vivid textually as "The Erl King," makes an interesting contrast to it in having a style where the performer gets no "help" from the accompaniment, but must furnish the dramatic development by changes of vocal style. Any comparison between folk style and what many people consider its opposite, art style, must consider the relative amount of complexity in each and the reasons for it. The former is an oral–aural tradition using material without identifiable authorship. The latter is a literary, written tradition drawing upon works whose authorship is known and acknowledged. "Barbra Allen" is available on many recordings; it is the most popular and widespread of the folk ballads in English.

PRIMARY LISTENING:
Hugo Wolf, "Abschied"
(record set)

By 1888, Romanticism had reached its peak and composers were off in a number of different musical directions. One was toward new harmonic devices that were often so dissonant that the concept of dissonance itself was about to undergo one of its periodic changes. Along with that went a tendency to avoid staying in one key long enough to become comfortable with it, at least as far as the average listener was concerned. You will recall that Richard Wagner was responsible for much of the aesthetic stance that led to this harmonic restlessness. Also, the melody and its accompaniment often seemed to be going their own separate ways. Much of this is found in a song called "Abschied" (A Farewell), composed by Hugo Wolf in 1888. Wolf was a great admirer of Wagner, and so one would expect him to draw some of his musical devices from his idol. A German composer, Wolf (1860–1903) composed songs almost exclusively, and he is considered by some to be the greatest of the Romantic song composers. Cosmopolitan and discriminating in his literary taste, he was strongly attracted to the best available poetry of the period, in his native German and in other European languages.

The text of "Abschied" suggests that some of the Romantic preoccupation with death, mystery, and the macabre is fading. At least in this poem, there is a refreshing sense of wit and self-mockery. It is by the German poet and pastor Eduard Mörike.

Unangelklopft ein Herr tritt
abends bei mir ein:
"Ich habe die Ehr', Ihr Rezensent
zu sein."
Sofort nimmt er das Licht in die
Hand,
Besieht lang meinen Schatten an
der Wand,
Rückt nah und fern: "Nun, lieber
junger Mann,
Sehn Sie doch gefälligst mal Ihre
Nas' so von der Seite an!
Sie geben zu, dass das ein
Auswuchs is."
"Das? Alle Wetter—gewiss!"
Ei Hasen! Ich dachte nicht,
All mein Lebtage nicht,
Dass ich so eine Weltsnase führt'
im Gesicht!
Der Mann sprach noch
Verschiedenes hin und her,
Ich weiss, auf meines Ehre, nicht
mehr;
Meinte vielleicht, ich sollt' ihm
beichten.
Zuletzt stand er auf; ich tat ihm
leuchten.
Wie wir nun an die Treppe sind,

Da geb' ich ihm, ganz froh gesinnt,
Einen kleinen Tritt
Nur so von hinten aufs Gesässe
mit—
Alle Hagel! ward das ein Gerumpel,
Ein Gepurzel, ein Gehumpel,
Dergleichen hab' ich nie gesehn,
All mein Lebtage nicht gesehn,
Einen Menschen so rasch die
Trepp' hinabgehn!

Without knocking, a man came
into my room one evening;
"I have the honor of being your
critic."
At once he took the lamp into his
hand,
Inspecting for a long time my
shadow on the wall,
Moving back and forth: "Now,
dear youth,
Do me the kindness of observing
your nose from the side!
You must admit that it is not
normal."
"That? Good heavens—actually!"
Great guns! I never thought,
All the days of my life,
That I carried such a world-beater
on my face!
The man spoke about different
things,
I don't know what else, I swear;

Maybe he thought I should
confess to him.
At last he stood up; I lighted his
way out.
As we were standing at the top of
the stairs
I gave him all in mischief,
A little kick
Just right, from behind, on his
bottom—
What a storm! What rumbling,
What tumbling, what hobbling,
I never saw anything like it,
Never in all my days did I see
A man go down the steps so
hastily!

Example 32
Wolf, "Abschied," *Songs on
Poems by Moerike.*
International Music Company.

Abschied.
A farewell.

Listening to this can be pretty frustrating if we expect it to sound as simple as a folk song or to use the same sort of harmonic ideas as Schubert. The rhythms sound cut up too, mainly because they are often following the rhythms of speech in a kind of recitative manner (Example 32). Until the end there isn't much of what we could call a tune, certainly nothing we'd whistle to pass the time away. A lot of the melody is just too disjunct to fall easily on our ear. The harmony is not only unsettled but downright dissonant until the last part of the song. And the phrasing has no sense of regularity—but neither does the poetry—in fact, some listeners might call this style "spastic"! Instead of furnishing a principally harmonic accompaniment with some stabs at text-illustration, as in Schubert's "Erl King," the piano here has a melodic life of its own. The vocal melody and the accompaniment are none too attractive by themselves; together they are quite graphic, if not pretty. Nor are there many repeated chords as in Schubert; the texture in "Abschied" is much more linear, often outright polyphonic. Notice, too, how frequently the piano is used for rhythmic and harmonic punctuation after having "laid out" for brief periods. The result is rather like a vocal–instrumental dialogue or discussion. Incidentally, you may realize that while the song is written for high voice, the singer is using a lower key. This is a common occurrence in vocal music. Our score examples are in the key that Wolf composed "Abschied" in. However, lots of people who can't sing that high still want to perform the song. The solution is easy: accompanist and singer just transpose it to a lower key.

The independence of voice and piano becomes most apparent when the visitor has been booted down the steps; this is text illustration, of course (Example 33). But the atmosphere changes at the end of the song. At "Never in all my days" the voice launches into a waltz-like melody while the piano furnishes an appropriate oom-pah-pah accompaniment. It isn't really a waltz by Johann Strauss, the Viennese composer of many famous examples, but it sounds like one. Wolf is having some fun here. No one being kicked down the stairs is doing a waltz, which is among the most graceful of ballroom dances, but the kicker feels good about it, so good that it probably looks just as satisfying as a waltz to him. This is a case of musical irony—the use of sarcasm to suggest precisely the opposite of the literal sense of the words or situation. To drive the point home, the piano is given a long waltzing postlude during which the listener can use his imagination to recreate the scene.

The important thing to realize about this ending is that the composer needs some cooperation from the audience in order to get his points across. Anyone who doesn't recognize a waltz is going to miss a lot of what is going on, not only musically but expressively

Example 33
Wolf, "Abschied." *Songs on Poems by Moerike.* International Music Company.

as well. Since irony has to be bounced off the literal sense of something, it can't work unless the literal sense is known. Wolf's waltz is a quotation *reference* which enables the knowing audience to use a lot of imagination. Any composer or performer who does this sort of thing is complimenting the audience, taking for granted a certain amount of sophistication on their part, giving them a chance to contribute something instead of hitting them over the head as though they were mules. In other words, there is some subtlety here, and some musical imagery, rather than totally obvious statement. This happens in all sorts of music; sometimes we miss it through lack of attention, lack of information, or lack of imagination.

SUPPLEMENTAL LISTENING   Other examples of quotation references occur in:

Robert Schumann, "Die beiden Grenadiere" (The Two Grenadiers), which quotes the French national anthem for dramatic association with patriotism. It is available on *Schuman Songs.* Deutsche Grammophon: 139110.

Duke Ellington, *Black and Tan Fantasy.* This is one of Ellington's earliest and most important compositions and one we will be looking at in detail later. In his original 1927 recording of the piece, he has some fun quoting from Chopin's "Funeral March" at the end—for no apparent reason except just good-hearted foolishness, although some listeners have taken it as a serious commentary. This recording is on *Duke Ellington: The Beginning.* Decca: DL–79224.

Composers of program music, with which we will deal in part 2 of the book, have used quotations frequently to invite associations in the listener. Often these serve a serious purpose rather than an ironic one.

A GLANCE AT HISTORY
In the same sense that the Classic period cannot be dated clearly (see chapter 8), the Romantic period and the artistic temper that defines it began earlier than 1800 and lasted longer than 1900, although the nineteenth century is generally considered to be the Romantic century. A glance through the list of musicians and other people given below will show that a number of them were active well into the twentieth century although their artistic style continued to be principally Romantic. But for purposes of easy identification, we can flow with the stream and think of Romanticism as being a nineteenth-century phenomenon.

The list of events below will reveal the enormous activity that was characteristic of the century. As a key-hole to history, they will pretty much tell a lot of the story. One of the most important characteristics of the period was the growth of nationalism and national outreach, most evident in the spread of colonialism. We are all familiar, I think, with the saying that "the sun never sets on English soil." That, in itself, is the nationalistic temper in a nutshell. All of this had its reflection in the arts, where composers, painters, sculptors, architects all attempted to develop a style that would identify the nationality of its origin. Notice the advent of Russian composers on the list, together with playwrights and authors. Part of this was the breakdown of Eastern European isolationism, but part was also a deliberate attempt to establish and share with the world a Russian sensibility in all the arts. Naturally, other nations were equally involved, including America.

The nineteenth century was the first in which composers, performers, and other artists were able to become true professionals, mostly out from under the wings of patronage. The list of musicians and other artists is as long as it is because of this urge to be self-supporting and the ability to manage that. Communication and travel among different countries encouraged the widespread sharing of all kinds of works of art as well as of political theories, philosophies, social customs, fashions, and even tastes in food.

Along with the success enjoyed by artists came the feeling that all of them, regardless of their medium, were very special people and not subject to the same moral codes as ordinary folk. As a result, the life style of many of them was quite exotic and even outré. Wagner, for example, not only lived a rather loose life sexually, trading partners with some abandon, but he also believed that because of his genius he should be supported in a style that he could not manage on the income from his compositions. He was not atypical; he had lots of company from artists who applied the same views to themselves.

In music, one of the strongest aesthetic stances was that of synthesis, by means of which a number of arts can be combined to create something new. It was because of this that there was such a vast emphasis on program music, which we will investigate later. Some commentators attribute that, however, to the attempt by composers to make their large-scale work intelligible to the masses—give them a story to follow so they will understand the music. Other combination genres were the art song, which combines music and poetry, and ballet, uniting music and dance as well as story. The latter was not a new genre but it was given immense attention in the 1900s by people other than the aristocracy who had supported it in previous eras. As we saw earlier, Wagner was enamored of the idea that his operas or music dramas were able to amalgamate music, words, action, and scenery into one indivisible whole. That would be synthesis at its fullest, and indeed Wagner is considered to be the epitome of Romanticism.

We will be dealing with romantic music of all sorts later. But for now, look carefully at the list of people and events given here for a full appreciation of the highlights of nineteenth-century action.

MUSICIANS:

Hector Berlioz: 1803–1869
Georges Bizet: 1838–1875
Alexander Borodin: 1833–1887
Johannes Brahms: 1833–1897
Anton Bruckner: 1824–1896
Frédéric Chopin: 1810–1849
Claude Debussy: 1862–1918
Anton Dvořák: 1841–1904
Gabriel Fauré: 1845–1924
Stephen C. Foster: 1826–1864
César Franck: 1822–1890
Charles Gounod: 1818–1893
Edward Grieg: 1843–1907
Fanny Mendelssohn Hensel: 1805–1847
Scott Joplin: 1868–1917
Franz Liszt: 1811–1886
Gustave Mahler: 1860–1911
Jules Massenet: 1842–1912
Felix Mendelssohn: 1809–1847
Modest Moussorgsky: 1839–1881

Giacomo Puccini: 1858–1924
Sergei Rachmaninoff: 1873–1943
Maurice Ravel: 1875–1937
Nicolas Rimsky-Korsakov: 1844–1908
Gioacchino Rossini: 1792–1868
Camille Saint-Saëns: 1835–1921
Erik Satie: 1866–1925
Franz Schubert: 1797–1828
Clara Schumann: 1819–1896
Robert Schumann: 1810–1856
Jean Sibelius: 1865–1957
Bedřich Smetana: 1824–1884
John Philip Sousa: 1854–1932
Richard Strauss: 1864–1949

Sir Arthur Sullivan: 1842–1900
Peter I. Tchaikowsky: 1840–1893
Giuseppe Verdi: 1813–1901
Richard Wagner: 1813–1883
Carl Maria von Weber: 1786–1826
Hugo Wolf: 1860–1903

AUTHORS, LITERARY FIGURES AND OTHERS:

Jane Austen: 1775–1817
Pierre Baudelaire: 1821–1867
Elizabeth Browning: 1806–1861

John Keats: 1795–1821
Rudyard Kipling: 1865–1936
Henry Wadsworth Longfellow: 1807–1882

Robert Browning: 1812–1889
George Byron: 1788–1824
Lewis Carroll: 1832–1898
Paul Cézanne: 1839–1906
Stephen Crane: 1871–1900
Louis Jacque M. Daguerre: 1789–1851
Charles Darwin: 1809–1882
Edgar Degas: 1834–1917
Charles Dickens: 1812–1870
Feodor Dostoyevsky: 1821–1881
Thomas Edison: 1847–1931
George Eliot: 1819–1880

Ralph Waldo Emerson: 1803–1882
Gustave Flaubert: 1821–1880
Paul Gaugin: 1848–1903
Sir William Gilbert: 1836–1911
Vincent van Gogh: 1853–1890
Francisco Goya: 1746–1828
Nathaniel Hawthorne: 1804–1864
Victor Hugo: 1802–1885
Henrik Ibsen: 1826–1906

Stéphane Mallarmé: 1842–1898
Karl Marx: 1818–1883
Claude Monet: 1840–1926
Friedrich Nietzsche: 1844–1900
Louis Pasteur: 1822–1895
Edgar Allan Poe: 1809–1849

Alexander Pushkin: 1799–1837
Pierre Renoir: 1841–1919
Auguste Rodin: 1840–1917
Sir Walter Scott: 1771–1832
George Bernard Shaw: 1856–1950
Robert Louis Stevenson: 1850–1894
Harriet Beecher Stowe: 1812–1896
Alfred Lord Tennyson: 1809–1892
Henry David Thoreau: 1817–1862
Leo Tolstoy: 1828–1910
Mark Twain: 1835–1910
Walt Whitman: 1819–1892
Oscar Wilde: 1856–1900
Emile Zola: 1840–1902

EVENTS:

California gold rush: 1849
Constructions:
    Brooklyn Bridge: 1883
    Erie Canal: 1825
    Panama Canal: 1914
    Railroads: begun in 1830s
    Statue of Liberty: 1886
    Subways: begun in 1895
    Suez Canal: 1869
    Transatlantic cable: 1866
Discoveries:
    Ether as an anesthetic: 1842
    Radium: 1898
    X-rays: 1895
Expansion of the U. S.:
    Alaska purchased: 1867
    Louisiana Purchase: 1803
Inventions:
    Reaper: 1826
    Sewing machine: 1846
    Telegraph: 1830s
    Telephone: 1876

Japanese trade inaugurated: 1850s
Monroe Doctrine: 1823
Wars:
   American Civil War: 1861–1865
   Boer War: 1899–1902
   Napoleonic conquests: 1793–1814
   Spanish-American War: 1898

Chapter 10
Twentieth-Century Song

The twentieth century has been a puzzling one in every way in the arts. In music, probably the most striking thing has been the increased tolerance for dissonance, both melodic and harmonic. Together with that has gone an outburst of rhythmic complexities of all sorts. We will be investigating all of these things in detail later, but for now let's look at three examples of the sort of song composition that is somewhat representative.

PRIMARY LISTENING:
Samuel Barber, "The Crucifixion" from *Hermit Songs* (record set)

Barber tells us that the texts for his set of ten *Hermit Songs* were taken from jottings found in the margins of medieval manuscripts from the eighth to the thirteenth centuries. The primary job of the monks who did the brief comments was to copy manuscripts, but obviously boredom or the need for a break from routine led them to make miscellaneous observations. Some are in poetry; others, like "The Crucifixion," are either prose or blank verse.

The text:

At the cry of the first bird
They began to crucify Thee, O Swan!
Never shall lament cease because of that,
It was like the parting of day from night.
Ah, sore was the suff'ring borne
By the body of Mary's Son,
But sorer still to Him was the grief

Which for His sake
Came upon His Mother.

The musical fabric here is quite stark, certainly appropriate to the words. There is some text illustration going on because the highest part of the piano seems to be imitating the "cry of the first bird" (Example 34).

Less obvious than that, though, are the musical references to medieval practice. If you will think back to our contacts with medieval music, you may remember that some of the favorite intervals were fourths and fifths and octaves. We did look at an example of free organum from the Notre Dame School, but earlier than that, singers were moving along in parallel fourths and fifths. That was actually the first type of organum, and it creates an even bleaker sound than the "Benedicamus Domino." Perhaps in an attempt to recapture that medieval sound to match his medieval text, Barber does exploit fourths and fifths in the melody line (Example 35). They are present in some of the chords, too. The cadence chord at "O Swan!" for instance is made up of fourths rather than the thirds with which we ordinarily construct chords. The same thing occurs at the last vocal cadence on "His Mother" (Example 36). Although this particular usage in this song is probably

Example 34
Samuel Barber, "Crucifixion"
(*Hermit Songs*).
Copyright © 1954 by G. Schirmer, Inc.
All rights reserved. Used by permission.

Example 35
Samuel Barber, "Crucifixion"
(*Hermit Songs*).
Copyright © 1954 by G. Schirmer, Inc.
All rights reserved. Used by permission.

At the cry of the first bird they be gan to cru - ci -

fy thee, O Swan!

Example 36
Samuel Barber, "Crucifixion"
(*Hermit Songs*).
Copyright © 1954 by G. Schirmer, Inc.
All rights reserved. Used by permission.

Mo - ther.

a reference to medieval music, the use of chords based on fourths rather than thirds is a compositional technique that has had some currency in our century. Such structures are known as *quartal chords*.

Listen very carefully to the accompaniment beginning at "It was like the parting of day from night," and continuing until the voice enters with "Ah, sore . . ." Using fourths as an important interval, there are several polyphonically imitative entrances of the same tune that the voice will sing—a sort of preparation for that most climactic part of the song.

There is a lot of dissonance, sometimes within the accompaniment and sometimes between the accompaniment and the voice. This would be very appropriate, of course, because the subject of the song is certainly a dissonant one. Listen to the very last chord of the song (Example 37). *That's* dissonant.

Barber composed the *Hermit Songs* during 1952–1953 and they were first performed in October of 1953 in Washington, D. C. For that performance, as for the one on our recording, Barber was the pianist and Leontyne Price was the soloist. Price, a black soprano, is one of the most renowned singers in the world. Black performers of "serious" music have had a difficult time being accepted into that world. It was not until 1955 that the famous contralto, Marian Anderson, was placed on the roster of the Metropolitan Opera in New York City, although she had had a distinguished career here and abroad for many years prior to that. Leontyne Price was well known at the most prestigious opera houses in the world for a number of years before her Met debut in 1961. Since that time, she has been among the most successful and sought-after artists, appearing with major symphony orchestras, in recital, and at all the leading opera houses.

Blacks have been successful in the areas of entertainment, popular music, and jazz for many years and have been accepted in those roles. However, they have won recognition as serious artists only during the last few decades, and even then their progress has been painfully slow. Look over the personnel of the next symphony orchestra you see live or on TV. You might be shocked at the

Example 37
Samuel Barber, "Crucifixion"
(*Hermit Songs*).
Copyright © 1954 by G. Schirmer, Inc.
All rights reserved. Used by permission.

scarcity of blacks although they are among the most talented musicians we have available.

SUPPLEMENTAL LISTENING

The best way to supplement this example is to listen to the rest of the *Hermit Songs*. They are on Columbia: ML4988. The texts are mostly quite brief and some of them are rather salty. Barber is more conservative than many of his contemporaries, but there are enough twentieth-century techniques to reward the interested listener.

PRIMARY LISTENING:
Barbara Kolb, "Automort,"
from *Three Place Settings*
(record set)

We've been looking at and listening to many different combinations of words and music: songs, chants, arias, choruses, whatever. There are still other ways in which to combine voices and music, however, and one of them is illustrated by our next listening example. It is a piece by the American composer, Barbara Kolb, composed in 1968 using a poem by Ronald F. Costa. The selection, "Automort," is from a set of three pieces called *Three Place Settings;* this is the last of those three.

The words will give you a good idea of why the narrator is upset:

In change, out food
Turn handle, handle stuck
. . . again . . .

In change, out food
Turn handle, handle stuck
Again . . .   . . . again?
In change, out food
Turn handle, jiggle handle, hit handle,
Pull handle,
Old change, new handle
Gotta change, find-a handle
Gotta hand on a handle, handle change,
Find-a, gotta, gonna, giva,
        GIVE UP!!!

"Mort" means death; the poem is obviously about the death of an automat, an eating establishment best known to New Yorkers, perhaps, where all sorts of food and drink are available in machines. It may also refer to those dispensing mechanisms one finds in service stations and elsewhere—the ones that seem perpetually out of order.

Instead of setting the words to a melody, Kolb has assigned them to a narrator. This leaves the music free to illustrate and comment on the narration. It's not only a different role for the voice but it also creates a different relationship between words and music. The latter is still an accompaniment, of course, but it has a role far less restricted than in our earlier examples. Nonetheless, both the chamber group and the narrator must observe the timing very carefully. Otherwise all correlation between text and musical illustration is lost.

The chamber group consists of a violin, clarinet, double bass, and vibraphone. The musical score looks about as erratic as the sound of the chamber group, and that's entirely justifiable in this composition (Example 38). Many twentieth-century composers have had to resort to new methods of notation in order to provide directions for performances that depart radically from the practices of the past.

We have noticed, beginning with the Classic period, an increasing tendency for composers to exert control over performances of their music by supplying more and more instructions for tempo, dynamics, and other elements. Look carefully at the score for "Automort." Every single note is accompanied by one or more symbols indicating the exact dynamic level, expression, or method of performance expected by the composer. This places enormous demands on the performer and the conductor. In the performance on our record set, Barbara Kolb is herself the conductor so we can be reasonably sure that she got the results she wanted! It should be clear why there is a small group and why there is only one person on a given instrument rather than sections as in a large orchestra.

What correspondence do you find between the words and the music in this composition? There is plenty of opportunity for text illustration here—the coin going in and the handle being jiggled, for instance. Does Kolb take these things literally? Or is there more a general sense of frenzy and frustration? In any case, do you find the total effect of words and music mutually supportive? How about the roles of dissonance and rhythmic complexity?

Barbara Kolb (b. 1939) has received many grants, scholarships, and awards for her work in composition. Among the most prestigious have been the Prix de Rome and a Guggenheim Fellowship. Most of her compositions have been for chamber groups of various kinds, sometimes with voice. She has taught at Brooklyn College and Wellesley College and her works have received numerous performances, and a number have been recorded.

Kolb is representative of a group of composers who have just begun to come into their own during the twentieth century: women. Although we have had women composers for almost as long as we know anything about music, they have had a real struggle to gain acceptance in what was long felt to be strictly a man's game. During some earlier centuries, it was even felt that a woman who composed

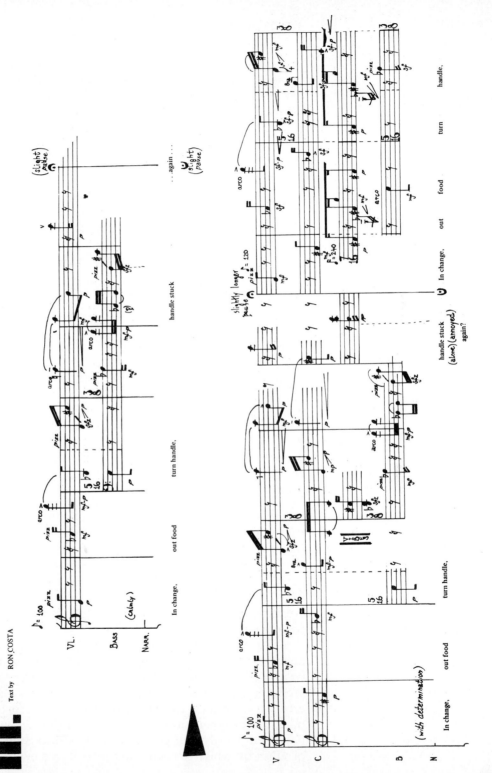

AUTOMORT

Text by   RON COSTA

or performed was of loose moral character. Even today in some parts of the world, the only women who are tolerated as performers are prostitutes. Some women composers have resorted to the use of a pseudonym (male, of course!) or to initials in order to disguise their sex. The same has been true of poets, novelists, painters, and playwrights, but happily that situation is changing and more and more women are taking their rightful place in the world of creative artists.

SUPPLEMENTAL LISTENING

It would be interesting to listen to the other two portions of *Three Place Settings*. The first two pieces are "I Think I'll Have . . ." and "Roast Peacock." The factor common to all is the subject of food. They have been recorded on Desto: DC–7143.

Among the welter of new musical procedures to emerge during the twentieth century has been a fascination for new and different sound-making machines. The most popular and widespread of these have been electronic and they have been used extensively in jazz and rock bands and even in country music. The initial experimentation in electronic instruments, however, was in the area of "serious" or "classical" music. Later in the book we will explore some of these developments more fully. Right now we will give some attention to a composition that combines the expressive use of the human voice with the startling varieties of sound that electronic machines can produce. The piece is *Visage*, a 1961 work by Luciano Berio.

PRIMARY LISTENING:
Luciano Berio, *Visage*
(record set)

We usually associate the voice with some sort of wordmaking when we think about communicating. Of course, we use our voices in many different ways. We hum when the spirit moves us. And naturally we laugh, cry, scream; there are many ways to use the voice expressively without words. Berio, an Italian composer born in 1935, asks the "singer," Cathy Berberian, to explore the entire range of vocalization *except* for words. Only one real word is used in the course of the performance—the Italian *parole*, which, paradoxically, means "words."

The opening sections of the piece seem to suggest a tortured attempt at speech, a series of labored consonants and vowels almost wrung from the vocalist. Behind what appears to be agonizing effort, we have combinations of electronic sounds, swishes, muted sirenlike effects. Gradually the voice transfers its efforts to a succession of purely emotional outbursts: fear, laughter. Finally one clearly pronounced word emerges, *parole*. Is Berio suggesting the laborious process by which speech itself must have evolved?

By turn the voice becomes sensuous, alluring, intimate, but without perceptible language to explain the mood changes. We hear a veritable parade of emotions: smug self-satisfaction, joy, strong tints of sexual gratification. Then, motivated by a burst of electronic sound, fear, weeping, pleading. More hysterical mixtures of electronic material superimposed on short, shattering guttural vocal expletives. The record set includes only the first 10 minutes of the original 21-minute performance. The final sections, not reproduced, are by turn terror-stricken, lyric, complacent, exploratory, seductive—the whole range of expressive vocalization at its most direct levels. The accompanying electronic manipulations produce sounds that are often biting, excruciatingly dissonant. The piece ends with a complex of such sounds, gradually fading into silence. Is all of this related in some way to new styles in the visual arts (Illustration 14)?

Much of what Berberian does *sounds* like speech, including all the inflections we use when speaking. But with the one exception

Illustration 14. TOWARD CREPUSCULE.
Hans Hoffman, 1963. "Crepuscule" means twilight or dusk. Does this help to give a meaning to Hoffman's painting? Or is the interplay of shade and design simply sufficient meaning? The vividness of the work and its avoidance of direct representational statement seems like Berio's use of the human voice for nonverbal expression in *Visage*. In any case, both works of art are arresting in their kaleidoscopic use of texture and sound.
Cincinnati Art Museum. The Edwin and Virginia Irwin Memorial Fund.

noted—there are really no actual words, only a sort of gibberish, unintelligible but intense in its expressive strength. The electronics complement, motivate, respond. But they do no more to explain the ideas behind all this artistic effort than does the vocalization itself.

Berio has little to add interpretatively to what the listener might supply for himself. He is attracted to electronic music principally because it offers the experience of discovering new sounds, combinations of sound, dimensions of the aural acuteness of the listener. The sort of thing that Berberian does with her voice he refers to as vocal gestures and inflections, valuable expressively because they carry the weight of associations and "shadow of meanings." Her sounds relate in some way to the electrically produced sounds, but each of us must find his or her own particular relationships. Depending upon our individual sensitivity to sound for its own sake, our individual imagination and experience, we will fashion our own meanings. Or do without, perhaps. But the form is certainly in the emotional surges themselves. No diagram will work here.

SUPPLEMENTAL LISTENING   This is a unique composition and, although there are many others that employ electronic instruments in various combinations, there is no real parallel to *Visage*. We will be dealing in more detail with electronic music later in the book and some of the illustrations will involve vocalization of different sorts.

A GLANCE AT HISTORY   Perhaps because we are so close to it in time, the twentieth century seems to be the most active, complex one in our history. Political unrest, for instance, has been a key factor in the conduct of national and international affairs. There has not really been a period of any substantial length that has not been marred by wars, some of incredibly long duration. The struggle among the wealth of political philosophies has been a real factor at this point, and it continues unabated.

Scientific experimentation and discovery, new medical techniques, the advent of atomic energy, the profusion of satellites and other invasions of space, new concepts of education at all levels—all of these have been seen as raising questions of moral and ethical integrity. They have inaugurated many concerns about responsible behavior and reassessments of objectives and the means with which we pursue them. Much of this ferment has been reflected in religious movements and counter-movements, including the astonishing proliferation of cults of all sorts, many particularly aimed at college-age persons.

And these many experiments and readjustments, including reactions to them, have found their way into artistic enterprises of all sorts. Architects have responded to the demand for greater functionalism by creating streamlined structures that predict the pace of contemporary society just as forcefully as did the heavenward-reaching cathedrals of the Gothic period and the ornate public buildings of the Baroque period.

The visual arts have been through innumerable crises of identity beginning with the Dadaists and continuing right into the present. Expressionism, nonrepresentational art, pop, art-as-experience, serialism, minimalism, surrealism—name it and you can find supporters for and practitioners of it.

The theatre and the movies have been equally invigorated by new concepts, techniques, and experiments. The abandonment of a story line in the traditional sense has been one favorite way to go. The theatre of the absurd, theatre of cruelty, surrealism, Dadaism, improvisatory theatre, futurism, happenings—all and more are part of the twentieth-century movie and theatre scene. As you notice, many of them overlap similar movements in the visual arts.

And so with music. The parallels between composition/performance techniques and theories in music and their counterparts in the other arts is quite strong. Expressionism is there, aleatoric music (chance music) is there to complement improvisatory theatre, happenings are there, and so are minimalism and even serialism as a compositional technique—a welter of experimentation and new developments.

All such movements in the arts are identified as avant garde, a sort of catchall designation for any artistic movement that attempts to reject traditionalism in some way. Naturally there are many types of avant-garde gestures, and each century has had its own leaders. But, again perhaps because we are still so close to all of this, our own century does appear to have provided us with more than the usual amount of such activity.

There is a paradox, too, in that experimentation can in some ways be seen as a romantic notion—the search for the unknown, sometimes even the unreachable. And yet the century has been marked by a down-to-earth reliance upon scientific inquiry as a means for attaining answers. Computers are taking their place in practically all the arts, for instance. Our creativity seems to rely more and more on machines, and that need not necessarily mean that our efforts are any the less creative. What it does mean is that we are coming closer to an amalgamation of technology and art in many ways.

The list below is very extensive, but it is far from exhaustive. The thing to keep in mind when reading through it (and wondering who all these folks are) is that each musician, artist, literary figure, and other individual is a significant one who has made an important contribution to the temper of the twentieth century. The wars are purposely undated; it would be a good exercise for you to track down those yourself, as well as to realize that many of them continue right into our own day.

MUSICIANS: Samuel Barber: 1910–1981   Luciano Berio: 1925–
               Béla Bartók: 1881–1945   Leonard Bernstein: 1918–
               Amy Cheney Beach: 1867–1944   Ernest Bloch: 1880–1959
               Alban Berg: 1885–1935   Pierre Boulez: 1925–

Benjamin Britten: 1913–1976
John Cage: 1912–
Elliott Carter: 1908–
Aaron Copland: 1900–
George Crumb: 1929–
Luigi Dallapiccola: 1904–1975
Edward Kennedy "Duke" Ellington: 1899–1974
Manuel de Falla: 1876–1946
George Gershwin: 1897–1937
Alberto Ginastera: 1916–
Enrique Granados: 1867–1916
W. C. Handy: 1873–1958
Hans Werner Henze: 1926–
Paul Hindemith: 1895–1963
Arthur Honegger: 1892–1955

Charles Ives: 1874–1954
Zoltán Kodály: 1882–1967
Ernest Krenek: 1900–
Witold Lutaslawski: 1913–
Elizabeth Lutyens: 1906–
Gian-Carlo Menotti: 1911–
Olivier Messiaen: 1908–
Darius Milhaud: 1892–1974

Thea Musgrave: 1928–
Carl Orff: 1895–1982
Krzysztof Penderecki: 1933–
Walter Piston: 1894–1976
Francis Poulenc: 1899–1963
Sergei Prokofiev: 1891–1953
Ottorino Respighi: 1879–1936
Arnold Schönberg: 1874–1951
Alexander Scriabin: 1872–1915
Ruth Crawford Seeger: 1901–1953
Roger Sessions: 1896–

Dimitri Shostakovich: 1906–1975
Dame Ethel Smyth: 1858–1944
Karlheinz Stockhausen: 1928–
Igor Stravinsky: 1882–1971
Virgil Thomson: 1896–
Vladimir Ussachevsky: 1911–
Edgard Varèse: 1883–1965
Ralph Vaughan Williams: 1872–1958
Heitor Villa-Lobos: 1887–1959
Anton Webern: 1883–1945
Kurt Weill: 1900–1950
Yannis Xenakis: 1922–

ARTISTS, LITERARY FIGURES, AND OTHERS:

Samuel Beckett: 1916–
Georges Braque: 1882–1963
Bertolt Brecht: 1898–1956
Albert Camus: 1913–1960
Willa Cather: 1873–1947
Anton Chekhov: 1860–1904
Joseph Conrad: 1857–1924
Marie Curie: 1867–1934
Pierre Curie: 1859–1906
Salvador Dali: 1904–
Marcel Duchamp: 1887–1968
Albert Einstein: 1879–1955
T. S. Eliot: 1885–1965
William Faulkner: 1897–1962
Sigmund Freud: 1856–1939
Robert Frost: 1874–1963
Ernest Hemingway: 1899–1961
James Joyce: 1882–1941
Wassily Kandinsky: 1866–1944
Malcolm X: 1925–1965
Thomas Mann: 1875–1955

Guglielmo Marconi: 1874–1937
W. Somerset Maugham: 1874–1965
Arthur Miller: 1915–
Piet Mondrian: 1872–1944
Eugene O'Neill: 1888–1953
José Ortega y Gassett: 1883–1955
Pablo Picasso: 1881–1973
Harold Pinter: 1930–
Marcel Proust: 1871–1922
Ranier Maria Rilke: 1875–1926
Georges Rouault: 1871–1958
Bertrand Russell: 1872–1970
Aleksandr Solzhenitsyn: 1918–
Gertrude Stein: 1874–1946
John Steinbeck: 1902–1968
Dylan Thomas: 1914–1953
Tennessee Williams: 1911–1983
Virginia Woolf: 1882–1941
Frank Lloyd Wright: 1869–1959
W. B. Yeats: 1865–1939

EVENTS: Civil Rights Movements: 1950s and 60s
                 Communism and its spread: beginning in 1918
                 Depression of 1929–1939
                 Discoveries:
                    Electronic charge: 1910
                    Insulin: 1921
                    Neutrons: 1932
                    Nuclear fission: 1939
                    Protons: 1919
                 Inventions and developments:
                    Computers: 1937
                    Dirigibles (commercial): 1910
                    Gene theory: 1950s and 1960s
                    Jet planes: 1937
                    Laser beams: 1960
                    Motion picture "story picture": 1903
                    Organ transplants: 1950s
                    Radio (crystal): 1901
                    Television: 1920s
                    Test tube babies: 1970s
                 Polar exploration: North 1909; South 1911
                 Recordings (commercial): 1900
                 San Francisco Earthquake: 1906
                 Space exploration: 1957 to present
                    Men on the moon
                    Satellites/communications
                    Space shuttles
                 Titanic sinks: 1912
                 United Nations founded: 1945
                 Wars:
                    Britain–Argentina
                    Iranian Revolution
                    IRA conflicts in Ireland
                    Israeli conflicts in the Middle East
                    Italian Fascist Revolution
                    Japanese–Chinese War
                    Korean War
                    Russian Revolutions
                    Russo–Japanese War
                    Spanish Civil War
                    Vietnam War
                    World Wars I and II
                 Watergate: 1972

Chapter 11
"Dies irae"–Classic vs. Romantic

Human beings are forever comparing one political system to another, one educational theory to another, one religious philosophy to another, one person to another. And when we get into music we like to do the same thing, especially with performers. Some of the hottest arguments we have are about whose recording of what piece is better or worse than someone else's.

Comparison can be an especially rewarding exercise if we are interested in trying to understand differences among musical styles. If we focus the comparison on music that has words, it can be even more rewarding, because we can come closer to interpreting the music through the expressive content of the text. We can pick one single set of words that a number of composers have used at different periods of musical history and try to make sense out of the various approaches.

The text we will use to do this has several advantages. One is that it has been around for a long time. It was written by Thomas of Celano, a thirteenth-century Franciscan friar who was a friend of St. Francis of Assisi. It is a poem called "Dies irae," usually translated as "Day of Wrath." Possibly because of its dramatic nature, it has been quoted and referred to by countless novelists, playwrights, and historians. Its inclusion as part of the liturgy for the burial Mass and for commemorative Masses has assured its survival to the present day. As a result, many composers have furnished music for it; we will be listening to several contrasting versions.

All cultures that we have any information about have come to grips with the fact of death. The more sophisticated cultures have developed correspondingly sophisticated religions and rituals that accompany them, and some of the most elaborate theories and practices have been concerned with death—and the possibility of some sort of existence after it. Much of the continued force of the Christian religion has its roots in the concept of rewards and punishments, and mostly those to come following life on earth. The "Dies irae" concerns just that—and there's the drama.

In order to put this particular piece in perspective, we need to understand the structure of the Mass of which it is a part: the Requiem Mass. It is a special Mass that includes the following portions when used for a musical work. Some of these portions are from the Proper, but because the Requiem is a special Mass, they are consistent no matter when that Mass is celebrated.

> "Introit"—the text begins *Requiem aeternam dona eis, Domine* (Grant them rest eternal, Lord); this is where the title "Requiem Mass" comes from
> "Kyrie"
> "Dies irae," the section that concerns us
> "Offertorium"
> "Sanctus" and "Benedictus"
> "Agnus Dei"
> "Communion"
> "Responsorium" (not always used by composers)

Thus we can say that a musician "composed a *Requiem Mass*," meaning that he added music to the words of the portions listed above. When the composition is performed outside a church in concert, which often happens, then we may say we are "going to hear the Verdi *Requiem*," for instance. In both cases, we are talking about the musical composition that uses the text of the unchanging parts of the Requiem. The "Dies irae" occurs *only* in the Requiem Mass—another factor in its highly dramatic content.

This is the sketchiest sort of background, but it provides what is essential to a discussion of the settings of the "Dies irae" we will be hearing. The listening suggestions are based on only the opening portions of the poem—the first 8 stanzas of the 19 that Thomas of Celano wrote. If you were to attend a Requiem Mass or a concert performance of one, you would hear all 19 stanzas. The excerpts that will be discussed are chosen for purposes of comparison and therefore represent only a small portion of each composer's "Dies irae."

The words of these first 8 stanzas:

1. Dies irae, dies illa,
   Solvet sacclum in favilla,
   Teste David cum Sibylla.
2. Quantus tremor est futurus,

   Quando judex est venturus,

   Cuncta stricte discussurus!
3. Tuba mirum spargens sonum,

   Per sepulchra regionum,

   Coget omnes ante thronum.
4. Mors stupebit et natura,
   Cum resurget creatura,
   Judicanti responsura.
5. Liber scriptus proferetur,
   In quo totum continetur,
   Unde mundus judicetur.
6. Judex ergo cum sedebit,
   Quidquid latet apparebit,
   Nil inultum remanebit.
7. Quid sum miser tunc dicturus?
   Quem patronum rogaturus,

   Cum vix justus sit securus?
8. Rex tremendae majestatis!
   Qui salvandos salvas gratis!
   Salve me, fons pietatis!

Day of anger, day of mourning,
When to ashes all is burning,
So spake David and the Sibyl.
Oh, what fear man's bosom rendeth,

When from Heaven the Judge descendeth,

On whose sentence all dependeth!
Wondrous sound the trumpet flingeth,

Through earth's sepulchres it ringeth,

All before the throne it bringeth.
Death with wonder is enchained,
When man from the dust regained,
Stands before the Judge arraigned.
Now the record shall be cited,
Wherein all things stand indited,
Whence the world shall be requited.
When to judgment all are bidden,
Nothing longer shall be hidden,
Not a trespass go unsmitten.
What affliction mine exceeding?
Who shall stand forth for me pleading,

When the just man aid is needing?
King of might and awe, defend me!
Freely Thy salvation send me!
Fount of mercy, save, befriend me!

The focus here is on the Day of Judgment, and much of the imagery is drawn from biblical literature. Very much in evidence is the theological position taken by St. Thomas Aquinas, who was responsible for formulating a lot of what persists in both Catholic and Protestant doctrine. Dante's *Inferno* uses some of the same imagery, as do many other famous literary works. The value to us here, however, is not theological. Regardless of what response we may feel to the religious or spiritual sentiments, the drama inherent in the situation is obvious to anyone.

Because of the type of poetry involved and its thirteenth-century authorship, the text is more metric than in much of the Catholic liturgy. The translator has tried to keep this scheme, even to including the same number of syllables as in each line of the Latin poem. Is it possible that the three-line stanzas are yet another analogy to the Trinity?

PRIMARY LISTENING:
"Dies irae," Gregorian chant (record set)

The music of our first "Dies irae" listening selection is the earliest music associated with the text: Gregorian chant, the character of which is already familiar to us. This music seems to swing along more metrically than the other examples of Gregorian chant we heard, though, and this may be in response to the meter of the poem.

The composer of the music (Example 39) is unknown; some think that it might be Thomas of Celano, the poet, while others think this may be the music of an old Advent hymn. We do know, though, that the tune and words were closely associated for many centuries and are still used frequently. Musicians composed Requiem Masses throughout the Renaissance and Baroque periods; some were by the best-known composers of their time. In most cases, however, they did not provide music for the "Dies irae," but relied upon the Gregorian chant version. Sometimes other voice parts were added to it, but in general when a Requiem Mass was sung, the "Dies irae" was simply chanted on the Gregorian tune. Was this because the subject matter was too "awful"? Too dramatic? Too varied in mood?

Example 39
"Dies irae" from
Requiem Mass.

Di - es i - rae, di - es il - la, Sol - vet ___ sae - clum
Quan - tus tre - mor est fu - tu - rus, Quan - do ___ ju - dex

in fa - vil - la, Te - ste ___ Da - vid ___ cum Si - byl - la.
est ven - tu - rus, Cunc - ta ___ stric - te ___ dis - cus - sur - us!

Tu - ba mi - rum ___ spar - gens so - num ___ Per se - pul - cra
Mors stu - pe - bit ___ et ___ na - tu - ra, ___ Cum re - sur - get

re - gi - o - num, Co - get om - nes ___ an - te - thro - num
cre - a - tu - ra, Ju - di - can - ti ___ re - spon - su - ra.

Li - ber scrip - tus ___ pro - fe - re - tur, In ___ quo to - tum
Ju - dex er - go ___ cum se - de - bit, Quid quid la - tet

etc.

con - ti - ne - tur, ___ Un - de mun - dus ju - di - ce - tur, ___
ap - pa - re - bit. ___ Nil in - ul - tum re - ma - ne - bit. ___

Perhaps just too closely associated with the Gregorian melody to encourage disrupting that union? In any case, the words and chant tune were known as a unit throughout Christendom, and, as we shall see later, composers often used the melody in other works when they wanted to remind the listener of death or judgment or funeral services.

The formal organization of the melody is rather complex, with a good deal of overlapping of musical ideas from part to part. In general the stanzas are treated in pairs, the music for the first of each pair being repeated for the second. At *Tuba mirum* a new musical idea is introduced, but the last two lines of its stanza return to music very similar to that used in the first 2 stanzas. At *Liber scriptus* the melody introduces another new idea, and the rest of its stanza and the one that follows are relatively independent of what has preceded them. At *Quid sum miser* the opening music is reintroduced. There is some variety, then, and some continuity. This kind of interchange continues throughout most of the rest of the music for the poem, altering to include altogether new music only for the final 2 stanzas. Using just the portion we are considering here, the first 8 stanzas, and making allowance for many similarities from phrase to phrase, we might diagram the form like this:

Stanza 1 = A
Stanza 2 = A
Stanza 3 = B (but with a lot of A in it)
Stanza 4 = B
Stanza 5 = C
Stanza 6 = C
Stanza 7 = A
Stanza 8 = A

Like many diagrams, this one is misleading. Notice, for instance, the similarity among the final three or four notes of many cadences in A and B. Also, you will hear within C some repetition at cadences. This indicates a great coherence, an unusual blending of unity and variety, factors that have inspired the admiration of musicians through the centuries. The range is unusually large for Gregorian chant; is this an element of drama to match the content of the poem? We can only guess. But we can all react to the long, sweeping lines and the nobility of the rhythmic flow. Does the use of three different musical ideas (A, B, and C) refer once again to the Trinity and its three persons? Do the musical continuity and unity reflect the interaction among—maybe even the "indivisibility" of—the persons? Each of us will interpret in terms of our individual preconceptions, and the answers will not be right or wrong; but the questions are worth asking if we are trying to get beneath the surface of the music and words.

The Gregorian chant is invaluable as a reference point for other settings of the "Dies irae." In spite of its musical characteristics, the focus is on heightened speech. There is no repetition of words, because in this liturgical style one statement is enough. Whatever drama is present is veiled in solemnity and disciplined by under-statement. By the end of the eighteenth century, however, the restraints of medieval mysticism had been left far behind, and in the search for clarity in all things the Age of Enlightenment was turning its attention to empiricism in science, political restructuring, and the questioning of authoritarianism. Those composers who produced a *Requiem Mass* no longer relied on the Gregorian chant, but created their own setting for the "Dies irae."

Mozart was one such composer, and indeed his *Requiem Mass* is by all odds the most famous from the Classic period. He does not treat the entire poem as one piece of music. In order to capture the changing moods of the text, he separates the poetry into six sections, each one arranged for different combinations of chorus, soloists, and orchestra and each one different in musical character. Our listening selection includes only the first two sections. The first is based on the opening two stanzas of the poem, beginning "Dies irae" (Example 40); the second uses the following 5 stanzas, beginning "Tuba mirum." The complete *Requiem* includes all 19 stanzas, of course.

PRIMARY LISTENING: Wolfgang Amadeus Mozart, "Dies irae" and "Tuba mirum" from *Requiem Mass*

Listen first to the music Mozart provides for the first 2 stanzas. This is another thing altogether than the understatement of the medieval chant. Here all the musical resources of the intervening centuries are brought to bear in enlarging on the dramatic content of Thomas of Celano's poetry. As in any other discussion of music, it is possible to objectify those resources, to describe and name them.

Concentrate on the rhythm—some of the tremendous drive lies in the incessant activity of the orchestra. Most of the instruments are even busier than the voices, which are certainly busy enough. Try to catch the effect of the instrumental syncopation on the words *irae* and *illa*. Notice, too, how the rhythmic motion of the orchestral interludes drives into the following entrances of the voices. The meter—duple—is very strong. Many musicians believe that duple meter is more virile than triple, which they interpret as gentle and graceful. Triple is used in a waltz, for instance, and duple in marches. At any rate, here the meter has a kind of insistent vitality to it. All of this informs us that for Mozart the entire sound system is a unit

Example 40
Mozart, "Dies irae" from
Requiem Mass.

Di - es i - rae, di - es il - la. Sol - vet

sae - clum in fa - vil - la, Te - ste Da - vid cum Si - byl - la.

Quan - tus tre - mor est fu - tu - rus, Quan - do...

rhythmically, working in concert to propel the music forward in an almost reckless manner.

The mixture of homophonic and polyphonic textures adds to the excitement. During the opening section, the voices moving homophonically pound on us, punch together, beat into us like hammers. But with the words *Quantus tremor* the sopranos and tenors begin a polyphonic dialogue which creates a more complex sound pattern. Back again to pounding for the next section, and following that a longer antiphonal segment during which the basses are answered by the other voices and finally, the women are answered by the men. The changes of texture work here as they do frequently in music. Attention is pulled in first one direction, then another. The words are placed in a number of perspectives, repeated and thrown at us from different angles, and inserted within varying masses of sound. Is this the way confusion and turmoil will affect us on the Day of Judgment? Apparently for Mozart there is some relationship.

What does the harmony add? The mode is minor at the beginning. What is accomplished by the first instrumental interlude? Does the key change? Major or minor? What does *each* interlude do harmonically? The changing splashes of musical color that are thrown at us each time the chorus reenters are another part of the continuing restlessness and excitement. Even though we may not be able to follow theoretically or be able to identify by names the various keys through which Mozart carries us, we can nevertheless hear that the keys change because the tonic note varies with each chorus entrance (see appendix 1 for theory of key centers). And we know that the changes are more varied than those we heard in "How Long Blues," for example, and that they run through a wider range of colors. There is more complexity in this harmonic style, and it works on our sensitivities in a different way.

How about the phrasing? There is quite a bit of balancing activity in this piece—one phrase, often quite short, being balanced by an answering phrase. Although this is most apparent in the antiphonal sections, it is evident throughout. This kind of phrase dialogue is common in the Classic period, where balance is one of the principal objectives in all the arts. The phrases are not all the same length, though—try counting beats. Is this a deliberate device to dramatize the unsettling idea of the "Dies irae" itself?

What is the purpose of all the word repetition? Is Mozart driven into this because he wants a longer composition than he can otherwise get out of six short lines of poetry, or does he want to emphasize the text by hitting the words more than once? The words are not only repeated, they are used out of order—in the antiphonal section when the basses are singing *Quantus tremor,* the rest of the chorus is going back to *Dies irae* from the first stanza of the poem. Composers frequently do this with poetry, and it's hard to know whether the reason is principally musical or whether they want the expressive strength of word repetition.

We have taken up the matter of form in connection with several compositions. Does this piece follow any of the patterns that were used before? Musically you *might* diagram it this way:

"Dies irae," etc. = A
"Quantus tremor," etc. = B
"Dies irae," etc. = A'
"Quantus tremor," etc. = B'
"Quantus tremor, etc. (antiphonal section) = C

But that would be pushing your luck, because both A' and B' are more similar in rhythm to A and B than in melody or harmony. And what does one do with the C section bringing up the rear all by itself? Obviously this piece won't fit into the kinds of formal patterns we have fitted earlier listening selections into. If you think back to the Introduction of this book, you'll remember the discussion of categories and classification and the traps that can be fallen into by using them. Form can provide that kind of trap, because we like to put things into slots and the idea of formal slots is very appealing. When it doesn't work, we tend to become frustrated. But regardless of any specific form, art seems to demand both some sort of unity and some sort of variety, and certainly this composition by Mozart fulfills those needs—but in its own way. We do have a way out in such cases: we can say a piece has *free form*. If identification is necessary at all, that term for musical structure in which there is no regular recurrence of material fits the music better than anything else. What relationship do you see between free form and through-composition, as in Schubert's "Erl King"?

Another thing to notice is that the organization here is sectional. The sections are rather well marked off from one another by strong cadences, changes of texture, and instrumental interludes. The tendency to sectionalize was strong in the Classic period in all the arts simply because it added an element of clarity and rationality to the way events were experienced. Even so today, in our lives: we section them. So many hours for sleeping, so many minutes for eating, so many hours to a working day. The list is endless—and each event has its own kind of cadence. We get alarmed about this too, and then we try to evade it in all sorts of ways by not setting the alarm, by taking an unauthorized day off, by changing routines during vacations—the list is again virtually endless. These are ways of freeing up the form of existence, mixing up freedom and sectional order. And we each do the mixing up in our own way—uniquely— like a creative artist. Form for discipline and control; creative change for freedom. We look for a good workable balance between them that makes sense to us individually—and doesn't create chaos for everyone else!

Right at the beginning of the next section of Mozart's "Dies irae"—the part beginning *Tuba mirum* (Example 41)—we find an old friend: text illustration. You might wonder why Mozart uses a trombone instead of a trumpet to announce the Day of Judgment. Trumpets had been around for many centuries, and Mozart wrote many parts for them, but here he uses a trombone. Maybe he wanted to match the range of the bass voice, or maybe he wanted the trombone's nobility of sound.

In any case, an attractive vocal-instrumental duet is set up, obviously intended to represent the call to judgment. The mode is major, and the large intervals in the bass solo are dramatic enough to remind us of the subject matter. The music draws very promisingly toward a cadence at the words *Coget omnes ante thronum*, and we are set for the end of something. Just at the crucial moment,

Example 41
Mozart, "Tuba mirum" from
Requiem Mass.

though, the tenor enters, and, adding to the shock, the mode changes suddenly to minor. Perhaps this is a way of dramatizing the word *mors* (death), perhaps it is merely a way to introduce a new musical idea, perhaps it is only a change of color—maybe it is all of these working together. But the process of frustrating the expectancy of a cadence is certainly an effective expressive device. We found this earlier in Wagner's *Tristan und Isolde,* you will recall. The device is called sometimes an *evaded* cadence, sometimes an *elided* cadence, sometimes a *deceptive* cadence, depending on the way it is used. The effect is to disguise the seams between sections, to keep the momentum going from one part to the next.

This pattern of elision is carried out each time a new solo voice is introduced, and it is effective in binding the sections together. It also contributes to the sense of formal freedom. Mozart uses harmony in much the same way as in the previous chorus—changing keys frequently, switching modes from major to minor and back. At the end, all four solo voices get together in a short homophonic quartet to bring the piece to a relatively calm close. So this is another free form, put together differently from the opening chorus but with internal logic.

Throughout the composition the orchestra makes a strong contribution to the musical development, providing much more interest than a simple harmonization does. Once again, this means that the composer is using all his forces completely, no one musical material being subsidiary to the others.

These two pieces are only a part of the entire "Dies irae," of course, and a smaller part of the entire *Requiem Mass.* As a complete work, Mozart's *Requiem* is one of the most revered compositions in Western music and one that is frequently performed. Most often such performances are in a concert hall, completely divorced from the worship service that provided the text. However, the work is of such a length and style that it can be used in a true Mass, assuming room enough for the orchestra, chorus, and soloists. It was used in that way as a memorial service for President John Kennedy in Boston on January 19, 1964. That service was recorded (RCA Victor:

LSC–7030), and because of its particular significance it is more than just an affecting musical experience.

In some ways, any work of art must be judged on its own merits, without reference to events in the artist's life that may have been important in shaping it. On these terms, the Mozart *Requiem* can hold its own and has done so for nearly two centuries. But sometimes there are circumstances surrounding the creation of an art work that add to its interest in other ways. Such circumstances illuminate it as a product of a particular human life, placing it in perspective within the events of one person's history. It is thus that we often assign special importance to a star's last performance. We put great interest in being present at someone's "farewell concert," or in seeing the last movie made by a deceased star, or owning the last record cut by Louis Armstrong or Jimi Hendrix. We are equally pleased to say that we heard someone "in a local club before she became a star."

Last works of composers tend to assume this extra significance for many people, and the *Requiem Mass* happens to be Mozart's last work. But the story surrounding it adds even more interest. In some ways, this story is equal to the best of any number of "mistaken identity" plots in the theatre.

The story is best told in the context of Mozart's whole, short life. Wolfgang Amadeus Mozart (1756–1791) was born in Salzburg, Austria. He was exploited as a child prodigy for his piano virtuosity, and toured Europe extensively with his father and sister. His interest in composition began at a very early age. He was commissioned for his first opera in 1771 at the age of 15, having already completed a number of symphonies and other works. His first operatic success was in 1775, and this was followed by the success of many other Mozart operas, including *The Marriage of Figaro, The Magic Flute,* and *Don Giovanni.* In addition to operas and 41 symphonies, he composed sacred choral works (many with orchestra), songs, concertos, and chamber and piano works. He is one of the most widely respected and prolific of composers, and a master of the Viennese Classic style in all genres.

Although widely acclaimed as a composer and performer, Mozart was unable to earn a reasonable living. After 1780 his financial problems became more and more severe, and he died poor. The *Requiem* was commissioned in 1791, the year of Mozart's death, by a Count von Walsegg—secretly, because he wanted to pass it off as his own composition in honor of his deceased wife. He paid Mozart in advance, but unfortunately the composer died before he had completed the work. He had been ill for some time, and there is evidence to suggest that he took particular pains with the *Requiem* because he thought of it as being related somehow to his own death.

Some parts of it were completed, some parts were in the form of sketches only, and some portions were not even started when he died.

His widow was faced with a dilemma. She was so poor that her husband was buried in a pauper's grave; Mozart was one of the first composers who tried to "make it" professionally without the support of a court or full-time church job. Since the fee had been paid in advance, Mozart's wife was afraid to turn over the incomplete *Requiem* for fear she would have to refund the money. Finally she decided to allow one of Mozart's pupils, Franz Süssmayer, to finish it without taking credit for it. When it was done, the score was turned over to von Walsegg's courier, and few people other than Mozart's widow, Süssmayer, and some very close friends knew that it was not entirely the work of Mozart. In due time von Walsegg copied out the score in his own handwriting, and in 1793 it was performed as his own composition in memory of his wife.

After many years and much shuttling from place to place, the original manuscripts were collected. Scholars studied them, haggled about them, and finally reached some agreement about just what was Mozart's work, what was Süssmayer's, and what was a combination. There is still bickering, of course. "Would Mozart have done it all this way if he had lived?" The answer to that one is easy, of course: "Probably not exactly this way." But how about "Would *this section* have been better?" That's not so easy.

PRIMARY LISTENING:
Giuseppe Verdi, "Dies irae"
from *Requiem*

The Italian composer Giuseppe Verdi (1813–1901) is identified almost exclusively with opera, and many of his works in that genre are considered among the finest in the Romantic style. Among them are *Rigoletto*, *La Traviata*, *Aida*, and *Othello*. And Verdi was not a religious man according to usual standards; some have identified him as an agnostic. But he was a man fully appreciative of the drama of faith and religious expression, and in 1874, nearly a century after Mozart's death, he composed a Requiem and dedicated it to Alessandro Manzoni, an Italian author, poet, and political figure.

That Verdi was a Romantic and principally an opera composer is clearly reflected in his treatment of the Requiem text. The composition was never intended for use in a church service. Its length, its theatricalism, the size of its performing forces, its considerable disruption of text—all identify it as a concert piece. They are also indispensable in creating its enormous drama and musical excitement.

The opening of the "Dies irae" (Example 42) is like the crack of doom. As in much music, the sound here is far more powerful than words about it could ever be—the force of the instrumental

Example 42
"Dies irae" from Verdi
Requiem.
Used by permission of European
American Music Distributors
Corporation, sole U. S. agent for Ernst
Eulenberg.

Example 42 continued

Example 42 continued

introduction and interludes, including the addition of syncopated timpani during the first interlude; the outburst of the chorus on its entrances, and the slithering vocal lines that sound almost like shrill moaning or even screaming. Then we notice the antiphonal work among the various chorus parts. Romantics loved emphatic dynamic contrast, and Verdi uses it: *Dies irae* is first like an anguished howling, later only whispers full of awe and terror, preparing for the trembling, almost breathlessly broken *Quantus tremor.*

The text illustration Mozart used for the section beginning *Tuba mirum* is intensified by Verdi. Brass is added to brass, rhythms become more and more complex, and finally the chorus enters echoing the words with a mixture of polyphony and antiphony that pushes into the final hysterical outburst on *thronum.*

Then silence. Verdi, the dramatist, knew how stunning silence can be as an expressive device. What has immediately preceded this has left us with no sensation of finality, and so we *know* that something else is going to happen. The composer continues the tension of suspense with sneaky little bass figures in a disjointed rhythm. Then, when the bass soloist enters with the single word *mors* (death), that word could hardly be more dramatic. What follows is an additional intensification—the idea of death being finally and utterly defeated.

This is a far cry from the medieval chant, and it carries the drama beyond anything the Classic period envisioned as appropriate. Again this is only a portion of the "Dies irae"; Verdi continues with it, as with the rest of the Mass, in just as dramatic and intense a style. His harmonies here and through the balance of the *Requiem* are extremely rich, colorful, and varied. This is opera in all except the action and staging paraphernalia.

One of the melodic devices that add to the wailing or moaning character of the voices is *chromaticism.* Chromaticism has several applications in music. Wagner's melodic and harmonic style is highly chromatic. In Verdi's "Dies irae" much of the chromaticism takes the form of melodic passages in successive half-steps; these can be heard and can also be seen in the score at the first entrance of the chorus. They are, you will remember, the smallest intervals used in Western music except for some esoteric adventures of an avant-garde sort.

By the Renaissance period chromaticism had acquired an expressive significance, and it was widely used to denote sorrow, pain, torment, and the like. In contexts involving such emotions it appears frequently as a mood-coloring device from that time to the present, although it has many other functions as well. If you listen carefully to individual instrumental and vocal lines you will hear a great deal of chromaticism suffusing the texture of the Verdi "Dies irae" listening selection. Undoubtedly it is employed partly because of the text and its suggestion of terror tinged with sorrow.

From the harmonic standpoint, frequent key changes create a kind of chromaticism of their own, and some of the restlessness of the "Dies irae" can be attributed to that device. In a symbolic sense, the use of chromaticism enriches the harmonic and melodic color of a composition; musicians, in fact, often refer to a composer's use of harmony as his "harmonic palette." Harmonic enrichment was one of the features of Romanticism and one way of increasing the emotional content. One would expect Verdi to use this as a "tool" of Romanticism as well as in the service of the textual mood, and he does. Classic composers like Mozart did not totally avoid chromaticism, but it was not exploited to the same extent as in the nineteenth century. The harmonic palette of Classicism tended more toward the emphasis of a few of the most important chords in a key. Because of this the range of harmonies, the types of chords, and the number of keys used were all more limited in scope than during the Romantic period.

As an experiment, if you play a guitar, try strumming along with the first chorus of Mozart's "Dies irae." If you have a few keys under control, you'll be able to get most of the chords, especially when the chorus is singing. Then try to strum with Verdi. Your fingers as well as your ears will tell you the difference.

In the same way that the harmonic and melodic materials are more complex in Romanticism, the rhythms are more diverse and dramatic. Also, the size of the orchestra is increased during the nineteenth century—a look at the scores will show this. Strings dominate the orchestral fabric of Classicism, although many winds and brass are used; in Romanticism, there are many more of each instrument as well as a number of additional types of instruments.

Another romantic trait was to try to erase some of the sectionalization that appears in much Classic art. The artists and composers sought to present the artistic experience as a unified whole, indivisible and complete in itself. This took many forms, but one that is easy to perceive in Verdi's "Dies irae" is the way one stanza of the text moves into the next without totally breaking as it does in Mozart. Although the mood changes and there is sectionalization to that extent, all 19 stanzas of the original poem are treated as a single composition rather than in several separate movements, as they are by Mozart. The experience is a continuous one, as in life itself, although there are changes and interruptions of mood—also as in life itself.

If we were to itemize some of the differences between Classicism and Romanticism in music, the contrasts would come out like this:

CLASSICISM	ROMANTICISM
Harmonically strongly oriented around a few important key centers	Harmonically wide-ranging and more chromatic
Melodically concise and relatively limited in range	Melodically varied and larger in range
Rhythmically clean and often quite limited or repetitive	Rhythmically diverse with more complex patterns
Tendency to avoid wide or sudden changes in dynamics	Dramatic use of dynamics over a wide range
Orchestra size relatively small; strings most prominent	Orchestra size large and made up of many different instruments; strings share almost equally with other classes
Tendency toward sectional organization with clear balance among sections	Tendency toward continuous organization with divisions disguised or even eliminated
Relatively objective presentation of material without overdramatization of either joyful or sorrowful moods	Relatively emotional presentation of material, including idealization of all moods— often even a glorification of both sorrow and joy

Such contrasts are often drawn in other arts too, and they are sometimes clearly supported by particular works (Illustrations 15 and 16).

But there is danger in this sort of analysis and description; it can lead to gross oversimplification. Many critics believe that all art throughout the ages can be identified as either Classic or Romantic—in other words, that these are the only two artistic tempers. This has an element of truth but also a danger of too much generalization. The two tempers are not really mutually exclusive. It is *not* an either–or proposition, and trying to make it that can lead to bad trouble. More important, does it matter?

It does matter to the individual in certain ways. To a *participant* in the musical or artistic experience, all that matters is that one feels or does not feel something. But we all need to try to understand ourselves, and it can help us do that if we recognize the push and pull between our Classic and Romantic tendencies. Do you like your drama subtle or large-scale? Do you like your art clarified or emotionalized? Do you value simplicity or complexity? Do you respond more favorably to organization or to relative freedom? In rock, do you prefer Van Haylen or punk?

Most of us are probably somewhere in the middle and only rarely get to the very extreme in either direction. But we do go in

Illustration 15. PORTRAIT OF MRS. PHILIP THICKNESSE. Thomas Gainsborough, about 1760. Compare the cool, Classic serenity of this portrait to the more active canvas of Raeburn's *The Elphinstone Children* (page 371). The balance between the viol on the left, the table on the right, the gentle curve of the body echoed in the arms—all contribute to the feeling of control and discipline so close to the objectives of the Classicists. Cincinnati Art Museum. Bequest of Mary M. Emery.

one or the other direction, depending on the day or the time of day or our mood or the most recent events in our lives. And we are lucky that there is not just one expressive level in music—or art in general—that is accessible.

Verdi's *Requiem* was not well received by everyone. There was considerable opposition to it because of the composer's well-known refusal to conform to approved religious concepts and practices.

Illustration 16. VIEW ACROSS FRENCHMAN'S BAY FROM MT. DESERT ISLAND, AFTER A SQUALL. Thomas Cole (1801–1848). The Romantic delight in turbulence and dramatic action are reflected in this scene. The artists of the period were enchanted with depicting the strength and fury of nature as well as its beauty. All are essentially beyond man's control and consequently an unending source of mystery and continuing fascination. Cincinnati Art Museum. Gift of Miss Alice Scarborough.

There was also disapproval because of the theatricalism and the *Requiem's* inappropriateness for cathedral use. It was unashamedly a concert piece. Many people had difficulty reconciling this fact with the very special and hallowed nature of the Requiem Mass as a ritual. As a result, there was a good bit of "tsk-tsking" about the whole question of an irreligious man putting his artistry into a religious work.

The paradox was not new then, and it is still very much with us today. Productions like *Jesus Christ, Superstar* and *Godspell* meet with much the same response in many quarters. Criticism is directed not only to the dramatic liberties with religious subjects. The use of "inappropriate" musical idioms is questioned just as vigorously. Rock and its associations with visceral response are too secular, go the arguments. Anyone who gets too upset can take comfort in the fact that this problem, too, is an old one. Martin Luther asked, "Why should the devil have all the good tunes?" And in his search for usable music for his congregations he turned to popular song for some of his chorales. During the fifteenth and sixteenth centuries, many musical settings of the Mass were based on a French secular

Illustration 17. THE CRUCIFIXION WITH VIEW OF TOLEDO.
El Greco, about 1602–1610. Like musicians, painters frequently indulge in a mixture of sacred and secular. El Greco is caught up in exploiting the Renaissance concern for perspective and local scenes—here the Spanish city of Toledo.
Cincinnati Art Museum. The John J. Emery Fund.

song, "L'Homme armé" ("The Armed Man"). There are numerous other examples. The truth seems to be that the lines between secular and sacred are just as fuzzy as they are in most of our other categories (Illustration 17).

Regardless of the appropriateness of Verdi's treatment of the Requiem text, it is apparent that he was serious about intensifying the religious mood in his own way. Whether or not the composition is suitable for church, it is certainly a glorification and idealization of the dramatic truth of the religious experience as Verdi perceived it.

SUPPLEMENTAL LISTENING   Other Requiem Masses of interest include Luigi Cherubini's two, one in C minor, the other in D minor. The first (1816) is for mixed chorus and orchestra; the second (1836), intended for Cherubini's own funeral, is for men's chorus and orchestra. Both are relatively dramatic and use much the same musically illustrative approach to the "Tuba mirum" section of the text. Three highly dramatic and colorful settings, illustrative of the Romantic characteristics pointed out above, are by Hector Berlioz (1837), Anton Bruckner (1849; final revision, 1894), and Antonin Dvořák (1890).

All of these composers were involved to some extent in opera composition except for Bruckner. Only Cherubini, however, devoted himself almost exclusively to that medium.

Chapter 12
Twentieth-Century "Dies irae" and Requiem

PRIMARY LISTENING:
Benjamin Britten, "Dies irae" from *War Requiem*

The next listening suggestion uses the text of the "Dies irae" in quite a different manner from Verdi's. It is the opening section of the "Dies irae" from the *War Requiem* by Benjamin Britten, which was given its first performance in 1962.

Britten's sense of the drama is just as great as Verdi's, but it takes off in a completely different direction. No outburst here, but plenty of fear. The use of brass to duplicate trumpet calls is familiar by now, although there is much more dissonance here than in either Mozart or Verdi. Also the patterns are more shuddering and nervous, not so forthrightly climactic as in Verdi. Here they pass from instrument to instrument almost frantically, chattering instead of glorifying the mood. Syncopation and other rhythmic complexities, alternations of texture, dynamic contrast—all are musical devices that Britten uses to convey his interpretation of the words. How about melody? Is the music tuneful or more like broken speech inflections? What is the effect at "Tuba mirum"? What musical factors create it? These choral parts seem like disjointed mutterings alternating with mob outbursts.

The meter of the chorus sections is worth some attention. If you try to regularize it or to tap your feet to its accents, you'll run into problems. This is an irregular meter, similar in conception to the one in "Everything's Alright." The metric division here is in sevens. The use of this sort of irregularity has become common in the twentieth century. The effect, as you know, is to add rhythmic confusion to the harmonic dissonance and the melodic rigidity. Most of us like our meters to group comfortably in twos or threes; irregularities frustrate us. Maybe that's what Britten intends. "Dies irae."

The meter, the increased dissonance, the stark musical texture, the concept of melody as something more than just tune—these are all twentieth-century devices, and they combine to illuminate the mood of the poem.

The most surprising and unusual element, though, is the insertion of a poem in English. This is what makes Britten's *Requiem* a unique and powerful work of art, musically and in many other ways. The words are by an English poet, Wilfred Owen, who was killed during Word War I, in 1918. Unlike many poets, novelists, playwrights, and other artists who have concerned themselves with the subject of war during a war, Owen damned the wastefulness of the wholesale slaughter more than he deified the self-sacrifice of the victims. In his own words:

> My subject is War, and the pity of War.
> The Poetry is in the pity. . . .
> All a poet can do today is warn.

It was all an inglorious business for him, and Britten shared the views he had expressed. Beyond the words of the poet, Britten saw the paradox that man had set up between his religious practices and his social actions. He recognized the Requiem Mass as the theological and ritualistic focus of a system of belief set up to frustrate death, or at least the apparent effect of death. He also realized that such social exercises as war hasten death and intensify its inevitability. It seemed to him, then, that men work against themselves and their beliefs and that this contradiction could be expressed through music and poetry.

The *War Requiem* is a large-scale work for orchestra, mixed chorus, boys' chorus, and soloists. The traditional words of the Mass are used, but inserted within or following each movement are verses by Wilfred Owen which illustrate the tragic dichotomy between religious and social practices. In its entirety this Requiem is a powerful and incisive plea for an end to war. What is on the listening selection is that portion of the "Dies irae" encompassing the beginning of the traditional Requiem poem, followed by the words of Owen. This is enough to illustrate the process and intent of the complete *War Requiem.* The portion of Owen's poetry that is involved in this segment is:

> Bugles sang, sadd'ning the evening air;
> And bugles answer'd, sorrowful to hear.
> Bugles sang.—Bugles sang.
> Voices of boys were by the river-side.
> Sleep mother'd them; and left the twilight sad.
> The shadow of the morrow weighed on men.
> Bugles sang.
> Voices of old despondency resigned,
> Bowed by the shadow of the morrow, slept.

The imagery of the "Tuba mirum," used by Mozart and Verdi also, is exploited throughout the section. Against it is set the symbol of the bugle, traditionally the call to arms but also (in taps) to rest and death. The "boys" of the poem are soldiers, of course, sleeping before the next day's battle and the likelihood of death. As in all great poetry, what is not explicitly stated is far more powerful than what is on the page, if the reader does his share. Britten's task was simply to provide a musical framework within which the text of the "Dies irae" and Owen's poetry could exert their paradoxical strength.

It is unfair to represent a work as integrated as the *War Requiem* by means of one brief segment. Throughout it there is such great irony, such enormous expressive intensity, so much richness of symbolism and imagery. It has been selected by a large group of composers, critics, and performers as the most significant musical work of the middle years of the twentieth century. If that evaluation is a just one, the reasons are to be found not only in its musical characteristics. It appeared during the turbulence of the sixties, and fully expresses much of the bitter disenchantment of that period of history. Great works of art present to each of us a new and more powerful vision of ourselves and the world than we are capable of seeing without their help. The *War Requiem* uses the concept and material of the Requiem Mass to achieve this goal, and it ventures far beyond the ritual to gain its force. Anyone who experiences the entire work cannot help gaining an enlarged view of the distortion created by the message of the Requiem Mass on one hand and the use of military power on the other.

Britten (1913–1976) is generally considered to be the greatest native English composer after Henry Purcell. An especially skillful user of polyphony, he was nonetheless comfortable in all textures.

Associated most strongly with vocal music, he was masterful in his use of solo and choral possibilities. He was often sharply dissonant but he seldom lost a sense of tonal control. Among his best-known works are the operas *Peter Grimes, Billy Budd,* and *Let's Make an Opera;* the *Ceremony of Carols,* and *The Young Person's Guide to the Orchestra,* the latter a work that we will soon meet and hear.

SUPPLEMENTAL LISTENING   There is no work that can supplement this one except the entire piece. But an intensely expressive composition entitled *Dies Irae,* without the traditional text, was written by Krzysztof Penderecki in 1967. Philips: PHS–900–184. The words are from a mixture of sources—the Bible, modern poetry, Aeschylus. It is dedicated to the victims of Auschwitz, so that, like Britten's *War Requiem,* it addresses the violence and torment that has typified much twentieth-century life.

Chapter 13
New Orleans Funeral Tradition

Not all cultures and cultural groups share the same concept of death and its aftermath—or the moods appropriate to it. For the New Orleans black community of the late nineteenth and early twentieth centuries, the ritual included jubilation as well as mourning, and some of that tradition persists still, though at a somewhat diminished level. On hand for the burial ceremony was a brass band. On the way to the graveyard the band provided a slow dirge, and the following marchers matched its beat with solemnity. But when the casket was delivered at the grave and the burial service was complete, the band broke into a new musical mood. Wingy Manone describes it:

> On the way to the graveyard, they all walked slowly, following the cornet player. The cornet player was the boss. Sometimes it took them four hours to get to the cemetery. All the way they just swayed to the music and moaned. At the graveside they chanted questions, such as "Did he ramble?" "Did he gamble?" or "Did he lead a good life until the police shot him down on St. James Street?" Then after the body was buried, they'd go back to town and all the way they'd swing. They just pulled the instruments apart. They played the hottest music in the world.[1]

[1]Nat Shapiro and Nat Hentoff (eds.), *Hear Me Talkin' to Ya*, New York, Dover, 1966, p. 16.)

PRIMARY LISTENING:
Traditional, "Oh, Didn't He Ramble," Bunk Johnson's Brass Band (record set)

One of the favorite pieces for the return trip was "Oh, Didn't He Ramble," and listening to the recording by Bunk Johnson and his band raises some questions about what Manone meant by the "hottest music in the world." It doesn't really sound all that "hot" to most of us today. Why not? Bunk Johnson (1879–1949), one of the earliest of New Orleans jazz musicians, was a native of that city and was black too, so his tradition was rooted in the kind of practices mentioned by Manone. So why isn't the music hot, then?

Mostly we have to conjecture and interpret, because we have no recorded examples of New Orleans funeral music that date from the period around the turn of the century. Like some jazz musicians, Bunk Johnson was recorded long after his prime. This version of "Oh, Didn't He Ramble" was cut in 1944 during a revival of interest in the earliest recorded jazz style, Dixieland, and a corresponding interest in the sources of that style. But he claims to be playing in the "old style," and so we seem to have a clue here to the sound of both pre-recording-era jazz and the funeral music out of which jazz came in part.

The first important recordings by black New Orleans jazz musicians were made in Chicago in 1923, and they were performing pieces meant for dances, not funerals. And in Chicago, not New Orleans.[2] One characteristic of such early Dixieland bands recorded in Chicago is the relative independence of the melody instruments, in particular the trombone, trumpet, and clarinet. Each performed a function. The trumpet (or trumpets, if there were two) carried the melody, decorating it as seemed appropriate and often adding a two-instrument dialogue. The clarinet, in a higher register, added a counter-melody that very frequently relied on broken-chord runs to emphasize the harmony. The trombone added a melody in a lower register, and that contribution was also based principally on the harmony. All of this supplied a kind of polyphonic texture. The rhythm instruments kept the beat going, a steady pulse against which the more complex rhythms of the melodies could work. This kind of steady unmetered pulse is known among jazz musicians as "flat four" because it is simply an unaccented four solid beats to the bar.

Now if you listen closely, you will hear that on our particular version of "Oh, Didn't He Ramble" what came to be characteristic of Dixieland is only in the beginning stage. The trombone and trumpet are often doubling one another, the trombone playing the melody an octave lower. But sometimes the trumpet decorates the tune a little, and sometimes the trombone adds a bit of fancy work, sometimes it

[2]The earliest jazz recording was made in 1917 by a group of white players from New Orleans who called themselves the Original Dixieland Jazz Band. They were living and performing in New York City at the time. Although they had learned their style in New Orleans from black musicians, they were playing for white dancing audiences far from the social climate of their native city.

moves away into some interesting harmony notes. At the same time, the clarinet is running chords and scales in a real, though embryonic, Dixieland style. The variations from chorus to chorus are never severe. In later Dixieland, as we will discover, the variations became much more daring and the entire texture more active. This may have been the result of the change from a community tradition to a more commercial function.

Johnson is working here with a marching band, of course, but can you hear the background out of which Dixieland style must have come? Are the basic elements here? If so, we can understand what Manone meant when he said "the hottest music in the world"—we just have to realize that he was talking about *that time*. And also realize that "hot" is a very relative term.

In any case, this is happy, swinging music. No doleful dirge, and no artistically elaborate commentary on the grimness and fears that are so often associated with death. Most of us can feel the spirit of relaxation that such a performance conveys. Is this merely a case of whistling in the dark? Or might there be a certain easy acceptance of death, maybe even tempered by the sense of release from a life in which the memory of slavery and social denigration have been all too dominant? Or perhaps merely a different concept of reality than those leading to the development of a religious ritual among other cultural groups? However we may account for it, it is refreshing to catch the mood of a funeral ceremony when bitterness and threat are not involved.

SUPPLEMENTAL LISTENING

One of the most familiar pieces associated with the New Orleans funeral tradition was (and is) "When the Saints Go Marchin' In," still very much a part of American popular music repertoire. It has been recorded often by Dixieland-style groups. Among the "hotter" versions are:

Louis Armstrong and the All Stars. Decca: DXSA–7206.
Pete Fountain and New Orleans All Stars. Everest: FS–257.

Less commercially oriented documentations of New Orleans musical style that is based on old traditions but still alive to some extent today are found on the five-volume set *The Music of New Orleans.* Folkways: FA–2461/2/3/4/5.

Pause for Vocabulary

Let's pause and recall some of the descriptive vocabulary we have tried to accumulate. In each case the listening examples were chosen to help you hear what happened in the music and then, through the related section of the text, to acquire the proper terms of description for the music. If you followed conscientiously this pattern of listening first, then learning to describe or identify, there should always be musical reference points in particular compositions to correlate with the terms. And the terms often relate not just to specific musical devices but to the most important characteristics of an entire piece.

Here are some of the terms we have encountered so far. They are listed under the areas to which they relate most closely. Notice, though, that some are important to music without being actually musically descriptive themselves.

MELODY Gregorian chant; plain chant; plain song
Range
Conjunct; disjunct
Gapped scale; pentatonic
Pitch
Intervals: half steps; microtones
Melisma; melismatic
Tonic note
Recitative
Unending melody
Raga
Chromaticism

HARMONY Organum
Figured bass (realization of)

Chords: Tonic (I); subdominant (IV); dominant (V)
Changes
Mode: major; minor
Dissonance; consonance
Key
Quartal chords
Chromaticism

RHYTHM

Meter: regular; irregular; triple; duple; polymetric
Note values; duration
Syncopation
Tala

TEXTURE

Monophonic
Polyphonic; imitative polyphony
Homophonic

FORM

Ternary (tripartite): A B A
Strophic
Phrase: regular; irregular
Cadence: evaded; elided; deceptive
8-bar blues; chorus
Aria; *da capo* aria
32-bar pop song: A A B A
Bridge
Binary: a b
Coda
5-part: A B A C A
Through-composed
Free form

MISCELLANEOUS

Mass
Antiphony
Ritual
Ballad
Ornamentation: trills, runs, etc.
Tablature
Timbre
Leitmotif
Monody
Text illustration
Improvisation
Reference; quotation

Avant-garde
Dynamics
Dixieland style

That is a wide-ranging list, but many of the terms in it will occur often enough to save a lot of time in the discussions that follow if we clearly understand them.

It might also be rewarding to recall the relatively unfamiliar instruments that were on some of the recorded examples:

Recorder
Krummhorn
Lute
Sarangi
Tambura
Tabla
Harpsichord
Electronic

Finally we have glanced at each of the major stylistic periods in the history of music. The period classifications that follow serve not only music but all the arts and the history of Western man as well. They are listed here in chronological order with approximate dates, both for review and for reference in further discussions (see also appendix 2). The dates are approximate simply because changes from one period to another are gradual and there is always a considerable overlap from one to the next:

Medieval: 400 to 1400
   Romanesque: 450 to 1100
   Gothic: 1100 to 1400
Renaissance: 1400 to 1600
Baroque: 1600 to 1750
Classic: 1750 to 1827
Romantic: 1800 to 1900
Twentieth Century—sometimes called contemporary

Part Two

Program Music

Chapter 14
Instruments of the Orchestra

What we will be dealing with in part 2, "Program Music," will be entirely instrumental. Some of the compositions will be using quite traditional orchestral instruments, some will use those same instruments in unusual ways and combinations, and some will employ newer electronic devices. In view of this complexity, it would seem profitable to detour slightly at the beginning of the section to deal with an introduction to the orchestra and the instruments that comprise it as they are used in the traditional manner (Illustration 18). Before digging into our listening example, you might want to refer to appendix 1 under the heading *Instruments and Scores* for a brief discussion of the types of instruments and some of their peculiarities.

The composition we will use for purposes of orientation is one by Benjamin Britten, whom we have already heard through his *War Requiem*. The piece is *A Young Person's Guide to the Orchestra*, a far less esoteric work than the former. The composition was commissioned to accompany a film, "The Instruments of the Orchestra," and was composed in 1946. Because it is so attractive in the way the instruments are presented, however, it is far more often heard these days simply as a concert piece. And although it was originally intended as a number to capture the attention of children, it is equally appealing and instructive to adults.

Illustration 18. THE UNIVERSITY OF KENTUCKY SYMPHONY ORCHESTRA, PHILLIP MILLER, CONDUCTOR. Like most university symphony orchestras, this one includes all of the instruments illustrated in Britten's "Young Person's Guide."

Commentary has been supplied to introduce each group of instruments and, within those groups, each individual instrument. Some live performances do utilize that commentary, and a number of recordings feature it also. Some do not. If the recording that you use includes the verbal introductions, much of the following discussion will be superfluous. However, many performances do *not* use explanatory words, and so the guidelines given below may prove helpful.

The format employed by Britten is a theme with variations (a form that we will explore in depth later) followed by a fugue. The theme is taken from a Rondeau in a play entitled *Abdelazar* (The Moor's Revenge), for which music was provided by Henry Purcell (1659–1695), England's most respected composer during the Baroque period. Britten makes very imaginative use of the theme so that the composition can stand on its own, completely apart from its value in providing an introduction to orchestral instruments.

PRIMARY LISTENING:
Benjamin Britten, *A Young Person's Guide to the Orchestra* (Variations and Fugue on a Theme of Purcell)

The theme consists of an opening chord outline in D minor followed by a series of *sequences*, a musical process not yet contacted as such by us. A sequence is one way of extending a short melodic idea, and it was very popular during the Baroque period and beyond, as we shall see in the course of enlarging our acquaintance with instrumental music. The process is not a complicated one. Rather than following the presentation of a short motive with a series of continually changing musical ideas or with a literal repetition of the motive, a sequence uses the motive in repetition but transposed higher or lower in pitch. Thus we have the continuity of a recurring melodic pattern but varied enough to avoid monotony—again, our unit and variety concept as a valid artistic principle. In Example 43, you will find the entire theme, and the series of sequences is blocked out with brackets.

Following the presentation of the theme by the entire orchestra, each section reiterates it: woodwinds, strings, brass, percussion, and finally the full orchestra in a final statement. Very few percussion instruments are capable of reproducing a melody. In light of that limitation, what portion of the theme do they use? The order of presentation by sections follows the same order that will introduce the individual instruments of each section during the variations.

Next is the series of variations, 13 in all. With respect to range, the instruments within each section are introduced from highest to lowest. The entrance of each new instrument or pair of instruments is preceded by a brief pause during which the narration occurs. Where there is no narration, the pause issues a warning that something new is about to happen. Some of the variations played by

Example 43
Purcell, Rondeau from *Abdelazar*.

the different instruments follow rather closely the original Purcell theme. Some vary sharply, because Britten is most interested in using the material to display the most striking capabilities of the different instruments. The order of entry is as follows:

WOODWINDS:
1. Two flutes in dialogue, joined soon by a piccolo
2. Two oboes in duet
3. Two clarinets in an antiphonal conversation
4. Two bassoons, at first in unison and then in call–response format

STRINGS:
5. Violins in a sweeping melodic line with inserted chords
6. Violas in unison
7. Cellos in unison
8. Double basses in unison
9. Harps, first in melodic duet and then in chordal dialogue

BRASSES:
10. Horns in call–response and chords
11. Trumpets in antiphonal dialogue
12. Trombones and tubas, sometimes in polyphonic imitation.

PERCUSSION:
13. In this order:
    Timpani (kettle drums)
    Bass drum and cymbals
    Tambourine and triangle
    Snare drum and Chinese block
    Xylophone (this one plays a tune)
    Castanets and gong
    Whip
    All together in concert

The composition is brought to a close with a fugue. We will investigate the fugue as a form carefully later; for now it is only necessary to know that it works a lot like a round, each instrument entering in turn with the same tune and in the same order as their appearance in the variations. This is, of course, yet another instance of polyphonic imitation. The melody being used is given in Example 44. The main difference between the order of appearance here and the introduction of the flutes and piccolo in the first variation is that the fugue begins with the piccolo rather than with the flutes. Every instrument gets its turn at the tune and each one has to compete with those that have preceded because *they* keep right on playing after they have had their turn at the melody. Thus there is a regular crescendo of activity as well as of volume and you have to keep your ears open to hear each newcomer. At the height of the jubilation, the

Example 44
Britten, "Young Person's
Guide to the Orchestra."
Copyright © 1946 by Hawkes & Son
(London) Ltd.; Renewed 1973.
Reprinted by permission of Boosey &
Hawkes, Inc.

brasses enter with the original Rondeau that Purcell composed, but nobody else stops—it's a real carnival of sound! The only difference in the theme this time is that it appears in major rather than in minor as at the beginning of the composition. This is to conform to the key and mode of the fugue.

The entire piece offers a wonderful chance to hear the orchestral instruments in their very best colors and displaying their very best abilities. Some things to look for are the hunting-call character of the horns (they are often used by composers to suggest the hunt); the military sound of the trumpets; the soaring lushness of the violins; the exotic sound of the oboe; the sensuous quality of the cellos and violas; the rather flippant quality of the flutes and piccolos; the nobility of the trombone and tubas; the almost comical quality of the bassoons. Dare I add the heavenly sound of the harps? All of this is deliberate on Britten's part because it is in this sort of expressive context that many composers have used these instrumental colors.

Perhaps a more musically explicit feature is the use of sequences in so many of the variations. Remember that sequences are important to Purcell's theme and so it is entirely appropriate for Britten to exploit them in his variations. You might try keeping up with the variations just to see if you can count the number of them that do use sequences. Also, how about the fugue melody? Is it sequential?

Nothing can substitute for the experience of attending a live orchestral concert and seeing the instruments in use as well as hearing them. The film for which the music was designed is available and if possible, you should try to supplement the listening experience with the visual experience of the movie. Remain aware while listening to the examples ahead of the use to which individual composers have put the possibilities of the various instruments, even when they employ them in nontraditional ways. That awareness can give you a good handle on some of the differences among composers and compositional styles.

Chapter 15
Music To Tell and Illuminate a Tale

The whole idea of program music is a Romantic one. The idea is that music without words can be so composed as to describe or suggest things outside of itself—can be given extramusical "meaning," in other words, can arouse certain emotional or pictorial responses that are consistent enough from person to person to make this "meaning" clear to all or most of the audience. Composers have assumed that, given some sort of verbal suggestion, music can even depict a series of quite specific events. One purpose of this part of our study is to try to reach some conclusions about whether this is true and to what extent. Each of us will probably come to our own decisions; in the process we should discover what composers have *thought* is possible, judging from the sort of things they tried to accomplish with program music.

The nineteenth century was not the first period to use music to suggest a nonmusical idea. In "Valli profonde," for instance, we found a musical figure that represented a snake. However, the words told us what it was and why it appeared at that particular place in the song. If the words are eliminated, if the work is not a song or choral piece, where does the suggestion come from?

One indication is in the title or in some association that the title may evoke or some series of events that the title may indicate. It is also possible for the composer or someone else to add a program or explanatory statement at the beginning of a composition. Sometimes sections or even entire movements carry their own descriptive titles.

In all such cases, extramusical events or expressive content of some sort is being suggested to "explain" the music.

The nineteenth century was the first to put great emphasis on such programmatic ideas, the first to develop them fully. This was partially due to the interaction of all the arts during the Romantic period. Poets wanted their words to take on the rhythms of music and even used the concepts of consonance and dissonance, for instance. Musicians wanted to depict in sound the same sort of expressive content they found in paintings—even the same subject matter. Ballet of the storytelling sort reached a new peak of activity; many present-day favorite ballets date from the nineteenth century, and in them the music as well as the dancers' movements develops the series of events. Art song and opera both reached new heights of intensity during the period. Opera especially, under the influence of Wagner, attempted total synthesis of words, music, dramatic ideas, and action in what the composer called the *Gesamtkunstwerk*—the total or unified work of art. Today too we often combine different arts—for instance, when we accompany a rock show with lights, stimulating visual as well as aural perception.

So it was quite natural that musicians should assume that music was capable of communicating rather definite emotional states or narrative situations that were not in themselves musical. All that was necessary was some sort of brief description or a descriptive title; the listener responded by supplying out of his imagination the appropriate program. In some cases the audience was expected to supply even a chronology of events with minimal help.

Is this possible? It's an enchanting idea, and for many people it works.

We will be listening first to a very few of the many pieces of program music from the nineteenth and twentieth centuries, chosen to represent the range of specific extramusical themes various composers came to grips with. Each piece requires the greatest amount of imagination we can bring to it. Without this the composer and his ideas operate in a vacuum.

PRIMARY LISTENING:
Richard Strauss, *Till Eulenspiegel*

The full title of Richard Strauss's 1895 composition *Till Eulenspiegel* is *The Merry Pranks of Till Eulenspiegel, after the old roguish manner—in rondo form,* and it is an attempt to portray a rather exact series of events. It would be enlightening for you to listen first to the piece of music, knowing only what the title might convey to you. Jot down whatever occurs to you as a story line or series of episodes, moods, or whatever. Then read the following discussion to see how much correlation there is between what you heard and felt and what Strauss had in mind. There may be some discrepancies, but that doesn't mean that Strauss failed, that you are insensitive or unimaginative, or that the idea of program music is faulty. In this particular case it probably means that there is a missing link in the chain of communication. The link here is Till Eulenspiegel, the character about whom the piece was written. Strauss knew who he was, and his audience knew who he was. We don't. And without that knowledge we can't possibly imagine what sort of pranks he might be playing or what the music is doing about them.

Strauss was German, and Till is a character out of German literature. He lived in the fourteenth century, and the audience for whom Strauss was writing was expected to know him well. Suppose a composer wrote a piece without words and called it *Little Red Riding Hood*. We would expect that this composer would use some sort of music that would represent the characters in the story, that the musical material would remind us of their personalities in some way, and that it would try to illustrate the various incidents in the folk tale. Because we know what to expect, we would probably be quick to make the proper associations, or at least most of them. We don't have the same sort of information about Till. Getting it should help us understand Strauss's composition better. Strauss was asked to provide a program for the first performance of his work but he refused, stating that the listeners could supply the program out of their imagination and their knowledge of Till's life and character. Later, however, Wilhelm Mauke furnished a scenario that has helped audiences fill in the sequence of events that Strauss refused to specify.

There is a little of Till in each of us. Like us, he is torn between conforming to "establishment" practice and revolting against it. Like us, he is trying to reconcile these two sides of himself. The nonconformist side of his personality expresses itself by playing tricks on people, especially those who seem stuffy and pretentious to him. Several of the episodes in Strauss's piece deal with those pranks. But Till is more than just impish. Like us, he is capable of falling in love. Unfortunately, because of his nature he is unable to conform to the expected conventions for lovemaking, so he loses the girl. One episode concerns that. Like us, he envies the apparently uncomplicated folk, the workaday people who accept things the way they are and fit their lives to them without alienating everybody. So like us, he tries to work things out inside himself, discover his true identity, find out who he is. One episode illustrates that. But he runs afoul of the authorities because he has mocked the wrong people, played tricks in the wrong places, defied the wrong conventions. He is executed and the final episode portrays that.

To get into *Till Eulenspiegel,* even knowing the specific episodes, we need to realize that each art form demands its own particular types of concessions from the audience. At the theater, we accept the fact that if the stage is set as a dining room, for instance, one of the walls is missing. If it were there, we couldn't see the actors. In looking at a painting, we know the surface is flat, but we accept the techniques the artist uses in order to create the illusion of space and depth. We see things, in other words, that are not really there. In sculpture we accept the fact that the action is frozen; we don't ask that the discus thrower complete his delivery. In ballet we expect to see action without words even though there may be verbal communication implied. In opera or musical comedy we expect the performers to sing where they would normally speak. All of these are concessions that we make to the creative artists who work in these media.

The concession Strauss asks us to make in *Till Eulenspiegel* is a relatively simple one. The musical material he presents at the opening of the piece represents Till. Till has two sides to his personality, and there are two melodies—themes—that inform us of that fact. The first is gentle, gracious, and appealing and is offered to us in the strings. This is Till the "nice guy." The second, given in the French horns, is relatively disjointed, reckless-sounding, and quick-witted. This is Till the prankster. Strauss and many other nineteenth-century composers believed that musical ideas could illustrate just such extramusical characteristics. Their faith was in the ability of sound complexes to carry moods. Unless we are willing to make a concession to that faith, there is no use pursuing Till further. If we can accept that premise, however, it is possible to discuss the musical devices that Strauss used in order to develop his story ideas.

How to make use of the themes? Well, if the theme is a person or a characteristic side of a person, why not place it in different environments of sound and see what effect is produced? If people change to meet changing situations, why shouldn't musical representations of them change, too? This is exactly the methodology behind Strauss's music. The device has a technical name, *theme transformation.* It was not original with Strauss, but it is very useful in a programmatic situation, and he took advantage of it. The main thing the listener needs in order to follow the progress of the musical tale is a thorough acquaintance with both themes—their melodic outlines and their rhythmic characteristics. Because they *are* transformed, the listener needs to be aware of what characteristics are changing.

Unless the original is kept in mind the transformation will go unnoticed, and with it the musical reference point. So the best way to begin listening is to play the two themes several times until they are well in mind. From that point forward, it is necessary only to know the sequence of episodes and musical materials, other than Till's themes, that illuminate each event. For convenience, let's call the gentle theme I and the frisky theme II (Example 45).

Once the themes are introduced, the following section is devoted to presenting them in different keys and by different instruments of the orchestra. This serves the functional purpose of "setting" them in our ears and minds so we can make the proper associations later. There is a lot of antiphonal and polyphonic work going on, setting up contradictions, dialogues, even arguments among sounds. Obviously Till is trying to decide what to do.

The musical argument comes to a long, sustained note preceded by a large dissonant interval dropping downward. This is immediately followed by a very frisky and abrupt restatement of theme I. The device is *diminution*—shortening (diminishing) the note values so that the music occurs more quickly and creates a new mood with the same melodic outline. It is a useful technique in program or other descriptive music. And we know the feeling: when we feel good or full of devilment we move faster. Here the suggestion is that the "pretty" and ingratiating character of Till can appear more mischievous given the proper environment, or even that it can be disguised to meet the needs of the moment.

Immediately we hear a kind of galloping rhythm; he has gotten on a horse. The music becomes wispy, sneaky; he's plotting something. At the cymbal crash, he has ridden into the market place, knocked over the pots and pans of the vendors, left them screaming, and run off to observe the havoc, even giggling a little about it. All of this is pretty graphic, anyone who has listened to the music that is used behind cartoon shows knows exactly how it works. Not very subtle, perhaps, but effective. This kind of thing is tied to realism,

Example 45
Strauss, *Till Eulenspiegel.*

and Strauss indulged himself in it periodically. Also, he liked to use the full capabilities of the orchestra and there is plenty of opportunity to do that here.

In the next episode Till runs into some priests, men of the cloth, and joins them. Their musical characterization is rather "square," sounding almost like a hymn. It phrases regularly, the harmonization is fairly simple, and it all sounds comfortably solid and conventional (Example 46). Unfortunately, Till breaks it up with his theme I, and the solidarity is lost. Never intrude on the clergy or try to mimic them in jest, even gently.

A long glissando in the strings informs us that our hero has fallen in love. The music, based on snatches of Till's themes, becomes increasingly lush and romantic. Theme II especially is affected: the imp is changed into an ecstatic Romeo. But gradually the mood changes. The music contradicts itself, stumbles around, is interrupted. Something isn't working out, presumably Till's love life. We hear theme I sounding out in heavily accented beats, assertively, even angrily. Here the theme transformation is the exact opposite of diminution. The note values are larger than those of the original tune, rather than smaller. They are thus augmented, so the device is called *augmentation*. Again, as Strauss uses it, there is a programmatic significance. Much of the thematic transformation throughout the composition is actually augmentation and diminution. In this particular instance it suggests that Till is determined but also disgruntled: he has to be what he has to be, love or not. In a great high frenzy, themes flying in the wind, he escapes from the trap of romantic conformity. But he sounds a bit edgy, nonetheless, even as you and I in the same situation—although it is not his nature to brood about it. He moves on to a new episode.

Next, Till encounters what Mauke called the "Philistines." The dictionary terms a Philistine a person who opposes artistic or poetic expression and one who blocks progress or progressive ideas. We would call such people "stuffed shirts" or "squares." They are natural targets of all such folk as Till, so he engages them in a discussion. They are so dull that they haven't even a tune, just a plodding kind of rhythm (Example 47). They are the voice of authority, not partic-

Example 46
Strauss, *Till Eulenspiegel.*

Example 47
Strauss, *Till Eulenspiegel.*

ularly interesting but with an immense amount of assurance and persistence. They thump. Till answers. They thump some more. Till answers. The conversation gets hectic; we hear them get out of joint rhythmically, and Till finally puts them to flight. We know this because his theme becomes stronger and stronger and at last overcomes the rest of the musical framework.

A spritely tune, phrased regularly, harmonized simply, suggests a group of peasants, perhaps dancing (Example 48). Against its symbol of the uncomplicated life of the ordinary man, Till begins to weigh the contradictions in his own personality. The following section of self-questioning is the most extended portion of the piece and possibly the most important from the psychological perspective. Throughout it we hear Till's themes in varying guises, arguing between themselves, trying themselves out in different forms and in contrasting contexts. We accept this as a musical device imitating the mental and emotional conflicts inside Till. We know how such conflicts and self-searching feel; they are common to all of us. Here Strauss is sharing his concept of how they *sound*. Gradually, however, the "real" Till emerges as we hear his theme II stated with great conviction in augmentation by the French horns. It is as though he were again saying to himself and to us, "You have to be what you are, no matter what." And because of the way Strauss presents the material, one has the impression that coming to that conclusion makes Till feel better, more secure, happier. He has "put everything together" at last.

At the very peak of his triumph, however, his theme is interrupted by a drum roll. The chords of the Philistines accuse. Till answers. The chords accuse again and again. Till's responses become more and more frantic. Finally there is no response at all. The Philistines have worn him down, and they condemn him to death. The drum rolls, the hangman pulls the lever, the bassoons and brass fall by a large dissonant interval (that's Till dropping with the noose around his neck), Till's spirit ascends, and his body is left swaying crookedly. Realism once again.

The final section is a reflective epilogue. Till's themes appear, but they are transformed into the most poignant kind of comment, tender and gentle and filled with affection. Only at the end does

Example 48
Strauss, *Till Eulenspiegel.*

theme II assert itself again; is Strauss telling us that nothing can destroy that part of Till (and us) that dares to defy unreasonable convention? All sorts of psychological implications are here. To each his own.

Much of this is program music at its most illustrative level. It is the kind of thing we associate most strongly with background music in TV and films; all we need to add is enough imagination to envision the characters and situations. There is a real sense of continuity— what happened five minutes ago affects and motivates what happens now in the music. One situation leads to the next, and the end depends to a large extent on the events of the musical past of the composition. Even the dissonant descending interval that precedes Till's first episode appears again at the hanging. Was its earlier appearance a musical warning that he would come to no good end?

This music places certain demands on the audience that music with words can avoid, because here we need purely tonal memory. Unless we remember the different themes and what they represent, we have entirely lost the reference points in the story. There is no overlay of words to direct us; only the dramatic episodes that we supply out of our imagination "explain" the musical development. The generic name for this sort of composition is *tone poem*, and its power, like that of poetry, is in suggestion and imagery. It is directed along specific routes, however, and for it to be most effective, the listener needs to recognize those routes. Only if we know all the associations that the title implies can we relate to the music fully.

Can music tell a story? Can it present a series of dramatic episodes that mean the same thing to everyone? Has it a language specific enough to eliminate the need for verbalization? Or can it merely add another dimension to a drama that is already programmed for us through knowledge or experience? When Strauss refused to supply the program himself, was he asking the audience for more than they could be expected to provide? There are no pat answers to these questions, none that will be valid for all listeners. But the answers each of us arrives at will help define what we believe music can do, how it can function, what we expect of it, what limitations we place upon it. What, in fact, we think it *is*, to some extent.

From the standpoint of form, you will recognize that the insertion of Till's themes between statements of other music represents that kind of variety within unity that we discussed earlier in connection with five-part song. Strauss himself identified *Till Eulenspiegel* as a rondo, and it does utilize the rondo principle— alternation of one musical idea with other different ones in a regular pattern. The manipulations are very complex, however, and we might ask whether the greatest value is in the program or the form. The answer, as always, will depend on one's orientation. For the theorist, the form is of vital importance. For the average nonmusician, the program probably exerts the most attraction. For Strauss, both were significant; otherwise why mention the form at all? Musicians tend to haggle about whether the music can stand alone, without the program, and this is an important question in terms of aesthetics. Can content (program) be isolated from form (organization)? Do they interact in some inseparable manner? Is one more important in some cases and the other more important in different cases? Does it matter to us as listeners? These are age-old artistic problems, and if you are a philosopher at heart, you might like to wrestle with them.

Famous and widely travelled as a conductor, Strauss (1864–1949) adopted the aesthetic stance of extreme realism with an emphasis on its shock value in his operas *Salome* and *Elektra*. The cruelty and sensuality of the former and the barbaric quality of the latter caused wide criticism and controversy. Other operas, among them *Der Rosenkavalier* and *Ariadne auf Naxos*, are more gentle and lyric in style. His many operas and symphonic poems are his most familiar works, but he also composed for chamber groups and piano and wrote many solo songs, some with orchestra accompaniment.

SUPPLEMENTAL LISTENING

Among other compositions that depict a series of events that may be familiar to listeners are:

Paul Dukas, The Sorcerer's Apprentice.

A young boy, working for a magician, is responsible for carrying buckets of water to fill the tub. One day, while his master is gone, he uses a magic incantation to command a broom to do the labor. Happily the broom obeys, but unhappily the lad cannot recall the words to stop the activity. In a panic, he chops the broom in half only to find that both halves are carrying water to the overflowing tub. The fiasco continues until the magician returns and recites the magic formula to stop. The French composer Dukas (1865–1935) composed for ballet and opera, but is best remembered for this symphonic tone poem.

Sergei Prokofiev, Peter and the Wolf.

This is a delightful tale for small instrumental group and narrator. Against the wishes of his grandfather, a young boy sets out to capture a wolf, engaging the assistance of some animal friends. All the characters in the story are represented by different instruments and appropriate musical themes. After some frightening episodes, the wolf is captured and led away to the strains of a rollicking march. The Russian composer Prokofiev (1891–1953) achieved wide recognition at a relatively early age and traveled to London, the United States, and France, but returned permanently to Russia in 1927. He composed opera (*Love of Three Oranges* and others), ballet, choral music, orchestral works, including six symphonies, and piano music, but his best-known work is undoubtedly *Peter and the Wolf.*

Maurice Ravel, *Mother Goose Suite.*

This was written originally for piano, two hands, but the most familiar version is an orchestral accompaniment for a ballet in five scenes and an epilogue. The first two scenes are based on the familiar "Sleeping Beauty" legend: a young princess pricks her finger on the spindle of a spinning wheel and is laid on a couch. The next three scenes are based on her dreams. The first of these, "Hop o' My Thumb," concerns the trials of a boy lost in the forest and trying to find his way home by following a trail of bread crumbs. The second concerns another princess, deformed by a witch, who meets a prince, the victim of an evil spell which has turned him into a green serpent. They are restored to their former beauty through their love. The third is the familiar "Beauty and the Beast" legend—again a transformation through love. The epilogue supplies a happy ending for the sleeping princess: Prince Charming awakens her with a kiss. Ravel (1875–1937) followed many of the Impressionist harmonic principles established by his fellow French composer Claude Debussy, but with a more fully developed melodic vocabulary. Like Debussy, he was considered a musical revolutionary by some of his contemporaries because of his unresolved musical dissonances and extensive chromaticism. (See Debussy's *Prelude to the Afternoon of a Faun*, page 207). He composed piano works, orchestral works (all programmatic), ballet, and songs, many with orchestral accompaniment.

Nicholas Rimsky-Korsakov, *Sheherazade.*

This four-movement suite is adapted from the oriental tale *The Thousand and One Nights*, in which the lovely Sheherazade saves herself from the sultan's threat of death by spinning yarns. The four represented here are "The Sea and Sinbad's Ship," "The Story of the Kalandar Prince," "The Young Prince and the Young Princess," and "Festival at Baghdad—The Sea." Musically, the movements are integrated through the use of themes representing the sultan and Sheherazade. Other musical material is used to elaborate on the events and individuals in the various narratives. Rimsky-Korsakov (1844–1908), a Russian composer, spent his early years in naval service but retired to accept a teaching position at the Music Conservatory in St. Petersburg. Under the influence of nationalism, he sometimes exploited pseudo-Easternisms. He composed orchestral works, including three symphonies, chamber music, songs, and many operas, but his most familiar work is *Sheherazude*.

Richard Strauss, *Don Quixote*.

The adventures of the don and his squire, Sancho Panza, are given musical representation in 10 episodes cast in theme and variations form. Each character is represented by his own theme, responding in varying ways to the situations in which he finds himself. The episodes are the most important ones in the Cervantes novel— jousting with windmills, the don's love for Dulcinea, the unhappy trip on the River Ebor, etc.

Darius Milhaud, *The Creation of the World*.

Conceived as a ballet, this work features 1920s jazz idioms to which the French composer Milhaud was exposed during a trip to New York's Harlem. As originally choreographed, the ballet suggested a primitive African concept of creation in terms of which the syncopated and jagged rhythmic and melodic lines were entirely appropriate. The music is striking enough in itself, without benefit of accompanying dance, to stir the listener's imagination, and has become a standard part of the orchestral repertoire. Milhaud (1892–1974) was one of "The Six," a group of French composers dedicated to breaking away from the German influence that had dominated musical style throughout the nineteenth century and to eliminating the vagueness of Impressionism. Other members of the group included Erik Satie (1866–1925), Arthur Honegger (1892–1955), and Francis Poulenc (1899–1963). All were closely associated with prominent French artists and writers of the period. Quite eclectic in style, Milhaud uses idioms from jazz and folk music as well as polytonality and sometimes polyphonic devices. He composed operas (including some for children), ballets, orchestral works, program music, concertos, choruses, piano works, chamber music, and many songs.

Chapter 16
Musical Description of Locale

The Czech (Bohemian) composer Bedřich Smetana (1824–1884) was devoutly nationalistic in his use of thematic material as well as in the programmatic intent of much of his work. His *Die Moldau*, first performed in 1875, is one of a cycle of six symphonic tone poems collectively called *Mein Vaterland* (My Country) and concerned with scenes and historical incidents of particular significance for Bohemia. His compositions include also operas *(The Bartered Bride)*, chamber works, piano pieces—including many with programmatic intent—choruses, and songs.

Smetana thus shared a general nineteenth-century fascination with nationalism and a corresponding pride in the cultural and historical heritages of the developing European nations. The century has sometimes been identified as the century of colonialism and nationalistic outreach of all kinds. The political and military turmoils of the eighteenth century had settled down somewhat, and the various nations of Europe were able to turn their attention to developing their particular identities. We might say they were interested in projecting their images.

Out of the temper of the time, then, came an increasing interest in folklore, political history, musical culture, and other artistic expressions of national importance.

PRIMARY LISTENING:
Bedřich Smetana, *Die Moldau*

The Moldau is Bohemia's greatest river, and this portion of Smetana's cycle is an attempt to portray in musical terms some of the scenes that one would encounter on a trip down the river. The various sections of the composition and the themes that portray them are given titles in the score. Unless they are printed in a program, however, or on a record jacket, the listener must furnish much of the programmatic background himself if he is to follow the progress of the music.

Like all rivers, the Moldau has small beginnings, two brooklets that merge to form the main stream. Smetana illustrates this at the start (Example 49).

Before long, we hear the theme of the river itself, broad and sweeping. It appears in minor, and we have discussed the minor mode as an expressive device in Martini, Schubert, and others. Do you assign some mood to Smetana's river theme (Example 50) because of its mode?

Notice the regularity of phrasing, the fact that the theme, after some manipulation, suddenly appears in major. Is this simply the use of color for musical interest and without programmatic significance? Is there some added feeling content that results from the mode change, that is, apart from any suggested change in the river itself?

A deceptive cadence introduces a new musical figure, hunting horns. People hunt in forests. If you know that the Moldau flows through woodlands, you make the immediate association that Smetana expects. If not, you might think that the composer just wants the horns to have something more interesting than the stabs of sound that they've played so far!

For many centuries the sound of the horn was associated with the hunt as well as with the ceremonies of nobility. The nineteenth century, enchanted as it was with associations of all sorts, exploited this one fully. By 1875, when the piece was written, valves had been

Example 49
Smetana, *Die Moldau*.

Example 50
Smetana, *Die Moldau*.

added to practically all the standard orchestral brass instruments, so that the horns could play something more melodious than the flourishes that Smetana provides here. But broken-chord outlines are traditional for brass calls to the hunt (as well as other functions: remember Mozart and Verdi and Britten in the "Dies irae"?), and this is the context Smetana wants.

The point to catch in terms of the program is that, given the proper awareness, the audience knows that the horn flourishes mean a hunt along the banks of the Moldau. Can you recognize part of the river theme sneaking in amidst the horn figures?

A new thematic idea introduces a section devoted to a peasant wedding. It is a country dance tune, fit for merrymaking, and suggests that at this point the river flows past a rural village where marital festivities are in progress (Example 51).

This in turn fades into a quietly misty section called "Moon-shine"—suggesting a gathering of nymphs. Here the principal musical material, other than a series of muted chords, is carried by flutes and other woodwinds. In associative terms, this is suitable to suggest the mystery of a nighttime frolic of otherworldly creatures. Woodsy folk—shepherds, nymphs, even Pan himself—play on reed pipes.

Again the music changes as the river flows out of the forest and into open country. The river theme appears in its original form, including the change of mode from minor to major. Again it is interrupted deceptively at its final cadence, this time to become more and more tumultuous as the river flows over the Rapids of St. John. This is the first appearance in the composition of anything resembling polyphonic activity, and even here it is not highly developed. Most of the orchestra simply supplies exciting rhythms and runs to suggest the passage of the river over the rocks of the rapids.

Just below the rapids the river broadens, as everyone in Bohemia knows. To depict this, the river theme sounds forth triumphantly in major, almost as though it had won some sort of battle that threatened it, however briefly. Out of the musical activity comes a new theme suggesting the ancient castle Vysehrad, near the

Example 51
Smetana, *Die Moldau.*

mouth of the Moldau. It is in the style of a chorale—noble, firm, and proud—as befits the kind of national landmark it illustrates (Example 52). The entire piece ends with a gradual fading of the river into the distance, on its way to the sea. Two thunderous chords bring the final cadence.

This is much less complex working out of programmatic ideas than we found in *Till Eulenspiegel*. As you may have noticed, most of the texture is homophonic, consisting of gratifying and illustrative melodies harmonized in an appealing manner and presented in a steady flow except for the insertions of the river theme before and after the St. John's Rapids episode. There is no interplay or cross-relationship of musical themes or any "working out" of them. There is no reason to set up that sort of argumentative texture. This is simply a presentation of music to support a variety of scenes, and if one is willing to accept the music as representative, there is no problem with the program.

Perhaps because of the relative simplicity of the texture and the presentation of themes, the program is not needed to the same extent—just sit back and enjoy the tunes. Or perhaps you want to know *why* a new idea is presented. Or you want the themes to appear and reappear with more predictability. These things *may* affect your response.

SUPPLEMENTAL LISTENING

Many other program pieces attempt a musical representation of scenes with which audiences might be familiar. Among the most popular are:

George Gershwin, *An American in Paris.*

Composed while Gershwin was a visitor in Paris, this work is only suggestive of the street noises and atmosphere of that city. It does not, in other words, attempt to portray any specific buildings, monuments, or areas. It does include what Gershwin called a "blues," perhaps indicating a spell of homesickness. An American pianist and composer, George Gershwin (1898–1937) achieved his first fame with *Rhapsody in Blue* for piano and orchestra. Most of his compositions make use of jazz idioms in some way. His opera *Porgy and Bess* is considered by many the first and greatest American

Example 52
Smetana, *Die Moldau.*

opera. His compositions also include music for many stage shows and numerous pop songs of high caliber.

Ferde Grofé, *Grand Canyon Suite.* This is an attempt to recreate in sound the grandeur and vastness of the Grand Canyon. It is in five parts, all relatively graphic in their tonal portraiture: "Sunrise," "Painted Desert," "On the Trail" (including the clopping of hooves), "Sunset," and "Cloudburst." Ferde Grofé (1892–1972) was also an American composer. He played and arranged for Paul Whiteman's band, attempting to make symphonic use of jazz idioms. *Grand Canyon Suite* is his best-known example of this.

Ottorino Respighi, *The Pines of Rome.* Four tone poems make up this attempt to capture specific localities in the city of Rome:

> "The Pines of Villa Borghese"—children at play in a pine grove.
> "The Pines near a Catacomb"—shadows obscuring the
> entrance to a catacomb and a chant sounding from its depths.
> "The Pines of the Janiculum"—a moonlit scene on Gianicolo's
> Hill with the song of a nightingale as one important motive.
> "The Pines of the Appian Way"—dawn on the traditional road
> of the returning military on their way to Capitoline Hill. A
> march tempo and trumpets add to the vividness of the imagery.

Ottorino Respighi, *The Fountains of Rome.* Similar in intent to *The Pines of Rome*, this work is a reflection of certain well-known fountains and the associations they arouse in the listener:

> "The Fountain of Valle Giulia at Dawn"—a pastoral scene with
> cattle grazing in the misty dawn.
> "The Triton Fountain in the Morning"—naiads and tritons
> chasing one another and dancing in the fountain.
> "The Fountain of Trevi at Midday"—a triumphant processional,
> complete with trumpet flourishes, of Neptune's chariot across
> the water.
> "The Villa Medici Fountain at Sunset"—the tolling of bells, the
> chatter of birds, and the whisper of leaves fading serenely into
> the silence of night.

An Italian Impressionist composer, Respighi (1879–1936) was strongly influenced by Russian idioms, intensified by his studies with Rimsky-Korsakov. Although he composed some theater pieces and chamber works, he is best known for his programmatic orchestral compositions (*The Pines of Rome, The Fountains of Rome*, and others) in the idiom of French Impressionism.

Chapter 17
Sound Painting

Almost exactly contemporary with *Die Moldau* is *Pictures at an Exhibition*, an 1874 work by the Russian composer Modeste Mussorgsky. It, too, has strong nationalistic overtones. Here the inspiration for the composition was not a series of locales along a familiar river route, but rather a series of sketches by Mussorgsky's friend Victor Hartmann. Hartmann had died in 1873 at a relatively young age, and the "exhibition" in the title was held in his honor and featured his architectural sketches, most of which had never been really utilized in buildings. Like many of his contemporaries in Russia and elsewhere, Hartmann had been involved in breaking with artistic traditions that came from other nations. He wanted to use architectural decoration with a Russian folk and historical background.

The composition is based on ten different sketches. It begins with "Promenade" which recurs intermittently throughout the work and represents Mussorgsky strolling from picture to picture. Our discussion deals with three sections only: the opening "Promenade," "Gnomus" (Gnome), and the ensuing "Promenade." If you were to hear the entire work, there would be musical descriptions of these other sketches:

"Il Vecchio Castello"
"Tuileries (Children Quarreling after Play)"
"Bydlo"
"Ballet of the Chicks in Their Shells"
"Two Polish Jews, One Rich, the Other Poor"
"Limoges, The Market Place (Great News!)"
"Catacombae, Sepulcrum Romanum—Con Mortuis in Lingua Mortua"

"The Hut on Fowl's Legs (Baba Yaga)"
"The Great Gate of Kiev"

The composition is best known in an orchestral arrangement made by Maurice Ravel, the famous French Impressionist. However, Mussorgsky originally wrote it for piano solo, and we will deal with that version.

PRIMARY LISTENING:
Modeste Mussorgsky,
Pictures at an Exhibition,
Original piano version
(record set)

Listen first to the opening "Promenade" (Example 53). You know all the terminology for describing this—the monophonic introduction followed by a clearly homophonic repetition. Certainly not a gracious or charming melody, and very likely this is deliberate: Mussorgsky weighed considerably more than 200 pounds, and this "Promenade" is an illustration of his stroll into the art gallery and approach to the first painting. Are the stodgy, relatively monotonous rhythms and the "fat" chords that define the musical texture meant as tongue-in-cheek self-parody? Notice the meter, too—back and forth between five and six beats to a measure. This gives a sort of uneven rock to the rhythm, and is probably intended to illustrate the composer's rolling gait. Mussorgsky was a completely down-to-earth person, and if this "Promenade" really is a subtle mockery of himself, he seems to be a man with personal integrity and a wry sense of humor as well. This is rather refreshing in 1874, when most artists were taking themselves very seriously indeed.

Mussorgsky (1839–1881) was interesting in other ways too. He was the most daring, primitive, and imaginative of the Russian group of composers known as "The Five," who also included Mily Balakirev (1837—1910) and Alexander Borodin (1833—1887). He spent much of his life in government service rather than as a professional musician. Musically he was never much of a financial success because he insisted on following his own best instincts in an age when most Russian musicians were imitating western European musical practices. Many of his pieces were edited by Rimsky-Korsakov in order to eliminate the "clumsiness and errors." Later, however, they were issued in their original versions. He composed

Example 53
Mussorgsky, *Pictures at an Exhibition.*

opera (*Boris Godunov*), orchestral works, piano works, and songs (*Songs and Dances of Death*). His most popular work is *Pictures at an Exhibition.*

The composer arrives at a sketch of a nutcracker fashioned like a gnome and designed so that the nuts are broken between the jaws. What reaction is Mussorgsky trying to project through music here? Horror? Amusement? Surprise? Revulsion? The dissonance and increasing chromaticism certainly suggest *some* reaction. Is Mussorgsky imagining how such a twisted creature might walk? Is there an attempt to illustrate the cracking of the nuts? The answers are yours (Example 54).

The reappearance of the "Promenade" tells us that the composer is on his way to the next sketch. The change of mood and key may mean he is reflecting on the sketch he has just seen, or it may simply mean that we are being prepared for a different key to be used for the following section of the composition, or perhaps both.

Why not investigate the rest of Mussorgsky's *Pictures* by yourself, throwing your imagination wide open?

The rock group Emerson, Lake, and Palmer featured Mussorgsky's composition in live performances and on disc. It is always interesting and instructive to compare different interpretations of the same piece. A pianist performing from Mussorgsky's score would probably follow the composer's performance directions quite exactly. What we would hear, then, would be a re-creation of Mussorgsky's ideas as exactly as possible within the limits of the performer's skill.

PRIMARY LISTENING:
Mussorgsky, *Pictures at an Exhibition*, Emerson, Lake, and Palmer (Cotillion: ELP 66666)

This is not quite the case with Emerson, Lake, and Palmer. Although performed on an organ rather than a piano, the initial "Promenade" is as Mussorgsky composed it; there is no change of notes. "Gnomus," however, is arranged by Palmer, and the following "Promenade" is arranged by Lake for organ, synthesizer, and percussion, and some of Mussorgsky's notes are changed. Most listeners will recognize with little difficulty that the second "Promenade" is shortened, although it retains Mussorgsky's musical ideas. Can you detect the kind of

Example 54
Mussorgsky, *Pictures at an Exhibition.*

enlargements that are made in "Gnomus?" Are all the musical ideas used by the group inherent in or implied in Mussorgsky's composition? In other words, are the changes made with concern for the composer's creative ideas? Are Mussorgsky's artistic intentions merely extended, or are they annihilated for the sake of novelty? Is the mood essentially Mussorgsky's or has it changed?

These questions carry some broad implications. Authors write books that are then translated into movies. What are the responsibilities of the producers, directors, and actors in that case? Movies are edited for television. What is lost or gained in the process of editing? Present-day performers record pop numbers that have been previously recorded by others; these are called "cover" recordings in the trade. When the originals are changed, as they usually are, what is gained or lost in the modifications? Are the originals intensified, watered down, almost obliterated? Paintings are reproduced in books or in prints. At what sacrifice or gain?

Performance differences normally go under the general category of "interpretation," and all performers need to do some of this. Orchestra conductors, singers, actors, and dancers are all faced with the necessity of interpreting someone else's idea unless they are themselves the composer, playwright, or choreographer. In music, the composer is at the mercy of his interpreters, of course; this is one reason for the increasing use of performance directions, including even tempo indications, since the eighteenth century. Composers became more intent on making their intentions clear and also increasingly wary of allowing performers too much freedom. Some of this grew out of the tendency of many Romantic artists to wring every drop of intensity out of each rendition. An additional factor was the Romantic vision of art as its own sole justification—and, by extension, the artist's divine right to full expression of his artistry. This feeling of having been touched by the magic wand of art carried over fully into everyday living, where the typical Romantic was extremely bizarre about observing the usual social and ethical conventions.

Think about our own time and the life styles of many creative artists and performers. Is the Romantic temper still alive?

If composers, the creative musicians, recognize the need to protect their creations carefully by providing detailed performance directions, who can blame them? As members of the audience, we often judge the *composer's* value mainly in terms of what we hear the *performer* deliver. Is this always fair?

Anyway, here you have Emerson, Lake, Palmer, and Mussorgsky. How do they all come out in this exchange of creativity, performance techniques, and arrangement?

SUPPLEMENTAL LISTENING
Enrique Granados, *Goyescas.*

This is a set of six pieces for piano named for scenes in paintings and tapestries of Goya, as well as for events of his period in Spanish history, the early nineteenth century. The composition features Spanish rhythms of a quite distinctive nature. The pieces were later used as the bases for an opera of the same name.

Sergei Rachmaninoff,
Isle of the Dead.

This extended symphonic poem is based on a painting by Arnold Böcklin bearing the same title. The island, north of the Bay of Naples, is of volcanic origin and covered with cypress trees. Rachmaninoff captures the sense of desolation and isolation together with the sound of waves lapping on the rocks. Following a lament for the dead, there is a quotation of the Gregorian "Dies irae."

The Russian pianist and composer Rachmaninoff (1873–1943) travelled widely, spending extended periods in the United States, which were interrupted by concert and guest conducting engagements in Europe. Although strongly influenced by Western musical practices, he did include material from his native land in some of his compositions. He composed orchestral works, including two symphonies, piano and chamber music, and songs. Rachmaninoff is probably best known for his Second Piano Concerto, a theme from which was made into an American popular song, "Full Moon and Empty Arms," during the thirties.

Chapter 18
Ballet

Strictly speaking, ballet music is not true program music when it accompanies the actual dancing. This changes, however, when the music is extracted and performed as a concert piece. Much of the music for ballet has become familiar to audiences in exactly this way. *Petrushka*, by Igor Stravinsky (Illustration 19), is in that category. Although it may be enjoyable for many people without any reference at all to the action for which it was conceived, some knowledge of the ballet's storyline does add another dimension.

As in many great works, the characters we encounter in *Petrushka* are analogies; they are prototypes of the human condition in its varying forms. Petrushka is the clown with the tender heart, vulnerable and open to hurt in spite of his grotesque appearance. The Ballerina is the vain, giddy, eternal feminine, long on looks and short on sensitivity and compassion. This was written early in the century. When we see how much stereotyping has occurred in the past, we can understand the reasons for women's lib. The Moor is the exotic sophisticate without depth of character or even much gray matter to guide his behavior—mostly brawn without brain. The Magician, the puppeteer who controls their fates, is the governing force behind all of us, maneuvering us into patterns and situations where our weaknesses can be exploited for things not in our best interest and often to our detriment. The conflicts among these four characters and what they represent form the basis of the ballet. The action takes place during the Shrovetide fair in St. Petersburg, and is in four scenes, or tableaux. All of this drama is fully developed in the complete ballet. The first tableau, the part we will be considering here, sets the stage for it.

Stravinsky originally conceived the music for *Petrushka* as an

Illustration 19. IGOR STRAVINSKY.

orchestral work featuring the piano. His plans were changed, however, when the great Russian ballet master Sergei Diaghilev, for whose company of dancers the Russian-born Stravinsky had provided earlier music, became interested in the piece. Together they worked out the plot and dances, and the first performance was given in Paris on June 13, 1911. It was generally well received. The title role was danced by Nijinsky, probably the most famous and spectacular ballet dancer of all time.

Because of the enormous rhythmic complexities of the score, rehearsals were chaotic for dancers as well as for orchestral personnel. Dancers need to rely on rhythm; their movements actually serve to make the rhythms visible. They had a bad time with *Petrushka* because of the irregularities. A great deal of time was spent in explanation, counting, grouping accents, etc., so that what the dancers did and the rhythms that the audience saw would be properly synchronized with the music that was heard. The dancers had been trained in the classical tradition, of course, and they needed to adjust in order to accommodate the new musical ideas. Modern dance allows much more freedom and room for individual interpretation, but it still uses the same principle of translating musical movement into physical movement. You can see this when you watch a musical variety show on TV.

Stravinsky (1882–1971) opened up entirely new ideas about rhythmic arrangement and made other important contributions also. In any catalogue of important twentieth-century composers he would most certainly be among those at the very top. He is considered, in fact, to be one of the few great innovators in the entire history of Western musical practice. He is unique in his imaginative use of orchestral color; his polytonality, the simultaneous use of contrasting, often conflicting key centers; his flow of musical ideas, invaluable for a musical tale-spinner; his rhythmic manipulation; his dissonant textures under an almost continuous string of changing melodies; and his interest in all sorts of musical expression including jazz idioms.

Stravinsky first achieved fame with *Firebird, Petrushka,* and *The Rite of Spring,* all commissioned by Diaghilev's Ballet Russe. Among his many stage works are *Oedipus Rex,* an opera-oratorio for speaker, soloists, male chorus and orchestra, and *The Soldier's Tale* for narrator, actors/dancers, and chamber orchestra; he also composed choral pieces (*Symphony of Psalms* on Latin texts from the Vulgate, and the Mass), orchestral and chamber compositions, and works for piano and solo voice. *Petrushka* was only his second successful work, but it is still regarded as one of the masterpieces of the century.

PRIMARY LISTENING:
Igor Stravinsky, *Petrushka,*
first tableau

It begins with the complexity of sound that one might well associate with a carnival atmosphere in which the activities of the crowd are largely uncoordinated. Much of the rhythmic diversity is due to a conglomeration of simultaneous but contradictory meters. To add to the confusion, the metric organization changes rapidly, often at successive bars (Example 55).

The first important change of texture and idea turns the focus on a group of drunken revelers. The musical illustration is just about as ponderous as their progress across the stage: they're having a great time, but they're not very graceful (Example 56). The stark homophonic format contributes to the aural image; the huge orchestra pounds in rhythmic unison. If you have listened carefully to the opening section you will have heard the preparation for this music being sounded in the low woodwinds. A section of relatively

Example 55
Stravinsky, *Petrushka.*
Kalmus score, p. 12. Used by
permission.

diverse and fragmented material follows, matched by similar activity
on the stage, but eventually an organ grinder is heard and our
attention is drawn to him and the dancer he accompanies. The tune
is one that Stravinsky heard in the street outside his room in Paris,
played on a hurdy-gurdy. In the ballet, the sound of the hurdy-gurdy
is reproduced with standard orchestral instruments. On the other
side of the stage a second dancer with a music box appears, and

Example 56
Stravinsky, *Petrushka.*
Kalmus score, pp. 14–15. Used
by permission.

before long the two dancers and their tunes are in competition
(Example 57).

Our attention, plus that of the crowd on stage, is diverted after a
while; the drunks return and the general mixture of activity resumes.

This time the general confusion is interrupted decisively with a
drum roll. The focus now is on a little puppet theater and the

Example 57
Stravinsky, *Petrushka*.

Magician who runs it. A long flute solo, played by the Magician, announces the beginning of the show (Example 58). Shuddering mystical chords accompany the opening of the puppet theater curtain as Petrushka, the Ballerina, and the Moor become visible, flopped over like rag dolls. The Magician touches them with his flute; they come to life and begin to dance (Example 59).

The music for their dance, which is somewhat extended and uses two principal themes, comes to an abrupt end, and a drum roll prepares the way for the following scene, which takes place in Petrushka's room.

As music only, apart from its function as accompaniment to ballet, the opening scene has a discernible form, the flow of musical ideas alternating in a logical order. As dance, ballet also reflects this concern for formal discipline but one needs an understanding of the appropriate conventions in order to comprehend it fully. For many people these formal features are not the most compelling elements. In listening to a concert or recorded version of Petrushka, non-theorists will probably be more attracted by the wonderful diversity of ideas and the interesting use of orchestral color.

Example 58
Stravinsky, *Petrushka*.

Example 59
Stravinsky, *Petrushka*.

In 1911 the musical complexity was daring, far more so than anything that had been widely heard before that time. The same is true of the exploitation of instrumental sound. The manipulation of rhythm and the continuing stream of short but striking melodic ideas were also innovations. All of these factors added together identify Stravinsky's style, and they exerted a strong influence over twentieth-century composition.

Some of the tunes in this and the composer's other works were taken from Russian folk song, but much of the music is original. Throughout his composing career Stravinsky turned his attention in many directions, always alive to new ideas and devices. In this sample his eclecticism is illustrated by his use of the hurdy-gurdy tune he heard in the streets of Paris. One segment of Walt Disney's *Fantasia* is based on a portion of another Stravinsky ballet, *The Rite of Spring*. That work followed *Petrushka* and was also introduced by the Diaghilev Ballet Russe. In *The Rite of Spring* the dissonance and rhythmic complexities are even more severe than in *Petrushka;* they are actually barbaric-sounding in keeping with the subject of the ballet. It would be difficult to overestimate the importance of Stravinsky's contribution to musical developments in the present century.

Although many listeners will find the music of *Petrushka* satisfactory without the ballet to watch, *Petrushka* raises some important questions about the ways we alter the original intent of much music. This work was conceived and performed as a ballet before phonograph records were widely available, so that one *had* to contact both the music and the dance as a unified work of art. Although many experiments had been made with wire and cylinder recordings during the 1890s, it was not until the second decade of the twentieth century that sound reproduction was efficient enough to attract a wide market. Even then most of the recordings were of individuals or small groups. Performers sang or talked or played into a horn, and the entire process was acoustical rather than electrical, which it became in the 1920s. After that time developments and improvements were rapid, and it was increasingly practical to record large instrumental and vocal groups.

The point here is that until the advent of the phonograph one had to either perform music or go to hear a live performance—or do without. Recordings are a mixed blessing. They make a wide variety of music available at minimal cost. They allow us to contact worlds of music that would be inaccessible otherwise. They give us the opportunity to hear great performers who would ordinarily be known to us by name only. They bring music into our homes, make it more convenient, enrich our horizons in innumerable ways. They even act as archives, preserving the art of performers who have died. Without recordings, for instance, we would have no legacy of the great folk, jazz, blues, and pop performances of the past. These are assets and we cannot belittle them.

At the same time, they eliminate much of the human element. We have only that part of the person that is represented by the voice or the approach to the performing instrument. One of the most severe losses is the physical movement that usually accompanies performance. The *sight* of an orchestra playing is almost as rhythmic as the *sound* it produces. The same thing is true of rock or jazz or country western groups. When we confine our experience to records, we either have to program the movement in our imagination or eliminate it altogether.

How about a piece like *Petrushka* in this regard? When we contact it through a recording only, we have cut away several elements. Not only do we not see the action of the ballet for which it was intended, we don't even see the members of the orchestra or the conductor; in a concert version, we would at least have *that*. Stravinsky never envisioned, of course, the need for a program or explanation of his musical score. When you see the ballet, *that's* the program—who needs words? All of that changes when the music is performed in concert version. And it is changed even more, in different ways, when it is recorded. It might be that a lot of the explaining we do would become unnecessary if we suddenly lost all the advantages of twentieth-century technology. Add something here, subtract something there. This seems to be the continuing paradox and conflict of progress.

SUPPLEMENTAL LISTENING   Many of the questions raised above apply to the repertoire of ballet music that has come into the concert hall. The following are popular compositions of that type with wide appeal and in different styles:

Igor Stravinsky, *The Rite of Spring.*

This historic work is in two parts, each subdivided into a number of dances. The main theme is of a pagan ritual in the course of which a sacrificial virgin dances to her death. Melodically and harmonically dissonant, the entire work is characterized by disjointed and barbaric rhythms. It was met at its first performance by an outcry of rage over its rhythmic complexity, dissonance, and barbaric textures, but has since become a standard of the orchestral and ballet repertoire.

Peter Ilich Tchaikowsky, *Nutcracker Suite.*

The *Nutcracker Suite* has become one of this composer's best-known works, performed widely as a concert piece as well as on stage, in movies, and on television. The plot of the ballet involves a little girl whose brothers break her Christmas gift, a nutcracker in the form of a man. During the night, she steals downstairs and enters upon a series of fantasy adventures. In the concert version, much of the original score is omitted and the performances consist of a series of dances, including "Dance of the Sugar Plum Fairy," "Arabian Dance," "Dance of the Reed Flutes," "Waltz of the Flowers," and others of a similarly descriptive nature.

Aaron Copland, *Rodeo.*

The ballet concerns the attempt of a young girl to compete with cowboys in a rodeo. Enamored in particular of a champion roper, she eventually gives up her athletic goals, dons feminine attire for a Saturday night dance, and wins her man. The most frequently performed sections for concert purposes are "Buckaroo Holiday," "Corral Nocturne," "Saturday Night Waltz," and "Hoe-Down."

Leonard Bernstein, ballet from *West Side Story.*

West Side Story is an urbanized, modernized version of Shakespeare's classic *Romeo and Juliet.* The ballet suggested for listening here depicts the growing tension created by opposing New York street gangs itching for a fight. Caught in the threat of unwanted violence, Maria and Tony (Juliet and Romeo) seek a refuge where they can be at peace with their love. Bernstein draws freely on contemporary musical idioms, including jazz. An American pianist and composer, Bernstein (born 1918) is perhaps best known for having been the conductor of the New York Philharmonic Orchestra. In this role he did much to introduce new as well as established works to audiences with previously limited exposure. He has written stage works (*On the Town, Candide*), symphonies (mostly programmatic), piano works, songs, and his own version of the Mass.

Chapter 19
Musical Quotation

PRIMARY LISTENING:
Hector Berlioz, *Fantastic*
Symphony, fifth movement,
"Dream of a Witches'
Sabbath"

The idea of giving programmatic titles to symphonies and their individual movements is generally traced to Beethoven, although some minor composers used this device before him. There had been a great deal of programmatic titling of shorter works during the eighteenth century. Beethoven's *Pastoral* Symphony, the Sixth, however, is the first important one of its kind. In it he suggests by titles the expressive direction of each movement. For instance, the next-to-last movement is entitled "Storm," and the last movement "Thankful Feelings after the Storm." The work is made up of five movements instead of the traditional four, another significant departure from convention.

In 1830, only three years after Beethoven's death, the French composer Hector Berlioz's *Fantastic* Symphony received its first performance. Like the *Pastoral*, it is in five movements, the last of which is the next listening selection. The composer himself furnished program notes, meant to be read by the audience when the work was staged: it was conceived as a dramatic presentation complete with actors and theatrical props. Modern performances of the symphony are almost always in a concert version, however, unaccompanied by any dramatic production. The notes are certainly still appropriate and help us to understand the program behind the music.

Each of the five movements represents an incident that takes place in the visions of a young musician after an overdose of opium. The dramatic situation came out of Berlioz's experience as a result of a tumultuous affair with the well-known English actress Harriet Smithson. Berlioz (1803–1869) is considered by some to be a pioneer of all the eccentricities that Romanticism stands for, including the intrusion of his private life and personality into his artistic creations. And his behavior was, to say the least, generally quite erratic. He studied both music and medicine, abandoned the latter for the former, and became widely acclaimed and successful. He composed the *Fantastic* Symphony in order to publicly shame Harriet Smithson, with whom he was passionately in love and whom he later married. Although this is probably his best-known work, he is also famous for his *Requiem*, for program overtures, for songs, and, although the work is not yet widely known, for his opera *Les Troyens*.

Running throughout all five movements and appearing in different appropriate transformations is a melody representing his beloved, a melody he called the "fixed idea" (*idée fixe*). This is used programmatically and worked into various musical situations where it can be exploited. The first movement concerns dreams and passions mostly directed toward the woman with whom the young musician is infatuated. The second depicts a ball where he runs into the girl. The third finds the young man in the country, where the sounds of nature and shepherds' pipes remind him of his lost tranquility. In the fourth, he dreams that he has murdered the lady and is sent to the scaffold. We are concerned here with the fifth and last movement. This is titled "Dream of a Witches' Sabbath," and Berlioz furnished the following program:

> He imagines himself at a Witches' Sabbath in the midst of a crowd of spectres, sorcerers, and other monsters who are gathered for his funeral. Unearthly sounds, groans, shrieking laughter, far-off cries, responded to by everyone. He hears the melody of his loved one but it no longer has its nobility and timidity. It is now an ungracious dance tune, trite and grotesque. She has come to the Sabbath orgy. A howl of joy greets her. She joins the orgiastic dance. Bells toll in a burlesque of the Dies irae. The witches dance. The dance and the Dies irae are united.

Like Stravinsky nearly a century later, Berlioz was immensely gifted in the use of orchestral sound. The manner in which he put it to programmatic use was of great influence throughout the rest of the nineteenth century. This is immediately evident at the opening of the fifth movement, with its eerie cackling of muted violins in extremely high register and the corresponding use of woodwinds and brass.

The first melodic outline to emerge strongly is the "fixed idea," representing the woman in question. The musical idea is the same one that has been used in the previous four movements (Example 60) but here it is grossly distorted by the use of grace notes, pitches

Example 60
Berlioz, *Fantastic* Symphony.

played almost simultaneously with the principal melody notes but at the very dissonant interval of a half step (Example 61). As the program indicates, the woman has become a witch and is greeted with great gusto by her sisters. She dances in a frenzied meter amid considerable dissonance appropriate to the situation. As the music subsides and the bells sound, the brass introduces the Gregorian "Dies irae" (Example 62).

As Berlioz hoped his audiences would be, you are sophisticated and informed enough to make all the proper associations because you know that piece. Following an extended manipulation of the "Dies irae," a new dance theme emerges which proceeds with growing intensity in a polyphonic dialogue with the "Dies irae." From that point on, it's everyone for himself (Example 63).

Probably none of us will ever participate in this kind of Black Sabbath celebration, but we can recognize here all the Romantic delight in the macabre as well as the love of association by imagery. To appreciate fully the use of the "fixed idea," however, we would need to experience the first four movements, which are just as graphic as this one.

The idea of transforming a theme, here the "fixed idea," in order to give it a new expressive dimension is actually already familiar to us from *Till Eulenspiegel*. That was a one-movement composition,

Example 61
Berlioz, *Fantastic* Symphony.

Example 62
Berlioz, *Fantastic* Symphony.

Example 63
Berlioz, *Fantastic* Symphony.

however. Normally, multimovement works contain different musical ideas in each separate movement. The device of having one theme occur in several movements is a useful one for the program symphony, and was utilized in many nineteenth-century compositions.

The way Berlioz employs the "Dies irae" is a different thing altogether. This occurs only in the last movement, and its importance for a Witches' Sabbath is entirely in terms of the associations it had accumulated through the centuries. We link it to death, to judgment, to punishment, to fear; superimposing it on a Black Sabbath ritual raises all kinds of controversial notions. But only if we know the tune. Programmatic works often quote familiar musical material in order to encourage associations, to raise images in the mind of the audience, and the composer needs our cooperation in order to complete his purpose.

SUPPLEMENTAL LISTENING

Among programmatic works that use musical quotations as reference points are the following:

Peter Ilich Tchaikowsky, *1812 Overture.*

Two of the principal themes in this work depicting the Napoleonic invasion of Russia are the French national anthem and a Russian Cossack song. They are pitted against one another musically to suggest the conflict between the opposing armies. In the musical struggle, as might be expected, the Cossack tune emerges victorious.

Aaron Copland, *A Lincoln Portrait.*

This piece includes narration taken from the speeches and writings of Abraham Lincoln. Stephen Collins Foster's "Camptown Races" and a popular ballad, "On Springfield Mountain," are both used in the work.

Camille Saint-Saëns, *Carnival of the Animals.*

This cycle of short pieces for piano and instruments is mostly fun-making. Several of the movements involve musical parody. To suggest tortoises, for instance, the well-known cancan by Offenbach is performed at a turtle's pace. Another movement, "Fossils," uses the theme from *Danse macabre*, a different work by Saint-Saëns that portrays the revels of skeletons.

Saint-Saëns (1835–1921) was a French pianist, organist, and composer. He achieved relatively early recognition and composed in a wide range of genres. Included among his compositions are things for orchestra, chamber groups, chorus, and solo voice. He also wrote operas (*Samson and Delilah* is his best known).

Symphonic works that use the same thematic material for more than one movement, although only in a most general sense of program, are:

Antonin Dvořák, Ninth Symphony (often called the Fifth), *From the New World.*

The first theme of the second movement may be one of the best-known symphonic melodies of all time. It has been set to words and has circulated widely under the title "Goin' Home." As a unifying factor in the symphony, Dvořák uses it only slightly varied as one of the themes in the third movement. Another of the third-movement themes is derived from the first theme of the first movement. Dvořák (1841–1904), a Czech composer, utilized much traditional Czech music as the thematic basis of his compositions. But also, from 1892 to 1895 he was the director of the National Conservatory of Music in New York City, and during that period he travelled throughout the United States assimilating native idioms, particularly those of the Indian and Negro. He composed songs, symphonies, chamber works, symphonic poems, and operas.

César Franck, D minor Symphony.

In this three-movement work, Franck suggests a general mood of religiosity in the most melodious of the themes from the first movement. It appears in each of the other two movements, varied slightly but still quite recognizable in musical outline as well as in expressive substance. There is also some sense of continuity in the reference to the introductory material in the first movement that occurs in the first theme of the second movement.

Born in Belgium and of German stock, Franck (1822–1890) spent his adult life in France. His main professional appointments were as organist at St. Clotilde Church in Paris and professor of organ at the Paris Conservatory. His style is highly chromatic and fully Romantic; Debussy once referred to him as a "modulating machine." He composed piano, organ, vocal, and choral (mostly sacred) music, the D minor Symphony, and *Symphonic Variations* for piano and orchestra.

Ludwig van Beethoven, Fifth Symphony.

The entire symphony is unified through the persistence of a distinctive rhythmic figure that occurs in varying melodic contexts throughout all four movements of the work. Introduced with great strength at the opening of the first movement, it was characterized by Beethoven himself as the sound of Fate knocking at the door. The third and fourth movements are given additional continuity by the absence of a break between them and further by the statement in the fourth movement of one of the themes from the third. This symphony will be discussed in detail later in the book.

Interlude: Away from Description and Toward Pure Sound

The programmatic works we have encountered so far as Primary Listening examples have had a common denominator. The musical material has had quite definite reference to persons or things or events, all of which could be well articulated. In all cases the description was specific enough so that any person willing to make the effort could relate in just about the same way to the progress of the pieces. Much program music needs to have this factor operating if it is to be successful *as program music*—in other words, if the extramusical ideas are to have the same meaning for everyone. To keep that meaning clear, the music must develop, as it has in these examples, along rather precise lines. This includes even an element of continuity and sequence. In several cases what happened at one place depended to some extent on an event that had been depicted or suggested earlier. The function of memory and thematic association is involved here: we can keep the events and personalities separated only to the extent that we can keep the various thematic ideas separated.

This corresponds to drama. If we fail to recognize the characters, how can we follow the development of the play? It is the same thing with reading a novel; character development and manipulation are two of the most difficult tasks confronting a novelist. And we, as readers, need to keep them organized in our minds or *we* get lost.

Music is more abstract, though, than either of these forms, and tonal memory is something we often fail to acquire or exercise except in very small chunks, like the tune of a popular song. In the course of one of those, we usually have to remember only one fairly short melodic idea. Usually the entire piece is based on only that. Larger works demand closer attention. Even though the direction of the action may be clear, it takes a certain amount of musical "cataloguing" to keep things straight.

Not all program music deals with such specific situations or with a defined sequence of events. Sometimes it is merely a mood that is projected, or an event so vague that responding to it becomes a highly personal and individual matter, and one that makes heavy demands on our imagination and sensitivity. This kind of music has developed especially in the course of the twentieth century until today we frequently come face to face with the question of whether there *is* still a program in anything like the traditional sense of the word, or whether we have arrived at the exploration of sound for its own sake. There are many twentieth-century compositions that suggest extra-musical, programmatic reference points in their titles, although such suggestion is often indistinct enough to be both puzzling and tantalizing. In such cases, one wonders if the program has become the flux of emotional response itself rather than the representation of people and things in a developing situation or series of events. In such cases, the concept of program must be modified to include works that function strongest as motivation for free associations in the listener, associations of a highly personal nature that may defy verbalization but that are no less real and significant because of that.

The selections we will now be listening to illustrate this process of the extension of and possibly even the extinction of the idea of program music in its original nineteenth-century sense.

Chapter 20
Impressionism

"The Afternoon of a Faun" is a poem by Stéphane Mallarmé, one of the leading French symbolists of the nineteenth century. It furnishes the program for Debussy's 1892 tone poem *Prelude to "The Afternoon of a Faun."*

Symbolism as an artistic movement was a reaction against the realism that had immediately preceded it. The intent was to suggest only, rather than to state. Especially fascinating to the symbolists was the search for a way of expressing the metaphysical and mysterious truths that could not be reduced to articulate exposition. In its simplest terms, symbolism attempts to use words or visual images to suggest those things which cannot themselves be verbalized or pictured. Because music is generally recognized as the art that is most abstract of all and the one that allows for less literal exposition than any other, it was natural that the symbolists should try to bring their own arts as close to music as possible. To this end, writers often employed language more for its characteristics of sound than for its descriptive capabilities. They attempted to capture the rhythms of music, also, and to exploit its coloristic qualities. Poets in particular were caught up in the movement, and Mallarmé was among its leaders. His "Afternoon of a Faun" was one of the most important and influential works of its type.

All of this is very ethereal-sounding. We are so accustomed to the use of words for descriptive purposes that we seldom get around to questioning their complete effectiveness. Try explaining, even to yourself, how love or desire or hate or unhappiness feels. In all likelihood, you will wind up simply comparing it to another situation, e.g., "Love makes me feel as though . . ." or "It makes me feel the same as. . . ." Trying to articulate emotional experiences is a hum-

Illustration 20. OARSMEN AT CHATOU.
Auguste Renoir. The absence of color in this reproduction eliminates some of the most exciting aspects of Impressionist art. Because Debussy had instrumental color as much in mind as harmonic color, we would lose a dimension in his music if, for instance, his *Prelude to "The Afternoon of a Faun"* were to be performed on a piano. National Gallery of Art, Washington D.C. Gift of Sam A. Lewisohn 1951. Reproduced by permission.

bling thing; we soon appreciate the limitations of language. The symbolists were faced with the same problem, and they sometimes tried to solve it by using language to suggest situations, often vague and ill-defined and mysterious, that would arouse, through reader response and imagination, the sort of feelings or concepts they were after. It was all a highly sophisticated artistic movement, perhaps most successful among artists themselves, but making the attempt to understand it is a prerequisite to fully understanding Debussy's composition. Because of his sympathy for the objectives and methods of the symbolists, Debussy tried to release in music some of the things the poet Mallarmé had tried to release with words.

A faun is a mythical creature, half man and half goat, drawn from Roman religious lore. In Mallarmé's poem, a faun is lounging in

the misty heat of midday, hazily reminiscing about nymphs and wondering whether he had really had an encounter with them or had just imagined it in dreams. The language is extremely sensuous, full of innuendo rather than direct statement, subtle rhythms and rhymes—all about as misty as the faun's recollections. The implications of the situation are far more important than the situation itself, as is always the case with symbolism. What individual readers make of it all is apt to vary widely with personal sensitivity and response. Debussy's "problem" was to translate this into sound.

In addition to symbolism, another influence on Debussy's musical procedures came from the painters with whom he was closely associated and whose aesthetic stance he admired. This group, including Monet and Renoir, were known as Impressionists (see Illustration 20), and they attracted a number of other artists who followed their lead. Among them was the American, Paul Sawyier (see Illustration 21). Their objectives were to capture on

Illustration 21. SEVENTH POOL, KENTUCKY RIVER. C. 1908–1913, watercolor, $13\frac{9}{16} \times 20\frac{7}{8}''$. Paul Sawyier (American, 1865–1917). Sawyier was an important American painter who adopted the Impressionistic style pioneered by Monet, Renoir, and others in France.
Collection of the University of Kentucky Art Museum. Gift of Mr. Paul Borders in Memory of Mrs. Theodore T. Jones, 79.50.2.

canvas the impressions, momentary and illusive, that our visual senses present in such fleeting ways. The technique they employed was to place pigment on canvas in splotches of color rather than in a series of lines to delineate the forms and figures. Because the oils were built up in relatively heavy layers, the light and shadow played upon them and added a fresh dimension to the paintings. There is a kind of sparkle to the Impressionists' work that is usually absent from canvases where the pigment is brushed on smoothly, creating a more glossy surface. Debussy was enamored of their craftsmanship, and some of what he does with musical sound can be related to their techniques. For this reason he is usually classified as a musical Impressionist, the first and most innovative of a large group of composers who followed his example in their own individual ways.

All of this has an interesting way of translating into music. Let's begin with symbolism as opposed to direct statement. Musical phrasing moves us from one place to another in a direct line, so to speak. We feel that we have arrived somewhere at the end of a phrase; we might even be able to draw a line to represent the contour of the phrase. This is directed movement, achieved by the process of start–pause, start–pause through a piece, and it is one way to control our responses. What happens if the phrasing is so irregular or so inconsistent that we lose a sense of direction and expectancy? We tend to "drift"—and this is one way to suggest rather than to assert. Debussy uses it.

We have considered tonic notes and harmony and how we feel a sense of completion when we return to the tonic after having been away for a while. This is another way to direct the movement in music. What happens if we set up no such expectancy, no real sense of tonic to depart from and return to? Again we have drift, and again Debussy uses it.

We have also considered the use of dissonance and consonance to encourage a feeling of tension followed by relaxation. Suppose dissonance is used in a different way, so that it never really resolves into consonance. Then we have lost still more of the sense of musical direction. Suppose, too, that the dissonance is so cloaked in warm, evocative instrumental color that we feel no sense of acute discomfort, as we did in Schubert's "The Erl King," for instance, but rather just a vague feeling of lack of resolution. This is still another way of obscuring the musical statement, and Debussy uses it.

Meter, we know, creates a feeling of decisive rhythmic movement, driving us from accent to accent. Suppose we eliminate much of that metric strength and introduce a sort of floating rhythmic movement without the assertive qualities of metric accent? We have still less direction imposed on our responses. Debussy uses this device too.

You may have guessed how all of this relates to the techniques of the painters as well as to those of the poets. We have compared harmony to color. Why not use harmony in such a way that it functions as splashes of color, not meant to pull us in one direction or another, but merely to stimulate us in a sensual way? Painters used color in that way to some extent when they put it on canvas in splotches rather than in large homogenous areas. In spite of this, however, their work was representational: they painted pictures of recognizable things and people. Because music is more abstract, Debussy could use musical color *just* for itself rather than as the color *of* something. Painters later did precisely that, of course, but this was not one of the objectives of the Impressionists.

Also, why not use an indecisive sort of melodic line made up of brief, intermittent snatches of tune rather than of long, clearly phrased successions of tones? The painters avoided linear formations too. Why not use the sound sensations of the moment for their own sake, rather than as a series of sound events with definite musical direction? The painters tried to capture such fleeting impressions and sensations in their medium.

PRIMARY LISTENING:
Claude Debussy, *Prelude to "The Afternoon of a Faun"*

So Debussy related to the verbal symbolists and to the visual Impressionists. In *Prelude to "The Afternoon of a Faun"* he is really asking us to drift imaginatively with the *suggestions* of the situation, nothing more. He is presenting us with a musical fabric that is just as sensuous as the poem, and with just as little objective statement; the invitation is to revery much like the faun's. The techniques are very deliberate ones, although their effect is of almost complete freedom from the usual restraints.

The initial melodic material is highly chromatic and avoids any feeling for harmonic expectancy (Example 64). The chord that is

Example 64
Debussy, *Prelude to "The Afternoon of a Faun."*

thrown across the orchestra by the harp following that statement is a dissonant one but voiced so that there is no harshness in it (Example 65). The use of the harp is idiomatic in Impressionism; it works like a veil across the sound image, shimmering in much the same way as the pigment on an Impressionist painting.

To accommodate dissonance used in this way, we need to partially redefine it so that we eliminate its suggestion of harshness or unpleasantness. Debussy's audiences needed to reorient themselves too, because this was a new application of harmonic techniques. In a discussion Debussy and a fellow composer, Ernest Guiraud, investigated the question of unresolved dissonance. Debussy played a series of chords, and Guiraud asked what they were. Debussy replied, "Incomplete chords, floating. *Il faut noyer le ton.* [In a musical context, "the tone must be submerged."] One can travel where one wishes and leave by any door. Greater nuances." Guiraud then played a dissonant chord of his own and said that it had to resolve. Debussy: "I don't see that it should. Why?" Later he stated that there is no theory. "You have merely to listen. Pleasure is the law."[1]

Not everyone, however, could make the necessary transitions, and Debussy was criticized in some quarters. This is the eternal problem that innovators face.

The initial melody of the *Prelude* occurs again almost immediately, but the harmonization is changed. After that, the music becomes more and more fragmented. Melodies begin to unfold and are abandoned. We are promised a tune but it never quite develops. And always there is an indeterminate sense of meter, languid and lacking in intensity. The orchestral colors are blended sensuously—woodwinds with horns, strings muted and mysterious, the harp veiling it all. This use of instrumental color is as important in an impressionistic composition as is the use of color in an impressionistic painting. Compare the black and white reproduction of Sawyier's "Seventh Pool, Kentucky River" (Illustration 21) to the color reproduction on the jacket of the book. A piano transcription of Debussy's *Prelude* would delete much of the music's strength in the same way that black and white cannot fully capture Sawyier's expressivity. Silences create reflective pauses rather than abrupt tension areas as

[1]Edward Lockspeiser, *Debussy: His Life and Mind*, London, Cassell, 1962, pp. 206–207.

Example 65
Debussy, *Prelude to "The Afternoon of a Faun."*

in Verdi's "Dies irae"; here they give us only a chance to wander a little further with whatever imagination we may be exercising.

Only after a relatively long period of drifting are we offered what seems to be a fairly well-developed melody (Example 66). This new material is used to create the closest thing to directed statement in the composition. Even here, however, the phrasing is irregular and the harmonic color shifts constantly. The rhythm floats rather than drives; it has a long, slow surge rather than a hand-clapping or foot-stomping urgency.

Eventually we hear a return of the original chromatic melody accompanied by broken chords on the harp and quiet sustained harmonies in the strings. But now the melody is in augmentation, unfolding very slowly in long note values—even more languorous and dreamlike than at first (Example 67). It suggests a feeling of added lethargy, perhaps like the faun's return to midday revery after the half-remembered visions of the nymphs.

The use of thematic material creates an old formal pattern—ternary. One might want to argue that the program itself, as vague as it is, justifies this: the beginning indecisive and faltering because of the faun's hazy mental attitude, the middle section reflecting his dimly recalled episode of passion, and the final portion coinciding with his gradual sinking back into the original mood of mistiness. The dancer Nijinsky found the music so attractive that he choreographed a ballet to be performed with it. Although it is seldom done any more, it proved to be popular at the time and helped give Debussy's musical ideas a wide audience. In France, particularly among younger artists, the general opinion was that Debussy's music was completely successful as an extension of Mallarmé's poetic language and objectives.

Debussy (1862–1918) is credited with originating musical Impressionism with the *Prelude to "The Afternoon of a Faun."* His style was strongly influenced by the Russian harmonic practice that he

Example 66
Debussy, *Prelude to "The Afternoon of a Faun."*

Example 67
Debussy, *Prelude to "The Afternoon of a Faun."*

heard while traveling in that country. He advanced piano technique through his new use of the pedal in support of coloristic harmonic effects. His musical vocabulary includes extensive chromaticism, harmonies derived from old ecclesiastical modes, unresolved dissonance, whole-tone scales, and parallel chords derived from them. He composed songs, piano works, orchestral works (some with voices) of a programmatic nature, opera *(Pelléas et Mélisande)*, and string quartets.

The harmonic vocabulary of Impressionism, with its tolerance for veiled dissonance and its rich chords, was appropriated by popular song writers and arrangers during the 1930s and early 1940s in America. It was entirely in keeping with much of the subject matter—moonlight romance, the poignancy of love, and love's loss. It worked well into the velvety sound of big band arrangements. Even the ballrooms enhanced the atmosphere. Their huge global chandeliers rotating their soft pastel colors, candle-lit tables, sweet-tasting cocktails—all reflected the pseudo-sophistication of the "good years" before American involvement in unending military conflict and civil disenchantment. Much of this remains today in the dimly lit cocktail lounges with electric organs and muted grand pianos. Perhaps our nostalgic fascination with the music and art of that era is motivated by the desire to forget the torment of the fifties and sixties, pretend they never happened, and recapture the moods of an earlier, less tortured social climate. The materials of Impressionism certainly help to reinforce the mood of nostalgia.

There is some evidence that the mood of the thirties and forties as it was expressed in popular music will persist for awhile. A boxed record set entitled *The Great Band Era* (RCA RD 25-K), marketed by *Reader's Digest*, recalls many of the hits of that period as they were originally circulated. One of the most famous of the bands was Glenn Miller's, and his mellow ensemble sound borrowed heavily from the instrumental blendings and other vocabulary of Impressionism. Even the titles of some of his hits reproduced on this set offer a clue to the mood: "Moonlight Cocktail," "Moonlight Mood," and his theme song, "Moonlight Serenade."

We like to identify national styles in art; this is one way of organizing and categorizing to which we have become accustomed. As a rule of thumb, we define the German mood as developmental, symphonic, involved with presenting and working out musical ideas, argumentation, and manipulation. German philosophy is much this way—digging around, rattling ideas until they wear themselves out. We see much German literature as "heavy," with all that the word implies. In contrast, we characterize French art as highly sophisticated, cosmopolitan, sensuous. Even the national food and drink are contrasted—hearty beer and sausages for the Germans versus champagne and soufflés for the French. The French language was for many years the accepted diplomatic language of the Western world, partially because of its subtleties and the many innuendos it can carry. German grammatical syntax, on the other hand, is a continuing problem for students because of its complexities. The French led the styles in fashion for many years because of the appeal they made to the most cultivated and aristocratic social groups. During the same years French attitudes toward sexual expression were widely regarded as more liberated and titillating than others—certainly less puritanical than our own. During the 1920s and 1930s a generic name for pornographic literature was "French novel." The French, then, were seen as leaders in the worldly arts.

Are these things involved in the differences between *Till Eulenspiegel* and *Prelude to "The Afternoon of a Faun"*? Art critics have suggested that they are and that they provide a clue to nationalistic variation. A contrast between gutsy expression and delicate but highly sensuous innuendo is pointed to. Few of us would argue against the use of *Prelude* as background music for a seduction scene in an elegant apartment, complete with soft lights and champagne, but who would use *Till Eulenspiegel* for such a scene? And who would use *Prelude* at a beer blast? Or is this all a gross, even dangerous oversimplification?

SUPPLEMENTAL LISTENING

Many Impressionist recordings are easily available, and almost any will illustrate the musical points made above. Among others:

Claude Debussy, *La Mer.*

Debussy's tone poem is in three movements: "From Dawn to Noon on the Sea," "Play of the Waves," and "Dialogue of the Wind and the Sea." There is no real attempt to portray actual scenes of the sea. Rather, as in *"Afternoon of a Faun,"* the listener is expected to contribute free responses of an affective nature, much as one daydreams while sitting on the shore watching the ocean.

Charles Griffes, *The White Peacock.*

Originally written for piano, this composition is widely performed now in an orchestral version. The composer was inspired by William Sharp's poem, most of which is dreamlike and vague, more oriented toward mood than specific event. An American composer, Griffes (1884–1920) spent most of his short professional life teaching at a boys' school near New York City. His compositions include works for piano and some symphonic tone poems. Typical are *The Pleasure Dome of Kubla Khan* (orchestra) and *The White Peacock.*

Manuel de Falla, *Nights in the Gardens of Spain.*

Scored for piano and orchestra, this composition is in three sections: "In the Generalife," "Distant Dance," and "In the Gardens of the Sierra de Córdoba." In the manner of much Impressionist music, the titles are not meant to arouse any specific programmatic subjects, but only moods suggested by them. Because of the composer's involvement with Andalusian folk song, many of the themes reflect its character, although none are direct quotes of actual songs. De Falla (1876–1946) was a Spanish composer and pianist who spent most of his professional career in Paris, where he was associated with Debussy and other Impressionists. His style exploits Spanish rhythms together with typical Impressionist instrumental color. He is best known for *Nights in the Gardens of Spain*. He also composed operas, ballets, piano works, and other symphonic program music.

Chapter 21
American Traditions

During the years when the nineteenth century was preparing to turn into the twentieth, Charles Ives was working out a musical language that was to identify him as the first important and typically American composer. Ives (1874–1954) was not a professional musician; his real business was insurance. He was immensely successful and became a millionaire. But the sort of musical practices he indulged in were less acceptable to his contemporaries. His work, including music for orchestra, chorus, piano, violin, and solo singing, anticipated most of the avant-garde characteristics that appeared later on in the twentieth century—except for the electronic idioms. Because he was independently wealthy, he was able to indulge his fertile musical imagination without concern for public approval and commercial success. It should be noted, however, that he won the Pulitzer Prize for his Third Symphony.

Ives was not at all enamored of what was commonly believed to be beauty of sound. His interest was much more in graphic expression; dissonance didn't bother him at all if it served his purposes. Rhythmic complexity of the most severe type invaded his musical textures, and he actually threw aside some of the time-honored procedures of notation (like the use of bar lines and key signatures) when those procedures failed to achieve his purposes. But in the area of patriotism he was a dyed-in-the-wool conservative, and he was very much in love with the sounds of America and the New England where he lived. Folk songs, gospel songs, hymns, and patriotic tunes all run through his music and serve for many of his thematic ideas. He was enchanted with the various contradictions in America, the almost cacophonous activity that was so much a part of our country at the turn of the century.

PRIMARY LISTENING:
Charles Ives, "Putnam's
Camp, Redding,
Connecticut," from *Three
Places in New England*

Practically all of these factors are illustrated in his *Three Places in New England*, a work he developed during the years from 1903 to 1914. Listen to the second of its three movements, "Putnam's Camp, Redding, Connecticut." Ives himself supplies the program:

> Near Redding Center, Conn., is a small park preserved as a Revolutionary Memorial; for here General Israel Putnam's soldiers had their winter quarters in 1778–1779. Long rows of stone camp fire-places still remain to stir a child's imagination. The hardships which the soldiers endured and the agitation of a few hot-heads to break camp and march to the Hartford Assembly for relief, is a part of Redding History.
>
> Once upon a "4th of July," some time ago, so the story goes, a child went there on a picnic, held under the auspices of the First Church and the Village Cornet Band. Wandering away from the rest of the children past the camp ground into the woods, he hopes to catch a glimpse of some of the old soldiers. As he rests on the hillside of laurel and hickories, the tunes of the band and the songs of the children grow fainter and fainter;—when—"mirable dictu"—over the trees on the crest of the hill he sees a tall woman standing. She reminds him of a picture he has of the Goddess of Liberty,—but the face is sorrowful—she is pleading with the soldiers not to forget their "cause" and the great sacrifices they have made for it. But they march out of camp with fife and drum to a popular tune of the day. Suddenly a new national note is heard. Putnam is coming over the hills from the center,—soldiers turn back and cheer. The little boy awakes, he hears the children's songs and runs down past the monument to "listen to the band" and join in the games and dances.
>
> The repertoire of national airs at the time was meagre. Most of them were of English origin. It is a curious fact that a tune very popular with the American soldiers was "The British Grenadiers." A captain in one of Putnam's regiments put it to words, which were sung for the first time in 1779 at a patriotic meeting in the Congregational Church in Redding Center; the text is both ardent and interesting.[1]

Compare the opening section of "Putnam's Camp" (Example 68) with the beginning of *Petrushka*. There is the same hubbub of activity, the same type of musical cross-purposes, the same metric complexity, the same general sense of dissonance as a textural element. In contrast to Debussy's use of dissonance, however, it creates an atmosphere of excitement and even confusion. What other factors may account for this?

II

Notice the appearance of two march themes, similar to the appearance of the two dancers in *Petrushka* with their contradictory accompaniments (Example 69). The difference is in the Americanism of the sound in Ives. Many of us cannot remember the time when the Fourth of July was accompanied by the brand of celebration represented here, but it was a very real part of the scene for Ives's

Example 69
Ives, "Putnam's Camp" from
Three Places in New England.
Copyright 1935 by Mercury Music, Inc.
Used by permission.

generation and several that followed. Today even firecrackers are outlawed except in commercial, professionally operated displays. But parades, speeches, flag-waving, and picnics all were once the stuff of which the Fourth was made, and this is the atmosphere that Ives is trying to recreate in sound. There is something peculiarly American about all of this. The sound itself is far more descriptive than words.

We know the application of the term *polymetric*, and this is one way to explain the musical complexity. Another factor is the simultaneous sounding of different key centers. This is *polytonality* or, when there are only two keys involved, *bitonality*. One person playing a guitar in G and another playing one in F would create the same sort of conflict. A pianist playing the right hand in F and the left hand in G would do it too. The effect is quite appropriate for the scene that Ives is dealing with. While he did not invent polytonality, he was the first American composer to exploit what became an important part of the harmonic experimentation of the twentieth century. Actually, Stravinsky builds one of his most important thematic ideas in *Petrushka* on the principle of bitonality. It occurs first in the second tableau, which was not discussed above. There it is used to represent Petrushka himself. Stravinsky and Ives were not borrowing ideas from one another, however, because there was no possible contact between them at the time. This is simply an example of the sort of opening up of musical horizons that marked the end of the nineteenth century and the beginning of the twentieth. Innovative ideas were common to all the arts as well as to many phases of political and social life in the West.

In *Petrushka* we saw the constant shifting of meter and even the simultaneous use of different meters; this was illustrated visually in Example 55. Ives's notational approach is somewhat different in "Putnam's Camp." He accomplishes the cross-accents by means of conflicting barring so that although the meters are the same in all orchestral voices, the bars begin and end at different times (Example 70).

Everyone will recognize the quotations of familiar tunes and the way they are worked into the musical fabric as reminders of the

Example 70
Ives, "Putnam's Camp" from
Three Places in New England.
Copyright 1935 by Mercury Music, Inc.
Used by permission.

locale and occasion. The most prominent one is "The British Grenadiers," to which Ives refers in his program notes (Example 71). Apparent, too, is the change of mood that illustrates the child's wandering to the hillside and the daydreams there. The fascination with sound as an expressive medium—that is, pure sound apart from melodic, rhythmic, and harmonic manipulation—is another characteristic twentieth-century mechanism. We found it in *Petrushka*, in

Example 71
Ives, "Putnam's Camp" from
Three Places in New England.
Copyright 1935 by Mercury Music, Inc.
Used by permission.

Till Eulenspiegel, in *Prelude to "The Afternoon of a Faun,"* and it is equally apparent here. Because this use of sound has become so much a part of the musical environment of our own time in the century, it is difficult to project back into a time when it was shocking and unacceptable to many listeners. Many critics engaged in debates about the differences between sound and music; noise and music became a focal point. Where does a piece stop being music and start being merely noise? Punk rock has come in for its share of similar criticism, as has the frenetic vocal style of many soul singers.

His untraditional use of orchestral instruments was one factor that inhibited Ives's acceptance in America until the century was well advanced—too late, really, for the composer to enjoy the status and recognition he deserved. His disregard of harmonic rules and conventional rhythmic practice alienated most of his fellow musicians also. Acceptance came only after his death, as is so often the case with imaginative and innovative individuals.

Thinking in terms of formal organization, you will recognize the general tripartite pattern, with the dream sequence as B. Here again, as in Debussy, it serves a programmatic as well as a purely formal purpose—an example of why many critics and analysts believe that content cannot be isolated from form, that they work together in some sort of inseparable way to define the expressive experience.

The patches of sound and the cross-relationships of musical texture are first cousins to several techniques associated with the visual arts. Collage is found in many twentieth-century works of art of the "wall hanging" variety. It is simply the juxtaposition of varying and often sharply contrasting textures side by side or even over-lapping. Burlap with metal with wood with silk, for instance, creates a collage, and the interest is in the textural variety rather than in any representational character (see Illustration 22). In still photography and movies there is a technique called montage, achieved by double exposure and resulting in two or more simultaneous images, some-times complementary and sometimes contradictory in nature. More

**Illustration 22. THE FORUM
6 P.M.**
Frank Gunter. This work is a
collage. The juxtaposition of
contrasting, even conflicting
textures like tin, wood,
newspaper, etc., is comparable
to Ives's patches of sound and
conflicting musical textures in
his "Putnam's Camp."
Collection of the University of
Kentucky Art Museum, Lexington,
Kentucky. Gift of the artist.

recently in films and television there is an interesting procedure that
results from the film-cutting process: a quick succession of related or
unrelated images flashed momentarily on the screen. This is the
source of many sight gags, but it has other more serious applications
as well, such as the representation of rapid memory recall. All of
these devices are related to what Stravinsky and Ives achieved in
sound in *Petrushka* and "Putnam's Camp." In both cases the
techniques strongly support the programmatic ideas.

   Still another association with sister arts can be suggested. A writing technique that came to be known as "stream of consciousness" grew out of the work of James Joyce in *Ulysses*. It was an attempt to reproduce the almost spastic way our minds work when our thinking flashes from situation to situation and from image to image without any real sense of continuity. The final (and most controversial) chapter of *Ulysses* brims over with this style of writing. There is some relationship to that style and the way themes wander in and out of "Putnam's Camp," sometimes even overlapping one another but never being fully developed.

Finally, we should recognize that the use of nationalistic musical quotes, by Ives as by most other composers discussed in this part, is an important part of much program music. Here the listeners bring all the associations with them in their back pockets. Assuming a certain stance toward patriotic song, for instance, nothing achieves the expression of patriotism quite as quickly and decisively as to quote an appropriate tune—except, possibly, waving the flag. Both this sound and this sight are symbolic, and they operate almost instantaneously, assuming that the audience is sensitive to the symbolism. Redding Center, Connecticut, is a place where things happened at a particular time and for particular reasons. Ives uses this information, translating it into musical sound for his own purposes, and the nudge he gives our imagination can move us into all sorts of interesting interpretations.

Only in relatively recent years has America taken Ives's work seriously. We have been slow in this country to recognize our own artists, preferring for many years to borrow our cultural values from Europe. Perhaps this is natural, since we are a nation of immigrants. Until recently it was traditional for performers to seek their training in Europe, to be "discovered" there and then return in triumph, success assured. During the earlier years of the century, especially in the twenties, many painters, novelists, composers, and singers spent their formative years across the Atlantic, mostly in Paris. Those were also the years of a developing art form that was to prove the most significant American contribution to musical style: jazz. But it was largely ignored here as an art, and often was even derided. Even today it is less familiar and understood than it deserves to be in the country of its birth. An occasional step is made, however. One was the introduction of a joint resolution in the U.S. House of Representatives and Senate on February 28, 1973, which reads: "Resolved by the Senate and House of Representatives of the United States of America in Congress assembled, That the national music of the United States is declared to be jazz." Although this reluctance to recognize and reward Americanism did not inhibit Ives, he was sometimes bitter about it. He was actually using national idioms, yet the vast majority of people could see his musical innovations only as distortions of convention. Determined to share his ideas, though, he published his own music with his own money, often adding explanatory comments to the editions. It's a good thing that he could afford to do so; we might otherwise have lost his music because of sheer neglect and disinterest. But it opens wide the question of public reaction to imaginative ideas. How many of them do we throw on the garbage heap of popular disdain and ridicule simply because of our ingrained prejudices and lack of vision?

SUPPLEMENTAL LISTENING

Charles Ives is unique, and many of the discussion points above cannot be duplicated in the music of other composers. However, there are compositions that do feature quotations from familiar musical Americana. They include these works by the American composer Aaron Copland:

Rodeo.

Originally a ballet, this is most often performed as a four-movement suite. Although not familiar to many listeners, some of the themes are taken from folk and cowboy songs. Included are "If He'd Be a Buckaroo," "Sis Joe," and "Bonyparte."

Billy the Kid.

Concert versions are usually of a suite drawn from the music of the complete ballet. As in *Rodeo*, there are references to cowboy songs scattered throughout the score. They include "Goodbye Old Paint," "The Old Chisholm Trail," and "Git Along Little Dogies."

Appalachian Spring.

The setting for this ballet, for which the composer won the Pulitzer Prize, is the countryside of Pennsylvania, in particular the section occupied by the Shaker sect. The principal quotation is of a Shaker song, "The Gift to Be Simple," which carries strong implications of the philosophy of that group and their mode of life.

Aaron Copland is a composer, author, and lecturer. His literary works include the popular *What to Listen For in Music*. His compositions feature American folk and traditional music, often used programmatically. Strongly conventional and "popular" in style, Copland is also capable of writing in dissonant, incisive, and very sparse textures. He is probably most famous for his ballets (e.g., *Billy the Kid, Appalachian Spring*), but his work also includes film scores (*Of Mice and Men*, others), orchestral works, symphonies, piano works, opera *(The Tender Land)*, and songs, including some folk settings.

Chapter 22
Beyond Programmatic Convention

PRIMARY LISTENING:
Krzysztof Penderecki,
*Threnody to the Victims
of Hiroshima*

With Krzysztof Penderecki's composition *Threnody to the Victims of Hiroshima* we move deeply into the twentieth century, programmatically as well as musically, carrying even further the innovations of Stravinsky and Ives.

From the mechanical standpoint, we are apt to infer from the instrumental sounds of *Threnody to the Victims of Hiroshima* that there is some electronic manipulation going on. This has become a common method of sound production since the advent of an electronic instrument, the Moog, and the use of electronic modification of all sorts in rock and background music for films. The roots of this style, however, are in experiments made by "serious" composers who were trying to achieve expressive results that were not possible with the standard orchestral instruments they had inherited. Out of these experiments came ways to utilize sounds produced electronically or altered by means of tape modification and the like.

However, all the aural dissonance and "distortion" in Penderecki's piece are produced with standard orchestral string instruments. In order to achieve the effects, Penderecki was forced to develop an entirely new vocabulary of notation, including directions for performance. Not only are the players required to produce unaccustomed sounds from unaccustomed parts of their instruments, but they are also asked to manipulate pitches of quarter-tones as opposed to the usual half-step intervals which to most of us are doctrine (Example 72).

Abkürzungen und Symbole
Abbreviations and symbols

Erhöhung um einen Viertelton sharpen a quarter-tone	ǂ
Erhöhung um einen Dreiviertelton sharpen three quarter-tones	ǂǂ
Erniedrigung um einen Viertelton flatten a quarter-tone	♭
Erniedrigung um einen Dreiviertelton flatten three quarter-tones	♭
höchster Ton des Instrumentes (unbestimmte Tonhöhe) highest note of the instrument (no definite pitch)	↟
zwischen Steg und Saitenhalter spielen play between bridge and tailpiece	↑
Arpeggio zwischen Steg und Saitenhalter (4 Saiten) arpeggio on 4 strings behind the bridge	⇈⇈
auf dem Saitenhalter spielen (arco), Bogenstrich über den Saiten- halter (in einem Winkel von 90⁰ zu dessen Längsachse) play on the tailpiece (arco) by bowing the tailpiece at an angle of 90⁰ to its longer axis	⊥
auf dem Steg spielen (arco), Bogenstrich über das Holz des Steges senkrecht zu dessen rechter Schmalseite play on the bridge by bowing the wood of the bridge at a right angle at its right side	⊤
Schlagzeugeffekt: mit dem Frosch oder mit der Fingerspitze auf die Decke klopfen Percussion effect: strike the upper sounding board of the violin with the nut or the finger-tips	𝆑
mehrere unregelmäßige Bogenwechsel several irregular changes of bow	⊓∨
molto vibrato	⌇
sehr langsames Vibrato mit ¼ Ton-Frequenzdifferenz durch Fingerverschiebung very slow vibrato with a ¼ tone frequency difference produced by sliding the finger	⌒
sehr schnelles, nicht rhythmisiertes Tremolo very rapid non rhythmisized tremolo	✕
ordinario	ord.
sul ponticello	s. p.
sul tasto	s. t.
col legno	c. l.
legno battuto	l. batt.

The notation is equally unusual. Instead of bars or tempos or standard symbols for note values, the instructions are given in terms of time spans: so many seconds of this, so many seconds of that (Example 73).

Some of the most unusual and startling effects are those that sound "picky" and percussive. The page of notation looks about as

Example 73
Penderecki, *Threnody to the Victims of Hiroshima.*

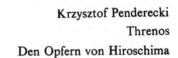

Krzysztof Penderecki

Threnos

Den Opfern von Hiroschima

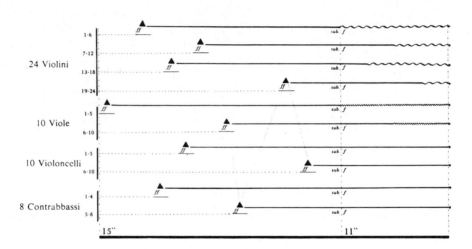

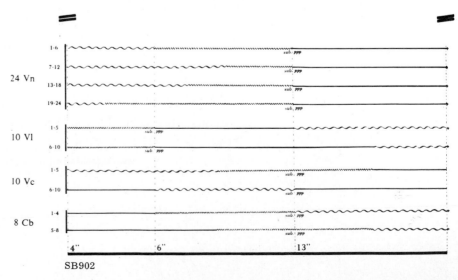

SB902

chaotic as the rhythmic patterns. As a result, we have an extremely graphic representation of the sound (Example 74).

An increasing number of twentieth-century compositions call for similar reorientation on the part of conductors and performers. Much of the scoring looks like schematic diagrams bearing little or

Example 74
Penderecki, *Threnody to the Victims of Hiroshima.*
Copyright © 1961 by Deshon Music, Inc., and PWM Editions. Used with permission. All rights reserved.

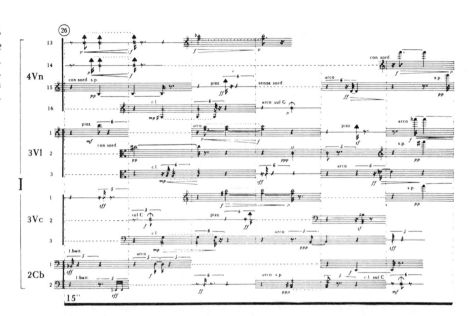

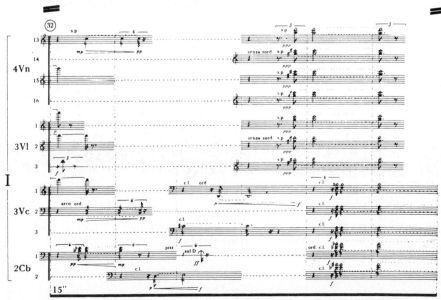

no relation to the notational symbolism that has been conventional for many centuries. This means that new skills must be acquired by people who make music, new signals attempted by composers, new ways found to evoke sound from instruments—even, in the end, new instruments. As we observed before, the very nature and effect of sound itself are being investigated more and more thoroughly as greater knowledge of acoustics is gained.

What expressive purpose is served by this approach to cacophony? Some words have assumed a very special kind of emotional significance in the world of the twentieth century. Hiroshima is one of them. It is not only a place and an event; it has become a symbol for total destruction itself and for the social, political, and military forces that precipitated it. Penderecki, who is Polish, called his composition a threnody and dedicated it to those who experienced at first hand the air raid that destroyed their city and many of its people. A threnody is a dirge or funeral piece, a song of lamentation. Penderecki's conception is an unusual one but perhaps the most appropriate expression possible for the event he is depicting as well as for the extensions of musical materials that had been made by 1956, the date of his composition.

There might be a number of suitable ways to structure a musical representation of the bombing of Hiroshima. One could approach it descriptively, beginning with the take-off of the plane and moving on through its trip to the city, the release of the bomb, and the resultant chaos. Given the advances in instrumental technique that had been made by 1956, including the advent of electronic music, a certain amount of realism could be brought to bear. Or a composer might want to deal with the residents of the city—the hustle and bustle of normal life, the interruption of the bomb's detonation, the search for shelter that followed. Both these approaches, and other possible ones, might portray a series of events in storytelling fashion, trying to capture the chronology of the action.

Penderecki's vision went beyond chronology or the action, however. His purpose was not to mimic the sound of planes or bombs or human screams. He was more interested in the emotional content of the experience—but not its glorification. Mozart and Verdi idealized and glorified the fear and awe of the Day of Judgment. But for Penderecki, as for many people, there was nothing about Hiroshima that merited idealization or that suggested the use of "normal" musical materials such as attractive melody, colorful harmonization, definable rhythmic manipulation. The event itself was abnormal, and normal material would not capture its essence.

Given the need to eliminate all but the bare emotional content of such a horrifying experience, what use can be made of sound? Apparently for Penderecki the sound itself must equate exactly with the ebb and flow of tensions, the tormented and frenetic urge to escape, the undirected sheer terror, the pain—the entire web of physical dissonance. And dissonance is Penderecki's tool. But here dissonance is used *as an objective in itself*—to assault our nerves as the events of Hiroshima assaults our psychic sensibilities. Every sound he entices from the orchestra of stringed instruments is meant to induce that single effect. How successful he was depends to a large extent on the sensitivities of his audience. Here are some written comments that were made by a group of college students who listened to a recording of this music without knowing the title of the composition. Their responses were in terms of affect, but not in reference to the situation of Hiroshima because they had no descriptive title to guide them. Compare them to your own reactions:

> Harsh. Terror. Excitement. Confusion. Grotesque.
>
> . . . jumble of every sound imaginable—unearthly. Loudest sounds assault me *physically*—made my eyebrows hurt.
>
> *Why* does there have to be music like this? The world could survive much better without it, I'm sure. My mind doesn't wander because I'm upset. My stomach hurts.
>
> *Violent!* Alone—running—fleeing—survival struggle—don't *like it!* Pain—sorrow—depressing—mysterious—too *powerful*—makes me feel mean and violent—don't care for it!
>
> A tense uptight feeling. It could make you go crazy if you listened to it for very long at a time. I don't like this piece of music. Sounds of death and fright.
>
> Confusion—questions—where are the answers? Running away—leave me alone—rat-race—let me think—where is there true and honest help? *Destruction*—where did everything go? Breaking apart. Can *I* help? Please stop. It's pressing me down—what about the others?

These are only a few examples, but they are typical. Remember that these students did not know the title of the piece, which has no fuller written program, and did not have any other clues at all.

The responses show that Penderecki communicated precisely what he wanted to communicate. They tell us that sound *can*, without words or program, affect us in certain definable ways emotionally and mentally. All that the title adds here is a specific direction: the reason for the response, its rationale. Collectively the student responses were the affective response at its most powerful.

Illustration 23. CHOCORUA II.
Frank Stella, 1966. Is this art? Nonrepresentational works in all media
have often prompted the question. It is as difficult to build fences
around paintings as it is to limit the definitions of music or its proper
range of expression.
Collection of the J. B. Speed Art Museum, Louisville, Kentucky.

Like any other emotional effect, the affective response varies widely in dynamics, and the strength of response that this composition calls forth would be inappropriate in many other contexts—the situation itself would seldom be so overwhelming. But the real point—and a difficult one to come to terms with philosophically—is that musical sound without words or program can apparently produce only a *generalized* emotion. Joy. Pain. Sorrow. Confusion. Peace. Only words or a program can tell us joy in what, pain for what reason, sorrow for what situation, and so forth. This is precisely why we say that music is the most abstract of the arts.

The question is often asked, "Is this really music? It's interesting and provocative as sound, but is it *music?*" That depends on what you mean by "music." Although the shape of Penderecki's work is unusual and less than tuneful, there is melody—pitch that sometimes sustains and sometimes changes. And there is rhythm. It is organized in new ways that are not based on a steadily recurring beat or on metric impulses, but still the *elements* of rhythm are present—sounds that vary in length; accents of some kind, however irregular or unpredictable. There is also harmony to the extent that there are different pitches sounding simultaneously. Some might argue that there is a difference between noise and music and that this is noise. Is a drum a musical instrument? It makes rhythmic noises. Some drums are tuned to a pitch, others are not. Do you *always* hear the drum as a part of the pitch character of a composition?

The more important question is "Can one define music at all?" It is easy to overlook the fact that definitions clarify but also limit. Once we have arrived at one, it gives us a useful handle for understanding things and ideas. But it also blocks out everything that doesn't fit that description. This can and often does effect a closure, a settling of the issue, as it were. But we have had to modify our definitions of many things and ideas. Are we still a democracy in the original sense of that word? How free is free enterprise in the 1980s? What is pornography? What constitutes marriage at present? Would anyone presume to describe, since Kinsey, sexual "normalcy?" What do we mean when we refer to a liberal education? The list of questions could go on almost interminably.

Much the same upheavals have affected our concepts of music. The things that distinguish the twentieth century in all the arts are the rash of experimentation and the development of new devices that enlarge not only the range of expression but its very direction (Illustration 23). In the wake of all the activity, we need to keep our definitions wide open; otherwise we are apt to close out a lot of exciting possibilities.

The student remarks raise an important related question about music in the world of artistic expression. Most people seem to have definite preconceptions about what is or is not acceptable as music. This is where our definitions get in the way. For some reason, most of us expect music to be pretty or appealing or emotionally warm or beautiful—we want to like it, in other words. We do not have the same attitudes toward many other arts. We accept violence and pain, suffering and tragedy, in stage, television, and screen productions. Often such subject matter attracts the largest audiences. Even Greek drama centuries ago was based on the concept that the tragic situation furnished a catharsis for the audience, a means of purging the emotional tensions that all of us are prey to. We empathize with the actors, and in the process we release some of our own suffering, frustration, and pain. In literature too we accept without question situations that are ugly, people who are despicable, settings that are depressing in their physical or spiritual squalor. Even our sense of humor is often triggered by harshness—we call it black humor. Violence in cartoon shows has been assaulted by many commentators; others have defended it as a means of working out our aggressions in a harmless way. We laugh uproariously when comedians insult one another or the audience or a public figure. All of these we find acceptable, although each has its basis to some degree in our most inhumane and least "beautiful" impulses.

Why do we insist on screening this type of expression out of music? Even with those situations that are themselves not beautiful—such as the situation described in the "Dies irae"—we prefer that the musical expression somehow beautify the content. Think back to the protest songs of the 1960s. Many were harsh denunciations of establishment practice, but all the music was pleasant and appealing. Much of it was even based on folk style.

Check again the student responses to *To the Victims of Hiroshima*. Some of them reject the music itself because of the emotional reactions it creates. After the title was announced almost everyone "accepted" the composition on its own terms. But they were accepting the *program*, not the music *for itself* or the emotional content *for itself*. Some refused to accept the piece even then: they felt that the subject matter was not suitable for musical representation. It is important to see that those who did accept the piece accepted it principally because of the programmatic association: they were tolerating the music only because the program was understandable. What this really means is that they were relating more strongly to the dramatic situation, as in a play or movie or novel, than they were to the expressive content of the music *as music*.

If music is indeed abstract and generates a sort of general

emotional response, why are we willing to tolerate only pleasantness? Is it because we need to have ugliness or pain or tension explained so that we know what motivates it? We are not that insistent with beauty. Whatever the reason, large masses of people have rejected enormous amounts of contemporary music because it is not "pretty." Is that, by itself, a valid reason to reject any artistic expression?

As this relates to program music, can naked emotion of any kind ever function as its own program? Are we willing to accept it without verbalization or explanation? Do we insist on reasons? Unless we are able to relate to emotional sound for its own sake, we will block out of our experience a great many contemporary compositions and performers. The next example is a case in point.

SUPPLEMENTAL LISTENING   Very few recordings raise all the particular associations that are discussed above. The same composer's *Dies Irae* does come close. That piece uses words, though, so the application is not exactly the same. On the other hand, there are compositions in which the unusual use of sound has a programmatic significance other than sheer expression. One such is:

Arthur Honegger: *Pacific 231.*   The title refers to a type of locomotive with which Honegger was much taken. Although the composer claims to be imitating the visual impressions and powerful sensations of the locomotive rather than its actual sounds, the work is quite realistic. It moves from a slow, laborious start (complete with hissing steam) through gathering momentum to high speed with driving rhythm. Honegger (1892–1955), a Swiss composer born in France, was first brought to wide recognition by *Pacific 231.* He was a member of the group known as "The Six," based in Paris. Among his compositions are a number of operas, ballets, symphonies and programmatic instrumental works, songs, and many film scores.

Perhaps no other stylistic movement in jazz has been so difficult to understand and relate to as the type that is best known as "The New Wave." Among those most closely associated with it have been John Coltrane and Ornette Coleman and, through their influence, Pharoah Sanders, Sun Ra, Cecil Taylor, Anthony Braxton, Albert Aylers, and Eric Dolphy. Their work can be somewhat related to that of academic composers like Penderecki in its emotional intensity and concern for greater extensions of the purely sound-producing possibilities of the instruments. Much of this can be traced to the artistic objectives of the New Wavers.

One of the leading exponents of the search for complete freedom from thematic and rhythmic constraints was tenor and soprano saxophonist John Coltrane (1926–1967), who began his career with big bands (Dizzy Gillespie and others) and later played with trumpeter Miles Davis. In 1960 he formed his own quartet, after which he stayed with the small-group format, although he changed personnel with some frequency. His style includes tremendously active bursts of sound, high-pitched and anguished tone quality, frequently static harmonic underpinning, and harsh but technically masterful and extended solo work.

Alto saxophonist and composer Ornette Coleman (born 1930) is one of the leaders in avant-garde, or New Wave, jazz. Sometimes rejecting the use of key centers altogether, he also seeks increasing freedom from the restrictions of predetermined thematic material. Although firmly grounded in "traditional" jazz style, his instrumental approach is characterized by a highly emotional tone.

For many decades, jazz improvisation took place within the limits imposed by form and harmonic progression. Although the type of melodic development that was indulged in was often sharply different from performer to performer, there was a consistency of adherence to the length of each chorus and relatively little attempt to extend the harmonic framework too severely. However, a number of the more restless players felt confined within such limits. Their ultimate goal was complete freedom from all thematic, harmonic, and rhythmic restrictions. Coltrane broke some of the chains, so to speak, when he became enamored of long passages during which he did little else than search at length for some apparently hidden implications in the music. Sometimes this was done quietly, sometimes with bursts of lightning sound, sometimes with nervously erratic slashes; frequently it was confined to a single chord or to a single series of scale tones. One wag reported that he had gone to hear the saxophonist play at a local club and all he heard was 45 minutes of one chord. Exaggerated as that may be, the implication is clear. The controls of harmonic movement had begun to crumble along with thematic reference and rhythmic regularity.

In 1960 Ornette Coleman gathered a double quartet of jazz musicians in a studio, and together they broke away from all limitations on spontaneous improvision. For over 40 minutes they worked individually and in concert totally without any preconceptions of material on which to base their performance: no themes, no harmonic restraints, no rhythmic limitations. The session was issued on a disc entitled *Free Jazz* (Atlantic: S–1364), and it was an important turning point in jazz style. Since that time Coleman has worked with numerous other musicians, and often their playing is an extension of the freedoms they first exploited in 1960. "Civilization

Day," from the album *Science Fiction,* is an example of that facet of the New Wave.

PRIMARY LISTENING:
"Civilization Day," Ornette Coleman, alto sax; Don Cherry, pocket trumpet; Charlie Haden, bass; Billy Higgins, drums (record set)

The opening burst of ensemble activity sets the tone for the rest of the piece. This is followed by a long free improvisation by Don Cherry on pocket trumpet. The only responsibility assumed by the drummer and bass player in such a context is to pick up what motivic ideas Cherry may project, respond to them, develop them in their own way. The music proceeds with such enormous speed and almost frantic interplay that these bursts of dialogue are difficult to isolate from the generally dissonant fabric. You can pick some of them up, though, if you listen to the relationship between the trumpet and bass.

Following Cherry's investigations, Coleman enters and continues the improvisations in much the same manner, with the bass and drums again responding as they wish. The cut on your record set contains only the first 5 minutes of the original piece, fading when Coleman is finishing up his solo. The final minute of the performance (not reproduced) is taken up with a drum solo and a final dazzling display of virtuosic passage work based on parts of the opening section as well as on motives that have been utilized in the preceding solos.

Quite apart from any breaking away from musical controls, many players of the New Wave became deeply involved in bursts of emotional sound, using their instruments in ways that often resembled human screaming, moaning, and crying. Some of that is perceptible on "Civilization Day," although not carried to the extremes found in many performances by other players. Like Penderecki's insistence on pure emotion rather than on easily defined form, these sounds suggest that emotional intensity becomes its own form, not translatable into symbolism other than its own.

The hazards for the listener are clear. There is no program even in the title in this music, as there was in Penderecki's, no clear way to "explain" the almost hysterical character of the playing at times. If one is unable to relate to the anguish in many of the sounds and at the same time cannot locate motivic threads to help integrate the music aurally, there is little else to cling to. Jazz had traditionally been built on a theme-and-variations principle, where the theme was fairly clear to both the listener and the performer. Eliminating that has placed the listener in a new dimension as far as his involvement is concerned. For this reason many musicians themselves no longer refer to this type of music as jazz, preferring to call it "black music." The implication is that this must come out of some experience unique to blacks. Although he did not have this particular piece in mind, James Baldwin, the widely read black novelist and essayist, did identify with the emotional intensity when he wrote:

> He stood there, wide-legged, humping the air, filling his barrel chest, shivering in the rags of his twenty-odd years, and screaming through the horn, "Do you love me? Do you love me"?
>
> The boy was blowing with his lungs and guts out of his short past; and somewhere in the past, in gutters or gang fights . . . he had received a blow from which he would never recover. . . .
>
> The men on the stand stayed with him, cool and at a little distance, adding and questioning. . . . But each man knew that the boy was blowing for every one of them. . . . [1]

In a similar vein, and one that reinforces the New Wave search for freedom, are statements that John Coltrane made about himself and some of the men with whom he performed frequently. Referring to Pharoah Sanders, he said:

> [He] is constantly trying to get more and more deeply into the human foundations of music . . . He's dealing in the human experience. . . . He's always trying to allow his spiritual self to be his guide. He's dealing . . . in energy, in integrity, in essences. [2]

Of the drummer Rashied Ali, Coltrane said:

> The way he plays allows the soloist maximum freedom. I can really choose just about any direction at just about any time in the confidence that it will be compatible with what he's doing. . . . he's laying down multi-directional rhythms all the time. [3]

Of himself, he said:

> You just keep going all the way, as deep as you can. You keep trying to get right down to the crux. [4]

Is this the program, then, this real-life anguish hammered into musical expression?

What we accept or reject as individuals is our own business. The extent to which we can relate, regardless of skin color, to nakedly emotional expression helps us locate the boundaries within which we are willing or able to tolerate what we conceive to be art. Jazz will change, programmatic concepts in music will change, and musical

[1] Quoted in Louis M. Savary, S. J. (ed.), *Listen to Love*, New York, Regina Press, 1973, p. 31.

[2] Quoted on liner of *Coltrane: Live at the Village Vanguard Again*, Impulse: AS–9124.

[3] *Ibid.*

[4] *Ibid.*

materials will change, because the social and artistic climate within which human beings express themselves will change. Our responses to musical experience will be determined largely in terms of our capacity to open ourselves to new horizons and a larger vision of ourselves and others. People make music and people listen to it. New Wave jazz, along with many of the more avant-garde idioms in "classical" music, does not have a large public. "Civilization Day" may go far to explain why. But before we reject such expression out of hand, it might be wise to ask on what basis we close out of our experiences all those that fail to fit inside the fences that we each build, in private, for our ears, our minds, and our spirits.

SUPPLEMENTAL LISTENING   Although the audience for the New Wave in jazz is not large, the devotion of its adherents has made it possible to issue many recordings with some degree of profit to recording studios and performers. A variety of listening experiences can be found on the following:

> *Free Jazz.* Atlantic: S–1364.
> *John Coltrane Live at the Village Vanguard Again.* Impulse: AS–9124.
> *Dollar Brand with Gato Barbieri: Confluence.* Arista: AL–1003.
> *Anthony Braxton: New York, Fall 1974.* Arista: AL–4032.

Chapter 23

The Uses of Percussion

With all the experimentation and the fascination with the possibilities of new sounds, it would have been strange indeed if someone had failed to investigate the use of percussion as a performing medium. Although the idea of a percussion ensemble is not a foreign one to many cultures, there had been no great emphasis on such music in the Western tradition until this century. Edgard Varèse's *Ionisation* is one of the pioneering works for such an ensemble. As the score indicates, the principal interest is in the rhythm, even though some of the instruments are pitched and some even capable of melodic passages (Example 75).

PRIMARY LISTENING:
Edgard Varèse, *Ionisation*

When melodic and harmonic considerations assume a decreased importance in the musical fabric, other elements naturally command more attention. In *Ionisation* timbre and dynamics enter strongly into the sound complexes, not only as areas of interest but also as means by which the form can be perceived. In order to exploit timbre fully, the composition was scored for a wide variety of instruments, including:

Two sirens, pitched differently
Two tam-tams (Chinese gongs), different in pitch
Gong
Cymbals

Example 75
Varèse, *Ionisation.*
Copyright © 1934 by Colfranc Music
Publishing Corporation, New York. By
courteous permission of E.C. Kerby
Ltd., Toronto, General Agent.

to Nicolas Slonimsky

IONISATION

(for Percussion Ensemble of 13 Players)

Edgard Varèse

Three bass drums, differing in size
Bongos
Snare drums
Cuban gourd, notched like a saw and scraped
Slap-sticks
Chinese wood blocks of three different pitches

Cuban claves (wooden sticks struck against one another)
Triangle
Maracas
Sleigh bells
Castanets
Tambourine
Anvils, tuned to two different pitches
Chimes
Celeste
Piano

That's a lot of material to create interesting rhythms with!

Although the diversity of rhythms and timbres is evident throughout, the piece does divide into sections in terms of certain dominant patterns that exert control over individual segments. The first recognizable one is the snare-drum figure against which other instruments weave their contrasting motion. It would be natural, too, to investigate contrasting and conflicting metric figures where the rhythm is so compelling an element. Varèse does this, and the resulting contradictions in accent add much to the music's development. Rhythmic groupings vary—sometimes against a basic pattern of three, a group of five equally divided pulses will appear, for instance. Throughout, the highly distinctive timbres help define and clarify the effect of all the manipulation.

The piece was highly controversial when it appeared in 1931. Many of those who felt the need to defend it compared its sounds to the cacophony of street noises, heard the sounds as a reflection of the apparently meaningless noise of a metropolis. Others saw the piece as a symbol of the conflicting tensions of a technological age and its tendency toward dehumanization in favor of the glorification of the machine. Still others simply felt a kind of excitement in the visceral effects of the rhythms.

Varèse himself (1885–1965) denies that his music is experimental in nature. Also, he throws the burden of "interpretation" upon the listener; sound and meaning are, he says, one and the same. The music is what it is. His fascination with the possibilities of sound led him into electronic music, and in that area too he was a leader in opening new fields of creativity. The relationship of all this to the New Wave in jazz is easy to see.

The fascination with percussion ensembles came late to Western music, though drums of all sorts have been used for many centuries as part of instrumental groups. In other cultures, however, "orchestras" made up exclusively of drums have traditionally been an integral part of the musical scene as accompaniment for dancing, ritual chants, festival occasions, and all the varied ongoing activities of communal life.

Among numerous other African tribes, the Yoruba have a highly developed art of this type. At least 10 different kinds of drums are available for use in the traditional tribal ensembles, some capable of being tuned. These have been used for communication over long distances, but they are not limited to that function. The next listening selection may convince you that a Yoruba percussion ensemble can be a pretty exciting affair.

PRIMARY LISTENING:
Salute to a Chief, Yoruba drums from Nigeria (record set)

You will notice here the same steady unaccented pulse that we encountered in the Juba dance from Haiti and also noticed in Bunk Johnson's "Oh, Didn't He Ramble?" This is one of the important features of rhythmic organization in Africa and one that apparently carried over when the blacks were transported to the Caribbean area and the United States. Also as in the Juba dance, you will hear a great variety of syncopated patterns against the steady beat, a result of mixing meters. Moreover, some of the mixed meters are themselves additive meters. We encountered a system of additive meters in the thumri song from India, but this device was not widely used in our own tradition until the twentieth century, when, for instance, Stravinsky used it in *Petrushka*. There is no great mystery about how additive meters work. The first two rows of the diagram below represent two different ones. The whole diagram illustrates their mixing with two different steady pulses. It is a very simple mixture that can nevertheless produce some interesting syncopation if the accents are put where they belong. The beat unit is the eighth note, and the metric groupings are given for that value.

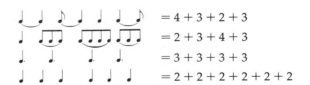

$$= 4 + 3 + 2 + 3$$
$$= 2 + 3 + 4 + 3$$
$$= 3 + 3 + 3 + 3$$
$$= 2 + 2 + 2 + 2 + 2 + 2$$

The first beat of each metric group should be accented, of course, and that's where all the complexity comes from. If you were to take part in a performance of this (and why not try?) or hear it performed, your foot would probably be tapping to the steady quarter notes in the bottom row while you beat out one or maybe two of the meters above it. Even your eye, though, can tell you how many different sets of accents are going to occur in just this brief example. And that's African metric arrangement: additive meters, irregular enough in themselves, are superimposed upon other metric schemes.

To further complicate matters the vocal parts, when they occur, are frequently in still another meter. It would be a miracle if our ears, unaccustomed to this kind of rhythmic maneuvering, were able to take it all in, much less get it down on paper accurately. But whether or not we can diagram it or reproduce it, we can still *feel* it, and that's the most significant thing about rhythm in any culture. African drummers learn these patterns by rote, using nonsense syllables to help them. As in many of our own ensemble performances, there is a leader who keeps things under control.

Aside from the sheer excitement created by this kind of percussion ensemble, there are other, richer factors that operate in African drumming practices. These go deeply into the spirit of tribal traditions, both social and religious. As in much of our music, there is a connection to the emotional needs of the people as opposed to intellectual requirements. The materials from which drums are made are carefully selected for their qualities of sound, but more than that, ceremonies are conducted in order to pacify the spirits that inhabit the trees from which they are made. Many of the drums, particularly those used in religious ritual, are decorated with symbols representing the patron deities of drumming. These symbols serve as focal points important to the worship of the drummers.

These practices and beliefs are grounded in myth, as are many of our own (Illustration 24). Not only the drumming but all of the music bridges the real world and the spirit world, helping to fill the universal human need to link the known to the unknown. Because of this spiritual emphasis in tribal music, the concept of performer and audience is foreign to the African. The making of music, with its pervasive and almost hypnotic rhythmic strength, is a communal affair, with the entire group responding and contributing to the experience. Those who have had the opportunity to attend worship services in black churches, especially in the rural sections of the South, recognize that much of this spirit persists even today. There is therefore no separation of art from life itself, a separation we are so often inclined to make in our own culture. The advantages should be clear to anyone who takes time to consider them. Just for a start, you might think about what needs are served by Varèse's *Ionisation* that make it a distinctly different enterprise than the example of Yoruba drumming.

Illustration 24. IBEJI FIGURES AND MANILLA CURRENCY.
Yoruba tribe, western Nigeria, Africa, nineteenth century. Ibeji figures are wooden sculptures of twins and are often used in tribal ritual worship because of the belief that magical powers reside in twins. Manilla currency are rings of metal worn on the wrist and used as a medium of exchange. The tendency among tribal cultures to emphasize the most striking physical features, to enlarge them even to the point of grotesqueness, is often mistaken for crudity or lack of sophistication. It would be a pity to miss the powerfully direct manner in which such art communicates or to ignore its intensity because it lacks the "prettiness" of much Western art work.
Collection of the J. B. Speed Art Museum, Louisville, Kentucky.

SUPPLEMENTAL LISTENING   A number of interesting African and Caribbean percussion groups, as well as some that have survived in America, may be heard on *African and Afro-American Drums*. Folkways: FE–4502.

Chapter 24
Expression with Electronics

The exciting sound-making possibilities of electronic equipment attracted more and more European and American composers during the 1950s and 1960s. The wide range of tonal colors and the equally diverse percussive effects were fertile areas for experimentation and investigation. The challenge of continuity in such pieces was always present as a formal factor, but new concepts of form itself evolved, and in fact are still being articulated.

One of the most striking compositions was produced by Edgard Varèse for the Brussels World's Fair in 1958. The title is really self-explanatory—*Poème Électronique;* it is our next listening example.

PRIMARY LISTENING:
Edgard Varèse, *Poème Électronique*

Some of the sounds were produced by the human voice, others by objects from the ordinary world—bells, for instance. Still others were made by electronic equipment like oscillators, modified by filters, loops, and all the paraphernalia of electric equipment. The result was classified as "organized sound." That's a paradox, really, since all music is organized sound of some sort. This is yet another example of problems of classification and identification.

The music was taped and played in the Philips Radio Corporation's pavillion at the fair. The pavillion itself was distinctive in design, and *Poème Électronique* was conceived so as to take advantage of the architecture. It was "broadcast" over 400 loudspeakers placed strategically around the structure and was accompanied by projected images. No attempt was made to correlate the sound and sight, and sometimes they were actually contradictory. The audiences, which were very large, reacted predictably along a line between total disgust and wild enthusiasm.

Each listener will draw his own conclusions. Most will be unable to find a formal pattern that relates to anything heard before. Some will conjure up all sorts of associations, and these will create what program there may be. Others will simply be fascinated with the varying complexes of sound for themselves alone. In Varèse's terms this is all appropriate, since his own descriptions of intent and content are vague enough to accommodate almost any interpretation. Like his *Ionisation*, the *Poème* was influential in projecting revolutionary ways of constructing sound patterns. Since that period there has been an astonishing amount of interest and activity in electronic production and modification of sound. The Moog and its derivatives are outgrowths of this. The kinds of background we hear in science-fiction movies are yet another. Listen to the music that accompanies TV shows; much that is going on there has its roots in works like *Ionisation* and *Poème Électronique*. The technological advances of the twentieth century are affecting more than our industrial enterprises. They have served our arts as well.

There are a number of different types of electronically produced or modified music. The following list of pieces is designed to stimulate investigation into some of the most common of these. For those interested in both the history and mechanics of such idioms, a helpful source is Jon H. Appleton and Ronald C. Perera, *The Development and Practice of Electronic Music*, Englewood Cliffs, N. J., Prentice-Hall, 1975.

Vladimir Ussachevsky (born 1911), *Sonic Contours, Sounds of New Music*. Folkways: FX–6160

This is an example of music produced from "natural" sounds electronically modified as opposed to sounds produced entirely by electronic devices. Ussachevsky was the first to exploit such music, the generic term for which is *musique concrète* (concrete music). In this case, the instrument is a piano recorded through a reverberation unit, a chamber designed to intensify and prolong the normal reverberation time expected of any given sound in a live setting such as a concert hall. This is a 1951 composition.

John Cage (born 1912), *Cartridge Music.* Time Records: S–8009.

In this 1960 composition, the sounds are produced in two ways: (1) by means of microphones applied to miscellaneous items such as wastebaskets and tables, (2) by assorted objects inserted into phonograph cartridges, e.g., feathers, toothpicks, slinkies. All the sounds are fed through amplifiers to loudspeakers, the volume being controlled by the performers.

John Cage, *Aria with Fontana Mix.* Time Records: S–8003.

Composed in 1959, the *Aria* and the *Fontana Mix* may be performed together or separately. *Fontana Mix* is made up of tapes that are capable of being used in a mix-or-match way to create different effects. The element of chance and experiment is therefore strong. The vocal *Aria* is in an extremely disjunct and rhythmically complex style, calling for an enormous range of vocal colors. Cage, active as an author, critic, and lecturer, is a leader of the avant-garde. His works include stage pieces, dance works, film scores, percussion ensembles, and composition for prepared piano (varying materials attached to the strings), among many other types.

Bicycle Built for Two, arranged by M. V. Matthews. *Music from Mathematics.* Decca: DL–79103.

This is an example of one of the many types of computer music, which was originally developed at the Bell Telephone Laboratories. In the idiom the acoustical properties of sound are reduced to numerical equivalents. These are then fed for storage into a computer. The composer selects the desired combinations, sends the program through the computer, and receives a numerical printout. This, in turn, is fed into a digital-to-sound conversion device which supplies an audio tape of the program. This is one of many ways to produce music entirely by electronic means.

Barry Vercoe (born 1938), *Synthesism. Computer Music.* Nonesuch: H–71245.

This is a more complex example of music derived from a computer program. This time the material is fed through a synthesizer. There are many types of synthesizers which vary widely in complexity and capability. In simplified terms, the synthesizer is a device used for generating, filtering, sequencing, etc., sound waves of all sorts. The most familiar types are those used by rock and jazz bands. The pioneer in this field was Robert Moog.

Edwin Dugger (born 1940), *Music for Synthesizer and Six Instruments.* Acoustic Research (AR): 0654 084.

This 1966 example represents one of numerous ways to combine synthesized sound with that of nonelectric instruments. In this case, the latter include flute, piccolo, oboe, clarinet, violin, viola, and cello. Although much more involved in such a piece, the basic concept, synthesizer with instruments, is the same found in many of the popular jazz-rock fusion groups such as Weather Report.

Karlheinz Stockhausen (born 1928), *Gesang der Jünglinge*. Deutsche Grammophon: 138811.	Stockhausen has been among the leaders of electronic music making for many years. His *Gesang der Jünglinge* (1956) exploits vocal sounds in every imaginable manner: there are consonants, pure vowels, tone mixtures, sometimes understandable words. These are used as part of the total sound in an instrumental sense rather than, except occasionally, as bearers of a text. Combined with this vocalization are electronically produced and synthesized sounds. Designed to be broadcast over loudspeakers, this is representative of that kind of musical composition that cannot be duplicated in live performance because of the enormous amount of electronic production, modification, and manipulation involved in achieving the tonal effects.
Aurelio de la Vega (born 1925), *Tangents for Violin and Tape*. Orion: OR–73128.	This 1973 composition uses forces that have become increasingly popular: a solo instrument with accompanying prerecorded tape. It features the usual repertoire of electronically manipulated sound on the tape with the violin interrupting and joining in by turns. The soloist is called upon to produce every conceivable sound that the violin is capable of, as well as much truly virtuosic passage work.
Kenneth Gaburo (born 1926), *The Wasting of Lucrécetzia*. Nonesuch: H–71199.	This is a prime example of the possibilities of combining concrete and electronic sounds. The concrete material includes voices in mixed ensembles as well as piccolo, bass trombone, and double-bass. The total effect of this highly rhythmic music is something like a strange mixture of rock and African tribal music overlaid on group hysteria. It is a 1964 composition.

Naturally, there has been a continuing interest in new ways to exploit electronic sound; the examples above are meant to simply introduce you to some of the concepts that have led the way. More recent recordings are available in abundance, although most of the principles have not undergone any radical development. The machinery itself is more complex and capable of greater variety, but essentially the sounds are either natural ones, sometimes modified electronically, or electronically produced ones. Is all of this somehow related to the new video games?

Part Three

Absolute Music

Chapter 25
Monothematic Forms: Theme and Variations

We have been considering music in terms of its ability to support extramusical ideas or events. We have been drawn, as well, into investigation of sound making of the most emotionally intense sort, as, for instance, in "Civilization Day" and *Visage*. In addition to these kinds of music there is a vast body of less highly charged musical composition for which there is no guideline to understanding other than the logical progressions of the sound complexes themselves. The generic name for this kind of music is *absolute music*. Hundreds of volumes on musical aesthetics, psychology, theory, appreciation, and what have you have attempted to explain how it works. The counterpart in the visual arts is what is called nonrepresentational art: it represents nothing but itself.

To reduce it to its most basic level, music is simply sound that occupies certain blocks of time. Since time itself is, we are told, an illusion, we define it frequently in terms of occurrences that give it a perceptible dimension. We say it takes a certain amount of time to drive from here to there. Events are scheduled to begin at one time, to end at another time. It takes 60 seconds to constitute a minute, 24 hours to describe a day. It is practically impossible for us to envision or define time without reference to some sort of event that marks its passage. We have said that music is the most abstract of the arts. In one sense this means that when there is no point of reference beyond it, when it is absolute within itself, then it is the stuff by which we are defining the period of time it occupies. It has no other meaning, and to rationalize it, we need to confine description and discussion to the purely musical events that occur. This, then, is music as a "pure" art. And like any art, it makes demands on us if we expect to capture it completely.

To construct an analogy: Think about visiting a large art museum. One of the items on display is a water jug from ancient Egypt. It is encased in glass, carefully lit, open to viewing from all sides. Does it leak? Who cares? It is no longer intended to function as a water jug. It is an art object and *that* is its function. It can be looked at from some historical perspective, but that's not what makes it beautiful. It represents a certain level of craftsmanship, but that is not its real value except to the craftsman. It may raise all sorts of associations concerning the cultural environment in which it was created and used, but that is peripheral to the reason it is on display. It is there mainly because somebody thought it was worth looking at for its own value, defined in terms of beauty of line, balance, decorative design, etc. When we study it from that perspective, we are treating it as an art object only, totally apart from the other points of interest it may have. If we are skilled lookers, sensitive to the sort of grace and artistic expression it embodies, we will not pass it by with only a casual glance. If we do, it simply means that for some combination of reasons we are unable to relate to it on its own terms. And it is possible that we will have lost something out of our experience because of that.

So with music. Many of us are reluctant to contribute a significant amount of effort to the experience of listening. We demand, instead, the most explicit sort of expressive content, something obvious enough that it takes little more than just being there to complete the communication. Little attention is required by such music, since the message can be gotten from even the most casual listening. And we are often content to share the performers' emotional climax (in some cases "orgasm" would be a more accurate description). Our tendencies here are not peculiar to music, though; they encompass most art media. We are told that the age level at which television is directed is something like 14 years—hardly a compliment to our subtlety of taste. Apparently sex and violence in movies are successful mostly in terms of how explicit they are—that is, how little imagination they demand of the audience. Novels often seem to make the best-seller lists in nearly direct proportion to how little untangling they demand from the reader. Even murder mysteries often rely on tricks rather than on any demand for thoughtful interpretation of evidence.

The alternative to such obvious and unsubtle expression is art that expects and requires a good deal of contribution from the observer or listener. In most cases, this means paying more than the usual amount of attention to what is happening. It means also the willingness to meet the work of art half-way in terms of emotional involvement, instead of demanding that the emotional content be so directly expressed that we are engulfed in it automatically. In many cases it means a willingness on our part to engage in an intellectual restructuring in order to reach an understanding of the "message," whatever that may be. Perhaps most important of all, it means that we must accept such art solely for what it is, without demanding that it remind us of something else or "mean" something else or find its justification in the ways it can be used for purposes other than its own.

Creative artists are very sensitive to the problem of communicating with a public that is often unable or unwilling to meet them half-way. The painter-sculptor David Middlebrook has put this very sharply into focus. He was discussing his own work and the objectives he had in mind and how those objectives related to the way people saw his art objects. He said that the objects "should become participatory things where one has to inquire further about their meanings. It means, of course, looking into your own mind" (Illustration 25).

Our ability to relinquish extramusical directions and suggestions helps us recognize our personal artistic needs. We have covered this territory before in connection with other compositions. With absolute music, however, the search for our individual responses becomes most demanding, and we have the best possible chance to discover the limits of our sensitivity and the extent of our capacity to contribute to the musical experience. We must throw away our crutches and try to walk alone with the music, as it were.

As mentioned in the Introduction, many musical procedures that are most strongly associated with absolute music do occur also in program music and music with words. There is nothing contradictory in the use of highly logical structures for their inherent artistic value, even though programs or words may be involved too. We have seen numerous examples of this already in pieces by Martini, Blood, Sweat and Tears, Debussy, and others. Therefore, although the thrust of part 3 will be directed toward absolute music, it will be profitable and interesting to take an occasional "side trip" in order to investigate some works that are vocal or programmatic but that use musical organizations we are studying at the time.

One final consideration before moving on. Music, as well as the other arts, is a reflection of life forces or events, and this is as true of absolute music as it is of music with words or program music. The difference is in the relative amount of abstraction. Tension, variation, structure, contrast, and repetition are all musical factors, and they sometimes point *into* the music rather than *away* from it in support

Illustration 25. DOOR OF PERCEPTION. Pierre Haubensak, 1973–1974. Like much other art of our own century, this painting places the burden of interpretation on the individual viewer. Is the artist telling us we are nonperceivers—blank walls? Or that there is nothing to perceive at all? Or that we each need to open our own door? There are many possibilities, but surely a strong one is that each of us must face the limitations of our own sensitivity and imagination. Collection of the J. B. Speed Art Museum. Louisville, Kentucky.

of an extramusical idea or event. The pattern of sound events becomes significant for itself alone, then. And to describe or discuss these events, we need to concentrate attention on them alone.

Our first experience will be with music that relies on a single piece of material for its projection and manipulation. Such a composition is called *monothematic*—one theme. There are many ways in which one basic musical construct can be utilized, and we will be exploring several of them. Much of the vocabulary and many of the concepts will be familiar because we have been considering musical procedures for many pages. The differences will be mainly in the terms' application, because the objective will be to identify those processes that contribute to the coherence between the form and whatever is being expressed, without which actually no art work can communicate except accidentally.

One of the cues to how little help we can expect from composers in the area of absolute music is found in the lack of expressive suggestion found in the title of such works. The word *symphony* tells us only that the work is a composition for orchestra containing several movements, usually four. There is no information about expressive intent, nor is there a suggestion of extramusical reference or meaning. As we will discover, there are cues that the initiate can generally rely upon, but mostly they concern the formal organization to expect and, sometimes, the tempo also. The attachment of the word *Surprise* to Haydn's Ninety-fourth Symphony was never his idea; it belongs to the listening public, refers to one chord only, and has little or nothing to do with anything that matters unless we are being kittenish about a single instance of sudden dynamic contrast that might startle us out of a nap. It occurs in that work's second movement, which is our next listening selection.

PRIMARY LISTENING:
Franz Joseph Haydn,
Symphony No. 94
(*Surprise*), second
movement, Andante, 1791

The only cue to what to expect at the beginning of that movement is the tempo marking, Andante, which indicates only the rate of musical speed. As a result, we look inside the music to find the means by which Haydn manipulates the material of sound in a logical way. What he is up to is nothing unusual. We have contacted the process before but in a somewhat different context. Haydn's composition is a theme and variations, which means simply that he presents us with a tune and follows it with a set of versions of it, similar enough to be recognizable but different enough to be interesting. In part 1 of this book we experienced improvised variation; Haydn's variations are fully composed. The procedure relates strongly to theme transformation, as in Strauss's *Till Eulenspiegel*, but our acquaintance with that technique was connected to musical enlargement of a programmatic idea. Haydn has no such illustrative objective.

His theme is in the major mode and uses melodic intervals that clearly outline the harmonic implications.

In the way of Classicists, Haydn fashions his material in nicely balanced regular four-measure phrases. The theme is in two parts, each repeated, so that we can diagram it A A B B and label it binary (Example 76). The "surprise" chord occurs after the repetition of A. What Haydn works with, is a 32-bar melody harmonized with great simplicity, involving no great rhythmic complexity, and constructed entirely in keeping with the Classic aesthetic ideals of clarity and balance. The very slight alterations of dynamics and orchestration that occur in the repeated A and B do not affect the form at all, of course; they merely add interest. To be really complete in our description, we should add that the A section of Haydn's theme is quite disjunct melodically but that the B section is fairly conjunct. One advantage to such a theme is that its simplicity allows us to carry it easily in our tonal memory, giving us a dependable reference for the variations that follow. And those variations? It would be fair to ask how severe they will be, whether the original form will be disrupted, whether the harmonic background will be maintained— lots of "whethers" are appropriate in meeting Haydn halfway.

The first variation does retain the form and even the melody of the original. What is added is an *obbligato*—added melody—taken in turn by strings and woodwinds in the A section and entirely by strings in the B section. Nor are there any harmonic surprises.

The first real shock is the change of mode at the start of the second variation (Example 77). Not only does Haydn jump suddenly into minor; he also adds a harmonic change in the middle of section A. And section A is all we hear of the original theme in this variation; B never does come around. In place of it, there is an abruptly active rhythmic section with a good bit of polyphonic and antiphonal activity between the strings and the woodwinds, much of which is built on the melodic material of section A of the original theme. The entire episode that substitutes for B is harmonically unsettled, as though Haydn were shifting gears frantically in an attempt to get things back under control. Which is exactly what is happening. Having been thrust without warning into minor for the opening of the second variation, we are now being maneuvered back into major

Example 76
Haydn, Symphony No. 94.

Example 77
Haydn, Symphony No. 94.

for the opening of the third. In a nutshell, this represents two different ways to change either key or mode. The first is by abrupt, unannounced, unprepared change. This happens all the time in popular music, particularly in the type that makes the pop charts. Listen for it. The second method is by *modulation*—gradual change often accompanied by a restless harmonic texture but resulting in a feeling of relaxation and satisfaction when the key or mode change is completed.

Which happens at just the right time for the start of the third variation. This variation returns once again to the form of the original theme. The repetitions of A and B are extensively altered by orchestration as well as by the addition again of obbligato lines, but after the relative turbulence of the modulatory passage, it is nice at least to be back on comfortable ground thematically and tonally.

The fourth and final variation has that kind of triumphant decisive character that endings often take on. Again there is considerable change in the repetitions of A and B although there is a kind of balance in that the opening A and the closing B of the variation are both solid and dynamically vigorous. By contrast, the "inside" A and B are much more lyrical in quality.

The closing section is not really an additional variation, but a *coda,* from the Italian word meaning "tail." You may remember that Blood, Sweat and Tears used a coda in "Lucretia MacEvil." Like that one, Haydn's coda brings things to a suitable end without too much suddenness and ties up the musical package. Many instrumental works of an extended type employ codas, and with some composers they assume a great deal of expressive and structural significance. Here the material for the coda is derived mainly from the original theme, principally the A section.

The entire movement is a good illustration of the Classic approach to the organization we call theme and variations. Only once, in the second variation, is the form disrupted or the harmonic background manipulated extensively. As a result of maintaining the Classic outlines of the theme's form, the entire movement takes on a sense of clarity and balance within its variation sections. Nor do we feel drawn very far off course. Even the most meager of tonal memories will suffice to keep us oriented musically. Although there is some dynamic contrast and the addition of much rhythmic activity to the modulatory section of the second variation, the feeling of control and discipline is evident. There is nothing here to stir us to the depths of our emotional beings, and this music wasn't really meant to accomplish that. We are comfortable with the music but at the same time, there is variety enough to sustain our interest—if we are listening with interest in the first place.

Franz Joseph Haydn (1732–1809), along with Mozart, is considered most representative of the musical style of Classicism. Haydn began his professional career as a keyboard performer and teacher in Vienna. In 1759 he secured the position of Musical Director and composer at the court of Count Ferdinand Maximilian Morzin. In 1761 he was attached to the court of Count Paul Esterhazy at Eisenstadt, where he stayed until the count's death. He was retained on an annual pension but moved back to Vienna. Although he thereafter visited several times in London, he consistently returned to Vienna.

Haydn is credited with establishing the formal procedures of the symphony and string quartet, although there was mutual influence between him and Mozart in this regard. Haydn composed many operas, oratorios (*The Seasons*, *The Creation*), sacred and secular choral works, 104 symphonies, overtures, chamber works, concerti, piano pieces, and songs, many with folk settings. He was one of the most productive composers of all time.

There are hundreds of movements from symphonies, string quartets, chamber works of all kinds, piano compositions, instrumental concerti, sonatas, and other types of music that employ the theme-and-variations format. The extent to which the variations depart from the original musical ideas cannot be generalized. One work of particular interest is a set of variations for orchestra composed by Edward Elgar, the English Romanticist. The theme in this composition is varied in ways meant to characterize individual personality traits of a number of Elgar's acquaintances. The people are not identified except by initials, however, and thus the "enigma" of the title. The title, incidentally, is Elgar's own. Many nineteenth-century composers used the variations in their works in as dramatic a manner as possible, so that the concept of varying the mood as much as the musical material became popular. Such compositions were known as "mood variations" or "character variations" to distinguish them from their less emotionally high-keyed relatives that relied more on objective musical manipulation.

Haydn's set of variations from the Symphony No. 94 has become so widely known and quoted as to be fair game for a musical burlesque. Burlesque was the business of the Hoffnung concerts, a series held in England. In almost every case the orchestra and its soloists programmed works that were familiar to concertgoers. Without such familiarity, the point of the fun making would be lost entirely. This is true of much humor, of course; thus parody and irony both refer to original material, usually serious, or to a real situation that serves as the focal point for mockery of some sort. If you are well acquainted with Haydn's variations, you will probably enjoy listening to the distortions created by the Hoffnung Orchestra.

PRIMARY LISTENING:
Haydn, Symphony No. 94,
second movement,
Andante, Hoffnung Festival
Orchestra (Angel: 35500)

Something goes noticeably—and studiedly—awry with the first variation—can you identify the "problem"? Numerous other disruptions follow, some based on metric alterations, some on mismanagement of cadential passages, some on misapplication of style, some on instrumentation. And some, certainly, on just plain foolishness. We are told that Haydn was a jovial sort, so it might be safe to guess that he would enjoy this kind of merrymaking with music, even his own.

Like Haydn's music itself, the Hoffnung version of the movement is performed from a score, meaning that the element of spontaneous improvisation is not present. The burlesque is worked out as carefully as the original composition; very likely it could not be as effective without such planning. There are vast areas of music, however, that exploit the principle of variation but in an improvisatory context, and to some of these we shall now turn our attention, with concentration on the purely musical devices involved in them.

SUPPLEMENTAL LISTENING

Mozart, *Variations on "Ah, vous dirai-je, Maman,"* K. 265.[1]

Other nonimprovisational themes and variations of varying complexity and in different styles are:

The theme here is a French folk song, better known to American audiences as "Twinkle, Twinkle, Little Star." Because of its familiarity, listeners will find it an especially easy piece to follow.

Charles Ives, *Variations on "America."*

This is for organ and is easy to follow because of the familiarity of the theme. After a harmonically restless introduction, "America" is played "straight," as most people know it. Ives then takes it through a series of alterations that utilize contrasting rhythms, harmonic manipulations including minor and dissonant "smear" chords, chromatic runs, and even some suggestion of a calliope. The piece is easy to keep up with, however, because the variations are separated clearly by full cadences.

[1]In 1862 the German musicologist, Ludwig von Koechel, prepared a thematic catalogue of Mozart's works, assigning a number to each composition. It has become customary to identify the works by those numbers.

Our first contact with Indian music was a thumri song with instrumental accompaniment. We used it as an example of improvisation within the confines of a musical system foreign to our ears and possibly even inaccessible to our complete understanding. Our main interest was in the expressive gap that so often keeps us from responding affectively to music outside of our own cultural sphere. The controlling musical elements were the raga and the tala although the performers improvised on those within the rather strict limits of the raga tradition. Because of the words it was not absolute music although the words were not an important part of the discussion.

India does have its share of purely instrumental music, without the "explanation" of a text, and *Maru-bihag,* our next listening selection, is such a piece. The performance on the record set is not the complete one but is extensive enough to give a clear representation of the musical characteristics. As is the usual practice, the title identifies the raga on which the performance, by a group including Ravi Shankar, is based. A raga performance can be seen, then, as a type of theme and variations process in which the raga is the theme. Shankar (born 1920) is probably the Indian musician who is best known in Europe and the United States because of his extended concert tours and his many recordings. A sitar virtuoso and composer who was trained in the traditions of Indian classical music, Shankar was among the first to perform it widely in the West. Articulate and cosmopolitan, he has done more than any other Indian musician to attempt to bridge the musical gap between Eastern and Western classical performance style (Illustration 26).

PRIMARY LISTENING:
Maru-bihag, Ravi Shankar, sitar, Chatur Lal, tabla, N. C. Mullick, tambura (record set)

The performing group here is a typical one for Indian music. The solo instrument is the sitar, the drone instrument is the tambura, and the tabla, a two-drum set, provides the rhythm, which is based on the tala.

Fortunately for us, Shankar acquaints us with the notes of the raga in its ascending and descending form and is even good enough to count off the tala. Raga *Maru-bihag* uses the basic notes shown in Example 78, although insertions of others within prescribed conventional restrictions are certainly possible, as you will hear in the course of the performance.

Other notes that may occur are always in an extremely weak position musically. Because of this, the notes played by Shankar as

Example 78
Maru-bihag.

Raga Maru-Bihag

Ascending   Descending

Illustration 26. MAN SURROUNDED BY LARGE ENTOURAGE.
Attributed to Sur Gujarati, late sixteenth century. The highly stylized art of India and the court traditions of the aristocracy combined to protect the conventions that still govern raga performances. Like Western Renaissance artists, the painter here is concerned with real people in action as well as with giving the scene depth of perspective. Compare *Adoration of the Magi* (page 38) and El Greco's *Crucifixion* (page 150).
Cincinnati Art Museum. Gift of John J. Emery.

illustration at the beginning of the performance (those in Example 78) dominate the performance. Notice that there is an interchange of F♮ and F♯ in the ascending form of the raga. The only time the F♮ is actually used, however, it is followed immediately by E, so its function in an actual performance is a highly prescribed one.

As indicated in our discussion of thumri song, because of tradition, usage, and cultural indoctrination each raga projects a mood peculiar to it, at least for the Indian who relates to the classical style. This makes it possible to retain the associations of certain ragas with particular ceremonial occasions, times of year, times of day. This raga happens to be an evening one.

One other thing to notice about Shankar's introductory remarks and musical illustrations is the intensity of the rhythmic burst that immediately precedes the first beat of the tala. That happens sometimes during the performance, too, and it might help you keep track of the tala if you are trying to listen analytically.

As is the usual practice, the actual performance begins with a cascade of notes on the sitar. This is the presentation of the raga material, its exposition, so to speak. This is followed by a relatively long, rhythmically free rhapsodic section in which Shankar seems to be exploring the notes of the raga. In the course of the exploration there is frequent use of microtones, inflected with great deliberation. This serves to establish the mood, evoking, as it were, the expressive characteristics of the tonal material. It has a subsidiary effect on many people, however, which is to create tension, relieved when the note is resolved to what appears to be a more restful pitch. Notice, if you hear this, how frequently the pitch manipulation occurs on B and resolves to C. This happens also in the approach to the C an octave lower. C is the tonic, and the tonic seems to operate in Indian music a little as it does in our music: we feel at home when we get to it. We can make the assumption, then, that ornamenting the approach to the tonic works in a kind of tension–release fashion. As in the thumri song, the tonic is strengthened by the drone of the tambura.

The opening free section of a raga performance is called the *Alāp*, an introductory passage in any raga performance. It lasts as long as the performer takes to investigate fully the notes of the raga, with particular attention to microtonal inflections at appropriate and allowable pitches.

The entrance of the tabla changes the direction entirely. From this point on the rhythmic impulse will invade both the sitar and the tabla. The rhapsody of the *Alāp* is left behind, and a new expressive dimension is substituted for it. The proper name of this new section is the *Gat*, an extended section during which the raga material is developed and manipulated. It includes also a sort of working out of melodic ideas—themes, as it were—that were presented in the Alāp.

In this performance the tala is *Jhāptal*. As Shankar explains, it is made up of alternating two- and three-beat metric units. This is additive, based on the same kind of metric concept that we found in African Yoruba drumming. The organization may be difficult to locate; there's much going on in the tabla besides simply counting off two- and three-beat groups. You may notice, though, that the heavy untuned drum is often used on both beats of the two-beat units. By contrast, the tuned drum seems to be more often active on the metric units of three beats. And *that* drum is tuned to the tonic note, like the tambura, so it adds yet another reinforcement to the home-base note.

Melodically there is much continuing investigation of the notes of the raga in various combinations, predominantly scalewise. This is another typical procedure in Indian music, in contrast to much of ours, in which the melodies are quite disjunct and frequently depart drastically from a succession of scale notes. But remember that the Indian raga is not *only* a scale or mode; it is also a melody. Variations, then, assume a largely scalar pattern because they are guided stringently by both the melodic and modal character of the raga. A lot of "teasing" is still going on with inflected notes, especially those that lead to the upper tonic. More tension, more expressiveness. Can we call it ornamentation, or does it have a deeper significance than that?

As the performance progresses, the rhythmic activity gradually increases. We are apt to interpret that as an increase in tempo, but if you tap your foot to the beats of the tala, you will realize that the tempo is constant. What happens is that more notes are being performed to each beat and that their rhythmic complexity is much greater and even includes an increasing amount of syncopation in both the sitar and the tabla. The excitement, then, is caused by more and more rhythmic activity rather than by changes in tempo. This happens in our own music, too, as you will discover if you listen analytically enough.

Shankar uses several approaches to developing his melody. One way is by beginning a melodic statement with a short motive, maybe five or six notes, and enlarging it by extension, that is, by adding notes to make it longer and more interesting. Sometimes he simply repeats the same pattern literally a time or two and then surprises us by using that as a beginning for a larger phrase. This kind of melodic development is another favorite musical device. We will find it used with great skill by Beethoven. Some critics describe his style as "expansionist," and we might put Shankar in that same category to some extent.

There are, then, a number of musical characteristics that distinguish raga performances from what we are accustomed to hearing in Western musical practice. At the same time, as I have indicated, there are some points of similarity. One striking difference is the absence in Indian music of harmonic movement except what takes place accidentally because of the drone instrument and the tuned drum reiterating the tonic. Many find this continuing tonic note disconcerting; for others the sound creates a sense of almost hypnotic peace. Certainly there is a very real function being served here: the tonic is a kind of "sound beacon," and nearly every phrase or combination of phrases finds its way back to this central pitch.

In spite of the numerous rhythmic and melodic variations, we are aware of a consistency of phrase length, especially if we define the phrases in terms of return to the tonic. This is partially related to the concept of the tala. It defines the phrase length simply because it is repeated constantly throughout the performance: 2 plus 3 plus 2 plus 3. That adds up to 10. So the entire performance is structurally organized around that unit of 10 beats. The fact that within this structure, which could easily become painfully restrictive, the performers are able to disguise the repetitions because of their improvisatory skill and their ability to keep some elasticity in the phrasing is a sign of their mastery. Except for certain types of music, our concept of phrasing is much more pliable in the West. But you might try carefully plotting the phrases in our popular music. You may be surprised to discover how consistently repetitive they are in their regularity.

SUPPLEMENTAL LISTENING

The trap in discussing music from any culture other than our own is oversimplification. There are many recordings of raga performances, and it has become very stylish to take an interest in them and to try to relate to them. This is all good, of course. Most of them (with their liner notes) will extend the discussion above. The following, which vary in complexity, are worth investigating:

Prabhāti: Swara Kākalī. Angel: S–36418.
Raga Piloo; Dhun; Raga Ananda Bhalrava. Angel: S–36026.
The Genius of Ravi Shankar. Columbia: CS–9560.

There are also many books with the express purpose of making the raga tradition understandable in the West. Some are popular in approach, others are quite scholarly. For those who would like to investigate on their own, the following are suggested:

Walter Kaufmann, *The Ragas of North India*, Indian University Press, Bloomington 1968. This is a scholarly book but in language that most informed laymen can understand.
Peggy Holroyde, *The Music of India*, Praeger, New York, 1972. This work, quoted from in the discussion of the Indian thumri song earlier in this book, includes much information on relationships between musical practice and philosophy, religion, social patterns, etc.
Ravi Shankar, *My Music, My Life*, Simon and Schuster, New York, 1968. This is a highly readable book, full of musical information but with the added dimension of the personality of this gifted performer shining through.

Fuki (a kind of grass) is a kind of duet coming out of a different cultural background but with traditions and conventions as strong as those of India or the ones that controlled Haydn. It shares with Shankar's *Maru-bihag* both the improvisation and the reliance on prescribed musical material upon which to build. It shares with both Haydn and Shankar the concept of variations growing out of relatively sparse musical motives. And as with Haydn, the use of obbligato is an important part of the musical process. This is a lot of sharing, but the differences are vast in spite of these links of concept and procedure.

The koto is one of the oldest of the world's instruments still in wide use (Illustration 27). It was imported from China sometime between the sixth and eighth centuries A.D., along with much of the musical system used to guide performers. It has 13 strings, each with its own bridge, and tunings are altered by moving the bridges. It is a large instrument, measuring about six feet long, and is plucked with picks made of ivory. There is a large body of literature written for the koto, much of it dating back many years. *Fuki* is a rather old piece, thought to come from the sixteenth century.

Both the words of the song and the melody of the instrumental part are composed and are a traditional part of the literature. The *tune* for the vocal line, however, is improvised by the singer. Both vocal and koto parts are performed by the same person. The result is a polyphonic texture, partially improvised.

The notation for koto music is far different from the type used in the West, although there is some slight resemblance to lute tablature from the Renaissance and Baroque periods. Anyone who

Illustration 27. KOTO.
The author of *Japanese Music and Musical Instruments*, the work from which this photograph comes, comments that in Japan, the koto is somewhat analogous to the parlor piano in the West, being most commonly heard in home performances of the type shown here.
William P. Malm, *Japanese Music and Musical Instruments*, Charles E. Tuttle Co., Inc., Tokyo, Japan, 1959. Reproduced by permission.

has learned to play guitar has probably worked from a kind of tablature, which as said earlier is merely a system that pictures the pitches in terms of the strings on an instrument. In guitar tablature dots indicate where the fingers need to be placed in order to get the proper chord. Lute and koto tablature are considerably more complex because there is a melody line to deal with, but the notation can be just as exact if one knows how to interpret the symbols.

The concept of harmony is not foreign to koto music as it is to Indian classical music. There are frequent simultaneous soundings of different pitches, sometimes resulting from a drone but just as often resulting from the addition of "harmonizing" notes to the melody. The function of harmony is not like its function in Western practice, however, in that there is no progression of chords within a tonal framework. Most often the organization is rhythmic and motivic; the compositions are conceived in terms of a certain number of beats in the piece and a melody built up of varying departures from a relatively short motivic base. This is what happens in *Fuki.*

PRIMARY LISTENING:
Fuki, Japanese koto music
(record set)

Our *Fuki* listening selection is only the beginning of the performance as originally recorded. In its entirety, the main body of the composition is made up of 128 beats divided into phrases of 16 beats each. If we arranged this in terms of our own $\frac{4}{4}$ meter, we would come up with the Classic phrase of four measures. This Japanese music is not conceived that way, however; and even the sensation of $\frac{4}{4}$ metric organization is absolutely missing, so that there is a much freer, more rhapsodic character to the sound. But each phrase of sixteen beats begins and cadences with the same motivic pattern, sometimes treated rather like a sequence, almost always varied in some ornamented or rhythmic way. The melodic line for the introduction and first two phrases looks as in Example 79. The koto actually sounds an octave below these pitches. The introduction is in addition to the 128 beats that make up the main part of *Fuki.*

The phrases are readily seen, as are the repetitions, variations, and sequential elements. The rest of the performance follows quite closely the process indicated in the notation given.

It is over this tune that the singer, using prescribed words, improvises his melody. This is actually only part of the first stanza of

Example 79
Fuki.

Note: ✕ = "bent" note

a seven-stanza poem. In a full performance of the work, each stanza would be accompanied by the koto using more and more elaborate variations on the original melody of 128 beats. The piece was conceived as a sort of game or contest song in which different performers took turns improvising vocal melodies to different stanzas of the poem. What they played on the koto, however, was the conventional melody as it has been handed down by tradition.

Again we are very conscious of what we call "bent" pitches in the blues tradition; they are indicated in the score by an *x* over the affected note. They are microtones manipulated by both the instrument and the voice in an expressive way. Here, as in Indian music, they are highly disciplined and controlled by tradition. The "bent" notes in the literature for the koto, do not normally vary from performer to performer except in very small details. Our own performers, of course, are free to inflect any note of their choice and to whatever degree they desire. Oriental languages, like many African dialects, are vocally inflected. Although Japanese is not inflected at present, it derives from Chinese, which is, and it is likely that there are strong Chinese influences on the literature of koto music and the conventions of its performance. Could we guess, then, that the practice of "bending" notes is usually derived from an extension of language inflection?

You will notice from Example 79 that C, D, and G are easily the most important pitches in the piece, which sounds to us a great deal as if it were in the key of C minor. The motives and cadences revolve around these pitches, and the final notes of the 16-beat phrases are all G. Thus the tonal relationships of the intervals we call the fifth (C to G) and fourth (D to G) are important. It has become a cliché in America, in fact, to suggest an Oriental sound by emphasizing fifths and fourths. This is another of our unfortunate tendencies to oversimplify matters. The same intervals are just as important in our own music from the medieval and Renaissance periods and have been exploited by innumerable musicians since Debussy. They also play a significant role in the music of Russia. This is worth a little thought in terms of our human delight in exotic sights and sounds—and our treatment of them from the most superficial angle. This discussion is also guilty of oversimplification, of course, since it omits the enormous implications of expressive intent and the force of tradition in all but the most skimpy terms; but without that sort of oversimplification we simply cannot even scratch the surface. We do need, however, to keep in mind that what we are doing here *is* only scratching the surface. It would be fatal for us to imagine that because we can describe some of the musical procedures of other cultures, we then "know all about" their music.

Anyway, *Fuki* is an obbligato, a kind of polyphonic duet, a kind of theme and variations, a kind of improvisation. And a glimpse of the careful, logical, finely fashioned detail that we admire in Japanese visual art, echoed here in musical art.

SUPPLEMENTAL LISTENING   As with Indian music, there are a number of recordings of koto music. There is not the same volume, however, perhaps because Japanese culture itself has assimilated so much from the West since World War II. Nor have we been as strongly drawn to Oriental philosophies as to those of India. Most of the recordings include liner notes that indicate the most important musical material being used. Two suggested recordings are:

Japanese Koto Classics. Nonesuch: H–72008.
The Koto Music of Japan. Nonesuch: HS–72005.

A study that is written in clear and accessible language is Willem Adriaansz, *The Kumiuta and Danmono Traditions of Japanese Koto Music*, University of California Press, Berkeley, 1973. In it the interested reader will find a full discussion of *Fuki*, together with other traditional compositions and performance conventions.

It is almost no hurdle at all, in terms of the use of a musical idea, to move from Haydn to Shankar to koto music to American jazz. What makes all of them sound different from one another is the musical material that each one uses, not the *concept* of varying that material in successive sections. Most jazz performances start out with a theme too, which means they begin with some sort of musical substance in hand. On this a set of variations is constructed. There are many ways to handle this process, but one of the easiest to hear is a solo improvisation, because there we are not apt to be distracted by the type of arrangement into which the music is maneuvered. As in any other improvisation, the individual performer will bring with him his own ideas, his own technical abilities, his own imagination. Because of this, we not only can relate to his work subjectively—we like it or we don't—but also can use the vocabulary of description to explain just what he does that makes his performance sound that way. But to understand this fully, we need to have the theme in mind as a point of reference for the variations that are being developed.

In jazz, two forms have been used more frequently than any others. They are not the *only* ones, of course, because many forms and many musical styles can be and have been used. But we are talking about relative frequency. The first of the forms is the blues, and we have discussed that in chapter 3. The second form is the 32-bar pop song, which we have encountered before, in Dizzy Gillespie's performance of "I Can't Get Started." If we think in terms of $\frac{4}{4}$ meters (the meter of most pop tunes), we will realize that we are dealing here with a form that covers 128 beats just as with the koto music. The way these 128 beats are organized, though, is very different.

The most common way to organize the 32-bar pop song (though not the *only* way) can be diagrammed like this, as you know:

A   A   B   A

Let's examine the form more carefully than we did before. All sections of the form are eight measures long. That means that we are going to hear the same material for 24 out of the 32 bars, since A is going to occur three times. The B section is the bridge, and the material there is quite different, often even using a different key from the A section. Because it is the part that comes around least frequently, it has often been made a very important part of the form and is often treated distinctively in performances. In the Benny Goodman Trio rendition of "Body and Soul" that is our next listening selection, it is handled in such a way that it stands out clearly, even for those people who might not know the original song on which the piece is based (Example 80). We'll see why and how.

PRIMARY LISTENING:
Sour, Green, and Heyman, "Body and Soul," Benny Goodman, clarinet, Teddy Wilson, piano, Gene Krupa, drums (Columbia: P 6–11891)

One other term is important in following and talking about a jazz performance based on any tune at all. As indicated in discussing "I Can't Get Started," the chorus is the whole theme, the whole song, the whole tune that is being used. In this case the chorus is the whole A A B A structure into which the song "Body and Soul" is cast. *Chorus* does not mean here what it does when we talk about the chorus *of* a song or about a piece being made up of a verse and a

Example 80
"Body and Soul." Composer: John W. Green. Authors: Robert Sour, Edward Heyman, and Frank Eyton.

chorus. Here the chorus *is* the song. A typical jazz performance will consist of a series of choruses, divided among the group and the soloists in whatever way they decide is satisfactory for them. Since the Goodman Trio has only two melody instruments, the piano and the clarinet, we can talk about the choruses in terms of what those two instruments are doing, how they divide up the theme between them, and what kind of improvisational variation they play when it is their "turn" to play. Also we can describe what each is doing when they are *not* playing the theme.

The first chorus is handled this way: Goodman on clarinet plays the melody for the A section and its repetition, while Teddy Wilson on piano furnishes the harmonic background with an occasional spurt of dialogue, most important at cadences. If you don't happen to know the original tune, you can learn it in a hurry from Goodman because his performance is a pretty "straight" one. This has no derogatory meaning in most jazz; it merely means that he is sticking quite close to the original piece without adding much ornamentation or getting off the tune very far.

Wilson plays the bridge, the B section. The piano is a much different instrument from the clarinet, and one thing that it can do that the clarinet cannot do is play more than one note at a time, which is one reason why the piano in a trio of this sort has the responsibility for stating the harmony. At the same time it can be used for melody, so it is versatile enough to present all the components of a piece of music. A melody instrument like the clarinet or trumpet or whatever, if it is going to deal with harmony, has to do it differently—by playing the elements of the chord in succession rather than all at once. That means that the harmony, for a clarinet, comes out sounding like a melody. This is the same thing that happened in the Haydn symphony, where the melody of the theme *implied* or *contained* the harmony because it was made up of chord tones played in succession (Example 76). Anyway, because of the nature of the piano and also because of Wilson's idea of what to do with the material of the bridge, he gets pretty far away from the original tune of that section. So far, in fact, that if you don't know the tune, you are not going to learn it from Wilson. You can hear the harmonic background of it, but Wilson runs all over the keyboard and pretty much abandons the melody of the bridge. If you happen to know the music of the bridge, on the other hand (which most listeners did when this record was cut in 1935), you will be in a position to admire how imaginative and creative Wilson's treatment of this B section is.

Goodman takes a break at this point, as you can hear. But he does come back in for the final statement of A, and once again he sticks close to the original material. And once again Wilson adds his commentary in his own way.

All of this taken together is the first chorus. So we say that the chorus is divided between Goodman and Wilson, with Wilson taking the bridge.

For the second chorus, the players reverse their roles: Wilson plays all the A sections and Goodman takes the bridge. Since you have heard the melody for A played straight by Goodman, you are in a position to see how far off the original tune Wilson gets during his solos. Also, since you have heard in the first chorus a fairly straight statement of the original harmony, you will notice that in this chorus Wilson adds some enrichment, some more colorful chords than there were the first time around.

In Goodman's treatment of the bridge you can hear *some* of the tune without much change, especially during the first four measures. But in the last half of the bridge, he gets fairly far off the tune, so once again if you don't know the melody for this section, you are not apt to learn it from this performance.

The final chorus is not a complete one. In fact, the trio omits the first two statements of A altogether and jumps right into the bridge after the end of the second chorus. The distinctive thing about this closing portion of the piece is that both players go off at a tangent and get away from the original song much more than in either of the first two choruses. Final choruses are often this way, and that's one thing that makes jazz so much fun to listen to. But it also puts a lot of responsibility on the listener if he or she is going to get with what's going on. To follow it well, the audience has to be constantly supplying the original tune for itself. In most performances, as in this one, each succeeding chorus gets farther away and the variations become more and more "far out." This is one reason why the well-known jazz critic Martin Williams wrote a book called *Where's the Melody?*[2] In all but the first chorus of this performance, it's a good question.

[2]Martin Williams, *Where's the Melody?* New York, Pantheon Books, 1969.

What this cut shows is several different conceptions of how to treat the material of a standard 32-bar pop song in an arrangement for a small jazz group. Also, it shows how the bridge section is pulled out for emphasis each time by changing instrumentation for it. And it shows, finally, the differences in approach that are possible because of the capabilities of the particular instruments—for example, that the piano can handle more of the musical fabric than any single melody instrument can do.

During the big band period of the 1930s and 1940s, Benny Goodman (born 1909) was known as the "King of Swing." He formed his first band in 1934 and shortly thereafter achieved great success.

He has toured abroad independently and under the auspices of the U.S. State Department. He has also played and recorded with small combinations—combos—made up of band members, as in this recording, and has appeared a number of times in performances of classical music as a featured soloist.

Coleman Hawkins (1904–1969) was one of the most influential saxophone players in jazz history, and his 1939 recording of "Body and Soul" was one of the most important cuts of its time. For one thing, the heavy vibrato he used was more emotional than most of the sax players were using at the time. But more important from the musical standpoint, his "Body and Soul" indicated a new direction for melodic improvisation. He combined the abilities to use his instrument to outline the harmony—run the chords—and to fashion an entirely new melody without losing the "sense" of the music's original implications. As a result, many jazz players memorized note for note his version of this piece as a departure point for their own improvisations.

PRIMARY LISTENING:
Sour, Green, and Heyman, "Body and Soul," Coleman Hawkins and His Orchestra (Columbia: P 6–11891)

The recording goes through only two choruses of the song. The first chorus is all Hawkins with a drum and piano accompaniment that does nothing except furnish the chords and background beat. For the first few bars Hawkins is pretty much on the tune. That lasts only a short time, however, because he soon starts to wander into his own ideas (Example 81). Comparing this version to Benny Goodman's gives us a good example of the differences that can exist between two skilled players with different ideas of improvisation and variation.

The orchestra comes in for the second chorus, but only to play the chords. With them in the background, we can fully appreciate how Hawkins both covers the harmony and fashions his own melody. The band drops out for the bridge, and Hawkins gets more

Example 81
"Body and Soul": Coleman Hawkins' improvisation.

(Coleman Hawkins - 1st A)

and more involved in his own ideas. When the band comes back in for the final A section, Hawkins gets quite dissonant in his solo, not only extending the range of the sax but also extending the notes of the chords. The piece ends with a very brief *cadenza*, a sort of free solo where the accompaniment drops out. The word comes from *cadence*, and the device is common to many compositions and forms that use a soloist with an accompaniment group. Many solo concerti, for instance, use a cadenza during which the soloist goes off into a virtuoso section that can last for quite a long time. The ending cadenza in "Body and Soul" is very brief, but it gives Hawkins a chance to explore by himself some of the ideas he has for bringing the performance to a close. And like most cadenzas, the rhythm is free and the whole feeling is rhapsodic.

These two performances tell us something about the differences in improvisational techniques between the East and the West. In the Eastern performances, conventional restrictions pretty clearly define what is possible for the performer, even to limiting the particular notes that can be ornamented and the manner of the ornamentation itself. There is a whole set of formulas, in fact, and learning them and how and when to apply them is one of the main tasks of the Eastern musician. This is not true in jazz to nearly the same extent, although there is bound to be a certain amount of interpreters' "copying" ideas from one another. Many influential jazz performers have been important precisely because they have gone beyond the conventions of their predecessors and developed new ideas of improvised variations. Not only were they skilled technicians, which means that they handled their instruments with more than the usual virtuosity; they also had much to contribute to the creative aspects of improvisation—new ways to use the harmony, new melodic ideas, sometimes new concepts of rhythm within which to work. These are the things that highlight the history of jazz and make it such a glorious part of the American contribution to the culture of the world. And because this kind of musical exploration and spontaneous creativity occurred *only* in jazz for many years, we can identify it as unique in the history of Western musical development. During the medieval, Renaissance and Baroque periods there was much improvisation as we have seen. Then, however, it was largely restricted to the choice of instruments and to adding decorative passages to pre-existent melodies. It did not involve structuring entirely new tunes "on the spot," so to speak.

So the idea of using a single thematic idea, melodically based, around which to fashion a longer musical composition or performance is a common one in the world of music. Different cultures treat it differently and different traditions and conventions control it to varying degrees. In all cases, however, it represents one way to bring coherence to music when there are no extramusical guidelines furnished by words or program. It is a way to organize sound so that it makes sense by itself, and it provides an element of control for the composer and performer as well as a focal point for the listener.

SUPPLEMENTAL LISTENING   Since the swing era, the 32-bar pop song has been among the most consistently used forms. In this age of nostalgia, there are a host of reissues of the big bands from the thirties and forties. Any of them will show different approaches to improvisation, since most of them feature choruses or portions of choruses assigned to soloists. At the same time, about two-thirds or more of the songs will use the A A B A form discussed above. One interesting set of composed variations on a 32-bar pop tune is George Gershwin's *Variations on "I Got Rhythm."* RCA Victor: LSC–2586.

Chapter 26
Passacaglia

Closely related to the type of theme and variations we have been discussing is the form known as the *passacaglia*. There are, however, some significant differences. The word comes from Spanish and means literally "to step in the street"; in this case "to step" means "to dance," and originally a passacaglia was a slow, rather dignified dance. As is so often the case, the function was abandoned and the musical organization assumed a greater importance; the association with dancing is almost entirely lost, but the formal arrangement has been used by many composers.

Your ears will tell you what that arrangement is. As always, the musical score (Example 82) will reinforce what you hear.

PRIMARY LISTENING:
Johann Sebastian Bach, Passacaglia in C minor for organ, 1708–1717

This is one of the easiest forms to hear because the theme is presented to us without any other musical activity to attract our attention. Bach's theme in this organ piece is one of those types that carries with it a strong sense of the harmony that will "fit" best; the first three notes, for instance, outline the key, C minor. The rest is a bit more subtle until we come to the cadence, which moves very firmly to the tonic. We have in this and other passacaglias an eight-measure theme, presented monophonically in the bass, or lowest voice, carrying certain harmonic implications that can be worked into the variations that occur above it through the rest of the composition. Notice, also, that the music is in triple meter. That particular feature comes directly from the dance out of which the form evolved.

Example 82
Bach, Passacaglia in C minor.

If you are a person who tries to keep up with the logical development of events, you will notice that there are 21 appearances of the theme. Another way of saying the same thing is that there is a theme with 20 variations. It is in the nature of a passacaglia that each variation is the same length—the length of the theme—and any departures from this are considered to be irregularities. That pattern of eight-measure repetitions is followed rigidly in Bach's composition. Also, due to the way a passacaglia is put together, if the theme is grounded in a key center with a strong sense of harmonic solidarity—if it is not, for instance, highly chromatic—then the harmony throughout is apt to be consistent and repetitive. Again this is the case in Bach's Passacaglia in C Minor. There are melodic movements in the various voices that tend to obscure this sometimes, and the cadences are treated in such a way that we sometimes lose the sense of arrival at the tonic just at the right time. But these add interest and relieve the monotony instead of destroying or changing the harmonic underpinning. Because of the control exercised by the theme, the passacaglia has an inherent trap that composers need to overcome: the danger of repetitious rigidity, and resultant boredom. The way out is through variations that add enough interest to somehow disguise the constant melodic and harmonic and even rhythmic discipline that the theme exerts.

One "out" is to vary the rhythm of the theme without destroying the melody and harmony. Bach does this several times, first during the fifth variation, the sixth appearance of the theme. In this case the rhythm is somewhat disjointed in the bass, but the first beat of each measure arrives strongly with the right note of the theme at the right time.

Another procedure Bach uses is to take the theme out of the bass and put it into another voice. This happens in the eleventh variation when the theme jumps into the highest (soprano) part.

The thirteenth variation has the theme hidden in an inside voice. And the fourteenth and fifteenth don't have it as a melody at all, but hide it inside a battery of broken-chord outlines. Beginning with the sixteenth variation, the theme is back in the bass, where it "belongs," and there it stays until the final cadence.

There are many other ways to vary the theme itself without losing it altogether; the ones described are just the particular ones that Bach uses in this particular passacaglia. Perhaps you can imagine others—or listen to other passacaglias to discover what else might be accomplished within the guidelines of the form.

Aside from varying the theme, this is an active and complex piece of music in spite of its basically repetitive nature, and like all complex things, we need to attack it from all angles if we are interested in digging into it seriously. But the music will reveal more than words, and will do it more quickly. Some complexities, and the exciting kinds of things that they reveal, just cannot be well articulated.

The Baroque period in which Bach wrote his Passacaglia in C minor was in general one of great complexity, and the arts of the time all show this (Illustrations 28 and 29). Refer again to chapter 5 for more details. You can hear a lot of this complexity in the Bach passacaglia. The organ is a particularly suitable instrument for this sort of texture. Besides the foot pedals, which can handle a melody if the player is skillful enough, there are usually at least two manuals (keyboards), often even three, and each is capable of producing very distinctive tone qualities if the proper registration (combination of pipes) is used. Thus it is possible to have three different melodies with three very different tonal characteristics all going on at the same time. This makes it relatively easy for our ears to sort them out. Some people are bothered by all that extravagance of sound. Others like to try to hear the variety of relationships. The point is that with so much happening, it takes repeated listening before we can really say that we've heard everything. The Passacaglia in C Minor gives you a chance to test your perceptivity. If it all turns out to be just too much for you, that is informative too: maybe you simply don't have a Baroque personality.

The German organist and composer Johann Sebastian Bach (1685–1750) was the most illustrious member of a large musical dynasty that extended for several generations before and after him.

His principal positions were:

Weimar, 1708–1717: organist and concertmaster of the court orchestra
Cöthen, 1717–1723: conductor of the court orchestra
Leipzig, 1723–1750: cantor (choirmaster) at Thomas School, which supplied musicians for the city's churches.

At all these locations, Bach composed music for the type of responsibility he fulfilled. In general, the Weimar compositions are for organ and keyboard, the Cöthen works are for instrumental chamber groups, and the Leipzig pieces are sacred choral compositions. He composed in practically all the known forms except opera.

Illustration 28. CARTEL CLOCK AND BRACKET. Jacques Caffieri, about 1745. The word "baroque" means rough (irregularly shaped) pearl and implies imperfection. As it was first used to apply to art and music, it was a negative appraisal of elaborate, often extravagant decorative detail. The interplay of swirling patterns here correlates strongly to the intricacy of Baroque musical polyphony. Collection of the J. B. Speed Art Museum, Louisville, Kentucky.

Illustration 29. FRENCH CANDLEHOLDER WITH LOUIS XVI APPLIQUÉ. Nineteenth century. Appliqué is ornamental addition to a figure usually in relief. Here the artist is re-creating some elements of rococo style, in vogue during the reign of Louis XVI, King of France from 1774 to 1792. The more delicate but fussier rococo style was an elaboration of the Baroque temper extended into the Classic period. Rococo and Classic artistic devices are somewhat contradictory, although they do share a concern for elegance of design and detail. Collection of the J. B. Speed Art Museum, Louisville, Kentucky.

His output was enormous and, with Handel, he is considered to represent the peak and summation of Baroque musical style.

Among his many strengths was his great control over the architecture of polyphonic forms. His *Art of Fugue* is the undisputed masterpiece of that genre. Representative of his stylistic characteristics are his *Brandenburg Concertos,* his B Minor Mass, his more than 300 church cantatas, his organ works, and the collection of preludes and fugues in his *Well-tempered Clavier.*

SUPPLEMENTAL LISTENING

Two other interesting passacaglias, one contemporary with Bach and the other from the twentieth century, are:

Arcangelo Corelli, *La Follia,* Opus 5, No. 12.

Although the bass line and the harmonic progression remain fairly consistent throughout this piece for string orchestra, there are a number of interesting departures. In contrast to the Bach passacaglia discussed above, the theme does not appear as an unaccompanied bass statement at the beginning but rather as one of several voices accompanying the melody, which was well known at the time and used by other composers. The relationship between the passacaglia and the chaconne, discussed in the next chapter, is very strong. A composition like Corelli's illustrates why many theorists make no distinctions between the two forms. Corelli (1653–1713) was an Italian composer and violinist who traveled throughout Europe, but most of his work was done in Rome. He was influential in establishing the violin technique and musical style that led into the use of that instrument as the dominant one in the orchestras of his period. His chamber sonatas and concerti grossi are representative of the mid-Baroque instrumental approach.

Aaron Copland, *Passacaglia.*

The process of statement and succeeding variations in this piece for piano is as described for Bach's Passacaglia in C minor. Because of the harmonic style, typical of twentieth century linear dissonance, the sense of tonal security is less apparent. But the theme is quite consistent. It changes registers with relative frequency, but it does remain perceptible, and so it offers a reference point that balances the otherwise dissonant contrapuntal texture.

Chapter 27
Chaconne and Blues

There is another monothematic form that is closely related to the passacaglia and that falls generally within the theme-and-variations concept. Although theorists differ among themselves about what constitutes a real passacaglia, many agree that strict observance of the form demands that the theme appear at the start in the bass voice and without accompanying harmony of any sort. A closely related form is the *chaconne*, also derived from a dance, the basis of which is a repeated harmonic progression. Sometimes the bass theme also remains the same throughout, as well as the harmony, and in that case there is a mixture of forms, passacaglia and chaconne. That's what happens in Johann Pachelbel's Canon in D major.

A bass theme that persists throughout a composition is called an *ostinato bass* (obstinate bass), a *ground bass*, or sometimes just a *ground*. We say that the composition is built on a ground or on an ostinato bass. When the harmonic pattern is also persistent, then we have one type of chaconne, and an easy one to hear.

A brief aside should be inserted here. A "real" chaconne not only uses a reiterated harmonic progression; it is also in triple meter and slow, and its bass theme is eight bars long. In Pachelbel's piece, we have some of the characteristics but not all of them. This is one more example of the confusion that our mania for identification and classification gets us into.

A further complication of terminology with Pachelbel's piece is that it is also a canon—a different matter altogether. *Canon* is a more esoteric name for a round (like "Row, Row, Row Your Boat"). The canon in this piece by Pachelbel is in the highest strings. The ground bass is in the low string bass, and the repeated harmony is in the harpsichord and the pizzicato strings. So there is a lot happening. To condense the description to its most basic terms, this is a sort of chaconne employing a ground bass over which there is a canon. We will be taking a close look at some canons in a later chapter; at this point, we are concentrating on the bass line and the harmony.

PRIMARY LISTENING:
Johann Pachelbel, Canon in D major (record set)

Try listening to see if you can enjoy the gentle interplay of the musical lines and at the same time be aware of the security given by the recurrence of the harmonic background (Example 83).

A German organist and composer, Pachelbel (1653–1706) served as court organist at Eisenach, Stuttgart, and elsewhere. He was well known for his treatment of chorales and thus an influence on the style of J. S. Bach. He composed suites, organ fugues, cantatas, and sacred choral works.

We are not sure when Pachelbel wrote this piece. Since he died in 1706, we do know that it was written earlier than Bach's Passacaglia, which was composed sometime between 1708 and 1717. The use of a ground bass and a chaconne theme was common in the Baroque period; there are many pieces called simply "Chaconne in C" or "Chaconne in G" or whatever. Also there are many pieces like "Theme on a Ground" or even just "A New Ground." Titles of that sort are never helpful in trying to understand the expressive intent of the composer. They identify only the form and give us some guidance in listening along those lines. In spite of this, the compositions frequently do project a strong sense of mood.

For some reason, Pachelbel's Canon in D major has been especially popular with college students, meeting with an almost universally positive reaction from them. Trying to understand why falls within the province of aesthetics. Whatever else it may involve, it surely involves the interaction of form and content. The form is not unique, and neither is the melodic smoothness; many works from all periods use conjunct melodies. The harmony, while interesting, is not particularly rich nor explorative—not nearly so rich, for instance, as that of "Body and Soul." And the rhythm, although varied, is nothing to get ecstatic about. So where does the mood of

Example 83
Pachelbel, Canon in D major.

tranquility and quiet freedom and sometimes even brief exultation come from? Does it matter? Does it matter to *you?* Aesthetics. A field with almost no answers but with a whole barrelful of questions.

Johannes Brahms, although a true Romantic in many ways, was also inclined toward Classicism in his attraction to intricacies of structure and the formal discipline that he exercised in his work. This makes him a "formalist," and he was one of the most skillful ones in the nineteenth century.

A German composer and pianist, Brahms (1833–1897) began his career as a protégé of Robert Schumann, who supported him in the Schumann periodical *Neue Zeitschrift für Musik.* Brahms's first wide recognition came as a result of his *German Requiem* (1868), which, typically, was Romantic in feeling but Classic in form. Because of his adherence to Classic clarity of form he was constantly at aesthetic odds with Liszt and Wagner. He is famous for orchestral, piano, and chamber works and for his original songs and settings of folk songs.

There is always a sense of structural concern in Brahms's compositions, and his Fourth Symphony's last movement, our next listening selection, is no exception. It is a true chaconne, although there is nothing in the title nor in the tempo marking to indicate this. All the latter tells us is that the tempo is fast and that the piece is to be performed with energy and passion (Example 84). As we expect in this form, the theme is eight measures long, the meter is triple, and the material is presented as a series of chords. One thing that the chords accomplish here, as in all other tonal chaconnes, is the establishment of the key, in this case E minor. (Notice, however, that the first chord we hear in the chaconne theme is not an E minor chord; the first two chords are actually leading us to E minor and that comes in the third measure. To complicate matters, the final chord in the theme is E major each time! What Brahms is doing is writing a sort of circular harmonic progression that leads us easily out of one statement of the theme into the beginning of the next. This is pretty heavy stuff, but if you are attracted to theory and/or the complexity of Brahms's musical thinking, it might interest you.) The music isn't going to stay in minor all the way through; for one important section it will be in E major. Also, because Brahms is very much of the nineteenth century, there is going to be an enormous

Example 84
Brahms, Symphony No. 4.

amount of harmonic enrichment, so that the consistency of key feeling that we had in Bach and Pachelbel should not be expected here. In every way, this is a tough piece.

PRIMARY LISTENING:
Johannes Brahms, Fourth Symphony, fourth movement, Allegro energico e passionato, 1885

Whenever complexity is the order of the day, one needs something to cling to in order to follow developments. There are several such things in this piece. If you listen very carefully—and perhaps even six or eight times—to the statement of the theme, you will hear an ascending scalewise passage in the flutes, reinforced by the oboe and partially by the trombones. This is an important bit of thematic material and will recur in different instrumental voices throughout the movement. At the same time you will hear a descending pattern in the low trombones (refer again to Example 84). That's important too, and it occurs often, although in differing voices. Another guideline is the fact that Brahms, being inclined toward Classic clarity, keeps the length of the theme consistent throughout; so if you count, count in groups of eight measures. Another help is the meter—triple—which is retained at all times. One confusing thing, however, is that the tempo, the rate of speed at which the beats and the metric accents occur, is *not* consistent. For one rather extended section, the beats are very, very slow relative to the fast opening tempo. But they are still in groups of three, and they cover a span of eight measures. Still another clue, if you are following the progress of the form, is the arrival of cadences in the varying key centers. Remember that a chaconne is oriented in harmony. Brahms is a tonal composer and so he uses his cadences to reinforce the strength of his key centers. Although you may need to concentrate very hard, you can possibly hear the movement to the tonic at the end of each eight-measure segment.

A characteristic of Brahms's style is the shifting of metric accents, so that even though he doesn't actually change the meter, it often *sounds* as though he is working with groups of two or four instead of three. That's merely a question of retaining three beats to a measure but grouping *accents* so that they fall in patterns of two or four. The proper name for this is *hemiola*. Again, this is hard to hear, but if you are the kind of person who wants to contribute something to the experiencing of art, you will be willing to do your part here.

One last clue to use in trying to understand the development of this music is the number of times the chaconne theme is stated. Can you figure this out for yourself? Brahms helps, by returning to the original form of the theme twice to remind you what the music is all about. Both of these returns come after some of the most complex passages. If you have been lost, they give you a chance to reorient yourself.

All of this has to do with following the form. Brahms's treatment of the form is so immensely complicated that one *needs* help in order to comprehend fully what he is doing, structurally speaking. And this raises an important question about the part organization plays in our experiencing of things. In this case, when keeping up with the form is such a problem, how important should it become for the listener? In other words, does the form matter? Is the organization significant to the experience?

Some things that have nothing to do with music—say, the organization of our government—are terribly complex mechanisms. Imagine them without patterns of procedure that exercise some control and discipline over the way they operate. If there were no formal pattern, could they achieve at all the things they are expected to achieve?

Somewhere in the middle, between total anarchy and total rigidity of control, there is a way to have the best of both worlds. Sometimes we call it "working within the system." All organizations if they are of any service at all to human beings, have rubbery places where some stretching can be done. But if the system is a good one, it won't break altogether. Isn't our government a little bit like this, with its allowance for modification and interpretation without annihilation of the underlying principles that keep it stable where it matters?

Maybe, for the creative artist, form works this way. And if we are to be rational participants in the artistic experience, maybe we need to understand something about the guidelines within which the composer works in order to understand exactly what kinds of things his imagination and craftsmanship are inspiring him to do. As with our government, if we fail to understand we are not able to work "within the system" at all.

For Brahms, the form does matter. And if we pay him the compliment of listening carefully enough to follow him through it, we will have learned something valuable about the creative process, and the listening process as well.

A very surprising relative of the chaconne is the blues. You might like to refer back to chapter 3 and "How Long Blues" to remind yourself that the blues is organized around a repeated series of chords. "How Long Blues" is an eight-bar blues, but the most important form of the blues for jazz was the twelve-bar type. In its "purest" form, it is organized like this:

Four bars of tonic
Two bars of subdominant

> Two bars of tonic
> Two bars of dominant
> Two bars of tonic.

When it is a vocal blues, there is an added feature and one that has something to do with form as well as with its popularity in jazz. It works this way:

> Two bars vocal—tonic
> Two bars instrumental—still tonic
> Two bars vocal, using same words as first two
>   bars—subdominant
> Two bars instrumental—tonic
> Two bars vocal, using different words from the first two vocal
>   sections—dominant
> Two bars instrumental—tonic

Thus the vocal part, taken from the viewpoint of its text alone, is an a a b form, although the tune of all three sections will be different. Depending on the performer, the instrumental sections are apt to be almost anything. A singer playing his or her own guitar accompaniment might just strum chords to fill in the breaks or might go off into some fanciful improvisational passages. The important feature of the form is that it has a built-in invitation to improvise during the recurring two-bar breaks between words. That's one way in which it thrived during the early years of blues recordings. Many famous jazz instrumentalists of all sorts were hired to "back" blues vocalists, and when they were of the stature of Louis Armstrong, their improvisations were often just as interesting and important to the piece as were the vocal sections. Also, when they were well known and skillful, they often took a chorus or part of one as a solo.

PRIMARY LISTENING:
"Bridwell Blues," Nolan
Welsh, vocal, Louis
Armstrong, trumpet,
Richard Jones, piano
(record set)

All of these things happen in the performance of "Bridwell Blues" on our record set. The only departures from the pattern given above are the movement to the dominant chord in the second bar and another two-beat insertion in the eleventh bar. The harmonic background is easy to hear on this recording because all the piano does is to beat out the chords, one to each pulse (Example 85).

The subject matter is a common one in the blues and one that every black could understand from his own experience or the experience of someone close to him. It's the age-old situation of conflict with "the law" (Bridwell was a jail), this time in the context of vagrancy. In 1926, when this was made, the recordings were designed specifically for circulation in the black community—in fact, they were called "Race Records," advertised by that term, and even

Example 85
"Bridwell Blues."

identified that way on the label. As a result, the texts spoke to common problems and experiences of that group. The fact that Nolan Welsh, the vocalist, is recounting his own actual experience (he uses his own name in one of the stanzas) adds an important personal touch. Many blues were autobiographical in content, and they furnish a valuable record of the singers' experiences as well as those of their community.

There are important musical characteristics other than the chord progressions that run through all blues, instrumental or vocal. One is microtonal inflections, or "bending" the note, which we have heard frequently in "ear" music from different parts of the world. Another related melodic characteristic is the interchange between certain scale degrees. That sounds complex but isn't. It only means that the third step of the scale is sometimes in the major mode and sometimes in the minor mode. In the scale of F, for instance, A and

$A^\flat$ are interchangeable—*but without destroying the basically major tonality*. This means that "blue notes," as the alternate pitches are called, are melodic factors, completely divorced from any harmonic concept. The same vacillation occurs often on the seventh degree— in F, that would be exchanging E for $E^\flat$ without upsetting the major harmonic background. Most melodic descriptions of the blues emphasize these two variable pitches, the third and the seventh, sometimes adding the fifth degree. In actual practice, however, *any* note can be bent, and frequently is. Unless one wants to get terribly complicated about melodic characteristics, it is necessary only to realize that microtonal inflections of the pitch are a feature of the blues. If they are missing, the blues loses much of its real character.

"Bridwell Blues" is full of such characteristics. Right at the beginning of the introduction Armstrong on trumpet begins to use alternate pitches and bent notes. Welsh employs the slurred sort of diction that was typical of many early blues singers, but the text was understandable to the public that bought the records even though we may have difficulty catching all the words now. Some of this is a result of the relatively primitive recording techniques. A lot of it has its history in the rural singers whose background was in field hollers and street cries. There is some carry-over of this in rock, incidentally, in spite of our advanced methods of recording: many times the text is almost indecipherable. Is this because other elements are more important for us, or is it because most of the characteristics of rock are derived from rhythm-and-blues, including the vocal approach?

In any case, in "Bridwell Blues" the pitch inflections are everywhere in evidence, and Armstrong's instrumental comments between Welsh's words are always in the mood of the piece. He did a lot of this kind of duet recording, and some of his reputation was based on it. He was paired with some of the biggest recording stars of his day, including the incomparable Bessie Smith, even after his magnificent technique and improvisational ability had made him a star among white audiences (Illustration 30).

New Orleans jazz trumpeter Louis Armstrong (1900–1971) was the first trumpet soloist to win international acclaim. His first important job was with King Oliver in Chicago in 1922. He was engaged as featured soloist with Fletcher Henderson's big band in New York in 1924 but soon returned to Chicago. There he made recordings with his Hot Five and Hot Seven groups. By 1929 he was well known enough to start bookings with various big bands, after which he toured extensively in the United States and abroad. During the blues craze of the 1920s he recorded with a number of blues stars, including Ma Rainey as well as Bessie Smith. He was active and immensely popular until the illness preceding his death.

As said above, our recording has the pure 12-bar form except for

Illustration 30.
LOUIS ARMSTRONG.

the brief harmonic variations in the second and eleventh bars of each chorus. Because of the relative consistency of the 12-bar chorus length and the harmonic changes that had become standardized, a recording like this one could be made without rehearsal. The guidelines were clear to everybody—how many bars of this chord, how many bars of that, which chorus was to be instrumental. Even the little harmonic pattern at the final two bars of each chorus had become standardized by this period (it was also there in "How Long Blues"), so that all the players knew what to expect and could work within it. When Welsh drops out for Armstrong's chorus, notice that the piano becomes a little more active. In many cases like this

the pianist would provide the two-measure breaks between what would normally be the singing sections. Richard Jones, however, never takes over, so Armstrong plays his own breaks to fill in the spaces of the form.

One last observation on the style of delivery in the type of blues that "Bridwell Blues" represents. Be conscious of the vocalist's almost speechlike treatment of the text, the relatively restricted range, the kinds of upward and downward inflections at cadences that we associate with speech. This is characteristic of many blues singers, especially those from a rural background. The tendency to treat the vocal line as a type of heightened speech is another common thread that leads from country to country and period to period. Peculiar to no individual style, it is probably an indication that singing itself is basically an outgrowth of speech—a way of intensifying it. There are many gradations between pure speech and pure song, so to speak, if we think of them as being at opposite poles. Popular singers of all types differ greatly in this respect. Compare Frank Sinatra with Bob Dylan, or even compare early Sinatra with late Sinatra. Do the differences relate to the differences between Handel's vocal line and the vocal delivery of the blues? In what way?

The transition from speech to song is particularly fascinating in the blues. African melodic style covers an extremely narrow range, and very often the vocal rhythms are more those of elongated speech than of song. The melodies do use enormous inflections of individual pitches, however, and that quality was never totally lost in America. In field hollers and street cries, two of the ancestors of the structured blues, we find a similar short-range and speechlike freedom of delivery. When an accompaniment was added, as with a guitar, more musical characteristics began to emerge. Harmony was one of them, naturally, but another was a more regular flow of rhythm. The musical elements, in other words, were beginning to exert more influence than the speech elements. The establishment of a form, as in "Bridwell Blues," complete with numbers of measures, harmonic progression, and metric rhythmic arrangement, forces a more musically oriented style on the vocal part. Speech inflections are left, and the range of most blues is relatively limited. But for the most part the form has become a musical one and must be described that way.

There is little disagreement that Bessie Smith (1894–1937) was the greatest of the blues singers, at least among those who were recorded at their prime and who appeared before a large public (see Illustration 31). Her background was rural (she was born in Chattanooga, Tennessee), and she began her career singing in carnivals and tent shows under the guidance of Ma Rainey, the first of the

**Illustration 31.
BESSIE SMITH.**

great women blues artists. After her first recording in 1923, Bessie Smith became widely known throughout the country, although practically all of her performances were given for exclusively black audiences. On those occasions when she did sing for whites (usually at small private gatherings), she did little or nothing to hide her disdain for them. Her heavy drinking and her unbridled sexual appetites resulted in innumerable legends, mostly derogatory and often used to reinforce the concept of the black performer (and by extension, the black community) as a less than desirable element of the otherwise spotless society of the country. This side of her life and personality has been exploited in the mania for sensationalism, at the expense of her real contribution, which was musical. Bessie Smith was important because she was a great singer and a great musician working within a tradition of enormous importance to the American musical scene. Lots of people, black and white, have been tortured by alcoholism and sexual impropriety without gaining any wide reputation because of that. The conduct of this singer's personal life is beside the main point of her tremendous musical contributions.

Many of her blues were spontaneous creations of her own, often autobiographical in the way that many blues are. As her popularity waned because of the encroachment of new musical styles and the restrictions of buying power at the height of the Depression, she turned sometimes to popular songs in an attempt to regain her public. Another type of expression that she used was undisguisedly earthy, even downright bawdy. "Empty Bed Blues" is typical of that strain. In 1928, when the recording of it that we shall listen to was made, the blues craze was fading into the sweeter style of the big bands, which were to sweep everything else before them in a few years. If we are to understand the piece and what it represents in perspective, the words (Bessie Smith's own) must be clearly understood.

I woke up this morning with an awful aching head.
I woke up this morning with an awful aching head.
My new man had left me, just a room and a empty bed.

Bought me a coffee grinder that's the best one I could find.
So he could grind my coffee 'cause he had a brand new grind.

He's a deep sea diver with a stroke that can't go wrong.
He can touch the bottom and his wind holds out so long.

He knows how to thrill me and he thrills me night and day.
He's got a new way of lovin' almost takes my breath away.

Lord, he's got that sweet somethin' and I told my gal friend, Lu.
From the way she's ravin', she must have gone and tried it, too.

When my bed gets empty makes me feel awful mean and blue.
My springs are gettin' rusty, sleepin' single like I do.

Bought him a blanket, pillow for his bed at night.
Then I bought him a mattress so he could lay just right.

He came home one evening with his spirit way up high.
What he had to give me made me wring my hands and cry.

He give me a lesson that I never had before.
When he got through teachin' me from my elbows down was sore.

He boiled my fresh cabbage and he made it awful hot.
When he put in the bacon, it overflowed the pot.

When you get good lovin', never go and spread the news.
He will double-cross you and leave you with them empty bed blues.

PRIMARY LISTENING:
"Empty Bed Blues," Bessie Smith, vocal, Charlie Green, trombone, Porter Grainger, piano, March 20, 1928 (record set)

This is a real twelve-bar blues, standard in every way. Gunther Schuller in *Early Jazz* has called Bessie Smith the first great jazz singer because of her approach to melody and rhythm. Try concentrating on the way she manipulates her rhythm around the beat, for instance, anticipating it, sliding in after it, using it for her own purposes but never losing the momentum that it provides. Her vocal inflections are magnificent, but they never inhibit the delivery of the text, even when she breathes in the middle of a word. One of her strong points as a performer, in fact, was her incisive manner of delivery, avoiding the slurred treatment of the words that had been typical of many earlier blues singers. There is a unique strength and drive to her singing. In public, she never used a mike, because her voice was dynamically strong enough without it. Neither does she resort to tricks of any kind. She was as honest and direct in her singing as she was in her life style. Much of her fame and much of the respect she has gained through the years are due to just this absolute integrity that shines through in all her work.

Charlie Green on trombone was one of her favorites, and this recording should give all the reasons. This is really "dirty" trombone, and given the subject matter of the song, nothing could be more appropriate. Each instrumental interlude is loaded with exactly the right response to the text that precedes it, and Green drags every bit of expressive nuance out of the horn. Porter Grainger on piano adds his own musical comments, changing style with the various choruses. But in spite of all the musical variables, the interest is in the text, on which the musicians merely elaborate.

This is an unusually long cut for the period. Most recordings were just about three minutes in duration because that's what you could get on one side of a 78-rpm record. This one happens to have been recorded on both sides. Obviously everyone was having a good time. Why cut the fun short?

By any standards that we might like to apply, this is a bawdy song—in most communities it would be considered inappropriate for radio broadcast even today, at least on AM stations—and so it raises questions that directly relate to the continuing controversy about the nature of pornography in all the entertainment media. What makes it unusually interesting is the fact that it was produced quite some time before rating systems were in effect and before there was wide public concern about the legality of censorship. Nor is it entirely unique: there was a considerable amount of this type of musical expression being circulated openly in 1928.

But most of it was on race records. And that should raise a few eyebrows. This was not produced by some crack-in-the-wall, fly-by-night, underground recording studio. It was produced and marketed by Columbia Records, one of the most prestigious record firms. Along with all other race records, it was advertised openly in journals—all black—and sold across the counter without any kind of censoring control whatever. There was no protest of significant proportions from anyone, nor any attempt to hide the product. The only whites who contacted it were the afficionado fringe, devotees of jazz and the blues, mostly those engaged in a professional way with performance. When it was broadcast on radio, which it was, it was done over stations that were patronized exclusively by blacks. In other words, this was a black singing for blacks, as much an in-group matter as anything could be, given the freedom of anyone of any color to buy the record or tune in the station.

A number of conclusions are possible, such as that in the midst of an otherwise circumspect sense of public and private morality, the blacks were a dirty-minded folk. That their sexual appetites were depraved and lacked the disciplines of civilization. That the jungle was still there.

Unhappily for such easy conclusions, though, there are other conditions to consider. There was no lack of the most blatant pornography in America—under the counter. In literature, "French novels" were easily gotten—for a usually exorbitant price. There was a large supply of "stag" movies, as specific as anything being produced today by the underground (and overground) film makers. Barroom ballads were sung at many social gatherings—for males. All of these things were patently off-color, though, and because of that they were banned, censored, forbidden, illegal.

The history of censorship has something interesting to add here. Think about the year that Bessie Smith cut her "Empty Bed Blues": 1928. Aldous Huxley's *Antic Hay* was written in 1923—and banned in 1930. D. H. Lawrence's *Lady Chatterley's Lover* was written in 1928—and barred by the U.S. Customs in 1929. Eugene O'Neill's *Desire under the Elms* opened in 1924—and was closed by police in 1925. John Cleland's *Memoirs of Fanny Hill*, written in 1749, was banned in Massachusetts in 1821—the first known obscenity case in America.

Not until 1963, when it was published by Grove Press and declared obscene by the Massachusetts Supreme Judicial Court, did *Fanny Hill* finally make its way to the top—the U.S. Supreme Court—where in 1966 it was allowed to circulate freely above the counter.

So there was a market and there were creative artists on hand to fill the demand, even as today. But official censorship, not just public indignation and wrath, was also on hand to protect the citizenry.

What does all this mean? For one thing, it means that pornography is not so easily defined, apparently (see Illustration 32). An editor of a recent collection of bawdy songs published by a respected university press has suggested that the difference between bawdy material and pornography is in the element of humor. In these terms, pornography is studiously serious, but the tongue-in-cheek humor of bawdy literature acts as a redeeming factor. It makes it fun rather than filth, in other words.

Other defenders of erotica refer to the use of symbolism rather than direct statement. There are no four-letter words in "Empty Bed Blues." Although there is no attempt to disguise the real situation, many allusions are couched in symbols. No one with imagination could suppose that Bessie Smith is talking about preparation of a breakfast drink when she sings about grinding coffee. Nor is the man in the song getting dinner ready when he boils her cabbage. But here the listener is being asked to supply something, and that's one function of symbolism. This contrasts rather sharply to some current films and books in which the sexualism and violence are so graphic that no demand is made on the creative imagination of the audience. This may have nothing to do with "redeeming social value"—according to the courts, the element that makes an otherwise censorable work of art acceptable—but it has a great deal to do with art.

Aside from definitions, always a plague, it might be valid to ask about double standards of morality. Was there such a double standard operating in 1928 that made it "safe" to openly circulate material like "Empty Bed Blues" within a certain predetermined market while at the same time restricting similar subject matter within a different market? Another question involves the use of courts of law, up to the Supreme Court, for control of "pornography": was even the law applied differently according to which racial category a work was classified under? We have made great strides as a nation in facing up to such dilemmas. There are still a lot of questions, though, and "Empty Bed Blues" raises a number of them.

As a musical form and a vehicle for improvisation, the 12-bar blues was absorbed by blues and jazz instrumental and vocal groups almost from the time of its standardization. The harmonic regularity and the control of phrasing in four-measure blocks gave the only

Illustration 32. THE TOWER.
Paul Cadmus, 1960. Open to
many interpretations, this
work will be seen by many
viewers as at least borderline
pornography. This perception
would probably be intensified
by conservatives if they were
aware that Cadmus was a
homosexual. Even so, the
tendency is to accept nudity
and associated expressions
more gracefully in the visual
arts than in other media.
Perhaps paintings and
sculpture are "redeemed"
because they are displayed in
the highly sedate atmosphere
of art museums or
(sometimes) cathedrals.
Collection of the J. B. Speed Art
Museum, Louisville, Kentucky.

necessary guidelines. All that had to be decided was the key; once that was agreed upon, groups could improvise for hours at a time, with or without singers, and they frequently did just that. It is difficult for those of us who lead more pedestrian lives to believe that a relatively large assortment of musicians can sit down and perform a piece entirely without rehearsal. And they couldn't unless the format were so clearly understood that each individual could find his way around in it without bumping into someone else. "Red Rooster" is evidence enough that it can be done.

Fortunately the initial discussion and rather sketchy performance directions were preserved on this recording. Howlin' Wolf, the singer (1910-1976), also had a less colorful name: Chester Burnett. A blues singer and guitar and harmonica player, he was brought up and indoctrinated in the southern rural blues tradition. Widely travelled, including in Europe, he appeared at many festivals and in numerous clubs. His style was one of the influences on English rock style, notably that of the Rolling Stones. Howlin' Wolf's inimitable vocal style may give you a clue to where he got the name that he performed under for many years. The men with whom he is working here are mostly English and associated with rock. They include Eric Clapton, Steve Winwood, Bill Wyman, Charlie Watts, and Lafayette Leake, among others. All of them are obviously very comfortable with what is expected of them in the context of this performance.

PRIMARY LISTENING:
"Red Rooster," Howlin' Wolf (record set)

Having gotten the "details" of musical direction out of the way, they all sail into "Red Rooster." This is a "straight" rendition of a 12-bar blues, meaning that there is no modification in the classic harmonic progression or in the length of each chorus. Although some of the instruments get caught up in rather repetitive motives, *all* of them are improvising. Notice particularly the piano and its variations from chorus to chorus.

A standard part of such group efforts was the insertion of an instrumental chorus amid the vocal choruses. This performance adheres to that tradition. And again, even though there are eight players involved, all of them playing by ear rather than from notes, there is no stumbling around. The controls are the form and the harmony; in spite of all the polyphonic activity going on, those guidelines are observed by everyone and that's where the coherence comes from.

Although many rock groups indulge in this kind of spontaneous improvisation, it is far more rare among them than among jazz musicians. One of the mainstays of the jazz repertoire has been the

12-bar blues. It has been the one form, in fact, that has persisted in jazz from the 1920s to the present day. You can verify that by visiting a jazz festival or a club featuring a small jazz group. It would be unusual to run into a group that did not do at least a few blues during the course of the evening, regardless of what titles they might give the compositions.

SUPPLEMENTAL LISTENING   There are countless examples of the blues in a group setting, with and without vocals. Among them:

> "Blues for Big Scotia," Oscar Peterson. Verve: 2-V6S-8810.
> "Blues for John," Joe Turner, Count Basie, Others. Columbia: G–30776.
> "Blues for Max," Dizzy Gillespie. Solid State: SS–18034.
> "Blues for Tommy Ladnier," Sidney Bechet. Blue Note: BST–81202.
> "Blues in the Dark," Dave Brubeck. Columbia: C–30522.
> "Midnight," B. B. King. ABC: ABCX–743.
> "The Sidewinder," Lee Morgan. *Blue Note's Three Decades of Jazz:* 1959–69. Blue Note: BST–89904.

Few jazz musicians have enjoyed the extended career of Edward Kennedy—"Duke"—Ellington (1899–1974), and even fewer have been so widely recognized for compositional excellence (see Illustration 33). His first club job of importance was at Barron's, one of the largest of the night spots in Harlem, in 1923. Because of his success there, he moved downtown later that year to take over at the Kentucky Club. He stayed there until December 1927, when he moved to the Cotton Club, again in Harlem but with an almost totally white patronage. It was perhaps the most important and famous of New York's nightclubs during the 1920s and 1930s. Because the Cotton Club featured an impressive floor show, Ellington was in a position to compose, to try out new ideas, to use his band in many different ways. And because of the steady employment even during the disastrous years of the Depression, he was able to offer his musicians economic security. In return, he gained a continuity of personnel not common for jazz bands. Some of his original members were, in fact, still in the band at the time of Ellington's death. The result was the development of one of the most integrated ensembles in the history of the art.

Black and Tan Fantasy was written and recorded several months before Ellington went into the Cotton Club. It was done in collaboration with Bubber Miley, a great trumpet player who contributed much to the style of the band and to the nature of its repertoire. The piece was a great success in its 1927 version and continued to be so

Illustration 33.
DUKE ELLINGTON.

popular with Ellington's audiences that he performed it repeatedly throughout his long career. The version on our record set was recorded live during a European tour in 1963, evidence enough of its durability.

PRIMARY LISTENING:
Black and Tan Fantasy,
Duke Ellington (record set)

Ellington precedes the performance with a rather elaborate piano introduction, not a part of the original composition. After this prelude, the *Fantasy* begins much as it was conceived in 1927. The basic material is that of the twelve-bar blues, but there are some interesting variations. In spite of all the manipulation of pitch and the interchange of natural and flat thirds and sevenths in the blues idiom, most blues are in the major mode. The opening trumpet and sax duet of 12 bars in *Black and Tan Fantasy* is in minor (Example 86). But remember that this is essentially a composition, not a blues improvisation. The chord progression is still the standard one for blues, though colored differently because of the mode. There are still four measures of tonic, two of subdominant, two of tonic, two of dominant, two of tonic, in the "right" order. Just for kicks, however, Ellington, throws in two beats of subdominant in the eleventh and twelfth bars—did you catch that?

After that opening 12 bars, we are suddenly into a new section, featuring a sax solo with ensemble accompaniment. The mode changes to major and the mood with it (Example 87). This section lasts for 16 bars, the second 8 of which are a repetition of the first 8. The musical example given here is taken from the original 1927 recording of "Black and Tan Fantasy." The sax player on the record set plays a slightly different version rhythmically while at the same time retaining the melodic outline of the original. Notice, though, his ornamentation on the repetition of the first 8 bars—that's jazz. Throughout this section the harmony is unusually rich, the key changes, and the whole thing has very much an "arranged" sound. This is Ellington the composer at work.

The rest of the performance is a series of blues choruses, some improvised, some arranged. If you follow them carefully, you will

understand how big bands can be handled so that there is a healthy mixture of spontaneity and control—and that's the secret of jazz when it is performed by a large organization. The first 12-bar chorus after the composed introduction is for trumpet solo with only bass, piano, and rhythm accompaniment—improvisation for everybody. The next 24 bars are arranged. The first 12 of these still feature the trumpet soloist but now with a brass section accompaniment built on a series of repeated rhythmic and harmonic figures. In jazz these are called *riffs,* and they are a useful device in this kind of context. In the next 12 bars these same riffs are picked up by the woodwinds with the trumpet contributing a sort of obbligato melody in the background. The next chorus is for clarinet with piano and bass accompanying—more small group improvisation right after an arranged section. Here, however, the harmony is somewhat enriched by Ellington at the keyboard.

Since this is a part of a medley of three pieces, as Ellington tells at the beginning of the cut, there is a transition to the next number. It begins with a rhythmically free soliloquy on the clarinet, settles into a 12-bar chorus over a standard blues harmonic progression, then drifts again into a relatively free rhapsody, and the orchestra is ready for the next piece.

The combination of improvisation and careful scoring here is typical of Ellington's approach to big band jazz. There are advantages, but there are also hazards. During the late 1920's, the development of jazz turned away from small Dixieland groups, with one of each instrument, toward larger bands with, for instance, three trumpets, a trombone or two, four reed instruments, plus piano and rhythm. This big band format and the carefully arranged style associated with it—swing—typified such groups as those led by Benny Goodman, the Dorsey brothers, Glenn Miller, and many others. Section work tended to replace many of the solo choruses, harmonic style became richer, and the emphasis was on masterful ensemble work. The soloists, with a few exceptions, became incidental to the total concept. Playing by ear along with skill at improvisation became of less importance than the ability to read music well and to blend into the section because so much of the music was fully scored—written out. The effect on the traditional jazzmen was dismal. Many of them were simply unable to read music well enough to contribute to the ensembles. Unless they could excel in a solo capacity, there was no work to be had except in low-paying, out-of-the-way spots. Many returned to jobs as dishwashers, day laborers, whatever they could find. Among the many victims was Bunk Johnson. Only with the revival of interest in Dixieland and the old-time performers during the 1940's did anyone make the effort to locate him and return him to the jazz scene.

But the blues remained very much a part of jazz repertoire, and many arrangements, even more elaborate than *Black and Tan Fantasy*, featured that form and harmonic-melodic style.

The original 1927 recording of *Black and Tan Fantasy* is available as a reissue on *Duke Ellington: The Beginning*. Decca: DL 79224. It makes an interesting comparison to the 1963 version discussed above.

One of the better-known pieces using the 12-bar blues is "One O'clock Jump," Count Basie's theme song. Basie's approach to big band jazz is considerably "hotter" and less moody than was Ellington's. Also it involves less arrangement. In his earlier years, when "One O'clock Jump" was developed, his band was geared to "head" arrangements, because this was the general approach in Kansas City, where he began his career. Head arrangements are those in which the performers agree on how to perform a piece but do not write down the notes. They are arranged in the players' heads, as it were. "One O'clock Jump" is a good example of the use of extensive riffs over a blues pattern.

There was a reaction against the sound of the big band and swing, and a new style of jazz came out of that reaction—bebop, sometimes called simply bop. One of the leading figures was Charlie Parker, and his argument with swing was not only the sound but also a much deeper psychological complaint. Through swing and its highly organized arrangements, jazz had become identified equally with white and black performers and audiences. Many black musicians felt that the process had been a "take over" or "rip off" of a musical idiom—jazz—that had been initiated by blacks and in some sense belonged to them. Parker (1920–1955) came out of Kansas City, where the heart of the band repertoire was still the blues and where the most popular style of arranging, even for big bands, was based on extensive improvisation. Behind the soloists the band did play in sections, but they used short, easily mastered riffs so that the arrangements could be put together with little or no rehearsal and thus retain a high degree of spontaneity.

Parker had played extensively with large bands and his solo work was highly respected. The arrangements used by the bands were restrictive, however, and he felt cramped and unable to "stretch out" completely with his improvisations. When he came to New York, he joined the jam sessions at a Harlem club called Minton's Playhouse where Thelonius Monk, Dizzy Gillespie, and others were experimenting with small-group jazz in a style that allowed great individual freedom and lots of room for extended solos. Later the players moved to 52nd Street, the heart of the mid-

Manhattan small jazz club district. There they developed fully the style that became known as bop or be-bop.

It was based on jagged, impetuous rhythms which emphasized the eighth note to such a degree that it virtually replaced the longer quarter-note as the controlling pulse. Many phrases began and ended on eighth notes, in fact, although the eighth is usually thought of as rhythmically weaker than the quarter. The term *bebop* is, in fact, a description of the rhythmic treatment of many phrase endings. The rhythm sections drove the bands hard, adding "bombs"—heavy drum stabs, irregular and strongly syncopated. The beat was kept with the string bass and the cymbal rather than with the heavier bass drum. Over these rhythmic elements, the melodies that Parker fashioned were based on the notes in extensions of the usual chords—ninths, elevenths, thirteenths—which added a more esoteric harmonic implication to the tunes.

The departures from usual band procedures made it difficult for anyone other than the bebop "in-group" to participate in the sessions. Many commentators have suggested that this was intentional: it was an exclusive style, elitist, protected against invasion by unwanted swing players. At the time, bebop was a unique movement in jazz for that reason. According to some of the players themselves, one of the purposes was the return of jazz to black musicians within a small-group format—a return, so to speak, to the Dixieland concept but with far more complex musical characteristics.

Here is a short excerpt from an article in *The New Yorker*, July 3, 1948, giving some of this background:

> Bebop, according to its pioneer practitioners, is a manifestation of revolt. Eight or ten years ago, many Negro jazz musicians . . . began to feel . . . that the white world wanted them to keep to the old-time jazz. They held the opinion that the old jazz, which they called "Uncle Tom music," was an art form representative of a meeker generation than theirs. They said that it did not express the modern American Negro. . . . It was at Minton's that the word "bebop" came into being. Dizzy was trying to show a bass player how the last two notes of a phrase should sound. The bass player tried it again and again, but he couldn't get the two notes. "Bebop! Be-bop! Be-bop!" Dizzy finally sang.*

*Quoted from "Profiles: Bop" by Richard O. Boyer. *The New Yorker*, July 3, 1948, pp. 26–32.

All of this was developing in the early 1940s. In this period there was a recording ban in effect that sharply restricted the production and broadcast of pop music, including jazz. The American Federation of Musicians inaugurated the ban because they saw the growing use of recordings and jukeboxes as a threat to members' employment. Also, Word War II was on, with its restrictions on the material of recording. Bop, then, was known to only a few musicians, and when the recording ban was lifted and the first bop recordings came out in 1945, the public was unprepared for the innovations. This was decidedly not dance music, it was decidedly not popular in nature, and it took a lot of careful listening to follow the intricacies of the improvisations. "Now's the Time," our next listening selection, was one of the earliest of these cuts. It is considered by many critics to be the definitive bop recording, and in it are all the dominant features of bop style.

PRIMARY LISTENING:
"Now's the Time," Charlie Parker, alto sax, Miles Davis, trumpet, Dizzy Gillespie, piano, Curley Russell, bass, Max Roach, drums, 1945 (record set)

"Now's the Time" is based on the familiar twelve-bar blues: remember that Parker and friends are interested in returning black music to the blacks, and the blues is rooted in the black experience. Following a short introduction, the blues begins, and it is handled within the format that became standard for bop performances. The first chorus is composed and is delivered with the melody instruments in unison—sax and trumpet here. This is the section known as the "head"—no relationship to head arrangements—and is the part composed by Parker (Example 88). Then the improvisatory choruses begin. Parker on alto sax has three in a row. Miles Davis on trumpet has two. One is taken by Curley Russell on bass and Dizzy Gillespie on piano. The last chorus is once again the unison one with which the piece began. It is, then, a very straightforward series of twelve-bar choruses based on the time-honored blues harmonic progressions—but with a difference.

Notice the chords that Gillespie uses for backing throughout; although they are essentially the tonic, subdominant, and dominant, he enriches them with added notes—but without destroying their basic function. This is the meaning of extended chords. Parker uses those extensions to fashion his own melodies. At the same time he

Example 88
Charlie Parker,
"Now's the Time."

uses all the rhythmic devices mentioned above. This takes careful listening, but you can hear it if you try.

Miles Davis is not really comfortable with the style, as you can hear. His musical inclinations were in a different direction and he was soon to break out of this context and get into what is called cool jazz, a style more suited to his particular technical abilities and interests. His two choruses are much more lyric than Parker's and far less abrupt rhythmically. Also, he tends to work within a more restricted range; he was quite young at the time and his full technical development lay ahead.

Especially during the chorus with Russell and Gillespie the harmonic extension is pronounced. Russell wanders throughout the chords, and Gillespie punctuates in unpredictable places and with greatly enriched chords. The closing unison chorus brings us back again to Parker's tune and ties up the performance satisfactorily.

The style attracted a relatively small group of enthusiasts—sharp listeners willing and able to follow the intricate improvisations. And it began a new trend in jazz audiences: they became smaller but more discriminating. The trend has continued until the present time: you never find a jazz performance on the charts.

What *is* on the charts is rock and its derivative styles. And that represents the culmination of a new popular music that ultimately replaced swing: rhythm-and-blues. It has black roots too. Following World War II, the black search for identity that finally came to full power in the civil rights movements of the 1950s and 1960s was anticipated by a change in the character of the vocal blues. Electric instruments—mainly guitars—and a heavy rhythm section were featured by black recording artists. These pieces replaced the former race records and like them were fashioned for the black market and broadcast over radio stations that catered to a heavily black audience. But a number of white performers were attracted to the invigorating rhythms and the generally intense sound of the music. Elvis Presley found his "Hound Dog" here, a piece introduced and featured by Big Mama Thornton. Bill Haley picked up "Shake, Rattle, and Roll" from Joe Turner. The Beatles covered Chuck Berry's "Roll over Beethoven." The list is endless. So the blues, only slightly disguised and intensified, came into the pop market and hit the pop music charts, in much the same way that big band swing, growing out of black Dixieland jazz, had dominated the pop market during the 1930s. Rock has gone off in numerous directions since then and will probably continue to do so, but its start was in rhythm-and-blues. It is impossible to overestimate the contribution of black music to the American (and world) pop music repertoire. The blues in its many and varied styles has been one of the most important factors.

To refocus a bit, the blues in its purest form is a type of chaconne, at least in concept: part of its organization is based on harmonic progression which is consistent in each chorus. Enrichments of this concept in the blues are usually a result of arrangement of some kind. The arrangements seldom get so elaborate that the basic feeling of tonic, subdominant, and dominant is lost. Within this format, however, the expressive range is almost limitless.

Chapter 28
Bluegrass and Country Music

Let's take a little side excursion to look at some other types of music that, while not monothematic, will help reinforce the chord progressions we've been examining in the blues. Among the many types of music that use that harmonic vocabulary is bluegrass. In the next listening example, you will see how the chords work along with a number of other musical characteristics that make bluegrass sound the way it does. The piece is "Blue Ridge Cabin Home," and it is performed by one of the "classic" bluegrass groups: Lester Flatt, Earl Scruggs, and the Foggy Mountain Boys.

PRIMARY LISTENING:
"Blue Ridge Cabin Home,"
Flatt and Scruggs and the
Foggy Mountain Boys
(record set).

Unlike the blues, this piece is divided into a verse and chorus (refrain), and the performance moves back and forth between those two parts. Both are the same length, 8 measures, which makes them easy to keep up with (Example 89). The introduction is simply the verse played on instruments without a vocal. After that, it's a series of vocal verse–chorus parts interspersed with instrumental verses featuring different instruments each time. To make certain that we're all hearing the same thing, this is the way it works:

Introduction: Instrumental (verse) with banjo lead (Earl Scruggs)
Verse: Vocal (Lester Flatt, lead, with Curley Seckler, tenor)
Chorus: Vocal (same singers as verse)

Example 89
Certain and Stacey, "Blue Ridge Cabin Home." Golden West Melodies, Inc. Copyright 9/18/64. Used by permission.

Verse: Instrumental with fiddle lead (Paul Warren)
Verse: Vocal (as above)
Chorus: Vocal (as above)
Verse: Instrumental with dobro lead (Buck Graves)
Verse: Vocal (as above)
Chorus: Vocal (as above)
Verse: Instrumental with banjo lead (Earl Scruggs)
Chorus: Vocal (as above)

The verse and chorus are so much alike that it's difficult to tell them apart. It helps to concentrate on the cadences; all the phrases are 4 measures long and if you listen carefully, you can hear the slight difference in melody at those points.

Although the chords being used are the same ones we found in the blues, they do not occur at the same places in this piece. To begin with, each part is 8 bars long instead of 12, so there's bound to be some difference. But that's not all. Remember that the classic changes in the blues operate like this:

MEASURE	CHORD
1	I
5	IV
7	I
9	V
11	I

But in "Blue Ridge Cabin Home":

MEASURE	CHORD
1	I
2	IV
3	V
4	I
6	IV
7	V
8	I

Where a measure is skipped in the chart, it means that the chord holds the same for the missing bar. Thus, the I chord lasts from measure 4 until the IV chord comes in at measure 6.

It is typical of bluegrass melodies that they cover a rather limited range and you will notice that this is true of "Blue Ridge Cabin Home." Some of this is due to the fact that the music is closely related to folk music—in some cases it actually *is* folk music coming out of oral tradition. Some of it is related to the instrumental style, too, which tends to emphasize the middle register of all the instruments rather than going up very high or down very low.

The rhythms are very active—another characteristic of bluegrass style. This is especially apparent when the fiddle and banjo are taking a solo; there are almost always at least four notes to a beat in the banjo and the same thing happens frequently in the fiddle. This is one of the elements that lends so much excitement to bluegrass music.

So much for the mechanics. The main melody instruments in any bluegrass band are the ones you hear in this recording: the fiddle, the banjo, and the dobro. The latter is a type of guitar with a metal plate that serves as an amplifier (but not electric). It is played with a slide and that accounts for all the bent notes, which create a close relationship to the blues. The dobro was introduced into bluegrass bands by the Flatt-Scruggs group and this piece was recorded at the first session to use the instrument. In many groups where the dobro is not used (and even where it is), the mandolin also takes an important solo role.

The banjo style in this recording is important in the history of bluegrass. It is a three-finger style of picking as opposed to the two-fingered style which is sometimes called claw-hammer or frailing. Scruggs is credited with introducing the method of playing into bluegrass bands as well as bringing in the five-string banjo. The fifth string is shorter than the other four and serves as a drone—you can hear it quite clearly on the banjo solo sections. As with some other drones we have encountered, this one is on the tonic note, and it causes a clash when the harmony moves to the V chord.

Much of this music is improvised. This is not as true of the vocal sections, which are quite repetitive, as of the instrumental solos. Notice that each solo instrument plays a different version of the verse; that's a clue to the fact that the players are not reading from a score but rather applying their individual creativity to the original tune.

One other feature of this style is worth noticing. During the vocal verse–chorus sections, all the instruments serve as rhythm backing with very little melodic responsibility. However, even though they are playing quietly and fading into the background, notice that there are some short bursts of melody that occur between phrases. This is yet another example of that old familiar call–response or antiphonal device. Not only does it add musical interest but it serves to drive the performance forward so that there is no lag at cadence points.

The use of the term bluegrass to describe a particular style of string band music grew out of the sound of the Blue Grass Boys, a group led by Bill Monroe, first recorded in 1946. That band included Flatt and Scruggs as well as Monroe playing mandolin and doing vocals, Chubby Wise on fiddle and Howard Watts on bass. Flatt and Monroe established the vocal style that was standard for bluegrass bands. Wise, Scruggs and Monroe did the same for their respective instruments.

Flatt and Scruggs left the Monroe band to form their own group, the Foggy Mountain Boys, in 1948. In 1955 they added the dobro to their instrumentation and it was by this group that the version of "Blue Ridge Cabin Home" was recorded. Bluegrass groups have changed styles a number of times since those early days, adding electric instruments and featuring different combinations than the "classic" ones. Purists insist on acoustic instruments only, however, and not all innovations in style are greeted with common enthusiasm.

Bluegrass was actually a movement to restore elements of an earlier style to country music, and its adherents argue that it is a purer and more traditional approach to playing as well as to the type of pieces performed. Country music, mostly because of the surge of commercialization that resulted from its first burst of popularity, had lost many of the folk roots from which it had originally sprung.

The earliest performers had been rural people steeped in tradition and familiar with ballads and other folk songs and dance tunes. They had been sought out and featured by record companies in 1922 and 1923 in order to combat the slump in record purchases brought on by the increased interest in radio. Like the blues, which were aimed at a particular segment of the population, country music (at first called old timey, mountain music, or hillbilly) was programmed to appeal to rural listeners principally in the south. Early performers included Eck Robertson, Fiddlin' John Carson, Dock Boggs, Clarence Ashley, Uncle Dave Macon, and many others, all of whom recorded mostly traditional folk material in a traditional folk style. Fiddle tunes, like "Sally Goodin" and "Arkansas Traveler," ballads like "The Wreck of the Old 97" and "Barbara Allen," and sentimental pieces like "The Little Old Log Cabin in the Lane" were among the pieces used—pieces as familiar to the mountain folk who listened as to the performers themselves.

Gradually, however, with the establishment of commercial radio shows like the Grand Old Opry and others, the performance style and repertoire took on a less traditional coloration. The advent of star performers like Vernon Dalhart (himself not a rural musician but performing in a pseudo-country style) further hastened the establishment of a less-than-oldtime approach. Family groups like the Carter family added still other dimensions to the country market. Perhaps the greatest commercial boost of all was the 1927 debut of Jimmie Rodgers and his blue yodel which catapulted him into the position of country music's first spectacular singing star. From that point onward, commercialization and the wooing of wider and wider markets were inevitable. The adoption of the electric guitar in the late 1930s took the music still further away from its folk beginnings.

Although they were not the only country groups to reject electrification in favor of acoustic instruments, the Bill Monroe Blue Grass Boys did set the pattern for not only bluegrass but the preservation of what many considered the "real" country music based in folk tradition. The style they inaugurated has become accepted with great enthusiasm, attracting many thousands of people of all persuasions to festivals throughout the United States and many foreign countries. Bluegrass is immensely popular in Japan, for instance, and it is not at all unusual to find a Japanese group performing in an American festival alongside old timers from the States as well as bands from Holland, France, Italy, and England. College campuses have given an especially warm reception to bluegrass performers and are, in fact, the seats of many festivals.

Record companies are marketing an increasing number of reissues of early country discs, mostly in anthologies. These are invaluable in helping to preserve this very important cultural legacy. Among the organizations that are entirely devoted to preserving and studying the tradition is the John Edwards Memorial Foundation at UCLA. Of the numerous books written about country music and bluegrass, two are outstanding: *Country Music USA* and *Southern Music, American Music,* both by Bill C. Malone.[1] It seems that at last serious scholars and students of American music are turning their attention to what may be, next to the blues, the repertoire and performance style most deeply rooted in our own national traditions.

Country music itself has worked its way into the very heart of popular idioms in America, no longer restricted to the rural population. The continuing success of "Hee Haw" on television is testimony enough to that fact. And with its wide acceptance and enthusiastic audiences have grown the number of superstars. No longer do the performers travel in small groups with little or no supporting equipment other than the instruments played by individuals. Instead, there are multiple truckloads of electronic machinery of all sorts, lights, amplification equipment, and often even stage scenery of a modest sort.

One star who has had spectacular loyalty from fans is Willie Nelson. He reached a wide audience in 1975 after having had a relatively large following on a regional level prior to that date. The song that launched him as a true star is our next listening example.

[1] *Country Music,* Austin, University of Texas Press, 1968. *Southern Music,* Lexington, University Press of Kentucky, 1979.

PRIMARY LISTENING: Willie Nelson, "Blue Eyes Crying in the Rain" (record set)

Typical of many country songs, "Blue Eyes Crying in the Rain" uses the harmonic background that we have discussed in connection with the blues and bluegrass music. The text is given below together with the chord changes indicated above the words.

I (E)
Every twilight glow I see
V (B)   I (E)
Blue eyes crying in the rain.
I (E)
When we kissed goodbye and parted
V (B)   I (E)
I knew we'd never meet again.
IV (A)
Love is like a dyin' ember
I (E)   V (B)
And only memories remain.
I (E)
And through the ages I'll remember
V (B)   I (E)
Blue eyes crying in the rain.

The piece is representative of that type of country song that is simple and direct, underplayed rather than flamboyant as are many of the genre. Notice that the instruments are all acoustic. Notice, too, that the form of the song is a familiar one: A A B A. The B section is given some prominence because of the addition of a harmonica (it sounds almost like a violin) to the first stanza at that point, and the addition of vocal harmony on the second stanza. Although the general style is reminiscent of an older type of country performance, there is a rather important concession to a more recent innovation: the use of double-tracking (overdubbing) in order to get the vocal duet on the second B section.

Nelson is typical of the country star whose spectacular success has led to great financial rewards. He has lots of company, of course; among many others are Loretta Lynn, Dolly Parton, Johnny Cash, and Tom T. Hall. As a tribute to the achievements of such performers, there are annual awards for the best male and female singers as well as the best songs and albums.

SUPPLEMENTAL LISTENING: For those who want to investigate bluegrass music more fully than can be done with one recording, the following album gives an excellent overview of the many styles to be found:

Hills and Home: Thirty Years of Bluegrass. New World Records: NW 225. The most recent and comprehensive anthology of country music is the one issued by the Smithsonian Institute: *The Smithsonian Collection of Classic Country Music.* R025 P8 15640. The set consists of 8 records covering recordings from the 1922 cut by Eck Robertson of "Sally Goodin" to the Willie Nelson piece discussed above. There are outstanding notes provided by Bill Malone, probably the most prestigious scholar of country music in America.

Chapter 29
Canon

Let us return to monothematic types and examine another way to organize music around a single musical idea which is already familiar to almost everyone. We call it a *round*. It makes fine social singing because anyone who can carry a tune can sing one part, and the result is chorus performance without anybody needing to think about harmony or about reading music. The harmony is a result of the concurrence of melodies, as it is in all types of polyphony; the round creates one type of polyphonic texture. A more "proper" name for the round is *canon*, which we are familiar with from Pachelbel's Canon in D major. There, however, the canon was only one of the things going on.

In seventeenth- and eighteenth-century England the canon was an extremely popular form. Then it was called a *catch*. Shakespeare refers to catches more than once in his plays and actually has his characters sing them to words that he provides. One instance is in *Twelfth Night*, when Sir Toby Belch says, "Shall we rouse the night-owl in a catch that will draw three souls out of one weaver?" This has a double meaning because musically, if there are three singers, they are "drawing" three parts from a single tune. Perhaps the continuing popularity of the form is due to the ease with which it allows a group of people to sing together and get a pretty sophisticated musical result even from the most unskilled.

Henry Purcell (1659–1695), who was one of the greatest of English composers during the early Baroque period—one of the greatest of all time, in fact—used the catch, among many other forms, in his composition. Often the pieces were intended for singing for fun in private clubs or in alehouses—barrooms—where groups of friends gathered for an evening on the town. Frequently the words were shady, sometimes downright filthy. Some writers of the time

Illustration 34. THE MERRY COMPANY.
Dirck Hals (1591–1656). This conveys the same spirit of gay ribaldry expressed in dozens of Restoration canons. Canons like Purcell's "Once in Our Lives" are one reflection of the freer atmosphere of the Restoration, an atmosphere expressed in Hals's painting. Compare this painting to Ter Borch's *A Music Party* (page 59) for another view of Baroque society. Collection of the J. B. Speed Art Museum, Louisville, Kentucky.

even suggested that they were not effective at all unless they *were* obscene. Others criticized them for that reason. Pornography and concerns about it didn't begin with X-rated movies (Illustration 34).

One of Purcell's less colorful texts, "Once in Our Lives," deals with a certain chauvinistic view of the marital relationship:

Once in our lives let us drink to our wives
Though their number be but small.

Heaven take yc best and the devil take the rest,
And so we shall get rid of them all.

To this hearty wish, let each man take his dish,
And drink, drink, drink till the fall.

PRIMARY LISTENING:
Henry Purcell, "Once in Our Lives" (record set)

The tune here is a lot more complicated than the one in "Row, Row, Row Your Boat," for instance, but the musical procedure is the same (Example 90). Most catches or rounds that we are familiar with tend toward harmonic sameness; often the chord seems to change no more than once or twice. "Row, Row, Row Your Boat" is one of that type, and so is "Three Blind Mice." Purcell's has much more harmonic interest. Also, he constructs it so that all voices come to a cadence strongly enough to make it easy to stop together and have a sense of completion. Each of the two-line stanzas ends on a different note of the tonic chord so that once all the parts are active, the cadences have a full chord sounding. The effect is quite satisfying harmonically. Canon, round, catch: still another way to structure music from a single bit of material.

In 1679 Purcell became organist at Westminster Abbey; later he was organist at the Chapel Royal. As court composer, he wrote much incidental music for plays as well as compositions for use on special days and anniversaries of royal personages. In conjunction with his duties at Westminster, he also composed a large number of sacred pieces. He composed opera (*Dido and Aeneas*, and others), music for stage works, anthems and other music for religious services, odes, catches, incidental songs, keyboard music, and chamber works.

SUPPLEMENTAL LISTENING

Purcell's extensive work includes examples of chaconne, passacaglia, and ground bass. An investigation of his style might well begin with the following:

"When I Am Laid in Earth."

Dido's lament from the opera *Dido and Aeneas*, composed for a girl's school and therefore confined to roles for treble voices. A chromatic descending figure is used throughout as a ground bass.

Example 90
Purcell, "Once in our lives."

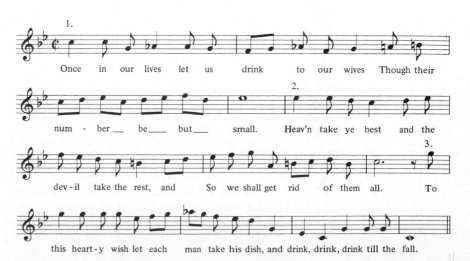

Once in our lives let us drink to our wives Though their
num - ber__ be__ but__ small. Heav'n take ye best and the
dev - il take the rest, and So we shall get rid of them all. To
this heart - y wish let each man take his dish, and drink, drink, drink till the fall.

A Choice Collection of Lessons for the Harpsichord or Spinnet.

The term "lessons" as it was used in this period indicated a series of keyboard pieces, normally for the harpsichord. An educational function might be implied, although this was not uniformly the case. This particular collection includes a chaconne.

Ode on St. Cecilia's Day.

This rather large-scale work for soloists, chorus, and instrumentalists represents the type of composition for which Purcell was responsible in his capacity as court musician.

The names for the canon describe this form quite literally. A canon is a rule, so that it must be composed according to law, or rule, in order for it to go together properly. In a catch, one part begins and the others, in imitation of it, try to catch their parts at the right time. A round goes on and on: it's eternal or infinite, like the perfect circle. But composing a canon that works out right is not an easy job. At one time puzzle canons were quite popular: the composer wrote the melody line on paper but without any indication as to when the various voices were to enter in order to make it come out right. The result was a kind of musical riddle and quite a challenge to the performers. And because of the complexity of construction, many composers have written canons as study pieces, exercises in craftsmanship.

Using the principles of canon poses an unusual problem. We hear music referred to as "the universal language," and that has an appealing ring to it, but it omits some important facts. All languages have syntax; without it no one could follow the flow of thought they express. In most cases, music lacks syntax. Very seldom do a series of melody notes *have* to be exactly what they are; numerous substitutions can be made without injury, as the process of variations bears out. Harmonization, too, is open to choice, as are the particular rhythms that a composer chooses. In canonic writing, however, some of that changes. Try singing "Row, Row, Row Your Boat" and let the different groups come in whenever they please instead of where they are supposed to. It will soon be apparent that here the syntax *must* be right or things will go completely awry. This means that composers using this kind of imitative polyphony need to work out their material carefully so that, once begun, the music can continue without mishap.

And so it is that composers often tackle the syntactical challenges in "practice" pieces. Having worked out the musical problems, then, they may use the solutions in larger vocal or instrumental works. Mozart left manuscript copies of a number of canons that served this purpose for him, and they give us a glimpse of him that most of his other music does not reveal. Because he was mostly interested in the *musical* problems to be solved in creating polyphonic texture, the words were of secondary importance. So he very often put nonsense texts to the canons. But also, there was an obscene streak in Mozart, and an enchantment with murky language shows up in some of his canons as well as quite strongly in some of the letters he wrote to relatives and close friends, which have very recently become available in translation. We are somehow reluctant to see the human side of our creative giants, preferring to imagine them as people whose feet never got dirty and whose thoughts were as pure as their musical or other artistic inventions. But in fact most of them were utterly human and prey to the same sort of off-color diversions that still spell out the nature of each of us to some extent. This side of Mozart's character was fully exploited in the award-winning play, *Amadeus*. Here is the text of his canon "Bona Nox," our next listening selection:

Bona nox, bist a rechter Ochs;	Bona nox, you're a stupid ox;
Bona notte, liebe Lotte;	Buona notte, dearest Lotte;
Bonne nuit, pfui, pfui;	Bonne nuit, pfui, pfui;
Good night, good night,	Good night, good night,
Heut müss ma no weit;	Now we must be on our way;
Gute Nacht, gute Nacht	Gute Nacht, gute Nacht,
Sh____ ins Bett dass's kracht,	Sh____ in bed till it crashes;
Gute Nacht;	Good night,
Schlaf fei g'sund	Sleep well,
Und reck'n A____ zum Mund.	And turn your a____ to mouth.

The version in our recording set is edited to adjust the number of syllables to the music as well as to modify the language enough to accommodate our sense of propriety.

PRIMARY LISTENING:
Mozart, "Bona Nox"
(record set)

Mozart was a cosmopolitan person, widely traveled and with the mind of a genius, and here he is throwing out a lot of different languages as well as a lot of just plain nonsense words, plus some obscenities. But he is also involved in a relatively complex canon. Notice, for instance, that there is nothing like the cadence structure of Purcell's catch. In Mozart's piece all the cadences are overlapped by activity in the other voices, so that here there is a very real sense of being able to go on forever—eternity expressed in musical terms (Example 91). The only way to stop is the way the performers here do: just agree ahead of time how many repetitions to do before dropping out. If one were faced with using stubborn or persistent performers, there might be no end to the piece. Stopping a canon like this is just about as hard as getting it started properly. But "Bona

Example 91
Mozart, "Bona Nox."

Bo - na   nox,   What a clum - sy

ox.   Bo - na   not - te,   you are pot - ty.   Bonne

nuit,   Pfui,   pfui; good_ night, good_   night; quite plain - ly you're

tight. Gu - te nacht, gu - te   nacht,crap in bed; you're crocked, gu - te nacht.

Soak   your   head   and   get   your   ass   to   bed.

Nox" does make a pretty good drinking song and is a cut above the average round musically.

Mozart doesn't seem quite so much a "long-hair" when we see this side of him, although his musical excellence comes through strongly.

SUPPLEMENTAL LISTENING   For obvious reasons, this particular canon has been given very few recorded performances. The version here is taken from a disc that includes others in the same vein, *Wolfgang Amadeus Mozart Is a Dirty Old Man.* Epic: BC–1366. An album featuring much of the same material, but done in the original language with translations in an accompanying pamphlet, is *The Comic Mozart.* Seraphim:: S–60050. Both selections contain pieces other than canons, some for solo, some for small vocal and instrumental ensembles. All are witty and urbane, and a few are downright naughty.

Louis Hardin, known professionally as Moondog (born 1916), did not write his canons as musical study pieces. His intention was to keep the rules of Renaissance polyphony intact but to put them into the context of some twentieth-century idioms. The purposes of his work and the work itself tell us as much about his personality as the Mozart canons tell us about his.

Moondog (Illustration 35) is blind as a result of a teenage accident. After considerable wandering in various sections of the

Illustration 35. MOONDOG.

country, he settled in New York City. His world is the streets of Manhattan, his life style that of the wandering minstrel sharing communal quarters where they can be found. Before he was "discovered" and recorded, his principal musical activity was composing canons and instrumental music structured on the forms of the past—chaconnes, passacaglias, short multimovement pieces in symphonic style. Because of his ideological roots in the Renaissance, most of his composition is based on polyphony—particularly that involving voices or instruments imitating each other—and is at its purest in the vocal canons. He dictated the notes of these canons to a friend, who wrote them down in manuscript form, had them duplicated, and sold them on the street corners of Manhattan. Moondog's dream was that people would sing them as a counter to the rock style that he could not relate to and that he considered to be noisy, undisciplined, and musically meaningless. He may well be one of the last of a long line of true troubadours reaching back in life style and musical style to the medieval period and even further. If he is thus a throwback, he nevertheless represents some of the richest portions of our Western musical inheritance, as well as some of the glory of our common humanity.

His first canon was "All Is Loneliness" (Example 92). The meter and the rhythmic style of the performance are of our own century. The melodic material and the polyphonic treatment are Renaissance or closely related to it.

PRIMARY LISTENING
Moondog. "All Is Loneliness"
(record set)

The meter is 5/4, and we have experienced it before. We usually refer to meters in which the number of beats between accents cannot be divided by two or three as irregular. This may have an actual physical basis; some music psychologists tell us that it has, because such meters make us feel uncomfortable rhythmically. Perhaps. Or it may simply be an example of the tyranny that indoctrination exerts over us. In any case, there is a rhythmic interest here, and a kind of swing to the music that doesn't translate well into words. It is its own thing. Notice that there is only one singer, Moondog. That doesn't make "All Is Loneliness" less of a canon. There are three melodic (canonic) voices, two being instrumental and one being human. Like all canons the piece is highly repetitive, and in this case that has a lot to do with the mood that the words project. In spite of the rhythmic diversity in Moondog's work, there is usually a sense of quiet and tranquility that distinguishes it sharply from rock, although it bears a relationship to some of the more gentle folk-rock repertoire and is very much like a lot of pure folk music.

Part of the purpose of studying and discussing and exposing ourselves to music is to learn what we can about human nature,

Example 92
Moondog, "All Is Loneliness."

All Is Loneliness - Moondog

All _____ is lone - li - ness here for me,

lone - li - ness here for me, lone - li - ness. _____

including our own. Can we learn anything at all here about Moondog? Remember that he is blind. Remember, too, that the streets of Manhattan are his home. He tells us that he wrote this canon while standing in the doorway of a building in mid-Manhattan. There are few places on earth where the noises are so overpowering and diverse, and the odors can be pretty hard to take: they represent the worst of the effects of what we like to call our "technical progress." There is a lot of pedestrian traffic in midtown Manhattan, a lot of jostling that can't be avoided. Sometimes the air not only smells awful but tastes awful. Serenity, peace, tranquility, order, clarity—none of these could describe the environment.

So why does Moondog compose the kinds of things that he composes? In no way could we suggest that he is reflecting his environment. Is he, rather, trying to bring some sort of sense and order into the chaos that surrounds him? Only his sense of sight is missing; if he had that, it would only add to the confusion of his other senses. Is he trying to block out with his music the cacophony that assaults him?

We say that the artist's job is to present us with a distillation of life. Lots of times that's exactly what artists do: they give us a vision of our world and its people that most of us are not quite sensitive enough to find on our own. Is that what Moondog is doing? Or is his world a substitute one?

One reason Moondog has so much respect for canons is that he considers them to be eternal; and they can go on forever, as noted above. We can't really get inside his head to find out all his motivations. But we can try to understand and to reach some rational conclusions about this example of the creative impulse and process, using the music itself as a guide.

SUPPLEMENTAL LISTENING   There is only one Moondog. But there are many Moondog canons, and they are on *Moondog 2.* Columbia KC–30897. His instrumental works, most of them using forms we have discussed above, are on *Moondog*. Columbia: MS–7335. The liner notes on both albums are by him and give great insight into his objectives and methods.

Sixteen years after Moondog wrote "All Is Loneliness" in 1951, Big Brother and the Holding Company, featuring Janis Joplin, recorded it. They were fresh from their first triumph at the Monterey Festival in California, and the recording launched a rather spectacular career for the group. It also put Joplin under full sail and on her way to become almost a legend in the world of rock—a symbol for everything that the music represented musically and in terms of life style.

PRIMARY LISTENING:
Moondog, "All Is
Loneliness," Big Brother
and the Holding Company
with Janis Joplin (record
set)

The label identifies the piece as Moondog's. Is it *his* "All Is Loneliness?" There are obvious musical changes. The 5/4 meter is gone, replaced by what is standard for rock—a regular meter. Canonic at first, the performance wanders into an added section that cannot be traced in any way to Moondog, musically or expressively. It is apparently there to deepen the original intent, to enrich or interpret or extend it somehow. Think about Moondog's artistic "roots" as he expresses them himself—his allegiance to the past and the musical devices that came to fruition in the Renaissance. Think about the mood of his piece, the kind of feeling it projects, the way it makes you feel when you listen to it. In the Holding Company–Joplin version, what is kept, what is added, what is lost?

At one point in her spectacular career, when what she had to say about her art assumed a great significance for many people, Joplin said:

> Young white kids have taken the groove and the soul from black people and added intensity. Black music is understated. I like to fill it full of feeling—to grab somebody by the collar and say "Can't you understand me?"[1]

[1] Ortiz Walton, *Music: Black, White and Blue*, New York, Morrow, 1972, p. 122.

Moondog is not black, and so this is not the music she was talking about. But she was talking about adding something to an existing tradition, and that is very much to the point here. Moondog uses the same sort of understatement Joplin heard in black music, for instance. Because of his traditions, his musical expression is peculiarly his in the same way that black music is peculiarly black. So what happens when we meddle with a tradition, add to it, subtract from it, extend it for our own purposes? Have we done a kindness? A disservice? Do we *need* to "add intensity"? When we do, have we replaced something valuable with something better?

The questions are universal ones, and how we answer them helps describe the world we fashion for ourselves, individually and collectively.

SUPPLEMENTAL LISTENING

The whole business of using someone else's composition has a long history in the pop music scene. When the piece has been recorded, successive recordings by other individuals or groups are called "covers." Joplin was a rock star. When she referred to adding intensity to black music, she was fully aware that many of her hits were rerecordings, covers, of material that had been made popular among blacks on their original releases. Sometimes the covers by her and others were done with integrity, sometimes with less than that.

Cover recordings were the principal way in which rhythm-and-blues was absorbed into rock-and-roll. If you have access to any of the pieces on the following list, you can examine for yourself both the practice and some of the abuses. The original rhythm-and-blues cut is given first, followed by the group that used the piece and the date of its release. All of the original rhythm-and-blues cuts are on a disc called *Pop Origins*. Chess: 1544. The original and its cover:

Lowell Fulsom, "Tollin' Bells"—covered by Paul Butterfield, 1968.
Bo Diddley, "Mona"—covered by the Rolling Stones, 1965
Howlin' Wolf, "Red Rooster"—covered by the Rolling Stones, 1965
Howlin' Wolf, "Killing Floor"—covered by Electric Flag, 1968.
Muddy Waters, "You Shook Me"—covered by Led Zeppelin, 1969
Little Milton, "More and More"—covered by Blood, Sweat and Tears, 1969

The list could go on indefinitely, of course.

Chapter 30
Prelude and Fugue

The term *well-tempered* has great significance for Western music. It involves tuning a keyboard instrument so that all the half-step intervals are the same size. This is an acoustical matter, essentially in the area of physics, and it is worth investigating. We are not going to take time for a lengthy explanation here, however, for we are more concerned with the *effect* of tempering, which was to make it possible for a keyboard instrument to play in all possible keys in our harmonic system and to move from one to the other smoothly and still be "in tune." In some important ways, tempering made it possible for musicians in our cultural environment to explore fully the element of harmony as we know it. For instance, the whole process of modulation at a keyboard instrument would be sharply restricted without tempering.

PRIMARY LISTENING: Johann Sebastian Bach, Prelude and Fugue in C minor, *Well-tempered Clavier*, book I, 1722

Partly, Bach's composition of the *Well-tempered Clavier* was to exploit the possibilities that tempering allowed. The pieces, preludes and fugues, are written in all the keys, major and minor, of our system. Most of the preludes are in the form of harmonic explorations and use the series of chord progressions to "define" the key. As a result, there is less melodic interest in the preludes than we might expect in music of the period. For instance, try singing the melody of the Prelude in C minor (Example 93), and you will realize that it isn't very exciting, even assuming that you can pick it out.

The Fugue in C minor is another matter altogether. The basis for it *is* a melody, and the way the melody is used makes it possible to give the piece the formal name *fugue*. The proper name for the

Example 93
Bach, Prelude in C minor.
Kalmus score, p. 6. Used by permission.

PRAELUDIUM II.

melody of a fugue is *subject*. There are three voices involved in
Bach's C minor Fugue, end even though they are instrumental rather
than vocal, let's call them soprano, alto, and bass. There is also a
tremendous amount of activity, which you will recognize as polyphonic activity. So we can say that the fugue is a polyphonic form
organized around a subject, and that it depends for its development
on the interplay of various voices and what they do with the subject.
The word "fugue" means "flight," and its antecedent was the canon.

The suggestion of flying may be a reference to the interaction of its various parts or possibly to the fact that the voices, once they have stated the subject, fly away into other material that seems less restricted.

We hear the subject first in the alto voice, followed almost immediately, but in a different key, by the soprano. Then, after a short section based on a series of sequences—called an *episode*—we hear the bass come in with the subject. This is all shown in Example 94.

The effect is something like a round or canon, but more complicated and developed. A round, for instance, has no episodes, only entrances of the melody. Neither does it change keys; normally all the voices are in the same key and everybody is singing or playing the same pitches when it is his or her turn.

There is another formal device that is important to the structure of a fugue. It takes careful listening to pick it out, but it can be seen easily in the score. When the alto is finished with the subject and the soprano begins, listen to (and/or look at) what it does. It continues with a tune *different* from the subject but one that goes along nicely with it. That is called the *counter-subject*, for obvious reasons. After the episode, which is meant to change the key back to the original one after the soprano has pulled us away from the key center, the

Example 94
Bach, Fugue in C minor.
Kalmus score, p. 8. Used by permission.

FUGA II.

bass subject is once again accompanied by the counter-subject, this time in the soprano. In a tightly organized fugue, this relationship between subject and counter-subject is consistent throughout the first section of the piece. What the first section accomplishes, then, is to introduce, by imitation among voices, the "material" of the composition. Also, it gets all the voices into the game. If the fugue involves two voices, you will hear two entrances of the subject. If three, as in this piece, there will be three entrances. A fugue can involve any number of voices; four is a popular number. Some have included as many as 32, which gets pretty complicated.

The initial section, the one that lasts until all the voices enter with the subject, is called the *exposition*—logically, because it exposes the musical material. What happens after that depends on how complicated the composer wants to get. It will always involve at least the use of bits and pieces of the subject—that is, motives derived from it—in some way. It will also always involve several episodes, the function of which is to prepare for various entrances of the subject in various keys. Because of the use of the subject or motives taken from it, there is a good bit of consistency about the melodic nature of a fugue, although the harmony will shift around a lot. The episodes are apt to be unsettled in feeling, mainly because their purpose is to *change* the harmony or key—to modulate—and the various entrances of the subject will feel more secure because they will be noticeably *in* some key or other. This is the old tension–release mechanism at work. And notice that the main musical device in episodes is the sequence, one of the many clichés in Baroque music.

Usually a fugue will end with a rather solid statement of the subject in one or more voices. In this case it is in the soprano, but it is immediately preceded by one in the bass. Do you catch the change to major on the final chord? This is another cliché in the Baroque period. The minor mode is defined in terms of the nature of the third step of the scale (as you will know if you have consulted appendix 1 on theory). When the third changes from minor to major, as it does here, we call it the *Picardy third,* so to be really accurate we can say that in many Baroque compositions the final cadence employs the Picardy third. It is just as good to say that the final cadence is in major instead of the expected minor. It's even better to *hear* it and to know that this is one characteristic of Baroque harmonic practice.

The Bach C minor is a fairly standard fugue, not very long and not very complex. The harpsichord, on which it is played, was a favorite instrument of the period (Illustration 36). It has manuals, like an organ, and the biggest ones have stops to push and pull, also like an organ, so that different timbres can be used in the different

**Illustration 36.
HARPSICHORD.**

voices. It is incapable of *crescendo* and *diminuendo* (increase and decrease of volume) except by means of adding or subtracting voices or changing stops. Look into this if you are curious. There are harpsichords around because they have become quite fashionable, even with some rock groups. Indeed, they can be purchased in kit form and constructed at home!

SUPPLEMENTAL LISTENING   There are two books (sets) in Bach's *Well-tempered Clavier*—48 preludes and fugues in all. Any of them will serve to illustrate fugal device and form.

When the Moog was first being developed and exploited, performers on it used many of Bach's compositions. This was a happy situation, because much of the music of Bach relies on extreme clarity of melody lines and their interrelationship and also has an inherently vigorous rhythmic basis, as does all Baroque music, and the Moog is able to make the most of both of these factors.

One acoustical property of the Moog is the possibility of an intensely *staccato* attack that is a little like the plucking attack of the harpsichord. However, it can be manipulated so that the sound lasts only a fraction of a second, so there is no blurring from extended reverberation. That feature can contribute to rhythmic incisiveness as well as to harmonic clarity.

In addition, there are an almost infinite number of tone colors that can be coaxed out of a Moog, all quite distinct from one another. The result is that each melodic line can be extremely clear and distinct from all the others. As listeners we can really hear the linear relationships and, if we put forth a little effort, sort out what is going on.

PRIMARY LISTENING:
Bach, Prelude and Fugue in C minor, Walter Carlos on the Moog (record set)

In Walter Carlos's performance of the C minor Prelude and Fugue on the Moog the original character of each movement is certainly there: these are the same notes that Bach wrote. There's a difference in tempo, though, and this is because of the way a performance is put together on the Moog. The whole thing is manipulated on tape, line by line, and then it can be speeded up or slowed down at will—at least that was the system when this particular cut was made—and this one was speeded up a lot! A performance on the harpsichord at this tempo would be nothing but mush, even if someone could perform it this fast. But even at this tempo the capabilities of the Moog make it possible to add more clarity to the performance of Bach than can be gotten from the harpsichord. Although it may change the original conception to some extent, this performance makes the structural features much clearer, and that helps us if we are interested in the way the piece is put together—the way the form is utilized, in other words.

Bach's "Little" Fugue in G minor for the organ is one of many that he wrote for the instrument. He himself was a skillful performer. During his lifetime, in fact, what fame he enjoyed, which was not much, was more as an organist and improviser than as a composer. The organ, like the Moog, is capable of many distinctive timbres, as we discovered with Bach's Passacaglia in C minor. Because of this, the musical devices are quite perceptible.

Bach, Fugue in G minor ("Little") for organ, 1708–1717

We hear the same successive entrances of the fugue subject as before (Example 95). Here, however, there are four, entering from high to low: soprano, alto, tenor, bass, in that order. There is the same use of an episode, preparing for the third entrance of the subject. At this point you might add a new bit of detail to your vocabulary. When the tune is in the key of the tonic (the key of the composition), it is called the subject, but when it is in another key, usually the dominant, it is called the *answer*, even though the shape

Example 95
Bach, Fugue for organ in G
minor.
Kalmus score, pp. 116–117. Used by
permission.

XVIII.

F U G E.

G-moll.

of the melody is almost identical. And in this piece (in contrast to the C minor Fugue) we say that the appearances of the melody are:

Subject in the soprano
Answer in the alto
Subject in the tenor
Answer in the bass

This is another instance of extended vocabulary of analysis and description. Your ear can't care less about what you call these things; your mind may be interested in getting everything organized in exact terminology.

The counter-subject in this fugue has the distinctive feature of a trill at one point, and the recurrence of that is a clue to the consistency of the use of that element of the form: you can pick it out of the fabric. Otherwise, things go along pretty much according to schedule for a fugue. The episodes rely heavily on sequences, which is a feature of this form and the Baroque in general. They are harmonically shifty. They use motives from the subject. Sometimes even the subject is divided between several voices instead of staying in only one.

All of a sudden, though, we are aware that the subject is in major instead of minor. It is first in the alto voice; then an episode leads to an entrance in the bass (Example 96). This is a nice bit of color change and not an unusual one. Some maneuvering then leads us back to minor, several of the episodes are relatively extended, and there are many more entrances of the subject than we had in the C minor Fugue from the *Well-tempered Clavier*. This simply adds up to a more extended composition and one that utilizes more developmental devices because of being longer. As the fugue draws to a close, however, we hear that final powerful statement of the subject in the tonic: we are home safe after all the harmonic wandering. Is there a Picardy third at the final cadence?

Once the form and its devices had become established and standardized, the fugue attracted composers of all persuasions. Sometimes they even constructed double fugues in which two separate subjects were manipulated simultaneously. Mozart, for instance, uses this device in the "Kyrie" of his *Requiem*, where he assigns one subject to the words "Kyrie eleison" and a second one to the words "Christe eleison."

Because of the particular nature of Romanticism, however, the demands of the fugue appear to have limited its use during the

Example 96
Bach, Fugue for organ in G minor.

Romantic period, except for a few notable composers. Brahms, for instance, used the fugue in a serious way, and some of the nineteenth-century composers for organ used it because of its particular adaptability for that instrument. In general, however, the Romantic period was more concerned with emotional fullness than with architectural complexity.

Then a disenchantment with exactly that fullness, which came to be called fulsomeness, occurred about the turn of the twentieth century, encouraging composers (and artists from other fields as well) to investigate seriously the advantages of structural clarity and logic as a counterbalance for extensive dissonance, abandonment of tonality, and increasing rhythmic complexity. And it was natural that they should turn to the fugue, the most highly developed of the contrapuntal forms and the one that offers the most challenge from the standpoint of organization.

Another important factor in the return to interest in contrapuntal forms was the nature of harmonic exploitation in the nineteenth century. So much attention has been paid to enriching the harmonic vocabulary that just about everything that could be done had been done in that direction. The reaction was a renewed fascination with linear relationships—polyphony.

PRIMARY LISTENING:
Béla Bartók, *Music for Strings, Percussion and Celeste*, first movement, Andante tranquillo, 1936

In the first movement of Bartók's *Music for Strings, Percussion and Celeste* we find an example of this interest. The very nature of the subject puts us into the twentieth century. Notice the enormous chromaticism; even the cadence notes alternate between B and B♭, inhibiting the sense of tonic. The range is very small; it covers only a fifth. But within that restricted compass there is a complete exploration of interval relationships as well as the use of every scale degree. Notice how the subject moves further and further away from its starting pitch on each successive phrase. This is, then, an exhaustive use of the concept of chromaticism. And along with the destruction, so to speak, of tonality there is a turning away from metric stability: no two successive measures use the same metric pattern (Example 97).

Listen to the counter-subject carefully. Is it consistent, as it was in both of the Bach fugues? If not, is it simply aimless, without structural purpose except to furnish linear interest? It would take a highly developed and esoteric analytical vocabulary to unravel this. What is readily perceived, though, is the melodic consistency of the subject as it enters in the four voices. But there is nothing of the tonic–dominant relationship that we found in Bach. Why?

Even though the nature of the sound is totally different, there is a sense of episodic movement interrupted by recognizable entries of the fugue subject. As a result, even though we lose tonality and metric clarity, we can cling to the melodic basis for the structure and the development of the form. If we need orientation, we have it here.

After a few episodes and subject entrances, we are conscious of a new procedure. The subject enters, but before it has gone more than five or six notes into the melody another instrumental voice begins in echo fashion. Then another, and another, as though too impatient to wait their turn. This kind of crowding of subject entrances is called *stretto*, and it is a way of treating the material that is very frequently used in fugues. The effect is one of greater intensity of dialogue than when the subject is fully stated before its next entrance. It may remind us of the discussions we sometimes get into where everybody talks at once and nobody gets to finish a sentence before being interrupted. By the way, think about how a round works: each person or group coming in before the preceding one has finished with the melody. Could you call that stretto?

After the stretto there is a section in which we hear the first violins repeating time after time a motive from the subject, insisting on it, while the lower voices react to it with their own individual lines. The dynamic level increases—a real struggle for dominance. The activity is entirely linear; there is no purely supporting harmony.

Out of the maze of insistence a unison note suddenly emerges, resolving the issues. Agreement at last. And it captures our attention because the tonal contrast is so great between this unified sound and the melodic arguments that preceded it. A new melodic idea begins to grow out of the unison. Descending swoops in the high voices are again followed by the new tune. And again descending slides (they are properly called *glissandos*), lowered dynamic level—and silence. If we are following closely, we are now prepared for something to happen, and it does: the new melody enters several times, and in stretto (Example 98).

But is it really a new tune—a new subject? Think about the melodic direction of the original subject. Remember how it moves upward away from the beginning note and then slips back down chromatically? What is the melodic direction of this new material in relation to the original? It moves down and slips back up chromatically. For every ascending interval of the original subject, this one uses a descending one. For each original descending interval, there is here an ascending one. Upside down, inverted, the way objects are inverted when we see them reflected in a lake or pond.

The procedure is a popular fugal device, and its name is an exact description: it is called *inversion*, or sometimes, *mirroring*. It is a form of variation, as are so many devices that we refer to as developmental in music. Like a reflection, it gives us a different view of the musical material even though it is essentially the same thing. Is it as though the composer were engaging us in a discussion and saying, "Let's approach the subject from another angle"?

After some exploration of the inverted subject, we hear—and this takes very close listening—both the original form and its inversion simultaneously, with the celeste throwing a veil of sound around them (Example 99).

Then further development, this time the original subject followed in stretto by the inversion, each being quietly inspected in turn. The

Example 98
Bartók, *Music for Strings,
Percussion and Celeste.*

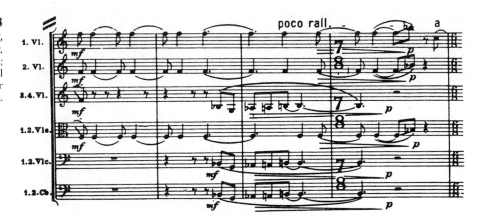

music fades into silence. Finally, a last appearance of the two forms of the subject, starting in unison, moving away in different directions, and coming slowly, deliberately back to the unison on which the composition ends (Example 100).

This is a husky piece of music, full of tightly controlled fugal devices. And yet, even with the obscured sense of tonality, the absence of metric regularity, and the pervasive dissonance, the melodic manipulations are perceptible. The structure itself furnishes us with aural guidelines that enable us to follow Bartók's musical ideas. This may be one reason that twentieth-century composers found contrapuntal procedures attractive. Melodic clarity, even though highly chromatic, guides our ear through the dissonance and the rhythmic complications.

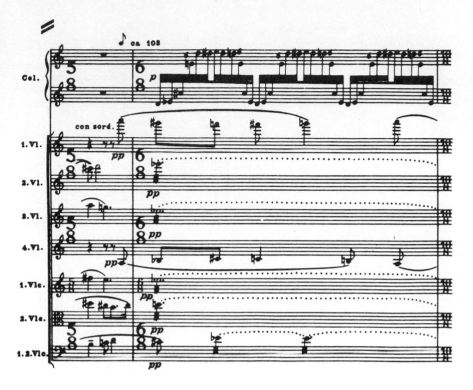

And the treatment of the material really does correspond to discussion. Intelligent discussion and argument expose varying points of view but without wandering off the subject entirely. Isn't this what Bartók is up to musically? Doesn't he present us with the unison passages in the middle in order to bring us sharply to attention, to capture our ears, so that his new version of the musical idea can be clearly presented?

The Hungarian pianist and composer Béla Bartók (1881–1945), after an initial short career as a concert pianist, abandoned the stage for research into folk song and for composing. He later took up the piano again and in 1927 came to the United States on tour. After returning to Hungary, he came to America to stay in 1940. His style covers a wide range from the conventional to the relatively esoteric. He is famous for his piano, chamber, and orchestral works, and for his settings of folk songs.

SUPPLEMENTAL LISTENING

Because of its combination of logic and complexity, the fugue is an interesting form to investigate. Here is a short list of works using the form that students have found rewarding:

Bach, Fugue in C minor for organ.

Bach intended this very complex fugue to be played following his Passacaglia in C minor, discussed in chapter 26. Too complicated to serve as an introduction to the form, it is interesting for follow-up study. It is a double fugue, and the first subject is the theme of the passacaglia. The second subject, made up of *staccato* eighth notes, acts as a melodic and rhythmic foil to the first.

Bach, *Art of Fugue.*

This is Bach's culminating work in the form, during the composition of which he died. The work is a series of fourteen fugues and four canons for unspecified instruments, plus two fugues for keyboard. All the pieces use the same subject, and it appears in every conceivable variation associated with the form.

Beethoven, "Great" Fugue in B♭ major, Opus 133.

Written for string quartet, this fugue is in the composer's most advanced and forward-looking style. In it Beethoven anticipates most of the harmonic expansion that was to characterize the music of the nineteenth century. Dynamic contrast plays an extremely important part in the development of the musical ideas.

Dmitri Shostakovich, Quintet for Strings and Piano, first movement.

The fugue here is preceded by a prelude which is quite extended and expressive. The fugue itself begins quietly with five entrances of the subject, four in the strings and the fifth in the piano. Later the strings and piano enter in stretto. In several places there are references to the thematic material of the prelude. Because Shostakovich (1906–1975) is of the twentieth century, the general texture is somewhat dissonant, although not as sharply so as in much of his other work. Shostakovich's style is somewhat uneven because of periods of harassment from Soviet government forces trying to induce conformity to state-approved artistic goals. He composed opera, ballet, and symphonies (some programmatic); chamber, piano, and vocal works; and film scores.

One of the most esoteric movements in jazz was what came to be called Third Stream. Among the leading groups was the Modern Jazz Quartet, founded in 1952 and led by pianist John Lewis. Third Stream is an attempt to unite the forms and devices of "serious" music with the improvisation and spontaneity of jazz. The players who were most strongly attracted to the style were those with a conservatory background or with a lot of comparable training and experience in chamber music. Jazz has had much influence on compositional techniques in the twentieth century, in America and abroad. Igor Stravinsky, Darius Milhaud, Aaron Copland, Charles Ives, Leonard Bernstein, and many others of equal stature have used some of the idiomatic material of jazz to enrich their own work. It was probably inevitable, then, that jazz musicians themselves would try to make their contribution to the forms that had developed through centuries of Western tradition. The fugue was one such form that exerted particular attraction for the Modern Jazz Quartet.

PRIMARY LISTENING:
"A Fugue for Music Inn,"
Modern Jazz Quartet with
Jimmy Giuffre, clarinet
(record set)

In "A Fugue for Music Inn" we hear a relatively early example of their exploration. The subject is a distinctive one, easy to hear, syncopated enough to suggest jazz. It is a classic four measures long. Except for that subject, which is written and agreed upon by everyone, the composition is based on improvisation, although a great deal of "working out" has gone into the preparation (Example 101).

The subject enters six times without episodes to separate the entrances, in spite of the fact that the key relationships we expect in fugues are there. In order of entry, the instruments are bass, clarinet, vibes (vibraphone), piano, clarinet, and vibes. There is no attempt to use a counter-subject in the way we found it in Bach, consistent throughout the exposition. Instead, each player fashions his own line individually once he has completed the statement of the subject.

Immediately following the six entries, we lose almost completely the sense of subject, although tiny bits and pieces of it persist through the next section, much as we might find motivic material in a fugue episode. The form of that section is associated with popular

Example 101
John Lewis, "Fugue for Music Inn."
Copyright © 1957, MJQ Music, Inc., New York, N.Y. (U.S., Canada, and Mexico). Used by permission. © 1958 MJQ Music Inc., assigned to Kensington Music Ltd., 85 Gower Street, London WCIE 6HJ. International Copyright Secured. Used By Permission (United Kingdom and Republic of Ireland). Melody reproduced by kind permission of Essex Music of Australia Pty. Limited (Australia and New Zealand).

music *and* jazz, and we have met it before: the 32-bar pop song form. Here the tune is original to this performance instead of the tune of a well-known song like "Body and Soul," which was a reference point in our earlier consideration of themes and variations. The clarinet is the soloist in this section, with the rest of the group furnishing an improvised polyphony to complement it.

At the conclusion of the 32 bars the vibes enter with the fugue subject, followed immediately by the clarinet. Another 32-bar segment follows, freely improvised but within the A A B A structure that is one of the most comfortable for jazz musicians.

Following that, the subject enters in inversion (Example 102): piano, sax, bass, vibes, and lastly the vibes again at the interval of a fifth. This last entrance of the subject in the vibes is really the beginning of another 32-bar episode, again in A A B A form. This is followed by a "settling down" passage that announces the final bit of fugal manipulation—an entry that features the subject in both its original form and the inversion, in stretto. That's pretty solid stuff for a jazz group!

The debt to fugal device is obvious. Everything is present that is needed to define the form. There are imitative entrances of the subject, key contrasts, episodes (in this case 32-bar segments in A A B A form) separating subject entries, even inverted versions and stretto. Here, however, the episodes suggest the tail wagging the dog: they are more extended than the subject statements on which the piece is based. This is actually not a bad thing. In a composed fugue, the composer is not bound in any way in terms of episode length. All he needs is enough time to change the key as he sees fit. When the episodes are improvised, as in this performance, the players need some guideline in terms of duration as well as harmonic background. The 32-bar pop song gives them just such a pattern around which they can structure their ideas. This form provides exactly the same sort of control here that the 12-bar blues gives improvisers when

Example 102
John Lewis, "Fugue for Music Inn."

that form is involved. The blues could be used in a fugue, too, as could any other form with which jazz musicians were aquainted, as long as it was standard enough to give the chance to improvise without anyone getting lost. When the form of the episodes is set, the entrances of the subject or its variation can be made on schedule without disrupting the progress of the music. Whatever final statements of original, inversion, and stretto there are are worked out ahead of time, of course.

So we have here a happy blending of deliberate composition and improvisation. In terms of the syntactical demands of fugue form, this may be the only procedure that could "work out" for improvisers. Continuing modulation such as we find in Bach episodes could not be handled satisfactorily unless the improvisational element was so highly controlled that it became negligible—and then where would the jazz be? At the same time, unless there were recognizable segments that involved the original subject, where would the fugue be? The Modern Jazz Quartet offers some of both worlds.

Music Inn, for which the composition was named, is a resort establishment in Massachusetts. Because of the interest of its proprietors, it was made available to jazz and folk artists in the 1950s. Seminars, performances, discussions, and other related activities were held and were open to the public. In some cases the musicians were offered an opportunity to simply explore new possibilities in their field, without the responsibility for providing entertainment that would bring in enough money to give them financial stability. In other words, they were subsidized so that they would be entirely free to dig into their "thing" without having to satisfy public demands or expectations. It was out of this kind of activity that the Modern Jazz Quartet seriously explored the relationship between jazz and traditional Western musical practice. And this raises some interesting questions.

The arts have always relied to some extent on patronage. At first the patron was the church, later the aristocracy; at present much support comes from governmental sources as well as from private contributions. Only the most popular of popular art idioms are self-supporting. The very use of the word "popular" is the key at this point. We need to remember that during the 1930s and early 1940s—the era of the big band and swing, when jazz was synonymous with popular music—jazz was completely self-sustaining. With the advent of the bop style, however, when jazz became a listener's music and a relatively difficult one at that, the economic status of the performers became pretty shaky. There was an afficionado element, but a small one, and no subsidies.

The subsidies came at first, and still come most, to those

musicians who related significantly to established practices and interests in "serious" musical styles. This is a continuing complaint among jazz performers, even though the idiom has become widely respected throughout the world. A few "stars" prosper; many competent musicians face the problem of limited opportunities for exposure and even more limited chances to experiment without threat of financial discomfort. This is less true with "serious" composers, many of whom are on the staffs of universities and colleges and able to secure grants from private and government sources. Much experimental music could not exist, in fact, without such support. The relative weight of attention given to jazz is small although there has been a trend during the last ten years to engage leading jazz musicians as college teachers. A growing number of universities are even offering jazz as a major subject area. But "popular" jazz artists like Louis Armstrong and Duke Ellington needed no subsidies. Groups like the Modern Jazz Quartet have received them, and they have also been welcomed on university campuses where the kind of thing they do relates strongly to the musical traditions emphasized there. Between the poles represented by these two types of jazz musicians, there is a sort of void that neither public support nor subsidy has moved to fill.

As an example of the confusion and problems, even the Modern Jazz Quartet broke up as a group in 1974 (although they have reassembled a few times in recent years for concert appearances). The vibes player, Milt Jackson, was the moving force behind that dissolution. He insisted that there was not enough public interest to support the kind of jazz that the group performed, with its major emphasis on linear textures, and he has suggested that lack of public interest may well be related to lack of promotion by recording and booking companies and by television. Other jazz musicians, many less esoteric than those in the Modern Jazz Quartet, have engaged in a new style: jazz-rock fusion. These include Wayne Shorter, Chick Corea, Herbie Hancock, and many others. Inserting heavy doses of rock does give the music a wider appeal, of course, but it also eliminates some of the improvisational spontaneity that has been a traditional feature of jazz. Add a little, lose a little. The strength of commercialization is a difficult, perhaps impossible, one to resist. And musicians need to eat, even as you and I.

SUPPLEMENTAL LISTENING There are other recordings by the Modern Jazz Quartet in which they tackle the fugue form. One of their more interesting pieces is "Three Windows." Atlantic: 1284.

In all the long history of Western music, only a few musicians stand apart from the crowd as innovators. Most of those few are important because of the way they manipulated materials already in wide use. Monteverdi was one such. He used sudden (the technical name is *unprepared*) dissonance, much to the distress of many of his contemporaries. Debussy was another. His dissonances failed to resolve to consonances as they were "supposed to." Stravinsky's rhythmic ideas were innovative. In each case, however, the material was there before them. Their contribution was in terms of how it was used. They did not, in other words, devise a new "system."

Arnold Schoenberg (1874–1951) did just that. He changed the course of twentieth-century music because of the way he rearranged the concept of tonality and the melodic order of music. His earliest work is in post-Romantic style, but he soon moved toward almost complete expressionism and a rejection of traditional concepts of tonality. He developed the system known as *serial composition*, also referred to as *12-tone* and *dodecaphonic* (*dodeca* means "12"). His concepts, grounded in contrapuntal practice, were best projected in chamber works, although his compositions include pieces for orchestra and a number of solo songs (Illustration 37).

The basis of Schoenberg's argument with existing systems of tonality was the tyranny of the tonic note, and with it the tonic chord. We have seen how compositions tend to draw back to the key tone, the tonic, at various points but most strongly at the conclusion. It is the "main" note, "home base," the point away from which music moves but to which it returns for completion. It is only because of this attraction that we can speak of a tonal system at all, within which melody and harmony work to define the key.

Schoenberg realized that in such a system one note exerted enormous control over all the other available ones, and he questioned the necessity and desirability of that. Why not work for complete independence of pitch? Why set up a complex of sound that dictated the supremacy of one pitch and one chord? Why not use all 12 tones of the chromatic scale in such a way that none of them assumed more importance than any other of them? How to accomplish this?

Several intervals, melodically speaking, tend to suggest movement to a tonic within the conventions that define Western harmonic practice. One is an ascending half-step, because it sounds like a tone leading to the tonic, like *ti* to *do* in our system of syllables. Another is an ascending perfect fourth or a descending perfect fifth, because either sounds like dominant to tonic. That's the favorite cadence pattern in most of the music we hear and have heard for centuries. It is the bass-note movement in countless pieces. It is *sol* to *do* in our syllable order. This is easy to check: have a bass sing or play that interval and have a soprano sing or play *ti* to *do* (in the same key, of course), and test the effect of completion.

Illustration 37. JEUNE FILLE DANS UN FAUTEUIL (WOMAN IN A CHAIR). Pablo Picasso, 1917. Like Schoenberg and other innovators in music, Picasso was a leader in using the established materials of the visual arts in ways that offered new insights. His objective was not distortion, as many might suspect, but rather clarification of form in terms of blocks and planes and space relationships. To relate to his work, it is necessary to abandon our preconceptions of what "real" objects "look like." In company with twentieth-century philosophers, dramatists, writers, and musicians, he encourages the participant to explore new, fresh visions of reality. Collection of the J. B. Speed Art Museum, Louisville, Kentucky.

To avoid the dictatorship of the tonic, then, one must avoid those intervals. That was one of the devices Schoenberg suggested.

Also, if the sense of tonic is to be subverted, it is better not to sound one pitch successively too often or to arrange the pitches so that they form a "normal" chord. In other words, stay away from all the pitch arrangements that raise associations with tonality as we have come to use and expect it. The "cure" is not difficult. There are twelve pitches available; each of them must be used before repeating any of them. But there must be no ascending half-steps, no ascending perfect fourths or descending perfect fifth, and no chord outlines. The twelve pitches are then a *tone row,* or series—and that's where the terms *serial composition* and *tone-row composition,* another alternate name, come from.

Having set up a particular series of pitches, then, what does one do with them? Just repeat them? Too monotonous. Change the rhythm? Still pretty monotonous—remember that we are dealing here with a melodic concept. Variations? Possibly, but what kind? Why not use the devices developed through the centuries by that most complex and syntactical and organized of melodically oriented forms, the fugue? There's the answer as Schoenberg found it.

Once the row has been established and presented, it may appear in almost innumerable versions as the composition develops. It may be transposed, each pitch raised or lowered by the same interval so that the row itself has the same shape but sounds higher or lower. It may be segmented, so that three or four notes from the row are manipulated in various ways without involving the rest of the series. It may be used in inversion, a device with which we are acquainted. Some of the notes may be sounded simultaneously as tone clusters while others (or even the same ones) are used to structure a melody above the chords. Since the basic row forms the material from which the composition is fashioned, almost any use can be made of it. It is the kernel of the piece, and to whatever extent the composition may be said to be tonal, it is the entire row rather than one single note from it that defines its tonality.

One fugal device that was particularly attractive to composers working within this system was that of *retrograde*—backward motion. The process had been a favorite one in the Baroque period also. In retrograde the material of the row was simply stated in reverse order as one of the variation techniques. Also possible is an even more esoteric treatment—*retrograde inversion,* backward and upside down at the same time.

Quite naturally the uniqueness and challenge of Schoenberg's system of serial composition caused a great stir. It also drew many disciples, among them Anton Webern (1883–1945). Webern was one of the more successful disciples of Arnold Schoenberg, and is best represented by his chamber compositions, where his highly dissonant but logical polyphony is completely exposed.

PRIMARY LISTENING: Anton Webern, Concerto *(Konzert),* Opus 24, 1934 (record set)

In the first movement of his Concerto (or *Konzert),* Opus 24, written for a chamber group of wind and string instruments with piano, Webern uses the device of retrograde inversion. The inversion follows immediately after the first presentation of the row. Although it is transposed, the pitch relationships are identical to those of the row (Example 103).

From this point the composition proceeds with highly involved manipulative techniques, always related to the original series of 12 pitches but within a devilishly complex context. Rhythms are as intricate as are the melodic and harmonic mechanisms. Webern was one of Schoenberg's most ardent followers, but added his own peculiar insights and creativity to Schoenberg's principles of organization. Webern was particularly fond of spreading the row among a number of instruments, sometimes even having each play only a single note in turn. This gives a very pinpointed effect, especially if the instruments differ distinctly in color. Some of that happens in this composition.

One needs a lot of help in hearing this sort of sound manipulation. A key to the character of the tone row is in the initial appearance. Notice that each of the four participating instruments has only three notes—a quarter of the row apiece, in other words. The figures have a relationship to one another: the first instrument is echoed immediately by a retrograde inversion of its material by the second instrument, and the same process occurs with the third and fourth instruments. The most striking feature of each figure is the highly dissonant largest interval involved. This same dissonant interval recurs throughout the piece, and our ears come to be drawn to it. There are also very distinctive rhythmic motives that occur often, and they too give us something to cling to.

In general, *dissonance* is a term without meaning here, as it was with Penderecki's *To the Victims of Hiroshima*. The entire texture is so saturated with musical movement that "doesn't sound right" that we need to abandon our preconceptions of dissonance–consonance relationships. There is no consonance against which to weigh dissonance, so the sounds are simply what they are and refuse to yield to relative or comparative terms. Understandably, serial composition has never held a wide audience, especially when it appears with the starkness of this piece.

In spite of the fact that many listeners react violently against such music—some call it pure chaos—it is actually more self-justifying than almost any style of composition. We earlier considered syntax in relation to canonic device. Here the syntax is actually built into the system itself. All the musical devices are controlled from the same germ, the row. No single note or combination of notes ever occurs by accident; each has a reason for being there at any particular time. All the material can be referred back to the opening tone row. Very few composers can give a logical reason for the direction of their melodies or for their choice of harmonies other than that they sound right to them. Here there is a structurally defensible reason for each bit of musical movement. It may be somewhat in the area of mathematics or physics, but it is rational.

What difficulties this music may present are aural ones. A favorite pastime of theorists is to trace the various uses to which the row is put in serial compositions. This kind of detailed analysis is done by eye, not by ear. For this reason, the music itself is often referred to as "eye music"—easier to see than to hear. Following its progress is somewhat like reading a map or deciphering an extended mathematical problem. Most of us do not have ears keen enough to keep up with the variations. Despite the completely logical syntax, then, we often fail to comprehend the sound. Interestingly enough, repeated exposure to such a piece does bring rewards to many listeners, especially those with an intellectual bent.

In spite of the problems it presents, serial composition seems to be here to stay. It has been modified by different composers so that the insistence on dissonant intervals is often less apparent. Most of the devices still follow polyphonic practice, however, perhaps because the procedures of counterpoint give both composers and listeners guidelines that might be missing in less linear textures. As a system, it is unique and one that has exerted great influence over much of the music of our century.

There is an interesting paradox in the fact that most jazz, although often largely improvised, is accessible to many listeners, even those who are relatively unskilled. On the other hand, compositions based on serial techniques do not attract a large audience, although the musical logic and craftsmanship are beyond question. There are many possible reasons; why not raise some questions? You might start with whether or not improvisation can be just as "logical" as the methods of serial composition. You might even get more philosophical than that and ask whether improvisation is just as compositional as any other kind of composition. What *is* composition, anyway?

SUPPLEMENTAL LISTENING   The following pieces will provide additional examples of serial techniques and raise other questions:

> Arnold Schoenberg, *Variations for Orchestra* and Quintet for
> Wind Instruments
> Alban Berg, Violin Concerto. Berg (1885–1935) was another of
> Schoenberg's better-known disciples. The Violin Concerto is
> notably easier to hear than many tone-row compositions
> because in it the row is made up partially of chord components
> of a "normal" type. As a result, the piece is much more
> consonant and even harmonically "familiar."

Chapter 31
Multithematic Forms: Movements of the Symphony

We have explored extensively several of the forms that are identified by their use of a single thematic idea, although some of them also featured contrasting material as well. There is a large body of musical repertoire in the Western tradition that uses more than one theme around which to develop. In this body, perhaps the greatest number of compositions are symphonies and related works. We have already discussed some of the uses to which contrasting musical ideas are put. Binary and ternary forms are multithematic in principle. So is the five-part song and even, on a small scale, the 32-bar pop song. So are the free forms, including through-composed songs. The concept, then, is not actually a new one for us, but we shall now deal with it extensively for the first time.

We shall be investigating several types of multithematic organization. One of the most important, and one that we have not encountered yet, is the one found in the first movements of nearly all symphonies. It also occurs in first movements of sonatas, concerti, string quartets, and other chamber works, and even in many single-movement forms such as the concert overture. The form goes by a number of different names—*first movement form, sonata form, sonata-allegro form*, and others. We will use *sonata-allegro*, but the name is much less important than the musical procedure. The *allegro* in the label comes from the fact that most first movements of symphonies, sonatas, and the other forms just named are in the fast tempo called allegro.

PRIMARY LISTENING:
Mozart, Symphony No. 40,
first movement, Allegro
molto, 1788

The procedure that identifies sonata-allegro form is not a terribly complex one, although many composers have treated it in a highly involved fashion. The form begins with the presentation of a musical idea, called here a *theme*, distinctive enough to provide the material for later manipulation without loss of substance. Normally, if a symphony is tonal, this first theme appears in the tonic, the key of the symphony. Mozart's Fortieth Symphony is in G minor, and so we hear the first theme in that key (Example 104).

Following a complete statement of the melody, we hear what sounds like the beginning of a repetition of it, but almost at once the direction changes. We enter a section without great melodic interest but with a lot of harmonic vacillation; obviously the music is taking us away from the beginning and trying to get us someplace else. As usual, there is a function involved. The section is called a *transition*, and its purpose is to change keys—modulate—in preparation for the entrance of a contrasting musical idea, which will be another theme.

A strong cadence marks the end of the transition, and following a brief silence (come to attention!), the second theme enters in the clarinet and bassoon but is taken over by the strings. The key, as well as the mode, has changed. The first theme was in G minor; this one is in B♭ major. Also, it is more lyric and even somewhat chromatic. The important thing is its marked difference from the first theme, a difference without which thematic contrast in a form as extended as this one could not be completely effective (Example 105).

The second theme is followed immediately by its repetition; this time there is no interruption until the final cadence is almost reached. Here, once again, it drifts off into a relatively unsettled

Example 104
Mozart, Symphony No. 40.

Example 105
Mozart, Symphony No. 40.

section but one that utilizes motives (short musical fragments) from the first theme. Some analysts refer to this as the *closing theme*, because it is the end of one of the sections of sonata-allegro form— the *exposition*. This is marked by another strong cadence. The exposition, then, consists of the statement of two contrasting musical ideas, bridged by a transition section and concluded with a closing theme. The purpose of the exposition is to reveal, or expose, the musical material in much the same way as the exposition of a fugue presents the subject.

For some reason that cannot be explained other than in terms of musical convention, most symphonic first movements from the Classic period repeat the exposition. This poses a problem for the composer. The key has changed for the second theme, as we have noticed. During the final section of the exposition, the composition normally stays in that new key. Since it is different from the key of the first theme, how is a composer to get back to the "right" key for the repetition of the exposition? There are a number of possibilities, including just jumping back into the first theme without worrying about the sudden change of key. In this symphony, Mozart's approach is a little more subtle than that. He simply throws in a single modulatory chord and away we go on the repetition. Since it *is* an exact repetition, we hear once more the chronology of the first section: the same themes, same transitions, same closing section, same final cadence, even the same modulatory chord.

What follows is the section called the *development,* and we will meet many old musical friends throughout it, devices that have been used in the fugue and in many of the programmatic compositions from part 2. But the modulatory chord originally designed to get from the key of the closing section back to the key of the opening theme will not work as a bridge into the development, so Mozart adds two other chords. And this is a clue that we are about to be led through a series of different tonal centers, again as in the fugue. The thread that binds all the harmonic wandering is the use of motives drawn from the first theme: we hear them in all sorts of alterations. Mostly we hear just the initial few notes; they are used as dialogue among sections of the orchestra in an antiphonal framework. They are even used upside down—in inversion—for a question-and-answer effect. They slip and slide into and out of a number of keys, getting further and further away tonally from the home key of G minor. Again as in the fugue, we hear a profusion of sequences, melodic as well as harmonic. The total effect is one of exploration, searching, argumentation, dialogue. If we are sensitive to harmonic instability, the result for us is a sense of uneasiness and drift and wonder about what will come next and where we will wind up at the end.

This is the exact nature of development. It is merely a musical working out of thematic material that the composer has presented in the exposition. Whatever expressive atmosphere the music creates is based mostly on our response to thematic discussion and transformation and manipulation. The argument is not about anything outside the music, as it was in *Till Eulenspiegel,* for instance. It is the highest form of abstraction, because it is only about itself: the music.

After Mozart has done what he wants to by way of developing the music introduced in the exposition—in this case, only the first theme—he has led us pretty far from the home tonality. Again, our sense of this is limited by our awareness of harmonic direction, and individual differences strongly define the degree to which we can each follow the procedures. But we can all follow the thematic contortions. And we can all sense in the music the chromatic sliding back to the key of the first theme that prepares us for the end of the development and the beginning of the next section, the *recapitulation.*

The recapitulation is exactly what the word suggests: a restatement of the thematic material in its original form or something very like that.

There is an important difference, however. If your tonal memory is a good one and your concentration level is high, you will realize that the transition between the first and second themes here is different from the same transition in the exposition. To what end becomes clear when the second theme enters: this time it is in G minor—the same key as the first theme (Example 106).

So why the transition? What purpose does it serve if not to modulate, change the key to prepare for the second theme? Balance of construction is probably the best answer, like the columns on many contemporary buildings that have no responsibility for supporting weight but are there merely to complete the visual balance of the architectural design.

The second theme is quite different in its recapitulated version because it varies in mode as well as key from its appearance in the exposition. So is the closing section, and for the same reason,

Example 106
Mozart, Symphony No. 40.

although much of the motivic nature is the same. A very short section closes the movement, using a slightly new musical idea, but one based on a motive from the first theme. This final summation is the *coda* (literally, "tail"), which we have encountered before.

Here is an outline that fits most sonata-allegros from the Classic period:

EXPOSITION

Theme I—key of the tonic
Transition—modulatory, often based on motives from theme I, often constructed with sequences
Theme II—key different from tonic but closely related to it
Closing section—stays in key of theme II, often using motivic material of one or both themes
Entire exposition repeated literally

DEVELOPMENT

Manipulation of thematic material; frequent, sometimes almost constant vacillation of key center; motivic dialogue; possibilities limited only by composer's imagination or intention; ends with transition back to key of theme I

RECAPITULATION

Restatement of exposition but with themes I and II in same key; transitions and closing section adjusted to accommodate unified tonality

CODA

Summary statement, often brief, to bring movement to a graceful conclusion

You will recognize that the underlying concept here is one of contrast. The contrast includes thematic material as well as tonal centers. Before people were stirred out of such associations as a result of women's lib and similar movements designed to destroy stereotyping, the first theme was referred to as "masculine" (because of its rhythmic vitality and often disjunct melodic movement) and the second theme as "feminine" (because of its more lyric quality). Since the character of the two themes is normally quite different, each of us can find our own label, if we like labels. Contrast is the name of the game, though, and in most movements of this type that element is pretty strong. The musical conflict set up in the development section is another important feature of the form. So is the regrouping of material in the recapitulation. Some commentators have likened the form to a drama, in which the characters are introduced in the first act (exposition) and placed in varying dramatic situations in the second act (development), which are finally resolved in the third act (recapitulation). The fact that the themes appear finally in the same key can even be related to the male–female analogy and to marriage, if you like your imagination to run wild!

There is a subtle artistic danger in this kind of thinking, though; it assumes that most people are unable to accept musical expression for its own sake, without referring it to some pseudo-programmatic context outside itself. When we are children, we are often asked to "be big elephants" or "be little tippy-toe fairies" to the accompaniment of absolute, or nonprogrammatic, music. This is usually defended as encouraging some sort of physical response to music. To each his own. But it would be nice if we outgrew this kind of reliance upon extramusical reference points as we matured. Musical dialogue, manipulation, argument, presentation, regrouping—none of these needs to "mean" something else. They should not always have to be "about something." If we persist in our description of music as the most abstract of the arts, we must be able to accept the abstract nature of the expression it conveys. Is this reluctance to let us develop our ability to deal in abstractions an insult to our intelligence and our sensitivity? What level are you geared to?

Mozart, Symphony No. 40, second movement, Andante

With the format of sonata-allegro in mind, you should be able to investigate the second movement of Mozart's Fortieth Symphony with little trouble. It follows exactly the same construction. Here you will discover that the first theme is presented in a polyphonic manner, imitatively, and is rather extensive, almost like a three-part song, but in principle the procedures are those of the first movement (Example 107). There are transitions, contrasting thematic ideas (Example 108), changes of key center, a development section with all the harmonic instability implied by that, and finally a return to the themes of the exposition.

One sharp difference is in tempo: how can we call this sonata-allegro form when the tempo is so slow? The answer is in the

Example 107
Mozart, Symphony No. 40.

Example 108
Mozart, Symphony No. 40.

concept of form itself—the way the different musical ideas are related to one another. As stated earlier, the *allegro* in the term *sonata-allegro form* refers to the tempo of the first movement, and the form is one that normally occurs there. But the organization, apart from any considerations of tempo, can and often does work for any movement.

You will hear, perhaps, other differences. Does the exposition repeat, for instance? Is the expressive atmosphere different? Why, or why not? Can you discuss the themes in terms like "masculine" and "feminine?" What about the coda?

The important thing, however, is whether or not the principles of organization that define sonata-allegro form are kept intact. The *uses* to which those principles are put by a composer will be various, even within the same work. But only if they are abandoned altogether can we say that the structure has changed significantly enough to require another label.

Mozart, Symphony No. 40, third movement, Menuetto: Allegretto, Minuet and Trio

The third movement does require another label. Although it involves a number of different themes, their arrangement and the relationships among them are not those of sonata-allegro form.

One of the important differences is the extensive use of repetition—literal repetition. Also involved is the lack of developmental techniques, musical discussion and argument, and "working out." This is appropriate, since the movement begins and ends with a minuet (Example 109), the minuet is a dance form, and we need some sense of regularity in a dance, even a relative lack of complexity, in order for it to function properly. As it was used in a symphony, of course, the dance became merely a reference point for form; no one expected the audience to jump up and turn the concert hall into a ballroom. Actually the minuet as it appears in symphonies has an accompanying trio, lighter in texture but echoing the meter and usually the tempo of the minuet while using contrasting music. For this reason, the entire movement is called Minuet and Trio.

The organization is very sectional, and each section tends to have a sort of independence, so that we feel almost a series of free-standing segments. What really connects them is a certain thematic similarity. This is our time-honored artistic process of unity–variety at work again.

To diagram a minuet and trio, we use familiar vocabulary and symbols:

A (Minuet)	B (Trio)	A (Minuet)
||:a :||: b a:||	||:c :||: d c:||	a b a

Example 109
Mozart, Symphony No. 40.

The symbol for exact repetition is the only new one:‖: :‖. It means only that all the music between the bracketed and dotted sections is repeated literally. This helps to account for the sectionalization as well as for the repetitive nature of the form.

Notice that in the A section, the Minuet, the musical ideas of a and b are very strongly related. The principal contrast is in key and mode, and Mozart is so skillful in getting from b back to a that we are almost unaware that anything different is going on. As a result, the integration is smoother than the formal outlines would suggest. This is a comment on Mozart and his ability to use form for his own purposes.

The change in texture and musical character at the beginning of the Trio is quite marked (Example 110). The melody is more gentle and the meter less strongly accented. The mode, too, is changed to major in contrast to the minor of the minuet.

The same chronology of presentation and repetition occurs here, but the texture is considerably thinner, as the word "Trio" indicates. In the very earliest use of trios with minuets, the trio was actually scored for only three instruments and then the title was exact rather than suggestive as in this movement. The d sections here are based on sequences, much as were the b sections of the Minuet, but the returns of c are given a somewhat distinctive quality because of

Example 110
Mozart, Symphony No. 40.

changes in instrumentation from strings to brass. The Trio, then, has the same sort of internal coherence and continuity that is found in the Minuet.

The return of A (Minuet) is altered only to the extent that there are no repetitions. In the movement as a whole you will recognize a three-within-three concept at work, including triple meter, but, we assume, without Trinitarian references. Perhaps you will have realized that the sonata-allegro format is also ternary in principle. This must be a compelling idea, since it recurs in so many contexts in the arts. Is this actually an extension of a theological concept. Or is it a satisfying way of organizing our ideas and perhaps even the basis for much theology itself?

Mozart, Symphony No. 40, fourth movement, Allegro assai

There is no need to explain the organization of the fourth and final movement of this symphony—it is an old friend. It would be a good challenge for you to sort out the themes and the progress of the form.

The symphony is far and away the most elaborate of the multimovement forms. Since its inauguration in the eighteenth century it has served a multitude of composers, and the manner in which its principles have been used is one means by which we describe period styles as well as the styles of individual composers. Although treated with relative objectivity in the Classic period, its inherent dramatic possibilities were seized upon by Romantics, as we shall see. Beethoven is frequently characterized as a "bridge" between Classicism and Romanticism. Much of this is apparent when we compare his Fifth Symphony with Mozart's Fortieth Symphony.

PRIMARY LISTENING:
Ludwig van Beethoven, Symphony No. 5, 1805–1807, first movement, Allegro con brio

The opening four-note motive of Beethoven's Fifth Symphony has become so well known that for many it typifies the man himself. Because its three shorts and a long relate to the Morse code for the letter V, it was used as a symbol for victory during World War II. It is often thought to be a representation of Fate knocking at the door; Beethoven himself is credited with making this comparison. Lots of other associations have grown up around it. Unfortunately, most of them are pretty superficial.

Although there is nothing dangerous about assigning extra-musical significance to the motive, its function in the first movement and throughout the symphony is far more interesting artistically. Like the presentation of any theme, it announces the material from which the music is to proceed. Its special power lies in its brevity and the strength with which it is announced. It is as though Beethoven were saying, "Here it is. This is the seed. From it this work will grow." And it does. Used as a sequential pattern, the motive provides practically all the substance of the first theme (Example 111).

In the transition, we hear the opening motive used sequentially, sometimes retaining its original melodic and rhythmic character, but sometimes used as a rhythmic device without reference to its initial melodic intervals. The opening mode is minor and, as in Mozart's Fortieth Symphony, the second theme appears in major, in this case E♭ major. It is introduced in the horns by a slightly varied version of the opening motive, then grows into a relatively lyric statement. But even while the woodwinds and violins are spinning this out, the basses are still busy with that motive (Example 112).

Without wasting a note or a moment, the music moves into the closing theme, still insisting on the original motivic idea. Beethoven seems little interested in spinning out graceful tunes; his musical inclinations were not in that direction, and he took his share of criticism for that. He is far more interested in developing, and we hear in this exposition his eagerness to present his musical ideas as concisely as possible so that he can get about the business of exploring their implications. His score does provide for a repetition of the entire exposition; this is convention at work. However, you will hear many performances of the Fifth that do not repeat; this has become the conductor's prerogative.

The development sounds like yet another beginning, but we are soon drawn into the kind of manipulation that takes us further and further away from home base.

It would be hard to imagine anyone getting more than Beethoven out of the brief musical ideas that make up his themes. They

Example 111
Beethoven, Symphony No. 5.

Example 112
Beethoven, Symphony No. 5.

are thrown around from instrumental section to instrumental section, backward, upside down, dissected, almost tortured. Dynamic levels change. Sometimes the music sounds actually angry, sometimes even tantalizingly hesitant. One of Beethoven's major contributions to the symphonic concept was his ability to exhaust his themes through development. The drama here needs no outside reference point; what happens to the music is dramatic enough.

When the transformations seem complete, Beethoven begins promising the recapitulation. There are false starts in varying keys, tension-creating waiting sections, dynamic contrasts. If we are informed enough to know symphonic process, we are apt to get pretty frustrated with all this stopping and starting. But Beethoven is not Mozart—he never does slip gradually into the recapitulation. Instead, when it finally arrives, we are almost slugged with it, as though that first theme were pounding us with a sledge hammer. This is dramatization of a high order—Romanticism at work.

In the recapitulation the final cadence of the first theme is extended by an oboe solo, totally without reference point in the exposition (Example 113). What is it doing there? Critics have worried with it for years. One wag has suggested that the oboe player is confused: he thinks the composition is an oboe concerto. Another has suggested that the brief interlude was written for Beethoven's nephew, Hermann Finkelschnitzer, who was able to play only within a narrow range and therefore got no opportunity for solo work—so Beethoven gave him this chance. Although facetious, either explanation just might be as good as the real one, which only Beethoven ever knew. This oboe solo does represent a breaking away from the limitations of form, though, and you might like to speculate on what implications this has in terms of the form-content controversies.

Apart from the oboe interruption, the recapitulation proceeds according to schedule, with one exception. The second theme would normally appear here in the key and mode of the first theme: this is one of the regrouping principles of the recapitulation. If we anticipate the conventions, then, we expect it to be in C minor. It is instead in C major, thus retaining its own individual character even though the key is changed from E♭, as in the exposition, in the interest of unifying the tonality of the recapitulation (Example 114).

Example 113
Beethoven, Symphony No. 5.

Example 114
Beethoven, Symphony No. 5.

Illustration 38. PAGE FROM BEETHOVEN MANUSCRIPT.
The fury that we hear in so much of Beethoven's music is reflected in this page of his manuscript for one of his piano sonatas. Also in evidence is his compulsion for reworking his ideas mercilessly.
Eric Simon (ed.), The Facsimile Series of Music Manuscripts, Dover Publications, Inc., New York, 1968.

There are more surprises. Instead of the brief coda we found in Mozart, we are given an enormously extended one that sounds precisely like another development. It is here that we see Beethoven as the master of symphonic technique. That technique is essentially a developmental one, a craft of manipulation, investigation, argumentation, and enlargement of musical idea, and it is typical of Beethoven that he uses it so fully here. It is as though he simply cannot turn his ideas loose, but needs to shake them and dissect them and worry over them again and again. It is in this regard that he exerted such great influence over the nineteenth century. Like Bach's in the Baroque period, his architectural skill stood above that of the crowd, and he used it to the utmost.

In the entire first movement we see this skill operating. The choice of an almost insignificantly tiny motivic idea and its logical

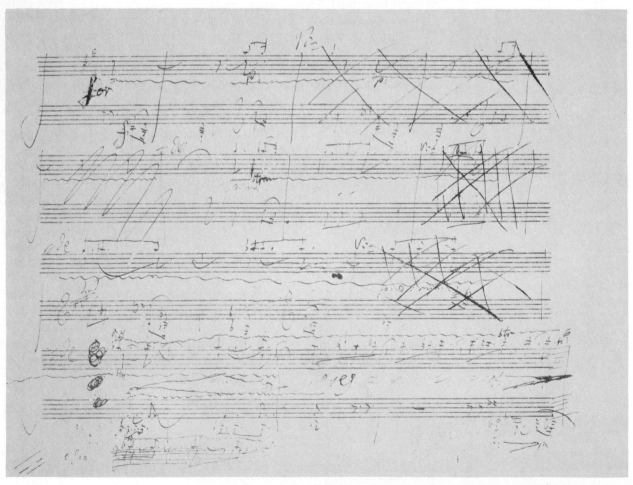

expansion into several different but related themes: Beethoven the expansionist. His impatience with transition and a corresponding intensity of presentation. His reluctance to expend great amounts of compositional effort on fashioning long, involved melodies. His immense imagination in the use of his themes. The drama with which he announces the recapitulation. The reluctance to have done with development even when the time is past in terms of strict formal chronology.

We see something of the man here. By the time he wrote the Fifth Symphony Beethoven was almost totally deaf. Not only did this make him more than usually irritable and impatient with the world and its folk; it also drove him inward where, undistracted by the sounds around him, he was free, perhaps even compelled, to wrestle with his music interminably.

We can understand some of this if we use our imagination. Think about how we sometimes get a tune stuck in our head early in the day and can't seem to get rid of it. Even worse is to remember part of it but to be unable to complete it. Beethoven's manuscripts suggest that he may have been tormented in a similar way. And when he became deaf, there were no other sounds to disturb his preoccupation with musical detail. He reworked his musical ideas over and over, even through the years—changing, erasing, starting again, changing again (Illustration 38). As a result, there is seldom any "filler" in Beethoven's music, few if any wasted notes. As much as that of any creative artist we know about, his belief in the nature of man shows through. He was a complete Romantic to the extent that he felt that man *could* overcome his torment, *could* triumph, *could* transcend the chains of his world. It is not difficult to hear this in his music.

Beethoven, Symphony No. 5, second movement, Andante con moto

The familiar concept of theme and variations furnished the format for the second movement of Beethoven's Fifth Symphony. There is a twist, however: instead of one theme there are two. There is nothing in the first theme to remind us of the symphony's opening motive (Example 115). There is, however, a tendency that we find often in Beethoven: an avoidance of cadential regularity, so that the theme

Example 115
Beethoven, Symphony No. 5.

spins out more or less continuously rather than arranging itself into small blocks.

The second theme is a direct "throwback" to the opening motive of the first movement. The relationship is more a rhythmic one than a melodic or harmonic one, and it is in this rhythmic guise that the motive will appear throughout the rest of the symphony. After an initial quiet statement of the second theme in the tonic, a brief harmonic transition prepares for its powerful reentrance in a related key. And, like the first theme, it spins out under the momentum of its own motivic ideas (Example 116).

The rest of the movement is a series of variations on these two themes, appearing alternately and becoming more complex in the process. Beethoven's procedures here are reminiscent of his developmental techniques. The variations are far more striking than mere ornamentation or mode change could make them. They are really character sketches which change mood and expressive content with each appearance. Again, dynamic levels and the teasing effect of segments that seem almost static add a sense of drama that is missing when variations are based on relatively simple transformations of the melody. Some critics have actually referred to this type of musical procedure as "character variations," variations that change the expressive quality of the theme rather than merely elaborating on the notes in an ornamental sense. Once more we discover the depth of Beethoven's invention and his ability to get beneath the surface of his music. And we see the Romantic tendency to use established forms in a more affecting way.

Beethoven, Symphony No. 5, third movement, Allegro

One of the innovations that Beethoven is credited with is the change in the third movements of some of his symphonies, not so much in form as in expressive intent and content. The minuet and trio was the traditional third-movement form of the Classic period. As you know from Mozart's Fortieth Symphony, it has a large ternary format in triple meter and is arranged sectionally. That includes a certain independence of individual sections. Related to Beethoven's tendency to characterize his musical figures, and to put them into a more dynamically expressive context, is his use of a scherzo to

Example 116
Beethoven, Symphony No. 5.

replace the minuet and trio in symphonic composition. The word *scherzo* means "joke.' Whether there is anything humorous about the third movement of Beethoven's Fifth Symphony is open to individual question, of course. What we hear most clearly is a change of tempo from moderate in the minuet to quite fast in the scherzo. Structurally, there is again a very perceptible three-part form. But inside that form there is a lot happening, and some of it is pretty different from a minuet and trio.

The A section contains two sharply different musical ideas, as we expect. Also as we expect, Beethoven presents them in a hurry, without spinning them out over a long space in time. The first idea (we will call it a as in a minuet) is an ascending broken-chord figure appearing in the bass and completed in the higher strings and winds (Example 117).

The b material is once more a reference to the rhythmic motive of the entire symphony, stronger and more virile than a for the sake of contrast (Example 118).

Only by pushing and pulling can we squeeze the music into a clear ternary format to equate with the A section of Mozart's Minuet. There is the same sort of interchange that we expect, but the chronology is a little distorted. We even hear the two thematic ideas overlapping at times. Moreover, there are segments that remind us of development—Beethoven indulging his manipulative inclinations again. But as with Mozart, a strong cadence on the tonic does announce the conclusion of A.

The B section is strikingly different and puzzling if we are oriented to expect a standard sectionalized trio such as goes with the older minuet. What Beethoven gives us is a largely fugal working out of a characteristically brief melody (Example 119).

The "subject" runs through a series of contrapuntal adventures, stopping abruptly, trying to get started again, finally succeeding, extending itself. There are repeats, even very literal ones, but the

Example 117
Beethoven, Symphony No. 5.

Example 118
Beethoven, Symphony No. 5.

Example 119
Beethoven, Symphony No. 5.

entire section is so integrated that we have no real sense of the kind of segmentation that repeated passages usually create. Also, we are accustomed, if we are looking for simply a fast trio, to a decisive cadence at the end of this part and a fresh beginning for the return of A. Instead, it sneaks back in almost before we are aware of its presence, gliding out of a very brief *pizzicato* transition in the basses.

Adding to the confusion is the changed character of A. It does avoid the extensive repetition of themes, and that correlates to the final section of the Minuet and Trio of Mozart's symphony. But changes in instrumentation and dynamic level and alternation between bowed and *pizzicato* passages combine to give the return a sharply different quality.

This movement, like the others, reveals Beethoven as the master of musical transformation, or development. The basic concepts of ternary arrangement that are associated with third-movement form are here. But within them, the music assumes new expressive as well as technical directions.

Beethoven, Symphony No. 5, fourth movement, Allegro

And now, where is the strong separation of movements we anticipate in symphonic style? In place of the anticipated conclusive cadence to finish off the scherzo, we are offered a long, low-level tension section clearly meant to prepare us for something to come. Out of it bursts the first theme of the last movement, a majestic statement in C major, another change from convention, because normally the finale of a symphony is in the key *and* mode of the first movement (Example 120).

There is no particular problem in following the presentation of themes in this last movement. However, because one idea grows so naturally from another, you may have some difficulty with feeling a sense of one theme stopping and another beginning. This is because of Beethoven's flow of material and his avoidance of "seams." This is apparent throughout the symphony, but nowhere is it so dramatic as in the transition from the third to the fourth movement and the exposition section of the finale. The enormous drive and sweep are one direct result of the musical continuity, the very evasion of the sectionalization that marked much of the music of the Classic period.

Example 120
Beethoven, Symphony No. 5.

There even seem to be more than the usual number of the themes. Critics argue about the number. But no matter, unless you insist on analytical exactness. As an expressive element, the continuity and drive are far more important. And notice that one of the themes uses the rhythmic motive again (Example 121).

The development section includes all the expected interweaving of thematic ideas and all the excitement that Beethoven's techniques bring to his work. What brings us up sharply, though, is the intrusion of one of the themes from the scherzo. And it comes at the exact time when we have been prepared for the recapitulation (Example 122).

Here is yet another application of "binding" techniques. Obviously there is a strong connection that Beethoven is trying to make between the character of the reintroduced scherzo material and the nature of the final movement. Is the latter an outgrowth of the implications of the former? Did the struggle in the scherzo fugal section and the changing character of the scherzo A section "mean" something extramusically that is resolved in the decisiveness of the last movement? But why rework it again by reintroducing the scherzo? Notice that we are given *only* the scherzo material based on the "germ" rhythmic motive, the section we identified as b above. Is this a reminder of the very opening of the first movement? There may even be an inherently but rather abstract expressive intent. Remember that the first of the fourth movement themes grows triumphantly out of the subdued transition following the scherzo. Here the recapitulation of that first theme grows out of a similarly subdued statement of the scherzo b theme. Is the expressive impact of the recapitulation stronger because of that?

The answers are interpretive ones, individual, not in the area of "right" or "wrong." But the ultimate danger would be to allow the drama of the music to be justified *only* in terms of a programmatic meaning. Beethoven does stand at the portal of Romanticism, and the dramatic character of his musical fabric entices us into seeking a program to explain the heightened expressiveness. In the absolute sense, no such program is necessary: the musical excitement is its own program.

Example 121
Beethoven, Symphony No. 5.

Example 122
Beethoven, Symphony No. 5.

At any rate, the musical progress following the scherzo theme is entirely on the track familiar to us in recapitulation. As usual, Beethoven has trouble releasing his composition. Even the final chords are typical. We have the sensation that he has ended a dozen times but without actually stopping.

The "disruptions" of form that are found in the Fifth Symphony are not the only ones found in Beethoven's work. In his Third Symphony, the *Eroica*, the first movement is notable for the introduction of an entirely new thematic idea in the development section. His compositions in all genres offer continuing surprises for the careful listener, one of many reasons why he stands out in the history of the music in the West.

One of the goals of the Romanticists was to erase the boundaries of experience, to seek the unreachable, probe the mysteries, minimize the limitations by which we are all somewhat bound. This underlies the whole concept of artistic combinations of previously segregated modes of expression, such as poetry and music in song, music and extramusical ideas in program music, and music and drama in opera. As noted before, the attempt was to portray experience as one unified, indivisible whole. In the Fifth Symphony, Beethoven contributes to this in a purely mechanical way by connecting ordinarily separate movements and carrying over thematic ideas from segment to segment of the symphony (Illustration 39). Berlioz carried even further the technique of thematic unity in his *Fantastic Symphony*, combining that device with literary and dramatic implications.

In another context, Wagner used the themes called *leitmotifs* to represent people, objects, and ideas in his operas. Their appearance in various transformations always relates to the dramatic situation, and thus the music itself becomes a real part of the drama. Wagner claimed Beethoven as a musical ancestor, and in terms of compositional procedures it is easy to see why.

And so the boundaries imposed by form itself began to stretch a little. Even though a structural concept, the form, was not entirely abandoned, it often became a vehicle for expressive intensity more than a simple means for organizing musical ideas. This is what we really mean by Romanticism, and you will easily recognize Beethoven's contributions to Romantic objectives and to the devices that were used by later composers. Largely because he was able to show the way, the multithematic form that we have called sonata-allegro was taken into the vocabulary of program music, where its particular nature was put to dramatic uses. But just as in Beethoven, the logic and discipline of formal process always allow the music to stand alone. The program may add a dimension to the experience as Beethoven's reference to fate may do for some of us, but the

Illustration 39. THE ELPHINSTONE CHILDREN. Sir Henry Raeburn (1756–1823). Like Beethoven, Raeburn lived during the period of transition from the Classic to the Romantic era. Although his figures are carefully placed for balance in the Classic mode, they are caught in action and highly idealized, as well as expressively represented. Cincinnati Art Museum, Bequest of Mrs. Mary M. Emery.

program cannot replace or substitute for musical coherence and continuity.

Ludwig van Beethoven (1770–1827) was one of the most important of the Viennese Classicists, but his work pointed strongly toward the Romantic period. Born in Bonn, Germany, the son of a drunken and irresponsible father, he was a greatly talented pianist in his youth. At the age of 17 he was forced to assume the responsibilities of head of the family, later even providing for the education and support of a nephew when Beethoven's brother died. In 1792 he moved to Vienna, where he tried to make a professional living independent of a court or church appointment; he did receive occasional sporadic assistance but never in large sums. Although he was successful and sold many compositions, he was always in financial difficulties.

In 1798 Beethoven began his battle with deafness. The problem worsened by 1801, and by 1802 he was faced with the fact of having to live without his hearing. Despite this, his greatest works were composed during the ensuing years. His production was enormous and includes works in almost every known genre. And no composer has gone further than he did in working out to the fullest the potential of his thematic ideas.

All of this came to focus in his last symphony, the Ninth. The final movement is set for orchestra, soloists, and chorus, to a poem by Friedrich von Schiller. It is an immensely powerful hymn to the concept of the brotherhood of man, united under God, reaching for the stars. In a master stroke of irony it was used in the movie *Clockwork Orange*, most often to accompany scenes of senseless and unmotivated violence. As is so often the case when quotations are used with skill and expressive richness, the reference point was lost on many of the audience.

SUPPLEMENTAL LISTENING   There is an almost limitless body of music that employs the formal principles of the Mozart and Beethoven symphonies we have considered. We will be examining some in the next few chapters, but at this point, you might like to listen to several other Mozart, Haydn, or Beethoven symphonies for the sake of comparison.

Chapter 32
Sonata-Allegro in the Overture

The dramatic possibilities of sonata-allegro form were drawn upon extensively throughout the nineteenth century. In the case of the concert overture (a term that identifies the piece as *not* an overture *to* something, such as an opera), the title gives the programmatic content. The listener is expected to contribute something to the interpretation of the program if that element of the expression is to communicate fully. This is certainly the situation in the Russian composer Peter Ilich Tchaikowsky's *Romeo and Juliet*, which the composer called an *Overture-Fantasy*.

PRIMARY LISTENING:
Peter Ilich Tchaikowsky,
Romeo and Juliet Overture,
1869, final revision 1880

A composer setting out to use Shakespeare's *Romeo and Juliet* for musical purposes might have a number of options from which to choose his course of action. One obvious one would be to present the chronology of the play's events in musical terms. This was not the route that Tchaikowsky elected. Instead he went to the heart of the drama and identified those elements that he felt to be most important to the development of the plot. Apparently for him, the love element, the conflict between the two families of the young Romeo and Juliet, and the attempt of Friar Laurence to mediate the tensions were the dramatic factors most readily translatable into sound.

In his last symphonies, Haydn had used a slow introduction for some of the first movements. During the years that followed, the Romantics had allowed the introduction to assume a great deal of expressive importance, perhaps because the first theme of the movement proper is quite striking when it emerges from a quieter, more gentle or brooding fabric. As it was most frequently used, the introduction employed its own thematic ideas and was therefore not considered as a part of the sonata-allegro form, although its themes did appear often in the development section. Tchaikowsky took advantage of the musical character of the introduction to present the theme associated with Friar Laurence. Solemn and choralelike, in the minor mode, it serves to establish the sort of mood that is appropriate to Shakespeare's drama (Example 123).

All the trappings of Romanticism are evident: the rich harmonic vocabulary, the exploitation of dynamics, the silences heavy with expectancy. Even the promise of something about to happen, and then the frustration when the music settles back down. There is, too, the tendency to develop right along with the presentation, to use the musical ideas at once in a manipulative way, but always including the vacillation of mood. By 1869 the orchestra had grown to mammoth proportions, and Tchaikowsky takes full advantage of this too.

Out of the almost morbid texture of the introduction emerges the first theme of the sonata-allegro form—conflict (Example 124).

In every way it is a sharp contrast to the introductory material. The jagged rhythms, syncopation, disjunct melody, and connotations carried by the minor mode all combine to project musically the sense of struggle and antagonism that we associate with the conflict between the families of the ill-fated lovers. This, then, is the first theme of the sonata-allegro form, and it adheres to the conventional character of such themes, but it also serves an appropriate programmatic purpose. Here, as in the introduction, there is more than

Example 123
Tchaikowsky, Romeo and Juliet Overture.

Example 124
Tchaikowsky, Romeo and Juliet Overture.

mere presentation. Compare it, for instance, to the appearance of the first theme of the first movement of Mozart's Fortieth Symphony, with its relative objectivity and single statement. Tchaikowsky presents his theme far more than once and increases its intensity with each repetition.

A gradual diminuendo and change of mood prepares for the entrance of the second theme: love. There are two definite and contrasting ideas within this theme. One is lyric, spun out, fully extended in the manner of a real tune (Example 125). The other, which follows immediately, is more a series of wavering chords (Example 126). Throughout the overture, these two ideas are associated and interwoven, and some critics have attempted to supply a programmatic significance to the contrast between them.

Perhaps because of the dramatic intent, we find no repetition of the exposition; there is no need for that here, and by the date when the overture was composed that particular convention had been abandoned anyway. Tchaikowsky is much more interested in proceeding to the development section, for here is where his drama can be best engaged.

Both the love and conflict themes and also the Friar Laurence theme are used developmentally and in the ways that we expect. They appear and reappear in all sorts of conflicting and changing musical contexts. The only thematic idea missing is the tuneful portion of the "love song"; the wavering chords do participate. The total effect of the development is one of struggle for superiority and presumably this is what Tchaikowsky is after. Which element in Shakespeare's drama will triumph? This is the programmatic side of the form—musical struggle and argument reflecting psychological struggle and argument.

Out of all the tension, the conflict theme emerges triumphantly. From the formal standpoint, it *has* to: it is the first theme and it will

Example 125
Tchaikowsky, *Romeo and Juliet Overture.*

Example 126
Tchaikowsky, *Romeo and Juliet Overture.*

appear first in the recapitulation. And this is equally useful from the dramatic standpoint. In the play, the conflict did indeed exert fatal power over the lovers, even with Friar Laurence interceding on their behalf.

We hear again the force of the first theme, intensified by repeated statements. But from it once more grows the love theme, this time transformed not only in tonal center but also in character. In the exposition the instrumentation selected by Tchaikowsky was relatively thin and light, innocent perhaps, certainly not saturated with passion. Here in the recapitulation, however, we have a full idealization of the flowing lyricism that was so much a part of the Romantic ideal. In each of its several succeeding statements the theme takes on greater intensity, until finally it soars out with full-bodied ecstacy. Is Tchaikowsky telling us that out of conflict the love has matured, become transcendent, richer and fuller? Or is he suggesting that because of its intensity it will survive in spite of the conflicts that threaten it? Or, program aside, is this a musical intensification that is its own justification?

The love theme does not prevail, however. Gradually it is swept away again by the conflict theme, stronger and more assertive than ever. It climaxes and concludes with great decision and finality. Once again the love theme appears, but this time distorted, in the minor mode, broken, fragmented. The changes here contradict the unity of key and mode found in classic use of the form but they do support the drama implied by the program.

The coda, as though to balance the introduction, uses references to the chorale style of the Friar Laurence theme, but in a far more ethereal and devoutly exultant way. With it is a final transformation of the love theme. Your imagination will supply all the implications.

What is the relationship here between form and content? Is either one the dominant factor? The question that will get most quickly to the heart of the matter is probably this: Could the music operate at its full expressive strength without the program to "explain" it? Or are music and program here so inextricably interwoven that one cannot be complete without the other? Is the experience, in other words, as the Romantics envisioned it—unified, indivisible, complete?

Tchaikowsky (1840–1893) began his professional career as a teacher in the newly founded Music Conservatory in Moscow. He gained some recognition as a composer, but his personal problems, mostly a consequence of being unable to resolve the conflict between his homosexuality and his marriage, resulted in a move to Italy. Supported by Nadezhda von Meck, a wealthy widow, he was able to concentrate on composition. Following a number of years in various European locations, among them Paris, he returned to Russia, where he spent most of the rest of his life, except for tours on which he conducted leading orchestras in Europe and the United States (1891). Although he was interested in Russian national idioms, which he sometimes used as thematic material, his work is completely Western and highly Romantic. He composed opera (*Queen of Spades*, others), ballets, three piano concerti, one violin concerto, six symphonies, program works, piano music, and songs.

SUPPLEMENTAL LISTENING   Other concert overtures that have been appealing and descriptive to many listeners are these two by Felix Mendelssohn. Both adhere to the sonata-allegro principle and provide opportunity to examine the relative weight of form and content.

Hebrides Overture (Fingal's Cave).   An early Mendelssohn work, this highly Romantic overture is an attempt to capture in tone the scenic majesty and mystery of the Hebrides Islands of Scotland. The imaginative listener will contribute his or her own images of waves against rock shorelines, the sound of birds crying, and perhaps a sense of the total feeling of the openness of the locale.

A Midsummer Night's Dream.   Based on Shakespeare's play of the same name, this work is also an early one, written when Mendelssohn was only 17 years of age. Those who are familiar with the characters and scenes in the play will recognize thematic material that suggests fairies, horns of hunters, the dance of the Bergomask, and even the brays of Bottom wearing his ass's head.

A German keyboard artist and composer, Mendelssohn (1809–1847) was a widely traveled, cosmopolitan, successful performer and composer. One of his most important contributions was that he revived public interest in Bach through his conducting of Bach's *St. Matthew Passion*, achieved only after considerable protest from Christians (Mendelssohn was a Jew). He composed many vocal works, including incidental choral pieces, oratorios *Elijah, St. Paul)*, songs, piano and organ works, five symphonies, and other orchestral music.

Chapter 33
Sonata-Allegro in Chamber Music

The same formal process that we have been discussing in the symphony and the program overture has served for chamber music of all sorts, as well: string quartets, woodwind quintets, brass groups. It has also served as the first movement form in many solo sonatas. What we will investigate next is its use in a trio for piano, violin, and cello.

PRIMARY LISTENING:
Fanny Mendelssohn Hensel, *Trio*, Opus 11, first movement.

We would expect that with a group of three instruments, all of which are capable of playing solo sections, a composer would divide the responsibility somewhat evenly among them. This is exactly what Fanny Mendelssohn Hensel does in her 1846 work.

Following a measure of piano runs, the violin enters with a rhythmically robust theme, the first of the sonata-allegro form. The theme is really in two parts and for the sake of clarity, we will call the first section Ia and the second section Ib. Both sections do appear importantly in the development and so it is well to keep them apart in our ears. For theme Ia, consult Example 127. We hear it reiterated in fragmented form on the way to Ib, which makes its appearance in the piano (Example 128). This section of the theme (Ib) is modulatory in nature, moving us from the D minor of the opening section to the key of the relative major, F, for the second theme. This is the same key relationship that we found in both the Mozart and Beethoven

Example 127
Hensel, *Trio.*

Theme Ia

Example 128
Hensel, *Trio.*

Theme Ib

symphonies we examined (see appendix 1 if these key relationships are confusing).

The second theme is quite lyric in spite of its use of rather wide leaps (Example 129). The violin and piano having shared the responsibility for the two sections of theme I, it is only fair that the cello should present us with the second theme—and that's precisely what happens. At the same time, the violin and piano have their chance, as well, setting up a real dialogue among all three of the instruments.

The closing theme appears first in the piano (Example 130), then the violin, and then argues mildly with motives from theme Ia as the exposition draws to a close. We have here, then, a well-balanced division of thematic material among the entire group. Hensel was a skilled pianist and, as we might expect, the piano parts are very demanding, even virtuosic, without at the same time overwhelming the violin and cello.

The musical conversations among the instruments continue in the development. It begins with bits and pieces of theme Ia shared

Example 129
Hensel, *Trio.*

Example 130
Hensel, *Trio.*

between the cello and violin while the piano provides an accompaniment alternating among rapid running passages, full chords, and arpeggios. Before long, we hear the second theme stated in the cello, followed by the same theme in the piano. This leads to a duet between the cello and violin in which the former uses a variation of theme Ib while the latter uses motives from theme Ia.

The recapitulation begins with theme Ia, but this time we hear it first in the piano rather than in the violin as in the exposition. Here, also, it is stated in full, rich chords—something that the violin cannot manage but which comes quite naturally for the piano. Theme Ib makes its appearance right on time but now it is in polyphonic imitation between the piano and violin. That bit of action fades into Ia, still in imitation while the piano keeps up its activity unabated. All of this leads to a dramatic four-measure flourish in the piano, driving us triumphantly into theme II with the cello and violin in resonant octaves while the piano provides a tremolo background. The closing theme is shared by the piano and violin, followed by a coda that features mostly material from theme Ia.

The only change in the recapitulation relative to the exposition is that the second theme appears in D major rather than in the original tonic of D minor. Does that remind you of Beethoven? Otherwise the key relationships are the standard ones, and the piece does move back into D minor for the final closing section.

And so we have here a composition, romantic in nature, that divides the musical responsibilities evenly among all three of the involved instruments. It makes skillful use of all the textural possibilities that such a combination can provide, while at the same time taking advantage of the formal guidelines to create a coherent work. We can admire Hensel's craftsmanship even though we may have a difficult time understanding why she should have had such problems bringing her artistry to the attention of the public. Let's look at those problems briefly.

Fanny Mendelssohn was born in 1805 into a wealthy, highly educated Jewish family in Hamburg, Germany. She was the elder sister of Felix Mendelssohn who became one of the most renowned and successful composers of the time. He relied a great deal on her guidance in his own work, largely because she had shared all the same educational opportunities that were afforded to him, including music instruction, and he fully recognized her competence.

Because her financial situation was so fortunate, she was not forced into a professional career in order to gain a livelihood. She was actually discouraged from such a course because her father not only insisted that she should not publish her music nor perform in public but that she should, on the contrary, "seek feminine contentment in the home." The attitude was an all-too-prevalent one at the time, and there is no doubt that many creatively gifted women in all the arts were denied recognition—and that as a result, we are denied the benefit of their art.

So restricted was Fanny's activity that, although she composed a number of songs, the first few of them to be published were published under her brother's name. It was not until after she married Wilhelm Hensel in 1829 that she published a song under her own name in 1837—with her husband's encouragement. However, it was fully nine years later in 1846 that she decided to publish more of her compositions, again encouraged by her husband and by offers from two publishers in Berlin.

Under a rush of new enthusiasm, she then composed her *Trio* in D minor, her only work for chamber group. It was also to be her final effort. The composition was written for her sister's birthday and was given its first performance on April 11, 1847, little more than a month before Fanny's death.

She was a friend of many of the leading musicians of the time and was known principally for the musicales given in her home and for her skill as a pianist. Robert and Clara Schumann, among many others, were members of an intimate circle who were well aware of Fanny's gifts. A mere handful of her works were published and several of those posthumously. Most of her large body of composition is available only in libraries here and abroad.

Because of the steadily strengthening women's movement in the United States, the work of many women composers of the nineteenth and earlier centuries is being uncovered, published, and recorded. Unfortunately the task of locating manuscripts that have been long hidden or forgotten is an arduous one.

SUPPLEMENTAL LISTENING   It would be rewarding to investigate the other three movements of Hensel's *Trio.* The entire work has been recorded on *Camerate Canada:* Crystal Records: S 642.

An anthology of compositions by women is entitled *Woman's Work:* Gemini Hall Records: RAP–1010. This is a two-disc set covering compositions from the Baroque era to the twentieth century and comes with a good descriptive booklet enclosed.

For another perspective altogether, try *Jazz Women:* Stash Records: ST 109. This two-disc set, complete with booklet, covers performances by women jazz players from 1923 to 1957.

Chapter 34
The Concerto

Still another genre that often employs sonata-allegro form in its first movement is the concerto, normally written for a solo instrument with orchestra. As in Hensel's *Trio,* there is often equal involvement of the orchestra and soloists, even though in the case of the solo concerto there is naturally more attention given by the audience to the "star" performer.

One of the structural features often found in the solo concerto is a double exposition—once around by the orchestra and then again by the soloist. Such is the case in our next listening exercise.

PRIMARY LISTENING:
Antonin Dvořák, Concerto for Cello, B Minor, Opus 104, first movement

The concerto begins with an immediate statement of the first theme in the clarinets in the tonic key of B minor (Example 131). It is taken up almost at once by the violins and then by the violas, bassoons, and horns in unison. Without too much delay, there is a massive statement by the full orchestra with the strings and woodwinds carrying the theme and the rest of the ensemble filling in the harmony. After these initial statements are introduced and we know what the theme is all about, there are some additional fragmented appearances which lead in a sort of settling-down section to the entrance of the second theme.

This is in sharp contrast to the rhythmically vigorous first theme. Not only is it in D major (the relative major), but it is very lyric, almost longing in quality (Example 132). The piece was composed in 1895, over a century after the Mozart Fortieth Symphony, and yet we are still observing the convention of contrast in the character of the first and second themes, and for good dramatic and expressive reasons. A vigorous closing section dies away and leads into the first entrance of the solo cello.

Example 131
Dvořák, Concerto for Cello.

Example 132
Dvořák, Concerto for Cello.

The preceding passage has brought the tonality back to B minor in order that this second exposition may parallel the tonality of the initial one in the orchestra. At this point, immediately after the statement of the theme, we are aware that there is a skilled performer on hand. Amid much virtuosic passage work, there is a lot of backing-and-forthing with fragments of the theme, arguments between the soloist and the orchestra, variations of the theme in rapid cello passages—all in all, a very developmental-sounding section although we are still in the exposition. This is a romantic characteristic—to present and then develop immediately rather than waiting for a new section. But it also serves the purpose of bringing the soloist into full play in an appropriate role of contrast to the orchestra. Once again, following all the activity, the pace subsides as well as the dynamic level and we are led into the second theme.

Again it is carried by the cello and, as in the first exposition, it is in the relative major, D. And once more we have dialogue between the soloist and the orchestra, additional virtuosic display, and again the sense of development. A majestic statement of the first theme, this time in D major and in the full orchestra, brings the double exposition to a close.

Whatever development there is begins with a very quiet statement of the first theme in the orchestral cellos and basses There is no need for a "real" development section because we have already had so many developmental devices during the second exposition. The main purpose here is to entice us back to a reappearance of the first theme. It does come, and it does feel like a recapitulation, but there is a twist. Rather than the vigor of the theme as we were first introduced to it, here it is quiet and reflective—and to our surprise, in augmentation (Example 133). And instead of being lodged in the orchestra as in the beginning of the exposition, here it belongs to the cello. A reversal of roles and another example of shared responsibility. Also, the key is a strange one—A♭ minor—which almost at

Example 133
Dvořák, Concerto for Cello.

once becomes G♯ minor. If you have consulted appendix 1, you will realize that these keys sound the same in a tempered system. All that is different is the spelling—our ears can't detect that without the help of our eyes. To be quite specific and as musically accurate as possible, we would say that the G♯ minor is the slightly altered VI chord in B minor, the tonic of the concerto. The romantic composers loved to use unusual key relationships and it wasn't long before they got away from the I, IV, V emphasis of the classic period. One of the ways they liked to enlarge their harmonic palette was to indulge in what we call third relationships—keys that are a third apart rather than a fourth or fifth. That's what is going on here. Dvořák is beginning the recapitulation in a key a third away from the tonic. A real romantic.

Sliding chromatically, the orchestra and cello discuss the themes, sometimes in augmentation, sometimes in the original note values. Again, the whole process sounds developmental but we finally arrive at the statement of the second theme in the orchestra. This time, though, it has changed key and is in B major rather than D major as in the exposition. The cello takes up the material, still in B major, adds more virtuoso work in a developmental context, and the section reaches a climax with a grandioso statement of the first theme, now in B major. Notice that with this reiteration of the first theme in B major, following shortly after the second theme in B major, there is that unification of tonality we found in Mozart's recapitulation. The only real difference is the use of an unusual key for the *start* of the recapitulation. By the end, we have a consistent tonality, and it is in B major that we stay until the end of the coda and the movement comes to a close.

A lot has happened since the establishment of sonata-allegro form in the classic period. By the end of the nineteenth century we have added an enormous amount of dynamic contrast to the forces available to the composer. Coupled with that is a fascination for frequent changes of tempo. Harmonically, there is much added chromaticism and a concern for wider exploitation of key contrasts. All of these factors are, of course, the composer's attempt to deepen the expressive content of the music.

As for loosening the bounds of form, there is a tendency to present thematic material and then proceed immediately to a development of it. What this accomplishes is one of the objectives of the romantic period—to create a seamless whole. Thus, instead of saving development for a separate section, and instead of clearly announcing the recapitulation, there is a more continuous working out of the principles of sonata-allegro but without reliance on the fences that often separated sections in earlier decades. We still have presentation, development, and re-presentation but certainly in a more free-flowing format.

And we do have that characteristic procedure of the solo concerto—a double exposition in the first movement. The genre is different from the symphony and many chamber works in that it normally consists of only three movements rather than four. Typically the first movement is fast, the second movement quite slow and lyric, and the finale again fast and vigorous. All three movements afford the soloist ample opportunity to display his or her skills. At the same time, the orchestra is assigned its fair share of the musical interest. It is not, in other words, merely an accompanying force.

Dvořák (1841–1904) was a Czech composer who enjoyed considerable fame throughout Europe and the United States during his lifetime. He began slowly, composing many works before gaining his first recognition in 1873 at the age of 32. He was drawn toward the then-current interest in nationalistic music along with his countryman Smetana (see *Die Moldau*, chapter 16) and used many Czech folk idioms in his composition. His reputation spread rapidly and he visited in England, Germany, and Russia beginning in 1884, often to conduct his own works.

In 1892, he became Director of the National Conservatory of Music in New York, where he stayed for three years. Fascinated with the music of the American Indians and the blacks, he composed a number of works in tribute to those styles. One such, probably his best known composition, was the Symphony in E minor ("New World Symphony"). The 1895 *Concerto for Cello*, which we discussed above, was the last work composed while Dvořák was in New York. The inspiration for that piece, however, was homesickness for his homeland. In 1895 he returned to Czechoslovakia and taught until his death in 1904.

SUPPLEMENTAL LISTENING: There are many popular concertos available on record. Some use a double exposition in their first movement, some do not. It might be interesting just to investigate a few to see how different composers have handled the opportunity for interplay between the orchestra and the soloist.

Sergei Rachmaninoff, Piano Concerto No. 2, C minor
Felix Mendelssohn, Violin Concerto in E minor

Both of these are highly romantic in style and harmonic-melodic material. For a more contemporary approach, try listening to:

Alban Berg, Concerto for Violin
George Gershwin, Piano Concerto in F major

The concerto grosso is the grandaddy of the solo concerto, although even that genre had antecedents in the concerto da camera (chamber concerto) and the concerto da chiesa (church concerto) of the earlier Baroque. As the term "concerto" was used in the very early Baroque period, it simply implied a piece for an ensemble of instruments of various kinds, sometimes with voices, and with one person to each part. By the end of the seventeenth century, however, the music had gotten complex enough that not everyone could handle it competently, and that led to a division of the performing group into soloists and nonsoloists. As you might imagine, this development was gradual but it was basically an indication that the concerto in its modern sense was being launched—but with some differences.

In the 18th century a division of responsibilities between soloists and larger ensemble became fully developed. The soloists, two or more, were placed in one group which was called the *concertino*. The rest of the group, larger in size, was called the *concertino grosso* (grosso means "large"), or sometimes the *ripieno*. In either case, it meant the entire ensemble of nonsoloists but sometimes they were joined by the soloists as well. A composition for such an ensemble was called a *concerto grosso* (plural: *concerti grossi*), and you can readily see its relationship to our present-day concerto for solo instrument and orchestra. The only real difference is that the concerto grosso utilized two or more soloists; we normally use only one. And the forms within the multimovement composition are somewhat different.

PRIMARY LISTENING:
George Frederic Handel,
Concerto in B♭ major for
oboes and strings, Opus 3,
No. 2.

Composed in 1734 while Handel was in London, the B♭ major Concerto for oboes and strings is the second of a group of six concerti grossi included in Opus 3. The concertino (the soloists) consists of two oboes, first and second violins, and cello. The grosso or ripieno consists of first and second violins, violas, and cello, plus a harpsichord playing the continuo part from a figured bass (check this out in chapter 3 in the discussion of "Tu se' morta" if you've forgotten these terms). The composition is in five movements—a concerto grosso from the high Baroque might have anywhere from three to six or more movements.

The first movement is quite brisk in tempo, is in $B^\flat$ major, and utilizes the violins in the concertino more prominently than the oboes or cello. The very opening introduces us to that favorite Baroque device: the sequence (Example 134). And that persists throughout all the movements, in some more obviously than in others, but always present as a way to extend melodic ideas beyond the motive stage. Notice that the solo violins are sometimes engaged in an antiphonal, call–response context with the large group, sometimes simply displaying their skills unaccompanied. The oboes are somewhat buried in the overall tonal fabric because they are so often doubling the melody of the ripieno. Toward the end of the movement, however, they do break loose with a brief passage of triplets (Example 135).

Following a short transition, the purpose of which is to modulate, the second movement begins in G minor. Everyone has a series of repeated notes except for the two groups of cellos in the ripieno which carry a call–response pattern on broken chords. After nine measures of introduction—the tempo is a *very* slow three beats to a bar, so slow that it feels like six—the solo oboe enters with a sustained, almost melancholy melody (Example 136). This movement, then, is very closely allied to the later solo concerto in principle. If your recording features a really competent oboist, that person will add a tasteful amount of ornamentation to the melody in the true Baroque spirit.

Following another modulatory transition, we are into the third movement, a lively fugue-like section (Example 137). We are back in

Example 134
Handel, Concerto Grosso for oboes and strings.

Example 135
Handel, Concerto Grosso for oboes and strings.

Example 136
Handel, Concerto Grosso for oboes and strings.

Example 137
Handel, Concerto Grosso for
oboes and strings.

B♭ and you will notice only an occasional use of the concertino group apart from the ripieno. Most of the time they are simply playing with the ensemble but having no less fun because of that. You might be aware again of the heavy reliance upon sequences.

There is no transition between the third and fourth movements—can you explain why? The fourth movement begins with the concertino carrying the entire responsibility for introducing the musical material (Example 138). They are joined shortly by the ripieno, however. The movement is in two parts, the second of which is merely a transposition of the first but with some variations added (Example 139). Again the concertino gets the section under way, is joined by the ripieno, and then the two indulge in a brief antiphonal exchange. The entire second part is then repeated literally.

The last movement is a theme and variations based on a two-part theme (Example 140). Each part is repeated in the original statement as well as in the succeeding variations. There is a rather balanced interchange of concertino and ripieno throughout, each contributing to the progress of the piece. You will recognize that there are two variations following the original theme, but it may be difficult to follow because of the extensive repetition. The second variation may sound a bit livelier to you because of the introduction

Example 138
Handel, Concerto Grosso for
oboes and strings.

Example 139
Handel, Concerto Grosso for
oboes and strings.

Example 140
Handel, Concerto Grosso for oboes and strings.

of triplets which gives the impression of a meter of $\frac{12}{8}$, somewhat more energetic than the "real" $\frac{4}{4}$ of the theme.

Concerti grossi vary in length and, of course, in instrumentation. The concertino in different instances utilizes practically all the solo instruments that were available. Some are naturally more virtuosic than others, but the principle remains the same for all.

SUPPLEMENTAL LISTENING

Handel has another set of concerti grossi scored for all strings, including the concertino. It is Opus 6, and there are 12 pieces in the collection.

J. S. Bach's contribution to the genre was a set of six *Brandenburg Concerti*. They are quite a bit more complex than Handel's and are scored for a variety of instruments in the concertino groups.

Another Baroque composer who provided a set of concerti grossi was Arcangelo Corelli (1653–1713). His is a group of 12 pieces, published as Opus 6, with the concertino groups using a variety of instruments.

All of the above are available on excellent recordings.

Chapter 35
Rondo

PRIMARY LISTENING:
Mozart, Concerto for Horn
and Orchestra in E♭ major,
K. 417, third movement,
Rondo.

So far we have looked pretty closely at these formal arrangements that occur often in the symphony and its related forms: sonata-allegro, theme and variations, and minuet and trio. The latter combination has a close relative, of course, in the scherzo. Another of the popular structures found in concerto or symphonic context is the rondo. Multithematic in concept, it is related to the three-part song and five-part song as well as to the minuet and trio. Like those, the rondo operates on the principle of statement-digression-restatement. It is most frequently found in the final movement of concerti, sonatas, symphonies, and chamber works, and it is in that position that Mozart used it in his Concerto for Horn and Orchestra.

A concerto for solo instrument and accompanying instrumental group offers considerable opportunity for musical conversation, as we have seen. In diagram terms, the opening statement of section **A** by the horn soloist is immediately echoed by the orchestra (Example 141).

Then without pause, B enters, again introduced by the horn (Example 142). This section is more fully developed than A. The **A** section consists of only an 8-measure theme, stated once by the horn and then by the orchestra—a total of 16 measures. The B section, on the other hand, consists of 30 measures through-composed and includes a relatively suspenseful transition section during which the group modulates to the dominant key. The use of transitions, sometimes quite extended, leading to the return of the **A** theme in rondos is one characteristic that distinguishes that form from the five-part song. Because of the tension involved in the harmonic manipulation as well as in the dialogue and interplay among motives,

Example 141
Mozart, Concerto for Horn.

Example 142
Mozart, Concerto for Horn.

there is a sense of dramatic fulfillment when the horn brings us back to the home key with the opening material of the movement.

Much the same series of musical events occurs during the next digression and return. C itself is actually in a sharply different key and mode (Example 143), and is followed by another return of A.

Not content with two departures from A, Mozart leads us into still another: D (Example 144).

This one is lengthier and more musically complex than either of the others and is typical of still another feature of rondo form. Perhaps because of the frequency with which the main theme occurs, the digressions from it tend to become increasingly extended and involved. Often they migrate to more distant keys, for instance, and employ more developmental techniques. Regardless of what the reasons may be, the effect is certainly to make us welcome the eventual return of A, by this time an old and familiar friend. You may remember the same principle at work in Martini's "Plaisir d'amour." The C section of that five-part song was fully twice as long as either A or B. In that piece, however, there were only short piano interludes between parts rather than the extended transitions that we find here.

To further enhance the musical interest and perhaps even the drama, the return of A that follows D is quite different from its other reappearances. Not only is it more subdued than usual, it is also somewhat disjointed. A coda, based on the main theme but in an accelerated tempo, polishes off the movement.

Example 143
Mozart, Concerto for Horn.

Example 144
Mozart, Concerto for Horn.

The full diagram for this particular rondo would look like this:

A   B   A   C   A   D   A—Coda

In principle, this alternation of musical material could go on forever, maybe even long enough to use up all the letters in the alphabet. In actual practice, however, very few rondos go beyond this, and many do not include a D section at all.

Like many other forms we have examined, the rondo has been used for programmatic purposes. You may recall that Strauss identified *Till Eulenspiegel* as a rondo and the form–content relationship worked very well in that case. The questions raised then, at a point when we were concerned more with expression than with form, might be worth reconsidering.

SUPPLEMENTAL LISTENING

Of the many rondos available on records, the following may be suggested to illustrate both the form and its use in the concerto context. They vary in complexity and are therefore challenging to the listener who is interested in broadening his horizons. In all three instances, the solo instrument is the piano:

Mozart, Rondo in D major, K. 382.
Mozart, Rondo in A major, K. 386.
Beethoven, Rondo in C major.

Chapter 36
Sectional Forms: March, Rag, Dixieland, Mozart

The march, like the minuet and the rondo, is put together in a series of contrasting sections. The nomenclature is a little different but not altogether. The varying musical ideas in a march are referred to as *strains*. The third strain, however, is called a trio; this is reminiscent of the trio that goes with a minuet. *Within* the section, however, there is a considerable difference.

PRIMARY LISTENING:
John Philip Sousa, "El Capitan," 1896 (record set)

Any John Philip Sousa march will illustrate the point. Try his very popular "El Capitan." Count the measures as groups of two beats each. This is logical, since we march on two feet. You will discover a real regularity. Each strain is a block of 16 measures, and in this march each strain is repeated (Example 145). The diagram, then, comes out like this:

AA   BB   CC   DD

The only exception is the second C, which is extended to form a sort of transition into D. The C is the trio section, and you will notice the

393

Example 145
Sousa, *"El Capitan."*

same changes of dynamics and key that typify that portion of the minuet-and-trio form. The big difference structurally between the march and the minuet is the relationship between A and the other strains or sections, because there is no regular recurrence of that section in "El Capitan."

Sometimes strains do return on Sousa's marches. Listen to another of his best-known ones, "Semper Fidelis," and see if you can find the pattern. Don't overlook transitions between strains.

Sousa (1854–1932) known as "the march king," was a bandmaster and composer. He left a large body of marches, which are still being widely performed. Another popular one is "Stars and Stripes Forever."

The overall sense of regularity in marches is of importance in planning the routines of marching bands at football half-time shows. The predictability of the sectional arrangement makes it possible to block out some of the intricate patterns of movement that are so much a part of such shows. Try watching and listening from a *formal* point of view; in many cases, you will discover a pattern of marching that coincides with the pattern of the music for the march.

PRIMARY LISTENING:
Scott Joplin, "Maple Leaf Rag," 1899, Joshua Rifkin, piano (record set)

Like minuets and marches, the piano rag has a definite structural concept behind it, although not every rag uses the exact pattern. Basically it is a series of strains, each with its own independence. Like the march, the strains are each 16 measures long but with four fast beats or two slow beats to a measure. The most usual arrangement is the one found in Scott Joplin's "Maple Leaf Rag," and it is (Example 146):

AA   BB   A   CC   DD

It is apparent that there is no regularity in the return of A, as there would be in a minuet or rondo. Also, the tendency to repeat strains is related to the march. We are not really certain what forces combined to shape the piano rag, but we do know some likely ones.

Example 146
Joplin, "Maple Leaf Rag."

Marches were very much around and very much a part of community activity in the latter part of the nineteenth century. In addition, banjo rags had been a part of the standard repertoire of the minstrel show, and they used a type of sectionalized organization like the minuet and march.

Undoubtedly these other forms of composition, very much in the Western tradition, influenced the format of the piano rags. The first one was published in 1897; Joplin's "Maple Leaf" was published only two years later. For whatever reason, the country was flooded with rags for the next 20 years. The term rag is a reference to the emphasis on syncopation found in the melodies: the rhythm is ragged, in other words. The rhythmic interest in most rags, as in Joplin's, is in the highly syncopated right-hand melodic lines. The left hand, often in an "oom-pah" style, supplies the harmonic background and the steady beats against which the syncopations work. This is related strongly to the style of both marches and minstrel show banjo rags. In a band, for instance, the tubas together with the percussion normally supply a steady beat, while the higher-melody instruments, principally trumpets and winds, carry most of the melodic interest. In a banjo rag the melody belongs to the banjo and the accompanying piano furnishes the harmonic interest and the pulse. The transfer to piano was an easy one; the responsibilities were simply divided between the hands. Thus the oom-pah bass with off-beat chords in the left hand and the melodic syncopation and interest in the right hand.

Ragtime originated and flourished most strongly in the midwest; Joplin (1868–1917), for instance, was from Sedalia, Missouri. Because of its particular style it attracted whites as well as blacks. It was especially useful as dance music in small dance halls and listening music in small bars, and thus it spread across the country. Many rags were published too, so it wasn't necessary to go to a bar to hear them; you could play them at home if you were good enough.

In New Orleans, the home base for many early jazz musicians, many of the ragtime pianists found employment in the city's red-light district, where they played as soloists or as leaders of small instrumental groups providing entertainment and dance music for the patrons. For outdoor music in New Orleans, particularly but not exclusively within the black community, bands were the most important performing groups, and these were usually under the leadership of the trumpet player. Bands were utilized for all sorts of social occasions, including funerals, as we've seen, and much of the performance was based on improvisation or embellishment of a familiar piece. The inclusion of rags in the beginning repertoire of jazz is an outgrowth of the mixture of the two traditions of the ragtime piano and the marching band, and it is one of the fascinating stories of musical Americana.

Among the black population of New Orleans, the social lines were decisively drawn. Downtown were the Creoles, descendants of house slaves and French or Spanish masters. Because of their work assignments and the intimacy of their associations with the slave owners, the house slaves came into close contact with Western cultural traditions, including music. Also, they gained their freedom readily and were trained in the sort of professional crafts that allowed them to prosper following the Civil War. Their children were highly educated in the Western sense, many of them going to France for that experience. They were the cream of the crop, so to speak, and that status was jealously guarded.

The uptown blacks were largely the descendants of the field slaves, kept relatively isolated from Western cultural traditions and able, then, to maintain what was important of their African backgrounds. This naturally included the folk expressions, the blues and field hollers and work songs and spirituals upon which their musical heritage was based. And all of these are improvisatory types, different even in concept from Western forms like the minuet and the march and, ultimately, the piano rag. So when the uptown blacks took to the streets to perform in the marching bands, they carried with them the love of spontaneous variation and the rough-and-tumble rhythms of their ancestry.

Segregation brought uptown and downtown together. All the paraphernalia of racial identification finally placed the Creoles in the same social class as all the rest of the blacks: degree of color meant little or nothing. Gradually, although skilled in the techniques of Western music, they lost their jobs in opera houses and white dance halls, replaced by whites who "belonged." They found their jobs then in Storyville, the large and prosperous red-light district named for alderman Story, who confined all the prostitution and related activity to one well-defined section of the city. And it was there that the Creoles and their blacker brothers blended their own particular skills to create jazz. The music they used was familiar: spirituals, gospel songs, piano rags, blues, marches. It was the performance style that made it jazz, the single most important musical style to come out of America.

The transfer of a piano rag into a jazz performance is no more difficult than the transfer of an accompanied banjo rag into a piano rag. The melody instruments, typically one cornet, clarinet, and trombone, do what they usually do, and the rhythm instruments do what they usually do. The melodies are polyphonically interwoven with one another in Dixieland style, and while the music of the rag is readily recognizable, the performance has the kind of complexity and concerted excitement that only a small jazz group can bring to it. Innumerable recordings from the 1920s, often referred to as "the jazz age," illustrate this. The style as well as the use of rags continued with varying degrees of intensity, and persists even today. Our next listening selection is a typical performance by the New Orleans Feetwarmers, recorded in 1932 when Dixieland style was already being overridden in popularity by the smoother, more arranged, and sweeter big band sound. It features the following personnel, all prominent players and most with roots in New Orleans traditions: Tommy Ladnier, trumpet; Sidney Bechet, soprano sax and clarinet; Teddy Nixon, trombone; Hank Duncan, piano; Wilson Myers, bass; and Morris Moreland, drums.

PRIMARY LISTENING: Scott Joplin, "Maple Leaf Rag," New Orleans Feetwarmers (record set)

If you follow their performance from the standpoint of form, you will catch on to the fact that the band uses the various strains for its own purposes. Scott Joplin's format and the diagram that described it will not work here. That's typical of jazz, because it is a *way* of performing music, not a *form*. So we have a mixture of Scott Joplin and the New Orleans Feetwarmers. Fair enough when improvisation is involved.

Dixieland grew out of the function of music within the black community, just as early blues and band repertoire of marches, gospel songs, and spirituals were a part of the ongoing life of the people who developed them. Storyville was closed down in 1917 because of an incident involving several sailors who were killed there. Many of its musicians drifted away into other sectors of the country, principally to Chicago at first. The end of World War I brought many Negro troops home. Disenchanted with the social and economic environment of the south and tempted by the promise of better conditions in the industrial cities of the north, they migrated there, only, unfortunately, to be confined to a ghetto situation. But the advent of prohibition in 1920 opened new arenas for jazz performance: the speakeasies of Chicago and New York City, centers of the gang lords of bootlegging and its associated vices.

In the process of migration and changing function, jazz became an entertainment medium rather than a community business. It has changed its nature frequently, almost always in response to changing social and/or economic factors. But it is still possible to hear it in something like its original form in places like Preservation Hall in New Orleans and in numerous clubs throughout the country. There is something ironic about even the thought of a place like Preservation Hall—in one sense the first style of jazz that we know about has become a sort of museum piece. One can imagine Buddy Bolden, one of the originators of jazz trumpet style, puzzling over why it would be necessary to "preserve" such a magnificently spontaneous musical expression. A study of jazz in America raises many tantalizing questions about the effect of social change on arts and artists. There is a wealth of written and recorded material, most of which has emerged only in the last 15 or 20 years, that will stimulate and inform anyone interested in investigating the subject.

SUPPLEMENTAL LISTENING   There are many fine anthologies of recorded jazz, well annotated and often arranged chronologically by style. In them, there are examples of piano rags that carried over into early jazz. Among them:

"Sensation Rag," Original Dixieland Jazz Band on *A History of Jazz: The New York Scene.* RBF: RF–3.

This group was the first to record jazz under that name. It was a white band from New Orleans and had learned the style there and carried it to New York.

"Froggie Moore."

This was a piano rag composed by Jelly Roll Morton, first recorded by King Oliver and later by Fletcher Henderson's Orchestra featuring Louis Armstrong on trumpet. It was one of the early classics of jazz repertoire and there are numerous recordings of it. One is on *History of Classic Jazz.* Riverside: SDP–11.

"The Pearls."

Another Jelly Roll Morton piano rag. Sometime after he recorded it on piano, he performed it with his own Dixieland group, Morton's Red Hot Peppers. Both versions are in a number of anthologies. One is in *Jelly Roll Morton; King of New Orleans Jazz.* RCA Victor: LPM–1649.

"High Society."

Originally a march, this piece also became a standard in the repertoire. Like the rags, it is arranged in strains and usually features a clarinet solo derived from a piccolo solo in the original march. It became traditional and is usually performed as a challenge to virtuosity and also usually exactly as first played by Alphonse Picou. *Jazz Odyssey,* vol. 1: *The Sound of New Orleans.* Columbia: C3L–30.

The eclectic Russian Igor Stravinsky was one of many "serious" composers who adopted some of the vocabulary of jazz, including ragtime idioms. Ironically, then, the style was being "preserved" in other ways than through such establishments as Preservation Hall. Although Stravinsky had never heard a rag actually performed, he did have access to printed copies, and with these as models he composed a piece for 11 instruments in 1918 called simply *Ragtime*. When it was published, it came out in two versions, one for instruments and the other for piano. In 1919 he wrote another piece for piano called *Piano-Rag-Music*. He also incorporated the style in several other of his many compositions.

This raises some interesting issues. Composers seem to have taken a stance different from much of the "ordinary" population in America where ragtime was born. Here, during this same period and continuing into the 1920s, there was a tendency to view ragtime as questionable if not outright disreputable because of its associations with bawdyhouses and barrooms. This attitude dominated many blacks as well as whites. Composers were apparently not as turned off by the associated moral implications; instead, they were fascinated by the purely musical excitement of ragtime's rhythmic and melodic styles and did not hesitate to take advantage of these in their own work.

PRIMARY LISTENING:
Igor Stravinsky, *Ragtime*
for 11 instruments (record
set)

Is Stravinsky's *Ragtime* for 11 instruments really ragtime? If we are going to be sticky about our definitions, we need to consider the question of formal organization. We would look for a series of strains of consistent length and for some repetition. Does Stravinsky give us these? Are they in the "right" order? Is there anything that resembles a trio?

Think about rhythm. We expect certain kinds of things to happen in a rag, mainly a steady pulse against which the syncopations can be most effective. How about *Ragtime?* Keep in mind that Stravinsky was notable for his interest in rhythmic complexities. Does he, perhaps, go beyond the expectations of ragtime but without losing the basic spirit?

What melodic features can be related to "Maple Leaf Rag"? And how about harmony? In a rag we look for some contrasts of tonality. Stravinsky's harmonic tendencies are toward dissonant textures, and so the sense of tonal center is not so easily perceived. It takes very careful listening, but it is possible to hear the bass providing a foundation by playing lots of skips in the chords as well as very often sounding out on the tonic, dominant, and subdominant notes in various keys. That's much like the left-hand part of a piano rag and also the function of the bass in a Dixieland group.

If enough of the *principles* of ragtime are retained, we would have to assume that Stravinsky was true to that style while still allowing his own creative imagination to exert itself. This is what really does happen, but because of the unusual complexity of his work, one cannot assimilate everything on brief acquaintance. This tells us something about "serious" as opposed to "popular" approaches to music. After one or two exposures to "Maple Leaf Rag" we can probably go away whistling at least a couple of the strains. If this were not true of all so-called popular styles, they would never get to be popular in the first place. More involved types of art are just not so readily assimilated, not because they are "better" but only because they are more complicated. So Stravinsky's *Ragtime* may never make the top 40, but the fact that he wrote it at all is a tribute to the appeal that less sophisticated musical styles had and continue to have for all people.

SUPPLEMENTAL LISTENING

Among the numerous compositions that use ragtime and jazz style, the following are suggested:

Stravinsky, *L'Histoire du soldat* (The Soldier's Tale).

This composition was taken from several folk tales of Russian origin. It is scored for mixed instruments with a narrator and includes various dances, one of which is ragtime.

Stravinsky, *Ebony Concerto.*

Dedicated to and introduced by the Woody Herman big band, the concerto is scored for a typical swing band of the period (1945). Musically it is a sort of parody on jazz, with distorted rhythms, melodies, and even blues of a sort. It is in three movements that relate closely to concerto principles. The forms are:

I. Sonata-allegro
II. Blues, but more in mood than form
III. Theme and variations

Darius Milhaud, *La Creation du monde* (The Creation of the World).

A series of episodes using what the composer took to be primitive African musical style flavored heavily with jazz idioms.

George Gershwin, *Rhapsody in Blue.*

This is a work for piano and orchestra, one of the standard popular classics. It was introduced by Paul Whiteman's highly successful orchestra with the composer at the piano. There is an attempt to combine the melodic vocabulary of the blues with a more sophisticated harmonic background.

PRIMARY LISTENING:
Mozart, *Eine kleine Nachtmusik*, third movement, Menuetto: Allegretto, 1787

Sectionalization in terms of varying musical ideas is the underlying formal concept of rags. But it is not peculiar to them, as we have seen. Wind the musical clock back two centuries to a minuet by Mozart, the third movement of his *Eine kleine Nachtmusik*. All the formal characteristics of Classic clarity are here together with the exact presentation of musical ideas that define the minuet. Except for the precision of alternation among sections, there is the same

Example 147
Mozart, *Eine kleine Nachtmusik.*

structural basis as in the march or rag. Even many of the key relationships are the same. And notice the repetition of the "strains" (Example 147).

To bring ourselves to a complete circle, we need to ask, then, if Stravinsky is one of that brotherhood that includes "Mozart and all that long-hair" but Scott Joplin and his fellow rag composers are in another world entirely. What is "long-hair," anyway? And, indeed, what is music?

If we are uneasy with our classifications, so much the better. It means that we are discovering breaks in our fences through which we can move into new pastures and catch the excitement of discovery. The world is full of music and it has always been that way. Break through. The grass is wonderfully green in *all* the pastures.

Coda: How We Hear Music

A study by two psychologists at a large and prestigious eastern university revealed that there are two principal ways that we hear music. Those with training actually hear better with the ear that sends its messages to that side of the brain that takes care of our analytical functions. Those without training hear better with the ear that connects to the side of the brain that handles our intuitive or affective responses. The purpose of this book has been to help get our heads together in a very real sense.

Both ways of hearing are valid. Analysis and description should never be allowed to obliterate what music can do for us emotionally. After all, that is what makes music an art in the first place. Without attempting to categorize, we should all recognize that a lot of the music that is available is really programmed for our emotions and it is on that level that we should experience it. Description can't reveal much of value to the side of our head that is working at those times.

Analytical thinking, however, is the path to understanding. Most of us do want to understand the world in which we live. That includes the people in it and the things that they have done to express through art the vision that may easily escape most of us workaday types. Coming to grips with those things is the job of the other side of our brain. All the words and all the suggested listening have been an attempt to stir that area up a little.

A few things should be clear. We can talk about all kinds of music, even though the differences in sound are vast. We can describe musical devices and the similarities among them, even though they are used in many different ways. We can identify in more or less exact terms how a piece of music is put together, even though a thousand pieces put together roughly the same way will still come out sounding like a thousand different pieces. We can talk about the use of melody, harmony, and rhythm, even though they work together or in isolation to create astonishingly different effects. And because of all this, we can investigate, even though what we discover may be different for each of us.

Because we are each different to some extent and that may be the most valuable thing about us. We cannot be stereotyped, and neither can music.

And it takes both sides of our head to really understand why.

Glossary of Terms

Note: Terms dealing with performance directions, especially for dynamics (volume) and tempo (speed), are defined in Appendix 1, "Theory and Notation."

Antiphony: One individual or group responding to another; call–response; a favorite jazz technique between soloist and group or between sections of brass and winds; a feature of much music from the earliest periods through the Baroque. Music with this feature is described as *antiphonal.*

Aria: Air; in opera and oratorio, used in contrast to recitative; normally a relatively tuneful extended composition for solo voice; during Baroque period conventionally organized in ternary form and called *da capo aria.* Cf. **Recitative, Ternary.**

Augmentation: Enlarging note values but retaining melodic outline; results in slower presentation of the melody. The term is also applied to intervals in connection with their relative size. An augmented fifth is a half-step larger than a perfect fifth, an augmented second is a half-step larger than a major second, and so forth. See Appendix 1. Cf. **Diminution.**

Avant Garde: Literally, "vanguard." Thus, any movement in the arts that supports reform or a rejection of traditionalism.

Ballad: A folk genre that employs a story in song. Although there are many types, the most traditional is the body of literature with Scottish and English antecendents which was catalogued by Francis Child.

Baroque: That period in history from about 1600 to 1750. In music, art, and architecture, the style was characterized by elaborate ornamentation and decoration, a profusion of curves and curlicues, and often included grotesque statuary and carvings.

Bebop (Bop): A jazz style fostered by Charlie Parker, Dizzy Gillespie, and others in reaction to the highly organized arrangements of swing. The objectives were to allow for longer solo improvisations over chord progressions borrowed from familiar popular songs but greatly extended and made more complex. Although different instrumentations are used, the original one featured trumpet, saxophone, piano, bass, and drums. Cf. **Dixieland, Swing, Third Stream.**

Binary: Two-part; diagrammed usually as A B, a b, or extensions of those; final material to appear is b. Cf. **Ternary.**

Bitonality: The simultaneous use of two contrasting key centers. Cf. **Polytonality.**

Bluegrass: A style of country music inaugurated by the Blue Grass Boys whose leader was Bill Monroe. The band included Lester Flatt, Earl Scruggs, Chubby Wise, and Howard Watts. The "classic" instrumentation is banjo, fiddle, mandolin, guitar, and bass; an important addition was the dobro, introduced by Flatt and Scruggs and the Foggy Mountain Boys.

Blues: From standpoint of form, an 8-, 12-, or 16-bar structure over a framework of tonic, subdominant, and dominant harmonies; melodically characterized by free interchange of major and minor third and seventh scale degrees, sometimes also inflections of the fifth degree; all pitches can be and are inflected in actual practice, however.

Bridge: The B section of an A A B A pop song form. Sometimes called the release.

Cadence: Musical movement marking the end of a phrase, section, movement, etc. Decisive or complete cadences use the harmonic progression dominant to tonic. Indecisive or incomplete cadences use a chord other than the tonic as the final chord—usually the subdominant or dominant. Deceptive or evaded cadences normally progress from the dominant to the submediant (V to VI), but any unexpected progression is possible.

Call-Response: A performance process involving the interplay between a leader and chorus, two choruses, soloist and group, or sections of a vocal or instrumental ensemble. Same as **Antiphony.**

Canon (or **Catch** or **Round**): Composition for two or more voices or instruments based on imitation; probably the commonest form of polyphonic composition.

Castrati: Adult males who had been emasculated shortly before puberty in order to preserve the quality of the child voice as well as to increase breath capacity. Inaugurated by the Roman church, castrati were highly exploited during the heyday of Baroque opera.

Catch: Same as **Canon.**

Chaconne: Composition in triple meter using as its basis an eight-meausre harmonic progression which is repeated throughout and over which variations are devised.

Chamber Music: Music performed by a small group with one instrument to a part, as opposed to sections of like instruments.

Changes: The chord progressions in a jazz performance.

Chords: Entities usually composed of three or more different pitches organized in a prescribed fashion. See appendix 1. See also **Quartal Harmony.**

Chorus: A vocal ensemble. In song form, a refrain as contrasted to a verse. In jazz terminology, a unit (blues, song, etc.) that is repeated with variations.

Chromaticism: As applied to a scale, movement by successive half-steps; in the harmonic sense, the use of pitches and chords outside the tonic scale; a characteristic of much music during the late nineteenth century and since.

Classicism: The artistic temper that places emphasis on formal logic, discipline, and clarity as opposed to intense expressive involvement. The period in music that best exemplified those ideals was the last half of the eighteenth century and the very early years of the nineteenth century. Composers who represent musical Classicism most completely include Mozart and Haydn. Cf. **Romanticism.**

Coda: Final section of some large forms; since Beethoven, it has often been extended to become an important factor in developing or regrouping material in sonata-allegro form.

Concertino: In a Baroque concerto grosso, the ensemble of soloists as contrasted to the larger group of nonsoloists. Cf. **Ripieno.**

Concerto: Composition for solo instrument with accompanying instrumental group, usually an orchestra; during the Baroque, a composition for a small group of soloists, accompanied by and/or alternating with a larger group.

Conjunct Melody: Melody that moves by neighboring scale degrees; melody having stepwise motion. Cf. **Disjunct Melody.**

Consonance: Those combinations of pitches that are perceived as being pleasant or acceptable. Theories of con-

sonance have changed rather drastically from period to period but are helpful in defining the aesthetic positions of various eras. Cf. **Dissonance.**

Continuo: Same as **Figured Bass.**

Country Music: A style of music introduced in the early 1920s to appeal to rural people. At first it was founded on traditional, mostly folk repertoire, but within a decade it had become highly commercialized. At present, it features music composed specifically for its performers.

Development: Manipulation of previously stated musical material; occurs most significantly in sonata-allegro and fugal forms, but may be used as a technique in any form.

Diminution: Shortening of note values but retaining melodic outline; results in quicker presentation of melody. The term is also applied to intervals in connection with their relative size. A diminished fifth is a half-step smaller than a perfect fifth, a diminished third is a half-step smaller than a minor third, and so forth. See appendix 1. Cf. **Augmentation.**

Disjunct Melody: Melody that moves by skipping rather than by scale degrees; melody with an angular movement. Cf. **Conjunct.**

Dissonance: Those combinations of pitches that are perceived as being unpleasant or unacceptable except in certain contexts. As dissonance has been used most consistently in Western music, it creates a tension which seeks release in succeeding consonance. However, theories about which pitch combinations constitute dissonance and consonance have changed from period to period. Cf. **Consonance.**

Dixieland: The earliest recorded jazz style, most often associated with black performers from New Orleans. The instrumentation was originally cornet or trumpet, clarinet, trombone, tuba or string bass, piano, and drums. Cf.. **Swing, Bebop, Third Stream.**

Dobro: A guitar with a metal plate for amplification (nonelectric) and played with a slide. The instrument is used most frequently in bluegrass bands.

Dodecaphonic: Same as **Twelve-Tone.**

Dominant: The fifth step of a scale and the chord built upon it. Also called V. Cf. **Tonic, Subdominant.**

Drone: A single reiterated pitch; associated with a number of musical styles including Indian ragas, banjo and fiddle music in the country genres, and the Scottish bagpipe.

Dynamics: Volume. See appendix 1.

Electronic Music: Music produced and/or performed on some sort of electronic device. This may be something as familiar and relatively uncomplicated as an electric bass or guitar. Jazz and rock bands have featured electric pianos, Moogs, amplified violins, etc., for a long time now, and their sounds have become familiar. On the more esoteric side are the many electronic "instruments" on which the sound is produced by means of signal generators like the oscillator. Together with tape recorders, a typical electronic music studio will include mixers, equalizers, reverberation units, and a wealth of other equipment to initiate or modify sounds. The simplest sort of manipulation is possible even in the home. For instance, speech can be recorded on a tape recorder at 3¾ speed and played back at 7½—Donald Duck, no less. For an introduction to the more sophisticated possibilities, the following album is an excellent start: *The Nonesuch Guide to Electronic Music.* Nonesuch: HC–73018.

Episode: Interludes between appearance of the subject in a fugue.

Exposition: The opening section of sonata-allegro and fugue forms, consisting of the presentation of thematic material to be utilized in the succeeding sections. Cf. **Development, Recapitulation.**

Extended Chords: Chords using intervals beyond the fifth or seventh; most common are ninths, elevenths, and thirteenths. See appendix 1.

Favola: Literally, tale; generic name for the first Italian operas.

Field Holler: Improvisatory solo piece initially used by slaves to communicate between fields; later used as type of free vocal expression; one of the forerunners of the blues.

Figured Bass: In the Baroque period, a bass line with figures (numbers) above or below it to identify intervals; one method of expressing harmonic structure; normally realized (filled in with indicated chords) at sight or, in edited music, by the editor. Same as **Continuo.**

Five-Part Song: Sectional composition, often for voice, diagrammed as A B A C A. Cf. **Rondo, Binary, Ternary.**

Fixed Idea (*idée fixe*): Melody meant to symbolize a person or an idea; often refers to such a melody in the *Fantastic Symphony* by Berlioz, who first used the term.

Free Form: Musical structure in which there is no regular recurrence of material. Cf. **Binary, Ternary, Rondo, Five-Part Song.**

Fugue: Polyphonic form based on presentation of subject, answer, and counter-subject in highly patterned procedure; involves also manipulation of those; developmental devices may include inversion, stretto, retrograde, retrograde inversion, change of mode, segmentation, others.

Gapped Scale: A scale that omits one or more of the seven pitches in a diatonic scale; associated most strongly with folk music.

Glissando: A gliding from one pitch to the succeeding one, usually over a relatively large interval; common device for stringed instruments, including guitars, and for trombones,

pianos, and some other instruments; in vocal music usually called *portamento.*

Gothic: The period from about 1100 to 1400 in the Middle Ages. Cf. **Romanesque.**

Gregorian Chant: Earliest type of Roman Catholic liturgical song; named for Pope Gregory I (590–604), who supervised and contributed to its standardization and editing.

Ground (Bass): Repeated melodic figure in lowest voice, usually eight measures or less, that remains constant throughout composition. Cf. **Ostinato.**

Harmony: The aural effect of simultaneous sounding of more than one pitch. See appendix 1.

Harpsichord: A close relative of the clavichord, both of which were forerunners of the piano. Sometimes using two or more manuals for variation in timbre and volume, the sound was produced by plucking the strings as contrasted to striking with hammers.

Hemiola: A rhythmic process involving a metric feeling of two or four but within an established meter of triple.

Hillbilly Music: The designation given to the earliest type of country music, dating from the early 1920s.

Homophonic Texture: Texture created when one melodic line dominates and is supported by accompanying parts in a relatively chordal fashion. Cf. **Monophonic Texture, Polyphony.**

Hours: Services other than Mass conducted during the Middle Ages and succeeding periods. They were: Matins, Lauds, Prime, Terce, Sext, None, Vespers, and Compline.

Improvise: Make up spontaneously; improvisation is consistently an element in jazz and much non-Western music; also typical of pre-Classic eras in Western practice.

Inflected Language: A language in which the pitch of a spoken word or syllable affects its meaning. Also called **Tone Language.**

Interval: Distance separating two pitches; applied to simultaneous as well as to consecutive sounds. See appendix 1.

Inversion: Applied to chords, the use of anything other than the root as the lowest sound; see appendix 1. In developmental process, particularly in a fugue, the use of melodic material upside down: for each ascending interval of the original a descending interval is substituted.

Key: The tonal center of a composition, usually defined by reference to the scale which includes the set of pitches used in a composition. The most important pitch in any key is the first note of the scale, called the tonic or key note, and the most important chord, the tonic chord, is the one built on that note. Most compositions in Western music end on the tonic note and, if they include harmony, on the tonic chord. The theory of keys is discussed fully in appendix 1.

Krummhorn: A Medieval and Renaissance instrument, forerunner of the oboe, which was characterized by a curve at its end. Krumm means "bent."

Leitmotif: A short musical motive used in Wagnerian music dramas to represent a person, object, or idea.

Lute: Stringed instrument from the medieval and later periods, notation for which employed tablature. It was particularly popular as an accompanying and solo instrument during the Renaissance and Baroque periods.

Madrigal: Vocal piece for small group, usually one voice to a part; most popular during Renaissance and early Baroque period; often used both homophonic and polyphonic textures.

Manuscript: Handwritten music as opposed to printed music; much early music exists only in manuscript form; manuscripts of original copy are valuable sources of information on composers even today.

March: Sectional composition, usually in $\frac{2}{4}$ or $\frac{6}{8}$ meter, made up of successive contrasting material; sections normally referred to as *strains*. Cf. **Rag.**

Mass: Series of liturgical prayers and statements forming basis of Roman Catholic and Anglican worship service; in a low Mass the liturgy is spoken, in a high Mass it is sung; the two principal sections of the Mass are the Proper, seldom set to music other than Gregorian, and the Ordinary, the section mostly used for compositions; the funeral Mass is known as the Requiem and is performed on All Souls' Day and on commemorative occasions.

Medieval: The historical period from about 450 to 1400, subdivided into the Romanesque and Gothic eras. Often referred to as the Middle Ages.

Melisma: The melodic figure that results from singing a number of different successive pitches on the same verbal syllable or word; one feature of certain types of Gregorian chant as well as some operatic arias, art songs, etc.

Melody: Tune; a series of pitches sounded in succession and occurring consecutively in time.

Meter: Arrangement of pulses or beats in terms of accented and unaccented units; regular meters are those in which the number of beats between accents is divisible by two or three; irregular meters are all others; additive meters are those with a succession of groups of pulses, often not consistent in number, as four plus four plus three plus two; additive meters are characteristic of much non-Western music including that of India and Africa. Cf. **Polymetric.** See appendix 1.

Metronome: A ticking device with a graduated scale of numbers designed to aid in the establishment of tempo. The scale is oriented to the frequency of impulses per minute.

Thus the tempo indication $\quad = 60$ means that there are 60 quarter notes to a minute, or one per second. Set the dial at the right place, turn on the metronome, and the ticks will occur at that rate of speed. Metronomes come in springwound or electric models, and, like watches, they vary in their degree of accuracy.

Microtones: Intervals smaller than a half-step; a characteristic of much non-Western music and the blues but also utilized by some avant-garde composers beginning in the late nineteenth century.

Minnesingers: German composers and performers of song from the Gothic period.

Minuet and Trio: Sectional form found most often as the third movement of Classic symphonies and related forms. Diagrammed as:

A (Minuet)	B (Trio)	A (Minuet)
||:a :||: b a:||	||:c :||: d c:||	a b a

Mode: A scale, defined in terms of the interval relationships among its various degrees; there were many modes in use in Western music until the Baroque; during the course of that period, all fell out of use except for major and minor.

Modulation: Change of key center, gradual.

Monody: Inaugurated in Italy at the beginning of the Baroque period in about 1600, the style featured a solo voice with instrumental accompaniment in contrast to the multivoiced polyphony of the Renaissance.

Monophonic Texture: Texture involving one single melodic line without accompanying harmony. Cf. **Homophnic Texture, Polyphony.**

Moog: A type of synthesizer named for its inventor, Robert Moog, this is one of a host of instruments on which the sounds are produced by electronic impulses of almost innumerable kinds. It has been taken into all sorts of ensembles, including rock and jazz bands. Moogs come in all sizes and shapes, but even the smallest is an enormously complex mechanism. One of the most valuable characteristics of all of them is their ability to create sounds of great clarity and distinctiveness. They are therefore even more versatile than what is perhaps their closest relative among the "standard" instruments, the organ.

Motet: Vocal composition in polyphonic texture based on liturgical or biblical text.

Obbligato: Added melody, usually higher than the material it is meant to complement.

Organum: Earliest known type of Western harmony; at first apparently consisted of parallel motion in intervals of fourths, fifths, or octaves; later, individual voices became more independent.

Ornamentation: Embellishment or a decorative musical figure; most frequent ornaments are the trill, grace note, and turning figure; in much music, inflected pitches are treated as ornaments, as in blues or raga performances; added runs are also sometimes thought of as ornamental in nature.

Ostinato: Repeated musical figure, usually in lowest voice, in which case it is called an *ostinato bass*, and short in duration; boogie-woogie piano is based on the ostinato principle. Cf. **Ground (Bass).**

Overture: Musical preface to an opera, musical comedy, or other stage work; as a concert overture, an independent composition, usually programmatic, employing the principles of structure found in sonata-allegro form.

Passacaglia: A musical form based upon a stated eight-measure theme in the lowest voice and repeated throughout; initial statement is followed by a series of variations mostly occurring in higher voices; theme may move to higher voices but most characteristically it remains in the bass.

Pentatonic Scale: A scale using only five different pitches as opposed to the diatonic scale of seven. One form of gapped scale.

Phrase: Segment of music concluded with a cadence; since the Classic period, regular phrases have been defined as four measures long; others are considered irregular. Cf. **Cadence.**

Pitch: The quality of a tone identified with reference to its frequency of vibrations. High pitches vibrate at a higher frequency level than low pitches. *A* has become the generally accepted reference point for determining proper pitch in most Western music. It is usually adjusted (tuned) to vibrate at 440 cycles per second and all other pitches are adjusted in relation to it. This is the pitch that is sounded in the process of tuning an orchestra and is sometimes referred to as "Concert *A*."

Plain Chant: Same as **Gregorian Chant.**

Plainsong: Same as **Gregorian Chant.**

Polymetric: Simultaneously using different, often conflicting, meters.

Polyphony: A texture exploiting two or more complementary melodic lines; the basis of early harmonic practice. Music with this texture is called *polyphonic.* Cf. **Homophonic Texture, Monophonic Texture.**

Polytonality: The simultaneous use of several contrasting, often conflicting key centers. Cf. **Bitonality.**

Pop Song: A type of popular vocal genre most prevalent during the period from the 1920s to the mid-1940s. The most frequently used form was 32 bars long in an A A B A format, but there were other organizations.

Prelude: A short, frequently independent composition preparatory to a longer piece or section; in the Bach Preludes and Fugues, it is used to explore the harmonic vocabulary of the key it is written in.

Quartal Harmony: A harmonic practice based upon chords constructed in fourths as contrasted to the more common use of thirds.

Race Records: Recordings from the 1920s featuring black performers and designed specifically for circulation to black audiences and purchasers.

Rag: A sectional composition related to the march in form; composed for banjo and piano or for piano alone; most popular from about 1895 to 1920; many piano rags were used for early Dixieland band performances. Cf. **March.**

Raga: The scale or mode on which the melodies of Indian classical music are formed; may be used for composition as well as for improvisation. Cf. **Tala.**

Range: Distance between the highest and lowest notes of a composition or a portion thereof.

Recapitulation: The third section of a sonata-allegro form in which the themes return following the development. Cf. **Exposition, Development.**

Recitative: Vocal music utilizing speech rhythms and relatively sparse melodic development; in opera and oratorio, it carries the narrative and dialogue sections as opposed to the aria, which is more tuneful and musically developed and carries the reflective or commentary portions of the text. Cf. **Aria.**

Recorder: An ancestor of the modern flute, used most prominently in the Renaissance and Baroque periods.

Renaissance: The period from about 1400 to 1600, often referred to as the Golden Age of Polyphony.

Rhythm: The branch of music that deals with pulse, meter, duration, accent, and the interaction of these. See appendix 1.

Rhythm-and-Blues: The name given to popular song developed, performed, and circulated among the black community beginning in the late 1940s; features forms and styles of the traditional blues but with heavy rhythm and electric guitars and other traditional jazz instruments; forerunner of rock-and-roll including the compositions themselves as well as the style. Cf. **Rock-and-Roll.**

Ripieno: In a Baroque concerto grosso, the large group of nonsoloists as contrasted to the concertino. Cf. **Concertino.**

Ritual: A prescribed order of worship or ceremonial observance.

Rock-and-Roll: A popular music style developed during the mid-1950s and based on black rhythm-and-blues. Cf. **Rhythm-and-Blues.**

Romanesque: The medieval era from about 450 to 1100. Cf. **Gothic.**

Romanticism: The artistic temper that places emphasis on expressive and dramatic use of musical materials and, in subject matter, shows a fascination for death, the supernatural, and mystery. The musical vocabulary of Romanticism includes exploitation of rich harmony, wide range of dynamics, soaring melodics, and elaborate, often extended development of thematic material. The period most strongly associated with musical Romanticism is the nineteenth century. That era is usually contrasted to the period immediately preceding it, identified as the Classic period, during which the artistic objectives were clarity, discipline and formal logic. Cf. **Classicism.**

Rondo: A composition, usually extended, characterized by the regular, patterned recurrence of a principal musical idea interspersed with contrasting material; may be diagrammed as A B A C A or as extensions and/or modifications of that. The process of alternating material in such a design is sometimes referred to as using the rondo principle, even though the composition itself may not be called a rondo.

Round: Same as **Canon.**

Sarangi: A stringed instrument used for solos and accompaniment in the raga tradition, mostly in North India. Cf. **Tabla, Tambura, Sitar.**

Scherzo: Replaced minuet and trio as third movement in Romantic symphony; organized sectionally by same principles as minuet and trio; usually in very fast tempo. Cf. **Minuet and Trio.**

Sectional Form: An organization of music characterized by sections of different musical material separated by relatively strong cadences.

Sequence: Repetition of melodic pattern but transposed up or down in pitch; also, harmonic progression that is used in the same manner.

Serial Composition: Composition using a tone row together with its varying alterations; based principally on fugal device; usually highly dissonant and complex. Cf. **Tone Row.**

Sitar: A stringed instrument used for solos and accompaniment in the raga tradition, mostly in South India. Cf. **Sarangi, Tabla, Tambura.**

Sonata: Multimovement composition, the first movement of which is usually in sonata-allegro form; composed for piano or for solo instrument often with piano accompaniment; in its earliest use, the term was applied to works that were meant simply to be played rather than sung.

Sonata-Allegro: The form associataed with first movements of compositions employing the sonata principle of organization; main portions are exposition, development, and recapitulation. Cf. **Development.**

Strain: Section of a march or piano rag, usually 16 measures repeated exactly or in slightly varied form.

Strophic: In song composition, descriptive of a piece that uses the same music for each stanza, or *strophe,* of the poem on which it is based. Cf. **Through-Composed.**

Subdominant: The fourth step of the scale and the chord built upon it. Also called IV. Cf. **Dominant, Tonic.**

Subject: The melodic material on which a fugue is based.

Swing: A jazz style associated with big bands from the mid-1930s to the present. The instrumentation featured sections of like instruments (trumpets, reeds, etc.) rather than the Dixieland and bebop use of a single instrument. Cf. **Dixieland, Bebop, Third Stream.**

Symphony: A multimovement form of the sonata type but written for orchestra; stabilized in form and principles of style during the Classic period; used extensively for programmatic as well as nonprogrammatic purposes since that time.

Syncopation: Generally, the placement of an accent on a normally unaccented beat or portion of a beat; syncopation is one important feature of jazz, African music, and much other Western and non-Western music.

Synthesizer: See **Moog.**

Tabla: The drum "set" used in Indian raga performances. It consists of two drums, one wooden and one metal, one of which is tuned to the tonic pitch. Cf. **Sarangi, Sitar, Tambura.**

Tablature: System of notation for stringed instruments that pictures the strings and in some way indicates where the fingers must be placed to produce the required pitches; used for the lute during the Renaissance and the Baroque period as well as for the guitar at present; customary notation for koto music in Japan.

Tala: Rhythmic system in Indian classical music; involves many different additive meters, e.g., five plus five plus two plus two. Cf. **Raga.**

Tambura: A stringed instrument used to produce a drone on the tonic note in Indian raga performances. Cf. **Sarangi, Sitar, Tabla.**

Tempo: The speed at which music is performed. See appendix 1.

Tempus: A Medieval concept (carried over somewhat into the Renaissance) of metric organization. Tempus perfectum (perfect time) was the equivalent of the present-day triple meter; tempus imperfectum (imperfect time) was the equivalent of duple meter.

Ternary (or **Three-Part** or **Tripartite**): In three parts, the first of which is also the last; diagrammed as A B A ; used as the basic structural and artistic principle of many forms. Cf. **Binary.**

Text Illustration: Presentation of a melodic and/or harmonic figure that attempts to pictorialize a word or phrase from accompanying text; a strong feature of Baroque musical practice. Cf. **Tone Painting.**

Texture: The relationship among the various instrumental and/or vocal pitches in a composition; usually categorized as monophonic, polyphonic, or homophonic.

Theme: A melody or tune; sometimes, as in a chaconne, a

harmonic progression; in its most general sense, a musical idea on which a composition is based.

Third Stream: A jazz style that attempted to combine the instrumentation and forms of Classical and jazz music. Cf. **Dixieland, Swing, Bebop.**

Three-Part: Same as **Ternary.**

Through-Composed: Descriptive of a vocal composition using different music for each or some of the stanzas, or strophes, of the poem on which it is based. Cf. **Strophic.**

Timbre: The "color" of a sound, based upon the strength or weakness, presence or absence of specific overtones or partials in the harmonic series of the fundamental tone. The variations in such factors account for the difference in sound between different instruments and voices.

Tonal: In a key or employing melody and harmony that can be related to a key center.

Tone Language: Same as **Inflected Language.**

Tone Painting: Generally thought of as text illustration, but may be extended to include implications of mood. Cf. **Text Illustration.**

Tone Row: The series, usually twelve notes, forming the musical material for serial compositions; originally selected to avoid tonal implications. Cf. **Serial Composition.**

Tonic: The principal note of a tonal composition; also the chord built on that note; the key tone. Also called I. See appendix 1.

Transposition: Transferring a melody and/or harmonic progression exactly from one key to another. Songs are often transposed to accommodate lower or higher voices than the original was intended for. One of the developmental or manipulative techniques in serial composition.

Trinity: A concept of the nature of God that makes indivisible the persons of God, Christ, and the Holy Spirit. The doctrine was adopted as the official one of the Roman church at the council of Nicaea in A.D. 325 and has been reflected in literature and art works ever since.

Trio: A composition for three instruments or voices. One section of a minuet and trio, usually in a key in contrast to but related to that of the minuet; sectionally organized, with repetition a common feature. A similar section in a march or rag.

Tripartite: Same as **Ternary.**

Troubadours: Poet-musicians of South France who flourished during the Gothic era of the Middle Ages. Cf. **Trouvères.**

Trouvères: Poet-musicians of North France who flourished during the Gothic era of the Middle Ages. Cf. **Troubadours.**

Twelve-Tone: Serial compositions using row of twelve tones.

Unending Melody: A Wagnerian principle of musical process which attempted to erase cadential "seams" by the use of elision, evasion, or false resolution. The result was a continuous flow of melody uninterrupted by sectional divisions.

Variation: The alteration of musical material, usually in such a manner as to retain recognizable characteristics of the original; composed as well as improvised; an important feature of many forms, e.g., theme and variations, jazz, Indian classical music.

Waltz: A dance in $\frac{3}{4}$ meter; extremely popular in Vienna during the nineteenth century but continuing there and elsewhere as a ballroom dance into the twentieth.

Work Song: A vocal piece, usually improvised, used by slaves and prison gangs to help coordinate physical effort; usually uses call–response patterns; antiphonal in principle; one of the forerunners of the blues.

Appendix 1
Theory and Notation

Any system of symbolism demands that we take certain things for granted and not question whether they might in themselves be entirely logical or not. Our alphabet is like that. So are the symbols we use in our number system and the sounds in our spoken language. Other symbols and sounds would work just as well to represent what is represented—as long as everyone agreed on the meaning of each. Only after accepting the symbolism we have at face value does the system begin to make sense internally.

And so with music. Several conventions must be accepted at the start. Here they are:

1. We name pitches by letter names, using only the first seven letters of our alphabet. We might just as well identify them by numbers or even some set of nonsense syllables. We don't do it; we use letters.

2. We notate music on *staffs,* horizontal groups of parallel lines and spaces, all of which we utilize. The lines and spaces tell us nothing at all about what pitch belongs where. But each different staff has a symbol at the far left (called a *clef* or *clef sign*) that *does* identify one line by letter name and pitch. Once we know that, all other lines and all spaces and pitch symbols take on a very definite relationship to one another.

3. The smallest interval that we have widely accepted notation for and that we normally use is a half-step. For anything smaller than the half-step we need a symbol that has not yet been developed and adopted by enough musicians to be in common usage. We can hear and even name a quarter-step and an eighth-

step; we don't have written symbols for them that are in general use. So we won't worry about them here.

If you will accept all of this, we can move on to how we name pitches and how they look on paper. Since most of us need a crutch at the beginning, we'll use the piano keyboard as a reference. And because they are the two most common staffs, we will start with the *bass* and *treble.* The pitches and their location on these two staffs are as shown in Notation Example 1. You can deduce what to call the lines and spaces that have no note on or in them.

The pitch C between the two staffs is *middle C*—because it *is* in the middle. It also happens to be the C closest to the center of the piano, but that has nothing to do with why it's called middle C. The clef sign on the treble staff, the staff on top, identifies the G above middle C: a useful clue here is the incomplete swirl on the second line from the bottom, the line where we find G. Logically enough, this *treble clef* is sometimes called the *G clef.* The clef sign on the bass staff, the lower one, locates the F below *middle C:* the clue there is the dots on either side of the fourth line from the bottom of the staff, the line where we find F. And this *bass clef* is sometimes called the *F clef.*

We do use one other clef sign; it identifies *middle C* itself. If you play only the piano or sing in a choir, you'll never need to know this

Notation Example 1   Bass and Treble Staffs

one. But if you try to read old manuscripts of music, you will. And if you play certain instruments in the orchestra, you will need to know at least the staff that is used for your instrument. The viola, for instance, uses the *alto* staff. The three staffs that use the *C clef* to locate *middle C* are shown in Notation Examples 2, 3, and 4.

Remember that the smallest interval we use is the half-step and

Notation Example 2

Tenor Staff

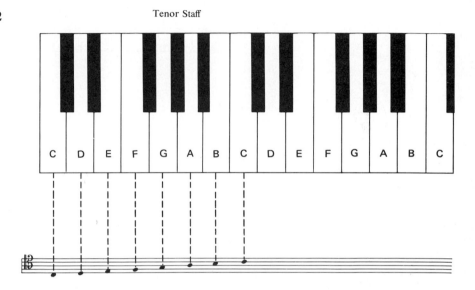

Notation Example 3

Alto Staff

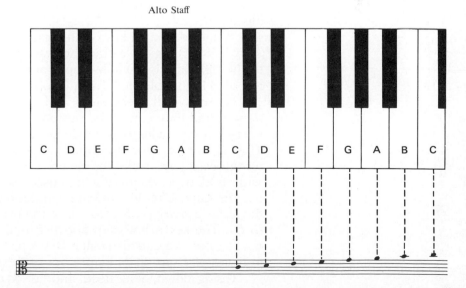

Notation Example 4

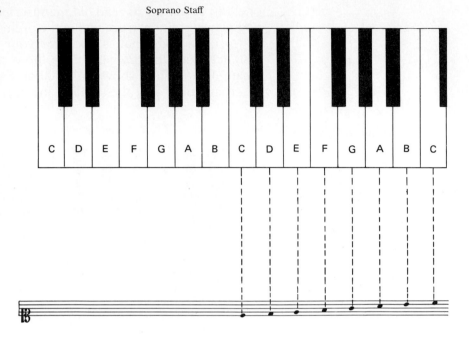

Soprano Staff

that on the keyboard a half-step is the distance from one key to the next nearest one, up or down. Color has nothing to do with it. From the white key E to the white key F is a half-step. From F to the black key just to the right of it is a half-step. From E to the black key just to the left of it is a half-step. From C to B is a half-step. And so forth, always.

When you skip a key on the piano keyboard, you move a *whole-step*, which is logical within the system. From E up to the black key to the right of F is a whole-step, from C down to the black key to the left of B is a whole-step, from G to A is a whole-step, and so forth.

Naturally, all these steps and the pitches they represent have names, and they can all be put on the staffs. Every pitch (and thus every key on the keyboard) can be called by several different names. This is not peculiar to music. A long stick can be a stake for tomatoes, a cane, a clothesline prop, or something to beat your mule with. It all depends on how it is used. So with music. If you want to use the same *letter* identification and move a half-step up, you add to the letter a *sharp* (♯). So from C to the black key on its right is from C to C♯. The key a half-step above B is B♯ (it looks like and is C, of course, but you can also call it B♯). A pair of half-steps up are shown in Notation Example 5. Figure out some more.

Going down, you need another symbol—a *flat* (♭)—but the system works the same way. From B to the black key to the left is

Notation Example 5   Half-Steps Up

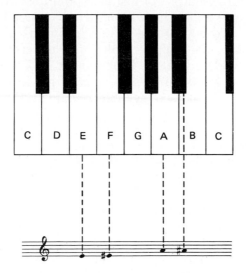

from B to B♭. From F to the next lower key on the piano is from F to F♭ (which is also E). Two half-steps down are shown in Notation Example 6. We can get into visual trouble here because left to right on the keyboard is up (always) but left to right on the page can sometimes be *down* pitchwise. Notice also in Examples 5 and 6 that on the staff the sharp or flat sign precedes the note it goes with. There are other symbols for pitch identification—double flats and

Notation Example 6   Half-Steps Down

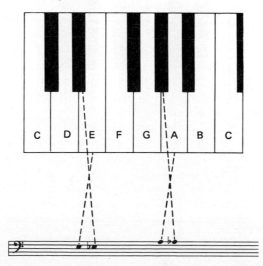

double sharps, for instance—but they are rather esoteric, and we can forget about them in this crash course in notation.

To put all this to use, let's think about *scales*. There are major scales and minor scales, the differences between which will be considered below. Probably we all know how a major scale sounds; this was drummed into us in grade school. Sometimes we sing a major scale with syllables. Going up, it's *do re mi fa so la ti do*—*do* to *do*, eight notes. That's an *octave* and the range of a scale. The C major scale, which starts and ends on C, is shown in Notation Example 7. Notice that it is made up of a series of half-steps and whole-steps, and that the half-steps are between the third and fourth notes, or scale degrees, and between the seventh and eighth notes (in the example these steps have a mark known as slur mark under them). All major scales are like that, regardless of what note you start and end on. For another illustration see Notation Example 8. To make the "tune" of the B major scale come out right, you need all those sharps, but the half- and whole-steps are still in the same relative places. In naming the pitches in a scale, we never skip a letter or use it twice in succession; in other words, each scale degree has its own letter name. A major scale beginning on F can look as in Notation Example 9. Here it covers part of two staffs. But it will all go on one staff, in which case it looks as in Notation Example 10. The black key is called and notated B♭ instead of A♯. This is because there already is one A and the scale needs to move on to some kind

Notation Example 7   C Major Scale

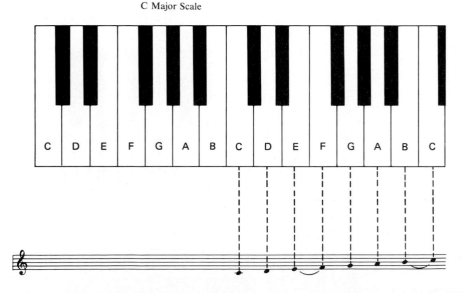

Notation Example 8

B Major Scale

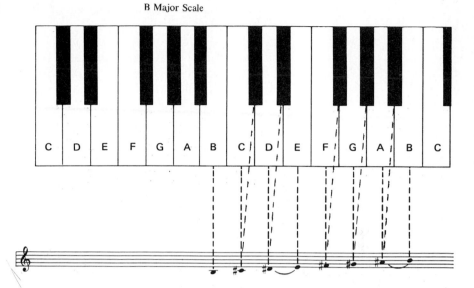

Notation Example 9

F Major Scale

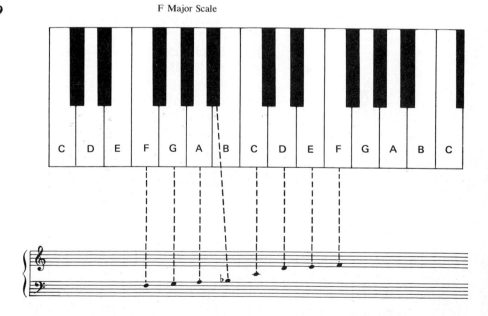

Notation Example 10

F Major Scale

of B—in this case B♭ because at this stage of the scale a half-step is needed.

By now you may be able to stop using the piano keyboard, except maybe to look back at it for reference, and when you can do that, you can come to grips with notation as an abstraction and begin to think more like a musician.

The major exception to this combination of half-steps and whole-steps in scales is in the scale we call *chromatic*. There, all the steps are half-steps and the pitches are identified by different names depending upon whether you're going up or down, as shown in Notation Example 11.

The scale is the material from which a composition is developed, and in composing, in order to avoid writing all the sharps and flats again and again, it became customary to put the necessary ones right after the clef sign. In terms just of scales, the sharps or flats following the clef sign tell the informed musician two things—what sharps or flats to use and what note to start the scale on. This is illustrated in Notation Example 12. If you want a major scale and you are going to use the flats that are given at the beginning of the staff here, you *must* begin on E♭—nothing else will work. Look at it in reverse, if you want to begin a major scale on E♭, you must use the flats that are given at the beginning of the staff. If this scale is the material of a composition, we say that the composition is in the key of E♭ major. Because of these relationships, we call the complex of accidentals (sharps or flats) at the beginning of the staff a *key signature*. The key signatures for the major keys we use are shown in Notation Example 13.

Notation Example 11   Chromatic Scale

Notation Example 12   E♭ Major Scale

Notation Example 13   Key Signatures for Major Keys

Now we have been dealing with major. A minor scale is another thing altogether. Most importantly, the half- and whole-steps are in different places. Notation Example 14 presents the scale of D minor, for instance, with slur marks between the half-steps; you can check this on your keyboard, if you're skeptical. In a minor scale, the half-steps are between the second and third and the fifth and sixth degrees.

But maybe you have realized already that the F major and D minor scales both use one flat, and the same one. They are made up of the same material, in other words. The difference is that in one scale F is the *tonic*—the starting note of the scale, the key note of a piece based on the scale, the note on which the piece will probably end—and in the other scale D is the tonic. We call them *relative* because they have the same bloodstream, as it were—the same pitches. Another way of putting it is to say that the relative minor of F major is D minor. It works the other way too: the relative major of D minor is F major. Every major key has a relative minor, and every minor key has a relative major. And the two members of each pair use the same key signature—naturally, since they use the same pitches. In Notation Example 15 are the key signatures for all the minor keys; match them up with their relative majors.

It is possible to start, then, on a given pitch, move up an octave scalewise, and have either a major or minor scale, depending on which notes you hit along the way. A scale that runs from F to F in major and one that runs from F to F in minor are called *parallel*. They are *not* relative, because they use much different material. But they do run parallel on the staff, as in Notation Example 16.

Notation Example 14   D Minor Scale

Notation Example 15   Key Signatures for Minor Keys

Notation Example 16   Parallel Scales

Although every key signature is used to identify a *relative* major and minor, there are not always similar letter designations for *parallel* majors and minors. Notice, for instance, that there is no A♯ major to go along with A♯ minor, even though we could *play* an A♯ major scale. Want to try to figure out why?

We've been working with pitch and how pitch relates to establishing a key and a mode, major or minor (see Glossary). For anybody who wants to come to grips with notation, it is necessary that the symbols for rhythm be understood also. But since they involve mathematics, they are a little easier; and there aren't so many of them.

The crucial rhythmic symbol is what we call a *whole note*. The rest of them are simply mathematical divisions of that. Here is how they work:

Very seldom do we get into note values as small as a sixty-fourth note, but the system can be carried on by the same process indefinitely. Relative to one another, the symbols tell you exactly how long to hold a note. For instance, a quarter note lasts twice as long as an eighth note and half as long as a half note.

A dot (·) after a note extends it for half of its value, so the following two rhythmic figures mean the same thing. In the second figure the *tie*—a slur mark between two notes at the same pitch—is a signal to treat the two notes like one.

We feel rhythm in beats, or pulses: we usually tap our feet or clap our hands to a beat. Rhythmic notation translates that beat into something we can see. The visual sign is the two numbers one over the other at the beginning of the staff, with the clef sign and the key signature. Probably because the rhythmic system is so closely involved with mathematics, the symbol is given in numbers. For many centuries the numbers have related to the system of organizing pulses into meters and gathering them into groups enclosed within vertical *bar lines*. This looks and works as in Notation Example 17. Here there are four quarter notes or their equivalent in each *measure* (the space between bar lines). This pair of numbers—the *meter signature*—is usually interpreted further to mean that each quarter note gets one beat, or that the beat is represented by a quarter note, to put it the other way around. The more different rhythmic values you use, the more complicated it all becomes. See Notation Example 18. If you add up all the values here, you'll find out that there are the equivalent of three quarter notes in each measure. Another very common meter is 2/4, and if you read much music, you'll run into it often.

People don't play or sing constantly; sometimes they pause. There are symbols for that too, which are called *rests*. On a staff, with their corresponding note values under them, they look as in Notation Example 19. Figure out the sixty-fourth rest yourself. You can dot a rest just as you can a note and extend it for half its time value.

With all this in mind, let's look at a familiar song. The way its sounds are transferred into notational symbols on paper is shown in Notation Example 20. The slurs connecting some of the notes mean that both of their pitches are sung on one word. Other than that, all the symbols should be familiar ones.

Notation Example 17   4/4 Meter

Notation Example 18   3/4 Meter

Notation Example 19   Rests

Notation Example 20   "Auld Lang Syne"

Should auld ac-quain-tance be for-got, and nev-er bro't to mind? Should
auld ac-quain-tance be for-got and days of auld lang syne? For
auld___ lang___ syne, my dear, For auld___ lang___ syne; We'll
tak' a cup o' kind-ness yet For___ auld___ lang___ syne.

Some meters that occur regularly are a bit complex. They go by the general designation of *compound*—meaning a combination of meters that make up something else when they are combined. The numbers in the meter signature still work the same way, but music itself *feels* different. The most common of these strangers is 6/8. In a song you already know, it looks and works as in Notation Example 21. If you sing this song fast, you will realize that you are feeling two beats in each measure. The meter signature, though, says that there are six eighth notes or their equivalent in each measure, and so you might assume that one eighth note represents a beat. Not so. Instead, three eighth notes are combined (compounded) into one beat. Some other meters that work the same way are 9/8, 12/8, 6/4, 9/4, and 12/4.

Harmony—along with melody and rhythm a member of music's triumvirate of basic materials—took a long time to develop in the West. At first, harmonic thinking was tied to melodic practice—polyphony—and the main thing that people worried about was getting the proper intervals—distances—between melodic voices. We can well think in terms of intervals too, for a while. Choose two pitches. Use the bottom pitch to start from; count *it* as well as the top pitch and all the lines and spaces between. That will give you the

Notation Example 21   "Row, Row, Row"

Row, row, row your boat, Gent-ly down the stream.___
Mer-ri-ly, mer-ri-ly, mer-ri-ly, mer-ri-ly, Life is but a dream.___

interval between the pitches. Notation Example 22 shows and identifies four intervals.

Intervals have qualities. Fourths and fifths and octaves are called *perfect* if both notes are in the major or minor scale of the bottom note. Thirds, sixths, and sevenths are called *major* if both notes are in the major scale of the bottom note. They are called *minor* if both notes are in the minor scale of the bottom note. Seconds are major if the notes are a whole-step apart, minor if a half-step apart. See Notation Example 23. All this is quite legal and not hard to figure out, although it may take some time and knowing key signatures helps.

Fourths and fifths are *diminished* if they are one half-step smaller than perfect; they are *augmented* if they are one half-step larger than perfect. See Notation Example 24.

Seconds, thirds, sixths, and sevenths that are one-half step smaller than minor are called diminished; one half-step larger than major and they are augmented. See Notation Example 25.

This is all tied up with conventions that have to do with "spelling" intervals—what to call them, how to put them on the staff. It has very little to do with what we hear. If you take the time to play

Notation Example 22   Intervals

5th   3rd   8th (octave)   6th

Notation Example 23   Perfect, Major, and Minor Intervals

perfect 4th   major 6th   minor 3rd   major 7th   major 3rd

minor 3rd   minor 2nd   major 2nd   minor 2nd   major 2nd

Notation Example 24   Varieties of Fifths and Fourths

perfect 5th   diminished 5th   augmented 5th   perfect 4th   augmented 4th

Notation Example 25   Augmented and Diminished Intervals

augmented 2nd   diminished 7th   augmented 3rd   diminished 3rd   diminished 2nd

some of these on the piano, you will soon discover, for instance, that an augmented fifth sounds exactly like a minor sixth and a diminished third sounds exactly like a major second, which is a whole-step. A diminished second sounds like one pitch! What this illustrates is that theory and written notation are a lot more involved than our ears lead us to suspect. Maybe that explains why so many early jazz musicians just settled for what sounded good and never did learn to read and write music or to analyze it.

After several centuries of thinking about intervals and how they went together, theorists developed the concept of *chords*. That meant they were thinking about three or more different pitches instead of only two, because it takes three different pitches to make a chord. As a result of our conventions, we normally construct chords in intervals of thirds up from a bottom note called a *root*. Three different pitches make a *triad*, and triads are the foundation of our harmonic system. The first note of the triad above the root is called the *third*, the second note, the *fifth*—they are so named because of their respective distances from the root. Another way of saying this is that a triad consists of a root, a third and a fifth. Triads have qualities as intervals do. If all the pitches are in the major scale of the bottom note, the triad is major. What happens if the pitches belong to the minor scale? See Notation Example 26. There are other qualities of chords; look into a good theory book if you are curious about them.

To use more than three different notes, you usually keep going up in thirds. In this case, you identify the chord in terms of the interval between the lowest (root) and highest notes, as shown in Notation Example 27. Larger chords have qualities just as intervals and triads do. But again this gets too complicated to elaborate on here. What we're trying to get here is the general idea.

Once we had accepted the concept of chords, it was a short step to develop a system of using them to harmonize a melody. That's when we got into homophonic thinking instead of purely polyphonic

Notation Example 26   Triad Chords

major   minor   minor   major   major   minor

Notation Example 27   Larger Chords

7th chord   9th chord   13th chord

thinking. Take any scale—say C major—and think about building chords with its material, knowing that you construct chords up in thirds and that you can do it from any root you choose. Triads built on the different steps of the C major scale would look as in Notation Example 28.

The chords have a mixture of qualities. The ones on C, F, and G are major. The ones on D, E, and A are minor. The one on B is diminished (figure out the intervals in it and come up with a rule about what makes a chord diminished). This variety means that we can wring a lot of harmonic color out of the material for C major. Likewise C minor, the triads of which are shown in Notation Example 29. When the mode changes, the qualities of the chords at particular places in the scale change too. So here the minor chords are on C, F, and G, and the major chords are on E♭, A♭, and B♭. The D chord here is diminished. Beyond this, harmonic practice in minor has an important trick to it that we'll consider below.

Within a key, we can identify the chords by their letter names, which we've been doing, or we can call them by the step of the scale they are built on, so that in the key of C, the chord built on C would be the I chord, the chord built on D would be the II chord, etc. Because of the particular developments that took place in Western harmonic practice, three chords in each key became immensely important in defining that key. They were the I, the IV, and the V. Another set of names for them is *tonic*, *subdominant*, and *dominant*, in that order. In the key of C major, they look as in Notation Example 30.

One thing that makes the I, IV, and V chords important in any scale is that they contain among them all the notes of the scale. If you want to harmonize (put chords with) any tune that stays in the

Notation Example 28

Chords on the C Major Scale

Notation Example 29

Chords on the C Minor Scale

Notation Example 30

I, IV, and V Chords in C Major

C — tonic — I   F — subdominant — IV   G — dominant — V

scale, then, one or another of these chords will fill the bill. Much music *does* stay within the scale of the key it happens to be in. This is true, for instance, of much folk music, country western, blues (except for inflected pitches and they do not change the key or mode), and rock and many church hymns and gospel songs. Because of this, these three chords form the harmonic vocabulary for thousands of songs of these types. They are easy to hear (good "ear" chords), easy to utilize, easy to learn on the guitar or piano. They are basic to our harmonic system. The further away one gets from them (the more one uses additional chords, in other words), the more complicated the harmony becomes, adding corresponding richness to the sound. That happened in Romanticism, for instance, and even more in Impressionism.

When using chords in minor, an adjustment is usually made to accommodate something that our ears apparently want to hear. In major, the harmonic progression from dominant to tonic (V to I) is the strongest, most decisive one we use in Western music, and it occurs often as the ending musical movement known as the final cadence. That particular progression was used almost always as the final cadence, in fact, from the mid-Baroque until about 1900, and even now is so used in folk, pop, and much other music. And the major dominant became so much a part of the musical scene that the use of the minor V chord in the minor mode was felt to be unsatisfactory. It didn't sound final enough. We like the sound of the seventh note of the scale going up a half-step to the tonic (*ti* to *do*), and so we want that note to be part of the V chord, which it isn't in minor. Easy to fix. Make the minor dominant chord major: just raise its third. Then it looks as in Notation Example 31 (notice that the I and IV are still minor). The sign ♮ (natural) is used to change a previously flatted or sharped pitch back to its "natural" (unaltered) position. In Notation Example 31, it changes the B♭ in the key signature to a B.

Just one other thing and we'll have covered the basic principles of Western harmonic practice. In 1722 a French theorist named Jean Philippe Rameau advanced the idea that you could turn chords upside down or mix the notes up (without changing them, of course) and still have the same chord. In other words, Rameau theorized

Notation Example 31   I, IV, and V Chords in C Minor

C – tonic – I   F – subdominant – IV   G – dominant – V

that the root did not have to be the lowest note played, the third the next highest and the fifth the highest. They could be shuffled around without losing their identity, much as students in a class can change seating arrangements without thereby becoming different people. That was a new idea at the time, and it changed the course of Western harmonic practice. The process is called *inversion* and it works as shown in Notation Example 32. The pitches—again of the same notes—can be spread out all over the staff and they still produce the same chord. See Notation Example 33. Notes that make up the chord may even be used in several different registers, spread out across two or more staffs, and they *still* produce the same chord. This is sometimes called *doubling*. See Notation Example 34. Mix and match. Scramble the notes up. The chord is the same, no matter what. So when you look at the score for a full orchestra, keep in mind that even with all those different instruments playing all those different pitches, they are still playing a chord of some kind, built on the principles discussed above—as long as they are playing tonal music, i.e., music that is harmonized with chords derived from the notes of an identifiable key.

If you feel adventurous, try chording along with a familiar tune—"How Long Blues," which is in your record set and is discussed in the text on page 53ff. It uses only the I, IV, and V chords. In F major, they look as in Notation Example 35 if you are going to work from the piano.

Notation Example 32   Chord Inversion,

F major   F major   F major

Notation Example 33   Chord Inversion,

F major   F major   F major

Notation Example 34   Chord with Doublings

F major

Notation Example 35   Chords of "How Long Blues"

I (F)   IV (Bb)   V (C)   I (F)

If you are really adventurous, try a more familiar piece and one that is in a different key. Here are the words and the chords that go with them. Can you find them on the piano?

I (C)
Silent night, holy night;
V (G)   I (C)
All is calm,   all is bright;
IV (F)   I (C)
'Round yon virgin,   mother and child;
IV (F)   I (C)
Holy infant so   tender and mild;
V (G)   I (C)
Sleep in heavenly   peace;
I (C)   V (G)   I (C)
Sleep in   heavenly   peace.

Now all of this is a scratch on the surface—like asking someone how to build a house and being shown some blueprints for the first time in your life. But you need to begin somewhere, with a house or with music theory. You can live in a house, enjoy it, and be comfortable in it without knowing a thing about how it was put together or how to read the blueprints, but how much more you'd know if you did know how to read them and build from them! For one thing, you could ask a contractor some intelligent questions. And maybe this bit of information about music theory and notation will lead you to some questions you'd like answered.

For instance, what makes Palestrina's music in the Introduction look so strange?

MISCELLANEOUS PERFORMANCE DIRECTIONS

There are a number of words and symbols in music that inform the performer how to go about following the composer's or editor's wishes. Many of these came into general use in the latter half of the eighteenth century—during the Classic period—when composers started trying to protect their music from overzealous or careless musicians. On the positive side, the use of such directions made it possible for performers to fulfill the creative vision of the composers. The Classic period, incidentally, was one when many composers were trying to support themselves as professionals rathar than by taking appointments as church or court musicians. And it also was a period of revolutionary stirrings. Can you make a connection anywhere?

As time went on, composers became more and more specific in their directions. As a result, there is now a vast vocabulary of performance instructions in use. The most common terminology is presented below; a good music dictionary will fill in the gaps if you are curious about things you run into that are not included here.

TEMPO

FROM SLOW TO FAST

Largo
Grave
Lento
Adagio
Andante
Moderato
Allegro
Presto

INDICATING CHANGE OF TEMPO

accelerando: gradually faster
stringendo: faster *and* louder
rallentando: gradually slower
ritard: gradually slower
meno mosso: slower immediately
morendo: slower *and* softer

Sometimes the tempo is given quite exactly instead of in these relative terms. The most specific way to indicate the speed is by means of a metronome marking. A metronome is a small instrument with a numbered scale and a ticking mechanism (see Glossary). In a metronome marking, a note and a number show how many of that kind of note there are per minute. For instance, ♩ = 60 means that there are sixty quarter notes per minute, one each second. Set the pointer of the metronome at 60 and you will hear sixty ticks each minute—if the metronome is accurate.

DYNAMICS

FROM SOFT TO LOUD

pp—pianissimo
p—piano
mp—mezzo-piano
mf—mezzo-forte
f—forte
ff—fortissimo

crescendo: gradually louder; also $<$
decrescendo: gradually softer; also $>$
sfz or *sf, sforzando:* sudden emphasis or stress: sometimes also $>$

A number of other performance directions have little or nothing to do with tempo or dynamics but are more general or sometimes, even more specific. A few of these are:

arco: bowed (directed toward string players)
pizzicato: plucked (also for string players)

· —*staccato:* detached, separated sound (for anyone, even singers)
ᵔ —*fermata:* sustained sound (indicates indefinite length of time except for sopranos and tenors, who hold on until their breath supply is exhausted)

INSTRUMENTS AND SCORES

There are some full scores quoted in this book, and they can be troublesome to an unskilled reader. They are there to satisfy the curiosity of those who might want to find out how the music for an orchestra *looks* as well as how it *sounds*. When we hear an orchestra, we hear the whole orchestra, not just the melody line, even though we may concentrate most on that. That's why the full score is quoted. Finding your way around in one is not easy. If you want to try, the following information is given in order to get you started.

Orchestral instruments are divided into groups (sometimes called families) of the following types: woodwinds, brasses, percussion, and strings, plus occasional instruments. The instruments, in their proper groups, are as follows:

WOODWINDS:	Piccolo
	Flute
	Oboe
	English horn
	Clarinet
	Bassoon
BRASSES:	French horn
	Trumpet
	Trombone
	Tuba
PERCUSSION (some are tuned, others are not):	Timpani
	Xylophone
	Chimes
	Glockenspiel
	Bass drum
	Snare drum

	Bongos
	Tambourine
	Cymbal
	Miscellaneous
STRINGS:	Violin
	Viola
	Cello
	Double bass
OCCASIONAL:	Harp
	Piano

That's a lot of instruments to get on a full score. Depending on the period and the intention of the composer, you may not run into all of them. For instance, Haydn and Mozart never even saw some of them because they were developed after these composers died. But in a composition that does use all or most of them, the arrangement on the page is of some help. The instruments are normally grouped in the same order as above, with a few exceptions. Reading from top to bottom of a score for full orchestra using all the instruments, you will find the following parts (like performance directions, scores usually use the Italian language to identify the instrument, so you may need to translate):

Flute and piccolo
Oboe
English horn
Clarinet
Bassoon
French horn
Trumpet
Trombone
Tuba
Timpani
Other drums
Xylophone
Piano (if one is used)
Harp (if one is used)
First violin
Second violin
Viola
Cello
Double bass

If there are voices, they usually come right before the strings.

You will notice, if you look at a full orchestra score, that the key signatures are all mixed up. So are the clef signs. This is due to an

Notation Example 36   Score of "Row, Row, Row"

idiosyncrasy of some of the instruments. These are called *transposing instruments* because when they play one note, a different one comes out. Naturally, the notation has to take this into account. One example will suffice to illustrate the problem.

Assume that you play the clarinet. Some are in A, which means that when you play the note the score says is a C, you get an A sound. The actual pitch is a minor third lower than the pitch you see on the page. If you are aware of this, you will understand why the clarinet in A plays from a staff with a key signature different than the ones the violins are using, for instance. The violins produce the pitch they read on the page. So if you had a full score for "Row, Row, Row Your Boat" and violins and clarinets played the melody, their lines of the score would begin as shown in Notation Example 36.

Not all the transporting instruments use the same interval relationships, unfortunately, so in a full score you will find more than just two key signatures at work. Also, you will find the violas and sometimes the cellos and other instruments playing from those bothersome *C clefs,* even though they are not transposing instruments.

As you can imagine, a conductor needs to know all this, and he or she also needs to be able to read in all the staffs and understand (and interpret) the welter of key signature. It gets complicated.

Even though you may never learn to follow the music on a full score—may not even *want* to learn—just trying a couple of times will increase your respect for the conductors you may see in action. They need to know a great deal more than how to wave their arms and acknowledge the applause of the audience.

The very first thing they need to know is how to read music. Want to join them? Dig in.

Appendix 2
Chronology of People and Events

The purpose of appendix 2 is to present an easily accessible chronology for the individual listings of people and events found under the "Glances at History" in the body of the text. In those listings, the information is divided into categories of musicians, artists, literary figures, other people of note, and events. The same divisions are observed in this appendix.

Here, however, there is a real chronology within each category rather than an alphabetical list as in the previous presentation. There is the added advantage of having within easy grasp the entire sweep of history that encompasses the medieval period through the present day.

Individuals, musicians and others are arranged in order by birth date. Events are given in order of their occurrence; where there is a span of years involved, the beginning year is used as an index. The only exception to this practice is the list of wars of the twentieth century. Because violence has been so great a part of our agenda during this period, it would be of some value to students to involve themselves in tracking the incidence of war, some of which is continuing even now.

ROMANESQUE PERIOD
(c. 450–1100)

MUSICIANS:

Boethius (c. 475–525)
Guido d'Arezzo (c. 995–1049)

435

CHURCHMEN IMPORTANT FOR MUSIC: Ambrose of Milan (Bishop 340–397)
Gregory I (Pope 590–604)

EVENTS: Third to sixth centuries: Barbarians overrun Europe
Fourth century: Monasteries inaugurated
476:     Sack of Rome
1066:   Norman conquest of England
Eleventh century: First Crusade

GOTHIC PERIOD
(1100–1400)

MUSICIANS: Léonin (12th century)
Adam de la Halle (c. 1240–1287)
Franco of Cologne (13th century)
Pérotin (13th century)
Guillaume de Machaut (c. 1300–1377)

ARTISTS AND LITERARY FIGURES: Roger Bacon (c. 1214–1294)
St. Thomas Aquinas (c. 1225–1274)
Dante Alighieri (1265–1321)
Giotto (c. 1266–1337)
Francesco Petrarch (1304–1374)
Giovanni Boccaccio (1313–1375)
John Wycliffe (c. 1320–1384)
Geoffrey Chaucer (c. 1340–1400)

EVENTS: 12th century: Universities established, including Oxford
12th century: Second Crusade
1215:   Magna Charta
c. 1254–1324:   Marco Polo (Journeys 1271–1295)
1309–77:   Avignon Captivity
1337–1453:   Hundred Years' War
1347–1350:   Plague of the Black Death (Bubonic Plague)

RENAISSANCE PERIOD
(1400–1600)

MUSICIANS: Guillaume Dufay (c. 1400–1474)
Jacob Obrecht (1430–1505)
Josquin des Prez (c. 1445–1521)
Giovanni Palestrina (c. 1526–1594)

Tomás Luis de Victoria (c. 1535–1611)
William Byrd (c. 1540–1623)
Thomas Morley (1557–1603)
Carlo Gesualdo (c. 1560–1613)
Claudio Monteverdi (1567–1643)

ARTISTS, LITERARY FIGURES AND OTHERS:

Donatello (c. 1386–1466)
Johannes Gutenberg (c. 1400–68)
Sandro Botticelli (c. 1444–1510)
Matthias Grünewald (c. 1470–1528)
Albrecht Dürer (1471–1528)
Nicolaus Copernicus (1473–1543)
Michelangelo Buonarotti (1475–1564)
Titian (c. 1477–1576)
Raphael (1483–1520)
Francois Rabelais (c. 1490–1553)
Benvenuto Cellini (1500–1571)
William Shakespeare (1564–1616)
Galilei Galileo (1564–1642)

EVENTS:

1492–1504:	Voyages of Christopher Columbus (c. 1446–1506)
1513:	Vasco de Balboa discovers Pacific Ocean
1519:	Invasion of Mexico by Hernando Cortes (1485–1547)
1520–1521:	Fernando Magellan voyages
1545–1563:	Council of Trent
1577–1580:	Sir Francis Drake (1540–1596) sails around the world

BAROQUE PERIOD
(1600-1750)

MUSICIANS:

Giulio Caccini (1548–1618)
Giovanni Gabrieli (1557–1612)
Jacopo Peri (1561–1633)
Heinrich Schütz (1585–1672)
Jean-Baptiste Lully (1632–1687)
Henry Purcell (c. 1659–1695)
François Couperin (1668–1733)
Antonio Vivaldi (c. 1676–1741)
Jean-Phillipe Rameau (1683–1764)
Johann Sebastian Bach (1685–1750)
Domenico Scarlatti (1685–1757)
George Frederic Handel (1685–1759)

ARTISTS, LITERARY FIGURES, AND
OTHERS:

Miguel de Cervantes (1547–1616)
Peter Paul Rubens (1577–1640)
Frans Hals (c. 1581–1666)
René Descartes (1596–1650)
Rembrandt van Rijn (1606–1669)
John Milton (1608–1674)
Jean Molière (1622–1673)
Blaise Pascal (1623–1662)
John Bunyon (1628–1688)
Baruch Spinoza (1632–1677)
Isaac Newton (1642–1727)
Jonathan Swift (1667–1745)
Jean Watteau (1684–1721)

EVENTS:

1609:	Hudson River explored and charted
1611:	King James Bible printed
1618–1648:	Thirty Years' War
1620:	Pilgrims landed on Cape Cod
1626:	Manhattan Island purchased
1635:	Académie Française founded
1636:	Harvard University founded
1640:	Bay Psalm Book printed
1649–1660:	Commonwealth/Restoration in England
1692:	Witchcraft trials in Salem, Mass.
1701:	Yale University founded

CLASSIC PERIOD
(1750-1827)

MUSICIANS:

Christoph Gluck (1714–1787)
Carl Philipp Emanuel Bach (1714–1788)
Johann Stamitz (1717–1757)
Franz Joseph Haydn (1732–1809)
William Billings (1746–1800)
Wolfgang Amadeus Mozart (1756–1791)
Luigi Cherubini (1760–1842)
Ludwig van Beethoven (1770–1827)

ARTISTS, LITERARY FIGURES AND
OTHERS:

Francois Voltaire (1694–1778)
Jean Jacques Rousseau (1712–1778)
Thomas Gainsborough (1717–1788)
Immanuel Kant (1724–1804)
Thomas Paine (1737–1809)
Jacques David (1748–1825)
Johann Wolfgang Goethe (1749–1832)

William Blake (1757–1827)
Robert Burns (1759–1796)
William Wordsworth (1770–1850)

EVENTS: 1769:   Steam engine invented
           1770:   Spinning jenny invented
           1774:   Oxygen discovered
           1774–1789:   Continental Congress
           1776:   Declaration of Independence
           1776:   Hydrogen discovered
           1781:   Articles of Confederation
           1787:   U.S. Constitution
           1787:   Steamboat invented
           1787–1815:   French Revolution
           1791:   Bill of Rights
           1793:   Cotton gin invented
           1796:   Electric battery invented

ROMANTIC PERIOD
(1800–1900)

MUSICIANS: Carl Maria von Weber (1786–1826)
              Giocchino Rossini (1792–1868)
              Franz Schubert (1797–1828)
              Hector Berlioz (1803–1869)
              Fanny Mendelssohn Hensel (1805–1847)
              Felix Mendelssohn (1809–1847)
              Frédéric Chopin (1810–1849)
              Robert Schumann (1810–1856)
              Franz Liszt (1811–1886)
              Richard Wagner (1813–1883)
              Giuseppe Verdi (1813–1901)
              Charles Gounod (1818–1893)
              Clara Schumann (1819–1896)
              César Franck (1822–1890)
              Bedřich Smetana (1824–1884)
              Anton Bruckner (1824–1896)
              Stephen C. Foster (1826–1864)
              Alexander Borodin (1833–1887)
              Johannes Brahms (1833–1897)
              Camille Saint-Saëns (1835–1921)
              Georges Bizet (1838–1875)
              Modest Moussorgsky (1839–1881)
              Peter I. Tchaikowsky (1840–1893)

Antonin Dvořák (1841–1904)
Sir Arthur Sullivan (1842–1900)
Jules Massenet (1842–1912)
Edward Grieg (1843–1907)
Nicolas Rimsky-Korsakov (1844–1908)
Gabriel Fauré (1845–1924)
John Philip Sousa (1854–1932)
Giacomo Puccini (1858–1924)
Hugo Wolf (1860–1903)
Gustave Mahler (1860–1911)
Claude Debussy (1862–1918)
Richard Strauss (1864–1949)
Jean Sibelius (1865–1957)
Erik Satie (1866–1925)
Scott Joplin (1868–1917)
Sergei Rachmaninoff (1873–1943)
Maurice Ravel (1875–1937)

AUTHORS, ARTISTS, LITERARY
FIGURES AND OTHERS:

Francisco Goya (1746–1828)
Sir Walter Scott (1771–1832)
Jane Austen (1775–1817)
George Byron (1788–1824)
Louis Jacque M. Daguerre (1789–1851)
John Keats (1795–1821)
Alexander Pushkin (1799–1837)
Victor Hugo (1802–1885)
Ralph Waldo Emerson (1803–1882)
Nathaniel Hawthorne (1804–1864)
Elizabeth Browning (1806–1861)
Henry Wadsworth Longfellow (1807–1882)
Edgar Allan Poe (1809–1849)
Charles Darwin (1809–1882)
Alfred Lord Tennyson (1809–1892)
Charles Dickens (1812–1870)
Robert Browning (1812–1889)
Harriet Beecher Stowe (1812–1896)
Henry David Thoreau (1817–1862)
Karl Marx (1818–1883)
George Eliot (1819–1880)
Walt Whitman (1819–1892)
Pierre Baudelaire (1821–1867)
Gustave Flaubert (1821–1880)
Feodor Dostoyevsky (1821–1881)
Louis Pasteur (1822–1895)

Henrik Ibsen (1826–1906)
Leo Tolstoy (1828–1910)
Lewis Carroll (1832–1898)
Edgar Degas (1834–1917)
Mark Twain (1835–1910)
Sir William Gilbert (1836–1911)
Paul Cézanne (1839–1906)
Emile Zola (1840–1902)
Auguste Rodin (1840–1917)
Claude Monet (1840–1926)
Pierre Renoir (1841–1919)
Stephane Mallarmé (1842–1898)
Friedrich Nietzsche (1844–1900
Thomas Edison (1847–1931)
Paul Gaugin (1848–1903)
Robert Louis Stevenson (1850–1894)
Vincent van Gogh (1853–1890)
Oscar Wilde (1856–1900)
George Bernard Shaw (1856–1950)
Rudyard Kipling (1865–1936)
Stephen Crane (1871–1900)

EVENTS:

1793–1814:	Napoleonic conquests
1803:	Louisiana Purchase
1823:	Monroe Doctrine
1825:	Erie Canal completed
1826:	Reaper invented
1830s:	Railroads begun
1830s:	Telegraph invented
1842:	Ether discovered as an anesthetic
1846:	Sewing machine invented
1849:	California gold rush
1850s:	Trade with Japan inaugurated
1861–1865:	American Civil War
1866:	Transatlantic cable laid
1867:	Alaska purchased from Russia
1869:	Suez Canal completed
1876:	Telephone invented
1881–1914:	Panama Canal constructed
1883:	Brooklyn Bridge completed
1886:	Statue of Liberty installed
1895:	Subways begun
1895:	X-rays discovered
1898:	Radium discovered
1898:	Spanish-American War
1899–1902:	Boer War

TWENTIETH CENTURY

MUSICIANS:

Dame Ethel Smyth (1858–1944)
Enrique Granados (1867–1916)
Amy Cheney Beach (1867–1944)
Alexander Scriabin (1872–1915)
Ralph Vaughan Willians (1872–1958)
W. C. Handy (1873–1958)
Arnold Schönberg (1874–1951)
Charles Ives (1874–1954)
Manuel de Falla (1876–1946)
Ottorino Respighi (1879–1936)
Ernest Bloch (1880–1959)
Bela Bartók (1881–1945)
Zoltan Kodály (1882–1967)
Igor Stravinsky (1882–1971)
Anton Webern (1883–1945)
Edgard Varèse (1883–1965)
Alban Berg (1885–1935)
Heitor Villa-Lobos (1887–1959)
Sergei Prokofiev (1891–1953)
Arthur Honegger (1892–1955)
Darius Milhaud (1892–1974)
Walter Piston (1894–1976)
Paul Hindemith (1895–1963)
Carl Orff (1895–1982)
Roger Sessions (1896–   )
Virgil Thomson (1896–   )
George Gershwin (1897–1937)
Francis Poulenc (1899–1963)
Edward Kennedy "Duke" Ellington (1899–1974)
Kurt Weill (1900–1950)
Aaron Copland (1900–   )
Ernest Krenek (1900–   )
Ruth Crawford Seeger (1901–1953)
Luigi Dallapiccola (1904–1975)
Dimitri Shostakovich (1905–1975)
Elizabeth Lutyens (1906–   )
Elliott Carter (1908–   )
Olivier Messaien (1908–   )
Samuel Barber (1910–1981)
Gian Carlo Menotti (1911–   )
Vladimir Ussachevsky (1911–   )
John Cage (1912–   )

Benjamin Britten (1913–1976)
Witold Lutaslawski (1913–   )
Alberto Ginastera (1916–   )
Leonard Bernstein (1918–   )
Yannis Xenakis (1922–   )
Luciano Berio (1925–   )
Pierre Boulez (1925–   )
Thea Musgrave (1928–   )
Hans Werner Henze (1926–   )
Karlheinz Stockhausen (1928–   )
George Crumb (1929–   )
Krzysztof Penderecki (1933–   )

AUTHORS, ARTISTS, LITERARY
FIGURES, AND OTHERS:

Sigmund Freud (1856–1939)
Joseph Conrad (1857–1924)
Pierre Curie (1859–1906)
Anton Chekhov (1860–1904)
W. B. Yeats (1865–1939)
Wassily Kandinsky (1866–1944)
Marie Curie (1867–1934)
Frank Lloyd Wright (1869–1959)
Marcel Proust (1871–1922)
Georges Rouault (1871–1958)
Piet Mondrian (1872–1944)
Bertrand Russell (1872–1970)
Willa Cather (1873–1947)
Guglielmo Marconi (1874–1937)
Gertrude Stein (1874–1946)
Robert Frost (1874–1963)
W. Somerset Maugham (1874–1965)
Rainer Maria Rilke (1875–1926)
Thomas Mann (1875–1955)
Albert Einstein (1879–1955)
Pablo Picasso (1881–1973)
James Joyce (1882–1941)
Virginia Woolf (1882–1941)
Georges Braque (1882–1963)
José Ortega y Gassett (1883–1955)
T. S. Eliot (1885–1965)
Marcel Duchamp (1887–1968)
Eugene O'Neill (1888–1953)
William Faulkner (1897–1962)
Bertolt Brecht (1898–1956)

Ernest Hemingway (1899–1961)
John Steinbeck (1902–1968)
Salvador Dali (1904–   )
Tennessee Williams (1911–1983)
Albert Camus (1913–1960)
Dylan Thomas (1914–1953)
Arthur Miller (1915–   )
Samuel Beckett (1916–   )
Aleksandr Solzhenitsyn (1918–   )
Malcolm X. (1925–1965)
Harold Pinter (1930–   )

EVENTS:

1900:	Commercial recordings issued
1901:	Radio (crystal sets) introduced
1903:	Motion picture "story pictures" introduced
1906:	San Francisco earthquake
1909:	North Pole exploration
1910:	Commercial dirigibles introduced
1910:	Electronic charge discovered
1911:	South Pole exploration
1912:	Titanic sank
1918:	Spread of communism began
1919:	Protons discovered
1920s:	Television invented
1921:	Insulin discovered
1929–1939:	Great Depression
1932:	Neutrons discovered
1937:	Computers developed
1937:	Jet planes introduced
1939:	Nuclear fission discovered
1945:	United Nations founded
1950s and 1960s:	Civil Rights movement
1950s and 1960s:	Gene theory developed
1950s:	Organ transplants introduced
1957	Space exploration begun
1960:	Laser beams discovered
1970s:	Test tube babies introduced
1972:	Watergate

The following wars have marred the social and political scene during the twentieth century. Some continue still. They are listed here alphabetically and you are invited to trace their dates.

Britain–Argentina
Invasion of Grenada
Iranian Revolution

IRA conflicts in Ireland
Israeli conflicts in the Middle East
Italian Fascist Revolution
Japanese–Chinese War
Korean War
Russian Revolutions
Russo-Japanese War
Spanish Civil War
Vietnam War
World Wars I and II

You should feel free to add others of your own.

Index

446